# Primitive

# Theology

### The Collected Primers of
### *John H. Gerstner*

(collected and edited by Rev. Don Kistler)

**Soli Deo Gloria Publications**
*...for instruction in righteousness...*

**Soli Deo Gloria Publications**
P.O. Box 451, Morgan, PA 15064
(412) 221-1901/FAX 221-1902

*

*Primitive Theology: The Collected Primers of
John H. Gerstner,* is © 1996 by Soli Deo Gloria.

*

ISBN 1-57358-045-7

*

The publisher is grateful to Baker Book House
for giving their permission to include
*A Predestination Primer* in this book.

# Contents

# A

# Primer

# on

# Apologetics

*A Study of the Defense of
the Christian Faith*

# Dedication

Without R.C. Sproul, Sr., this little book would never have been published; but without R.C., Jr. and Bob Ingram it would have never have been fit to publish. However, reader, please note: Just because these good young friends made my rough draft legible doesn't mean that they share any of the blame for what you are now able to read.

John H. Gerstner

# Contents

# Introduction

## A Definition of Apologetics

Apologetics means a reasoned defense of anything. The apologetics we are interested in is a reasoned defense of Christianity.

One no sooner mentions a reasoned defense of Christianity than he hears a thousand Christian voices asking: Since when does Christianity need a reasoned or any other kind of defense? We all remember the famous Baptist preacher Charles Haddon Spurgeon likening the Bible to a caged lion which needs only to be let loose to prove his power. Those who meet him need the defense, not the lion. Reason, Spurgeon said, needs defense, not faith; the word of man, not the Word of God.

I haven't heard any *amens* yet, but that is probably because sophisticated Christians don't express their feelings that way. But they do use expression of their feelings as the only necessary proof of their faith. When they say they know that Christianity is true, what they mean is that they feel it is true. The truth, at least religious truth, for them is a matter of the heart. Some intelligent people hang their minds with their hats in the vestibule when they come to church. When I speak on apologetics in some churches, I can see the congregation wondering if the old absent-minded professor has forgotten he is in church and is imagining that he is still lecturing in the seminary.

Evangelical Christians, most of them, do *know* that Christ rose from the dead. Do you know how they know that Christ still lives? "Because He lives within my heart," they sing. That proves it. A full heart, not an empty tomb, is the ultimate apologetic.

Who needs arguments when he has experience? The

"argument from experience" carries all the apologetic freight. One "encounter" can overthrow a thousand objections or substitute for a hundred arguments.

# 1. Contemporary Fideism

It is neither lame brains nor idiots who are opposed to reasons. It is not unreasonable people who are violently against reason for religion. Karl Barth was certainly the greatest theological genius of this century. He wrote the longest series of theological volumes in any century. Before he reaches page thirty of the first volume of his *Church Dogmatics*, he is asserting that what is philosophical is not Christian and what is Christian is not philosophical. He does not say "apologetical," but that is what he means, as demonstrated in an experience of one of my professors.

Julius Seelye Bixler, under whom I studied what was called "theology" at Harvard in the early 1940s, once visited Karl Barth. On Barth's desk he saw a copy of *The Reasonableness of Christianity*. Bixler, interested because he had studied under its author, he asked Barth what he thought of the book on his desk. "No good" was the answer.

"Have you read it?" Bixler asked.

"No," responded Barth.

"How, then, do you know that it is no good?" Barth then explained that he had read the first few pages where the author promised that he would show the reasonableness of Christianity. Barth then knew the book *couldn't* be any good. For him, Christianity was not "reasonable."

The father of this kind of thought (or nonthought) was the nineteenth-century melancholy theological Dane, Søren Kierkegaard. He simply could not stand the neat synthesis of Georg Wilhelm Friedrich Hegel. He blew the whistle in the name of paradox and Christianity has never been the same since.

The grandfather of the Barthian anti-apologetic Christianity (if one skips *the* quintessential father of the whole movement, Immanuel Kant, as too technical) is Blaise Pascal, who had reasons for Christianity that the mind knows not of.

## 2. Objections to Apologetics

It is not too difficult to see why intelligent people don't want to use their intelligence defending or proving Christianity. It is hard work. You have to prove, prove, prove to an age which is intellectually lazy and hostile to biblical truth. Jonathan Edwards, preaching from Psalm 94:8, demonstrated this in his sermon "Man's Natural Blindness in the Things of Religion."

One will do hard work when he thinks it necessary, but who works hard when it is thought *unnecessary?* Most Christians deem reasoning unreasonable. Reason isn't just a rocking chair business, though even that is harder than it may appear. But defending Christianity rationally means research in dusty libraries (where I, for one, got a heart attack), and among even dustier archeological ruins. These aren't nine-to-five jobs, forty hours a week. Apologetics is a lifetime endeavor for many, and the object of study for others. Meanwhile, for every answer Christians give, the doubters are ready with two more questions. It is just not commonsensical, not to mention reasonable, when the whole apologetical enterprise is unnecessary.

Second, few think about your conclusions and fewer stilll follow your arguments. You do it all for people, most of whom wonder why you do it at all. Their interest is elsewhere. You are accused of elaborately answering questions people aren't even asking.

Third, you stir up more opposition than you make converts. You often read of some who never doubted Christianity until they listened to an apologist argue for it. While you are rationally pointing them to Christ, they are looking for loopholes in your argument. And whoever heard of anyone being reasoned into the kingdom? At times you certainly do wonder if the best use of reason is not the non-use of reason. The case for Christianity should be a case of neglect.

Fourth, even the Bible itself seems, at places, to be against a rational defense of itself. Not many wise are called says Paul (1 Corinthians 1:26). And it was after Paul's most learned sermon on Mars Hill that he resolved to know nothing but Christ and Him crucified (1 Corinthians 2:2). I have encountered hundreds of Christians who insist that their conversion had nothing to do with apologetics.

Fifth, the titans of the church often seem opposed to apologetics. Augustine is cited as saying, "I believed in order to understand." Warfield called Anselm "Christianity's most analytic intelligence." But the author of the ontological argument is almost always remembered also as saying, "I *believe* in order to *understand*." Even Thomas Aquinas, usually regarded as Christianity's greatest apologist, was condemned by Francis Schaeffer and thought to be a fideist by Mascall. One writer says he reasons like an attorney who knows his opponent is guilty and only needs reasons to prove what he knows without them.

I could go on digging my own grave, but I might go over your head even as the dirt goes over mine. Enough's enough. At the bottom of the pit, as I start to climb out, I can only gratefully thank God that He once said, "Come now, and let us reason together" (Isaiah 1:18).

## 3. Spurgeon's Lion

Let me return to Spurgeon and his lion, or Scripture as its own apologist. This proposition certainly sounds sound. What could be more self-evident than if the Bible is the Word of God it must be able to prove itself? God must be capable of proving to His creatures that He is God. He would not seem to need a creature to prove to other creatures what the Creator Himself could not prove. It would seem to be as silly as pointing to a caged lion and proving by its anatomy and build and claws that it is capable of killing weaker animals, including man. History has shown that, when let loose among these creatures, the lion has

many times proven his irresistible power. No more need
be said. History has proven the obvious. Why argue the irrefutable?

Indeed, the Bible has times without number proven its
power to convert and convince of its divine origin and nature. Who can deny what has happened? Or who could be
sillier than the one who debates the *fait accompli*? It is like
the story of the old critic who pointed out all the bad taxi-
dermy of the "stuffed owl" in the barber shop. The stuffed
owl's stepping down from his perch was deemed sufficient
evidence to dispel the criticisms.

Why, then, apologetics? Why not persuade, or compel if
necessary, every one simply to read the Bible? Everyone
then would be instantly convinced that the Bible is the
Word of God and know that the religion it teaches is divinely inspired. There would be no more skeptics, cynics,
doubters, unbelievers—or apologists.

Some Christians do believe that that is the conclusion
Paul came to. He had made a mistake at Athens by reasoning with the Greeks. Only a few were reached. When he
came to Corinth he resolved to preach Christ and Him
crucified (1 Corinthians 2:2). It meant no more apologetics
for Paul, Christianity's greatest reasoner.

Even the apologists agree with the anti-apologists, it
would seem. We all, or almost all, admit that no one was
ever won to Christianity by apologetics. Some of us even
admit that its tendency is to harden the opposition to
Christianity. The more irrefutable our arguments, the more
alienated are those we would win by them. If there ever
was a self-defeating enterprise, this would be it.

Why not let the lion loose to destroy all before him, beginning with the apologists?

The first argument against Scripture as its own apologist is that we all meet the world before we meet the Bible.
We know something before we come to know the Bible. It
is in the context of our knowledge of the world that we first
encounter Scripture. Its claim to be the Word of God must

be weighed by what we know of the world into which the Bible comes.

Second, the Bible itself assumes this. Its first sentence is "In the beginning God created the heavens and the earth." It assumes that we already know that there is a God and tells us that He is the Author of us, the universe around us, and the Scriptures. If we had no idea of the meaning of the word "God," we could not grasp the message of the Bible or would deem it fictional. Atheists cannot believe the Bible from Genesis 1:1 on, because they know that its alleged author does not exist.

Third, if you cannot, independently of the Bible, prove the existence of God, you cannot prove the atheist wrong. You cannot prove the atheist wrong because he claims that all evidence in the existing universe is against the existence of God and you do not refute him. You "believe" in this "God" of the "Word of God" on "faith" without any evidence that "He" exists. If you take the God of the Bible on faith without evidence, then without evidence you or anyone else, including the atheist, may believe anything he wants including the nonexistence of your so-called God. He may also, like Alice in Wonderland, take any word in any sense he pleases, thus making all human conversation about God (or anything else) meaningless—or meaningful, no one would ever know.

Fourth, if you cannot, independently of the Bible, prove the existence of God, you cannot prove the Bible to be the Word of God. If you claim that the Bible is the Word of God, it must be the word of the you-know-not-what. When this so-called God of the Bible speaks to us claiming to be God, when we have already proven by all the evidence available that there is no evidence of God, we know at once that whoever or whatever this is who so claims, he or it is not God. This "God" purports to be the Creator of heaven and earth. Heaven and earth we know; but we also know when this claim is made that there is no evidence of any "Creator" of the heaven and earth.

Fifth, in fact, if it can be proved that there is no God, that proves that the Bible is not the Word of God. All of the Gospel collapses if there is no God, for the Gospel rests on the Bible as the Word of God, which it cannot be if there is no God. So far from the Bible proving that there is a God, the Bible proves itself not to be the Word of God, as there is no such being. If the Bible stands as evidence of God when there is no God, it fails at what it purports to be. Its very claim, so far from establishing it, demolishes it. If I claimed even as I write this, to be writing the Word of God, without any evidence for so claiming, my very claim would prove my writing is not what it claims to be. The Bible as the Word of God so claimed would be just as futile. The only difference is that my claiming is hypothetical while the Bible's claim is actual.

Sixth, worse than not being the Word of God, the Bible is fraudulent throughout since it pretends to be the Word of a God who does not exist. Christianity is not merely not true; it is a lie from Genesis to Revelation. Christians become of all men not only most miserable (1 Corinthians 15:19), but most deceitful. They zealously spread over the whole world their grand deception. Their religion inveighs against bearing false witness, but their Bible is nothing but false witness. They even die for their lie.

If then we merely let this lion loose, it would turn out to be a paper lion.

Is there no truth at all in Spurgeon's famous lion? Was it only a-*lyin*? There is no truth at all in it as a substitute for apologetics. As a sequel it is profoundly true. Once God is proven to be true, independent of Scripture, and the Scripture is then proven to be the Word of that God, then the Holy Spirit revealed in that Word of God does make that Word come alive in the hearts of men. With their new hearts they "experience" the power of this Lion of the tribe of Judah.

## 4. An Apology for Apologetics

So I must make an apology for apologetics. I must give reasons for using reasons. I have to argue for argument. I am constrained to prove the necessity of proving. First, all the half-dozen-plus arguments against arguments are, after all, arguments. People have to use their head to attempt to justify not using their heads. It does not take a superior intelligence to see that that is not very smart. In fact, it is what we call a contradiction, using one side of the brain against the other (which isn't a brainy thing at all). It is an intellectual sawing oneself off the rational limb on which one sits. If you can't see that having to have a reason means you must have a reason for everything, I'm afraid I can't give you a reason for anything.

Second, if anyone can and should always ask "why", there can and must be a "because."

People who have no reasons for their actions we call insane. "Why did you come in out of the rain?"

"I dunno," says the lunatic.

Third, when sane people appear to be against reason, they rarely are. When Tertullian said he believed because it is absurd, he was giving a reason for faith. What he meant by that arresting statement was that revelation coming from an infinitely wise God could be reasonably expected to be beyond our limited intelligence. What was needed was only to know that it was God who was revealing. Then the human mind would know (whether it could understand the revelation or not) that it was true. Though it appeared absurd it was true. If it appeared absurd, and came from infinite intelligence, that is an argument in its rational favor. Jonathan Edwards frequently wrote that "mystery" (the not fully understood) was to be expected in divine revelation.

My spouse has her own wifely way of reminding me of this principle on the earthly level. She constantly keeps well in my line of vision a printed motto that reads: "I refuse to have a battle of wits with an unarmed opponent."

Fourth, Christianity claims to be true, and truth is something that needs proof. If claiming were all that is necessary, Christianity is established. But even believers, not to mention unbelievers, are not and cannot be satisfied with that. As Chillingworth put it, "I am certain that God has given us our reason to discern between truth and falsehood, and he that makes not use of it, but believes things he knows not why, I say, it is by chance that he believes the truth, and not by choice; and that I cannot but fear that God will not accept this *sacrifice of fools.*"

Even when Christians appeal to experience they mean to make that an argument. Wilbur Smith's lengthy and learned work in apologetics devotes no less than a hundred pages to the "argument from experience." The less-learned Christians may not phrase it that way, but one can see that they are appealing to reason even when they do not know how to formulate it in the form of an argument.

What they are thinking is:" I have this kind of experience which could only come from God. Therefore I know it does come from God. You can take my word for it (as evidence of it)." That is an argument if the hearer can take the writer's word for it. But unless there is some evidence presented to the hearer, what may be evidence to the experiencer cannot be evidence to the non-experiencer. There is no problem in reasoning here, but a problem in communication.

This is especially true when the witness is unlearned and the witnessed-to is learned. I read once of a Moody Bible student who witnessed about Christ in her life to a University of Chicago professor. The learned professor, by his questions, soon had her (unable as she was to answer or even grasp his probing) not convincing him, but doubting her own salvation. She was right and he was wrong, but she didn't know her apologetics. She, having the proof but not knowing how to formulate it, was led to think she didn't have it.

Fifth, Christ proved that He was who He said He was. "Believe Me for My works' sake" (John 14:11). He claimed that what He did proved what He said about Himself, or about anything.

Specifically, when He said to the paralyzed man, "Your sins are forgiven" (Matthew 9:2), this implied His deity because, as the Pharisees present noted, only God can forgive sins. Thus He claimed deity. Then He went on to prove it by telling the paralytic to take up his bed and walk. When the man did what he was told, Jesus' claimed divinity was proven. Who can instantly cure a paralytic by a mere word except one who is God or has the power of God? Since Christ had already acted as God in forgiving sin, His displayed power had to prove His own deity and not merely the power of deity. This is proof of the deity of Christ that no rational human being can rationally deny.

Sixth, the Bible proves its own inspiration, but not through begging the question or by reasoning circularly. As generally reliable documents, the four gospels bear witness to a miracle-working Jesus Christ. His enemies did not deny it, and our contemporaries have no arguments against it. Since His status as a divinely certified messenger is established, His testimonies must be true. No one, but no one, denies that He believed that the Bible was the Word of God.

Seventh, apologetics demonstrates that the Creator is God, that God certifies His Son, His Son certifies His Word, and the Word certifies the Gospel.

## 5. Why We Cannot Start with the Starter

"If you don't start with God, you will never arrive at God" is the conviction of many otherwise solid thinkers. They contend you must begin with God to finish with Him. God is beyond finite comprehension. What the finite mind ultimately comprehends is the finite, never the infinite, a seemingly commonsense connection. What is fixed in Latin stone is usually the wisdom of the race: *Finitum non capax infinitum.* What is more evident than that "the finite cannot contain the infinite"?

First, one objection to this contention is that, wise as it seems to be, it self-destructs. If the finite cannot grasp the infinite, it cannot grasp the idea of its own ability. One knows something about God if he says that he knows nothing about God. This is something, if it is nothing. "God knows I'm an atheist."

The atheist would say, "I know two things: first, I know God, and, second, I know that He does not exist."

A second objection to starting with God is the company you keep if you do. It is those who say you cannot know God that you are thrown with if you seek to know God. These friends must make up their minds if they want us as fellow travelers. They cannot say that we cannot know God and then start with knowing God, as they profess to do.

They are fully aware of this silliness and confidently assert that they are not guilty of it except in the minds of really silly people. They say that since God cannot be known by the finite mind, God Himself (if He would be known) must reveal Himself to the finite mind. Then the finite mind can know God, who can make Himself known to whom He will, even though he cannot know Him.

But this defense is sillier than the original folly. If the finite mind cannot know the Infinite Being, the Infinite's attempt to reveal Himself to it would be infinite folly. If even God cannot square circles while they remain circles, how could He engage in the more impossible task of making finite containers hold the Infinite without changing their finite capacity? It does not make any difference whether you speak of univocal or analogical thinking, a finite container incapable of the Infinite cannot contain it without being changed from what it is to what it is not.

A third objection to starting with the Starter is that you don't know the Starter at the start. Even those who think you should start with the Starter admit this. They say you should assume, presuppose, or postulate His existence. That admits that you do not naturally and logically begin with Him. These presuppositionalists have somehow come to know Him, not by presupposing Him obviously. They now, however, submit presupposing Him at the outset as the only way to know Him. They feel they did not learn of Him *a-posteriori*, though they must have tried. They have found a successful way of knowing God to be— by presupposing Him, rather than trying to reach Him by observation of the world in and around us.

The presuppositionalist is in a bind. If he starts strictly with a presupposition without any proof, then he begs the question whether there is a God. He simply asserts the answer to the disputed question without any argument— even against those who offer arguments for atheism. Everyone *except* the presuppositionalist recognizes this as an unreasonable approach.

If, in defense, the presuppositionalist says that by presupposing God one has an answer for all mysteries and proof that He must exist, while the *a-posteriori* approach leads only to a blind alley, he is not presupposing God but proving Him. Whether the argument for presuppositionalism is sound or not is not the question. It destroys presuppositionalism and makes it into post-suppositionalism. That is, after discovering that all other efforts at finding answers are futile, this is found to be the only rationally successful approach. If it is tested and proven, it certainly is no mere presupposition. It is not accepted as a presupposition, as is supposed to be the case, but demonstrated as the only rational way to know God. It may be different in procedure from using the theistic proofs, but not in nature. Instead of arguing for God from cosmological, causal, teleological, or ontological considerations, one argues from the futility of all these approaches and the success of presupposing. One may consider the approach successful, but in no way presuppositional.

I will mention but one more objection to presuppositionalism. To be presuppositional is necessarily to be dogmatic. If you assume God at the outset, you cannot listen to objections because they would have to be considered temptations. Emil Brunner, who had a presuppositional streak in him, considered entertaining questions to be "demonic doubt." If God is entertained and believed as a presupposition, He cannot morally be doubted. To engage in debate becomes an unpardonable sin of possibly attributing to the evil one the presuppositional truth of God.

I have already shown that if a presuppositionalist tries to prove God thereby, he has sinfully left his presuppositionalism. Here I am saying that if he does not defend his position he cannot escape anti-rational dogmatism. The presuppositionalist is always between the devil of demonstration and the deep blue sea of irrationalism.

We cannot start with the Starter until we have ended with the Starter (Creator) of the universe. Man has to start where he starts. When he does so, as I have shown, he will end where he started—the mind of God. Once man knows God, thereafter he begins all his thinking with Him. The fear of the Lord is the beginning of all wisdom (in distinction from knowledge).

This is a well-known and well-worn formula: the order of knowing is the reverse of the order of being. We begin our knowing where we are and end it where He is. He is eternally first in the order of being. We learn by the reverse order of knowing. We must begin with autonomy and end with theonomy. We are a law to ourselves until we learn that that law comes from outside ourselves. From thence to the end of eternity it is: "Speak, Lord, for Thy servant heareth."

## 6. Starting with Self-Consciousness

Lest we take steps before the first step, let us begin at the beginning rather than at the end. We begin with ourselves in a surrounding environment.

We are conscious of ourselves as distinct from what surrounds us. If we deny consciousness, as is the habit of some today, it can't be denied in the vast majority who claim it. In fact, virtually every human being claims it, and that cannot be denied even if a few among us deny it in themselves. Self-consciousness is a highly private matter experienced by the general public. Now when the general public claims a private experience, we usually say that becomes common knowledge. And how does one refute common knowledge by the private convictions of a very few? How can one person know what a million do not experience? A million persons cannot say what I, one person, do not experience. My experience is my experience and a million others cannot take it from me. When the million experience it, how can one take it away from so many? This makes it the experience of the race. The thinker cannot doubt that, but must doubt or disregard the few who deny it in themselves.

How does the one come futilely to deny the many? He could be sick, or deranged, or joking, or making himself famous, or something or other. One thing he cannot be, he cannot be right. It is already proven that normal human beings are conscious of their personal existences. A person cannot be a human being and not be a self-conscious human being. We human beings so recognize and testify. Therefore these oddballs are playing linguistic games trying to fool us. Perhaps they have succeeded in fooling themselves. *They* may even be taken seriously, but what they are *saying* cannot be. It may be, as Norman Geisler writes in another connection, "sayable" but not "thinkable."

Human self-conscious existence is undeniable, but what about continuing identity? How do I know that this writer at seventy-five is the same person of whom he was conscious at five? at thirty-five? Consciousness is still the infallible answer. I am conscious that I am I at seventy-five. I was conscious that I was I at five and thirty-five. I am also conscious that it is the same I, in spite of all my external changes at five, thirty-five, and seventy-five. I am conscious of myself at seventy-five; true, I am not now conscious of myself at five. But I am conscious now at seventy-five that those were my experiences at five. I am conscious of being the same person, though now older. Call it a "stream of consciousness"; I am conscious that this is my stream of consciousness, not yours.

Jonathan Edwards broke with John Locke at this point. Edwards felt that God could create another person with these same experiences and thus create the illusion of identity. But since God is a God of truth, He would not make another person conscious of my experiences as his own (which they were not). Even less could He make this other person responsible for my experiences.

But I am here guilty of introducing God before He has introduced Himself. My excuse is that I was thinking of Edwards taking exception to John Locke when both were theists.

So far as my own exposition is concerned, I am conscious of me at five, thirty-five, and seventy-five. There is no reason to assume that it is other than as I am conscious (no God at this point being considered because we have not yet arrived at His demonstrated presence). When that point is reached, He will be found to be a God of truth, and the above observation will be relevant.

So there is an "I" and billions of other "I's", each one conscious of its own being and surrounding being. As yet we are not conscious of any deity, but only of ourselves and our surroundings. This is our universal *pou sto*; where I stand, where you stand.

Here I stand, but I cannot stand still. I must move on because, unlike the rocks around me, I am a thinking I. I am conscious of my being and at the same time that I am not the source of my being. Nor are my parents the source of my being for they were incapable of being the source of their own being. So what is the source of my being? It cannot be my environment, since even my most immediate environment, parents, is not the source of my being. In fact, my environment needs explanation of its being as much as I.

Why not "let it be"? Why can things not just be as they are? And as they have been? Is that unthinkable? Am I not thinking it, right now? Do not millions of others past and present not live and die with that notion? Why not let it be? Why is any explanation necessary for what is, and is to be, and has been?

Why the questions "Why?" or "How"? In a certain sense we all do "let it be." We all live with the "why" and the "how." We are all part of what is, and we necessarily let it be as it is. But we find that that which is includes our own question-asking nature. Part of that which is is a part which asks "why", and how it is as it is, and you are as you are, and things are as they are. Why not let it be? Because we are part of the being which must know how and why it came to be as it is. If you would let it be, you would not help man get the answers it is his nature to demand. He will die of intellectual suffocation if you do not get the information to him that he must have. That is the only way that you can "let it be."

Man knows that he has a cause of his own being. He depended on his parents, and he depends on other sources for his continued existence. But man knows that those sources are not adequate explanations even of his moment-to-moment, temporal being. That his father's sperm and mother's ovum could unite to form him in his zygote and fetal form is only telling him (superficially) what happens. It does not tell him how it produces another rational human life. The father has no power of his own will to produce the sperm. They are produced when he wills certain sexual activity. He knows his willing that activity does not produce the activity nor the sperm that is ejected from his body. So with his mother and her ova.

Man knows that, though everything needs explanation, what is visible does not explain anything. There is power in and through everything, or that which is would not come into being nor remain in being. The observing mind of man notices. The inquiring mind of man wonders the how and the why, including how and why the mind came into being asking "how" and "why." Let it be. Let it be. But how and why does it be? Let it be that man cannot be man without asking these questions, nor be a happy man without their answers. Let it be that man is a being who lives by asking questions and getting satisfactory answers. Otherwise he merely exists.

So existing as men who want to be, we have asked questions. What are the answers man finds on which his being depends?

It must be as the Greek poet Aratus said, quoted by the biblical writer Paul (Acts 17:28): "In Him we live and move and have our being." We have already seen that we cannot live and move and have our being in ourselves. It must be in someone other than ourselves.

# 7. Finishing with the Starter

Without question, the existence of God is the greatest question that can be raised. God, which we all understand to mean the ultimate being, must be the one to whom we all owe our existence and all that goes with it—gratitude, love, and fear.

Some philosophers think that this question was new to philosophy. Plato seemed to imagine that he started the inquiry. Whether that was so, in philosophical circles, following Plato almost all had some theory of the nature of the ultimate being. However, they seemed to view it as impersonal, precluding gratitude, love, or fear.

I find it incredible that our most thoughtful people would not immediately realize that, if there is an ultimate being, He must be personal. According to the apostle Paul, all men reflecting on the "visible things" immediately see that they reveal a personal God (Romans 1:20). Their subsequent primitivism of worshiping the creature rather than the Creator was traceable to their unwillingness, not incapacity, of having the divine person in their thinking (Romans 1:21f). "God gave them over" to this "reprobate mind" (Romans 1:28). Paul must be implying that the philosophers, though not crass idolaters, also suffered from this same human indisposition. It is, after all, not mankind's self-judgment. If they are willfully culpable in behaving as they do, it is not surprising that they do not readily admit it. Furthermore, if knowledge does "puff up" (1 Corinthians 8:1), philosophers would, by vocation, be even more inclined not to confess willful ignorance.

Philosophers (some, at least) would be surprised that I'm surprised that they do not think of an "ultimate being" as necessarily personal. Some, such as Schopenhauer, wonder whether they themselves are personal and if there is any meaning to such an occult term. If one means by the term "personal," a rational entity with any sort of "free" choice, all behaviorists are sure there are no such persons in this world that scientific observation can locate. That conviction grew out of the causal fixity of the world which seems, to these thinkers, to preclude any beings beyond, not to mention ultimately beyond this world.

The behaviorists have a point. If there are no persons in this world, we nonpersons would not likely suspect an Ultimate Person behind us.

So, I guess, before we can imagine an Ultimate Person, we must see if we can find a proximate one. I must start with me. I cannot start with God who, if He exists, could tell me that I am. But He cannot tell me that I exist until I first know that He exists. This means that if I am to know whether He exists or not, I must know that I exist.

"I" am one of those self conscious entities with "free choice" that the behaviorists assure us do not exist. So it is "I" against the behaviorist who says that I do not exist. To his credit, he also says that *he* does not exist. "I," he says of himself, "do not freely choose to say that I do not exist." He says it just the same. Who is this behaviorist "he" who denies his own existence? He looks like the same kind of person I and my wife and other people I know are. But he says that he is not the kind of people we are, nor are we the kind of people we think we are.

This conversation becomes rather frustrating. But that is *our* fault, the behaviorist tells us. We have not done our homework. If we had studied in the psychological laboratory with him, we would know that we are not.

So to the laboratory I must go to learn that I never went to the laboratory, never could or ever would go to the laboratory. In the laboratory the I who I thought I was is found to be a bundle of flesh, bones, nerves, and a brain. It is by this learning network (no epiphenomenal or subphenomenal "I" there) that this imaginary "I" learns that I am nothing but this network that does the thinking and the feeling and the "free choosing" that "I" wrongly suppose is an "I."

A host of nonbehaviorist psychologists and neurosurgeons have not neglected their homework. They have gone to the same split-brain laboratories and they found "me" there. Behold, my son was lost and is found again. They resurrected me in behaviorist laboratories where I had been executed. Sir John Eccles has shown that I am. "I" am, it seems, a left-brain, predominantly rational I. It seems I have a right brain also associated more with my intuitive, feeling conscious "I".

Grateful as "I" am that my friends raised me from the dead in behaviorist laboratories, I suspect that the behaviorists never got "me", but only burned me in effigy. Indeed I don't think that they ever "got" even themselves, but they engage in mock mayhem. They suffer from a suicidal death wish (that may not be unassociated with this God hypothesis of which we are speaking or were until the behaviorists so rudely interrupted).

The reason I and you and the behaviorists never go into their laboratory is because it is "we" who go. "We" cannot go as behaviorists. Before and after any experiments I and you and they (we) choose to experiment. Surely *we* learn much from these researches. We learn more and more about ourselves. If we were not selves, *we* could not learn anything in or out of a laboratory. This the behaviorists themselves teach us. If they are only a brain network, they could not teach us or themselves anything. There would be no one to teach or learn. Computers never teach us anything. Their programmers teach us much by computers. But computers learn and teach nothing. They are a network of chips. The behaviorist is a network of cells. Networks of chips and cells learn nothing and teach the same. It is their users, their I's, who know it all. If the behaviorist as a network of cells went into the laboratory, he would come out as ignorant as he went in. That the behaviorist learns and teaches anything is because he is not a behaviorist. He cannot be a behaviorist and know anything. The behaviorist often knows and teaches much—because he is not a behaviorist.

After this intellectual interruption, let us go back to fruitful intercourse with the beyond. We had been saying that it is natural and logical to believe that the ultimate being is personal. If ultimate being is ultimate, it must account for the proximate. No one will deny that. Neither will anyone, once the distempered behaviorists have been pacified, deny that the proximate includes personalities such as human beings. So this much seems obvious—the ultimate must account for the personal. Not so obvious to many is the supposition that it is logical to believe that Ultimate Being explains personal beings by being personal Himself.

For most contemporary thinkers this is gross overstatement, if not arrogance. Many see insurmountable objections to the mere notion that the ultimate may be personal. For one thing, the ultimate must be infinite. If not, there could be something else which could be ultimate or share ultimacy. But this would destroy all ultimacy. Shared ultimacy is a contradiction in terms. How can there be two

or more sources of all things? There would then have to be
a Source of the sources, the one and infinite Source.

It is argued, then, that since the ultimate is necessarily
infinite, it cannot possibly be personal. The infinite must
include everything. If it does not include everything it is not
infinite. If it does include everything it cannot be personal,
because everything is not personal. The personal is not everything. It may be something, but it cannot be everything
and be personal still.

Everyone agrees that if something is not personal it is
not God. And if it is infinite it is not personal. So if it is the
infinite ultimate or source, it is not God. If God is not infinite He is not God. He does not exist. This is what Zeis has
in mind when he says that God *necessarily* does *not* exist.
He is as sure of the nonexistence of God as theists are aware
of His existence. Apparent reason is on Zeis' side. There is
no God and Zeis is His prophet. We are all His prophet for
we all agree by definition that if God is He is infinite. Hear, O
Israel, the Lord thy God is no God.

We have been brought in out of the "heat." God, we
were saying, must be the Ultimate, the Source, the All. We
were warming our hearts in that thought when the "fire"
went out. Someone turned off the stove. We turned off the
stove and froze to death. Now we are a part of the frigid infinite. For us, only the ashes of God; ourselves, a part of the
ultimate cold. Death in all around I see. More apathy to
Thee. My Jesus, 'twas better never to have loved at all.
Cursed be Thy name.

No wonder philosophers are not a happy lot. They
know better than to rejoice. They, unless they are "fool-
osophers," as the fundamentalists say, know too much
ever to be at peace with themselves or their universe. 'Tis
folly to be wise, we say.

The philosophers know they think. The rest of us think
we know. So we are blessed in our ignorance; they are
cursed in their knowledge.

After this apostrophe to the ultimate, let us have

another look. All this came about because we concluded that the ultimate, the source, must include all and could not therefore be personal, be God. In desperation we must consider whether God has to be infinite or whether He can be after all (forgive the pun). When we came in out of the heat it was because we saw (or thought we saw) that God could not be infinite, and, therefore, could not be God. There is no God and Zeis is His prophet, the prophet of the dawn that never can be (Isaiah 8:20). Were we bewitched? Can't there be a finite God after all?

Try as we will we cannot think of, let alone worship, a limited God. How can He be our help in ages past when surrounded by totality? He would need help forevermore. He just might need our help. He would need us as much as we need Him. He would have to need us *more* than we need Him. We never had to keep up the appearance of being a God. That is His "thing." He needs prophets. We don't—we are prophets. In this case, we are prophets of doom, but prophets still. Poor God, a has-been. Help wanted: an ex-God? Not likely.

Okay, goodbye, Rock of Ages. Can God be infinite? Can He be God and "be all"? Is this crazy, or can God be the infinite finite God? Is it crazy to think of an infinite God? Crazier to think of a finite God? Or craziest to think of an infinite-finite God? Nuts! Why not?

We are new at this business of thinking like a god. Infinity is not our cup of tea. But we do know something about personality. We are persons. If we know anything, we know what it is to be a person. We may not know where we came from or where we are going, but we do know what we are.

I (we) know one thing. I am a person who has a finger. My finger is not a person, but it is a part of me and I am a person. Impersonal person? No, I am a person with impersonality like my impersonal finger. It is not a person, but I would not be a person, at least not a normal person, without it. It does not make me less a person. Rather, without it I would be less a person. So it adds to, not subtracts from, my personality. The older I become the older my finger becomes. We grow together. We go together. Then comes the separation at death. At least, separation comes if I can be a person without my finger. Of course, I know living persons living in this world without fingers, without most of their body. So it is not impossible for human personality to exist apart from the impersonal. But the point is that it is possible for our personality to live with the impersonal.

The grand conclusion: I am a person with an impersonal finger. It is not a contradiction for me to be personal and impersonal. My finger does not detract from personality. It is not incompatible with my person. It is not a contradiction in terms. What an amazing discovery; only a nonphilosopher could make it!

Yet, I hadn't thought of it when I was thinking about the Ultimate, the Source, God. Yet, I could see a human person along with a finger, but I couldn't see God along with His finger. I was thinking and saying all sorts of silly things about God and His finger that I couldn't tolerate close to home. I could see myself with ten fingers and still a self, but I destroyed God for one finger.

How silly can I get? Infinitely silly. I imagined that ten fingers could not destroy a finite person, but one could destroy an infinite person. I tremble when I think of the saying that God doesn't care for the worship of fools. I was a fool's fool—denying God's personality for what didn't detract from my own.

So we can come back into the divine "kitchen." God can be personal and infinite. But is He? We have seen that the Ultimate or Source is personal if we who come from the Ultimate are persons. But we stickled momentarily at His being an *infinite* person. Now that we see the possibility of that, at the same time we see the certainty of His infinite personality.

Now that we see clearly again another stickle crosses our vision. God has pain in His finger! His appendages do not destroy His personality, but do they destroy His happiness? He must be, we have seen, an infinite person, but is He an infinitely miserable person? I know I would be if I had an eternal boil on my little finger.

No one, but no one, denies that God has a pain in His fingers. If He is an "infinite all" He has all the pain and the pain of all. If so it would seem that the "everblessed" is the eversuffering God.

But this raises a problem not only for God, but for man. If God is all and in all, He must will all. He is, as seen, the Infinite One. As such He must be unlimited by anything. If He is everything, everything is His. How can He find fault, unless it is with Himself. But how would He find fault with Himself when all is as He wills it? It could not be otherwise. If He wanted it otherwise it would *be* otherwise.

So if there is a pain in His finger, He must want that pain in His finger. How else could it get there or remain there? But that is where we come in. It pains us to think that God suffers. Not that we suffer His pain, but it becomes our pain because we can't understand how a person who ordains everything according to His good pleasure could be pleased to have pain.

We, unlike masochists, never choose pain unless we're not truly human. Even then we learn to like pain because we know no other way of coping with it. But God doesn't have to cope. He is the one who makes all things cope with His almighty will.

If God wills His displeasure, it can only be because He is pleased to do so. So it cannot be displeasure because it is His pleasure to will it. He takes pleasure in pain. Pain is pleasure for Him. He must enjoy pain or He would not will it.

But if God enjoys pain it cannot be pain. Pain, by definition, causes suffering. But this "pain" does not, cannot, make God suffer because it pleases Him. When we have pain we suffer and try to escape the pain. If this were pain for God (who is a rational being), He would do what we rational beings would do if we could. There is no "if He could" with God, so there can't be any pain in God.

That relieves our pain too. At first we suffered intellectual pain trying to imagine how the God of all could suffer any pain. Now His pain is gone because we see that His pain never was. Our mental pain is cured and we're free to suffer our real pain and not God's imaginary pain.

There is, however a theological "Catch 22." We see that there can't be any pain in God, but seeing that shows that the only pain is ours. And how can God get pleasure in our pain? Has God been delivered from masochism only to be found a sadist? He seems to have all the makings. He has all the power and we His creatures have all the pain. He gets pleasure out of our pain. We have saved Him from pain by taking it upon ourselves. We are God's savior.

We feel good about ourselves by blaming ourselves. As King David's soldiers said to him, "You are worth ten thousand of us" (2 Samuel 18:3). We say to God, "You are worth all of us."

But if we are so virtuous, why does God let us suffer? Is it to save Him? That raises a real question about the existence of God. He seems to be the guilty one who causes all suffering in His creatures. They are merely creatures, but they do all the suffering. He must be the Creator, the Ultimate Source of them and their activities. But it is they and not He who suffers. They don't seem to "deserve" suffering, but they suffer. He seems to "deserve" suffering, but He does not suffer. He seems to suffer, but, as we have seen, it is only seeming and not suffering. Theirs is the suffering and no seeming. The Judge of all the earth cannot do wrong, but it certainly seems so.

At this juncture we will understand why Pascal was not interested in the God of the philosophers, but rather the God of Abraham, Isaac, and Jacob. The latter God is interested in grace and love and mercy instead of abstract qualities that seem to lead to just such embarrassments as we are presently facing.

But, of course, there are not two Gods. The one God is the God of the philosophers (natural revelation) and the God of the patriarchs (special revelation). Plato's problems have to be solved in Plato's natural world and Abraham's in Abraham's supernatural world. The one God is the God of both worlds, as Plato believed and Abraham knew.

Let us return to the world of the Greeks and forget the Hebrews for the moment. The natural world reveals that God is holy and just. We creatures of this world know that our moral sense can only have come from our Ultimate Being. All things must come from Him for there is no other place to come from.

We humans are created in such a way that we think, feel, make judgments and decisions. We think of a particular act, for example, feel approving or disapproving of it morally, judge it to be what ought or ought not to have been done, and decide that the doer was praise- or blame-worthy if the act corresponded to his intention. Reward or punishment ought to follow.

Let us now revert to that pain we were so painfully discussing. Pain is painful to discuss initially. Let us suppose that the doer of the act mentioned was found by our moral judgments to have been blameworthy and deserving of punishment, which would have to cause some kind of pain to be real (effective) punishment. In that case, the pain would please us. If no punishment followed, that would pain us. In the first case the offender would suffer pain deserved and would please the moral beholder. In the second case, pain would be spared the one who deserved it and pass to the moral beholder who did not deserve it.

We know that there are two kinds of pain in the world: deserved and undeserved. God, therefore, is pleased to allow (decree) good and bad pain. Just and unjust pain pleases Him? All we can say at this point is that it pleases Him to allow just and unjust pain. He could conceivably be angry with one and happy with the other. Or He could be indifferent to all—only pleased with His permission of all.

How do we know which? First, God gives all of us this moral nature described. Second, He must Himself, therefore, be morally concerned. Third, He must be disposed to virtue, not vice, because He disposes His moral creatures to virtue, not vice. This is evident because we approve the right and disapprove the wrong inwardly in our consciences and outwardly in our protestations. Fourth, He makes us suffer inwardly and outwardly when we choose what we know to be wrong. He makes us pleased with ourselves when we choose what we know to be right. He, therefore, shows that it is in accordance with His moral nature to love the good and hate the evil. Our answer to the question of how God must feel about just and unjust pain is plain. He is pleased with just and displeased with unjust pain, but pleased to allow each.

That brings us to the point that God is pleased to permit or decree what displeases Him. Once again He seems pleased with what displeases Him (as He seemed to be happy to inflict pain on Himself). Once again, this is only a seeming tyranny of words (which are our only vehicle for expressing ideas). If it pleases God to decree what displeases Him, there must be some "seeming" here, some play on words, some *apparent* contradiction. It makes no sense as it is expressed. So we must find the right words or the fuller explanation of the otherwise wrong words.

Let's try again. Here is evil or wrong which displeases God. Yet if He were displeased to have it exist He would not let it exist. So, clearly, He is pleased to let evil exist. God is not displeased with evil's existing; yet He is displeased with evil. Displeased with evil, not its existing!

How can these things be? It must be that God will bring something out of evil's existing that pleases Him and is therefore good. So evil is bad and against God's nature, but its existing must be good for the purpose God has. So the evil is bad, but not the good God brings out of it. He could not bring good out of evil without evil's existing. So it is good that evil exists, though evil as existing is bad. This is the divine method, not divine madness. God has seeming pleasure with evil, but actual displeasure with evil. His pleasure is only in what comes out of it, and therefore ultimately has pleasure in evil's existing. So God has no pleasure in evil; but, more properly and fully stated, God has pleasure in evil-existing-for-the-good-God-would-bring-out-of-it. That makes sense—good sense. Not a bad use of the bad. God's intelligence and morality are vindicated when properly understood.

So we see that God is holy though His world is unholy. God is in His heaven and much is ill with the world. Nevertheless it is good that it is ill.

So much for God's good use of evil in His world. We can see how God triumphs in and over evil in the world, but how did He bring it into the world in the first place?

One thing we know about that "who dunnit?"—God didn't! We know He didn't for a very good reason—the best of reasons—He couldn't. God cannot do evil. The Bible says so. But you knew that before the Bible told you. And you'd know that even if the Bible didn't tell you. We discovered that a few pages back. God made us, and even we know that we are made to do good and only good.

You say, "Yes, it is according to our created nature to do good and not to do evil. But, behold, we do evil! If our nature is like His and His like ours, He is able to do evil as well as good. Where do you get this idea that God cannot do what mere creatures originally made in His nature can do? If the way of the human transgressor is hard, it ought to be easy with Him. Certainly it can't be impossible. All things would appear possible with God. And remember, you just said it pleases God to allow evil to be. Why would He not get even more pleasure in doing it?"

God cannot possibly do evil because it has no appeal to Him. He is good, as we have already seen. We had better expand that statement. He is good and only good. As long as

He is good, only good, and nothing but good, He simply cannot incline to evil; and what He cannot incline to, He cannot choose, and what He cannot choose, He cannot do.

Can God not change? We creatures in His image can. Why can't He? Or do we always have so much more ability than our God? We can sin and He can't. We can change and He can't. We can choose sin and He can't. I'm beginning to feel sorrow for God. I feel like a certain poet who felt sorry for God because He would never ever enjoy a surprise. He knows everything and can't learn anything. We keep on learning, but God can never ever learn even one new thing.

But enough of this now. Let's concentrate on this one point beyond the point we are on. Why can't God, even if He can't now incline toward evil, change sometime and catch up with His creatures in this area, if not in all other areas?

We can change because circumstances change for us. But they never change for God. The Athenians used to wait around to hear some new thing. But there are no new things for God to react to. Everything is eternally old hat for Him. How can He ever change when nothing ever changes for Him? We have pasts, presents, and futures. God lives in an eternal "now."

This all comes under our very first point—the infinitude of God. He is unlimited by anything. And you need not feel sorry for God for all the experiences He cannot have. The only reason He cannot have or do anything is because there is nothing to change to, and He cannot choose or do evil because evil does not exist. There is nothing to choose.

Evil, or sin, is simply choosing what God forbids. For example, consider the killing of a person not deserving death. That is called by God and man "sin" or a "crime" and is, accordingly, punished. Those who know there is a God say this is a sin because it is a violation of the command of God. But we have already seen that it is not a violation of the will of God. Nothing is a violation of the will of God who brings everything to pass according to His will. Remember how He is pleased to ordain even what displeases Him? And, too, He is pleased to be displeased in different senses of the word.

This is what I mean by saying that evil does not, cannot, exist. It is all a seeming. Whatever God brings to pass is good. Everything that happens God brings to pass. Or, whatever happens is God's ordaining. Nothing not of God's ordaining ever has, ever does, or ever shall come to pass. In all the vast expanse of time and space, there is no time, no space, for evil to be.

What of suffering? I ask. What of suffering? You expostulate, "That is certainly evil, isn't it?"

I reply, "Of course not. It is good, perfectly good; the best, the very best. There would be evil only if there were no evil in this universe of ours." We know there is no evil in suffering because God ordains it (we know this because it happens). If we are moral we concur in it. We could not be moral if we did not concur in what God does. So, in a sense, we ourselves decree suffering, even if we are the ones who suffer.

If we do concur in suffering, however, we cannot suffer. Those who approve of suffering, because God approves of suffering, are moral persons; and moral persons are free from suffering, or from the pain of "pain." They know that such "pain" is good and are glad to have it. Pain is painful only for those who deserve it; and that makes the righteous rejoice.

For example, I have a bronchial restriction. As I write this my breathing is a little heavier than most of yours as you read this. But, since God has ordained this, I am glad to have heavy breathing. I don't envy you, though I carry a spray in my pocket to make the breathing easier. And I am also happy when I breathe easier, though I would still be happy if I didn't.

"This is nonsense," you say. Is it nonsense always to be happy when that is what all men are always seeking?

You reply, "Normal persons are seeking relief from

misery in order to be happy; not to be happy in misery. I reply: I mentioned above that I, too, carry my spray.

Who is the fool? The one who seeks relief but is happy even when he doesn't find it, or the one who seeks relief but is miserable when he doesn't find it? A rhetorical question, isn't it?

You hang in there because you'll not give up your misery easily. You say that I must be a masochist who enjoys suffering when it is you who are a hypochondriac. I enjoy not suffering. I have no "pain" that I cannot spare. Is that so bad? The masochist is miserable, he admits, but will not let his misery go. I gladly let my misery go. I don't even let it stay because I know that all that comes comes from God and is good for me. There is no evil coming the moral man's way. He knows it. There isn't any evil coming the immoral man's way, but he doesn't know it, or at least admit it.

So, we have given God a clean bill of existing in good moral health! God not only exists, He is existence. "In Him," as Paul says, "we live and move and have *our* being."

The real question is not whether God exists, but whether man does. If God does not exist, man does not exist. It is because we exist that we *learn* He exists. But it is because He exists that we *do* exist. As the little girl said, after praying for almost everybody on shipboard by name, "And take care of Yourself, Lord, because if anything happens to You, we're all sunk." Being is the reverse of the order of knowing, as the saying goes. God is the Alpha of being, but the Omega of being known. First, God is; second, man knows. First, man knows; second, God is. Does God's existence then depend on our knowing? For God to be is to be perceived? By man? Of course not. You cannot know in the order of being. That is the order of God.

"Wait a minute," someone says. "You (I, that is) have overlooked something. You began by *assuming* some Ultimate Being. Then you went on to argue that this Being must be personal and discussed this person's relation to man and evil and so on. But you never proved that there had to be an Ultimate Being. Granted, if it exists, you have proven that it must be a personal existence. But don't you have to prove that it exists? You'll admit, will you not, that many philosophers see no reason for positing an Ultimate Being?"

The point is well taken. I rather assumed that everyone immediately recognizes that there is an Ultimate Being and that the really vital question is whether that is the personal Being we call God. I know that there are philosophers in our day who seem to think that there can be infinite regress, and even things starting out of nothing. We are only now sobering up after a long existential anti-rational binge. Some have not yet returned from their lost weekend. So I do owe my readers proof that no one can rationally deny an eternal Being.

Some modern thinkers will challenge right there at the word "rationally." Why, they ask, does all knowledge have to be *rational*? Why can we not know by feeling and intuition and other "right-side" of the brain experiences? They observe that rational knowing is connected with the "left side" of the brain, but there is a right side as well, and this is the source of non-rational experience. One Christian, the Arminian theologian Ware, even leans toward right-side thinking as a way of justifying Arminian doctrine versus the more rational thinking of Calvinism.

What do we say to these modern patterns of thought? First, they aren't new patterns of thought, but new knowledge of the way the brain works that are being used as new arguments for old ways of thinking. We mentioned Pascal, above, who thought this way long before anyone knew about the two-sided brain and its detailed functioning.

The answer we gave to Pascal is the same as we give to Ware and Sperry, et. al.: "Thank you for your very useful researches, but it changes nothing about the way we think. It only gives us more detailed information about the process and its source."

Wherever thought comes from, and whatever the relation of mind/soul and brain, thought always has begun, and always will begin, with intellectual ideas of objects. We have a notion of being and first beings and beings, for example. Unless we have that, there can be no thinking. Whatever we feel or intuit about it, to deal with it intellectually it must first come from the mind in the form of ideas, notions, or concepts. Once we grasp these notions we can reflect on them and draw conclusions about them—accepting them as true or rejecting them as false.

For example, suppose I feel good or bad about the idea of being or Ultimate Being. I must first have an intellectual notion of being or Ultimate Being. I can't feel about I know not what. William James challenges me there: "You feel afraid of something jumping out of the bushes at you, though you don't know what it is or even whether it is. You feel dread without knowledge and before knowledge."

This illustration of primal nonrational feeling actually illustrates my point with a vengeance. The frightened person is not afraid of nothing. If he knew there was nothing in the bushes he wouldn't be afraid of nothing jumping out at him. It is because he thinks of something: thief, rapist, drunk, bat, skunk, he knows not which, that is why he is scared. True, William James once said that we're afraid because we run, not run because we are afraid.

True, William James said it, but what he said is false. The person fled because he *thought* something was chasing him, and then his fleeing may have seemed to confirm his fears. But even James would know that as soon as he learned that nothing was chasing him he would wonder why he was running, and, if not insane, would stop when he realized he was running from nothing.

Feelings must follow thought in the first place, though thought can be influenced by feeling in the second place. As truly as the second follows the first, so the feeling must follow thought, even if it were an imaginary thought about nothing.

So we all have thoughts about being, and one of these

thoughts is that it must always be. Being must always be. How do we know that? Because that is all we can think. We cannot think of being not being. That is, we cannot think of nonbeing. If we try to think of nothing, it becomes something—something *called* nothing, but not nothing. If nothing is anything, to think of it is something or we could not think of it. Jonathan Edwards was right in saying that nothing is what the sleeping rocks dream of. Note that even the rocks have to be *sleeping* to *dream* of nothing. Edwards didn't say this, but he must have thought that human beings had to have rocks in their heads to think they could think of nothing. If you think of nothing it must be no thinking.

So if there is nothing, we can't know it, imagine it, feel it, or have anything to do with it. It is out of the realm of existence for us. For us human minds, being must exist. There cannot be nothing in our world of conceiving.

A last gasp of hope may arise here. Can't we think of beings for whom nonbeing does exist? Suppose there are such beings. What difference does it make to us? Moreover, we have shown that this Ultimate Being, if it does exist, has a moral existence. If He has made us unable to think of nonbeing, nonbeing cannot exist for us. A moral God is, as shown, incapable of immoral activity such as lying or deceiving. So we know that if God exists, nonbeing does not.

So being must be eternal because we cannot think otherwise. But some think the "Big Bang" could have come out of nothing. Not only nothing can come out of nothing (*ex nihilo nihil fit*), but we can't even think of the nothing out of which it is supposed to come. That is zapping a zero.

A high school teacher of mine once said that the greatest question of all is *why* there is something rather than nothing. Since that time I have seen much purpose (the *why*-ness) for something. The greater question is *how* there can be something rather than nothing. The answer to that is even easier. There must be something because there can't be nothing. Nothing can't be. Something must be. How simple! How sublime!

This is a way of stating what usually is named the "ontological argument" for the existence of God. This is really a theoretical argument for eternal being from which we deduce and/or induce many of its characteristics that add up to deity. Anselm wrapped these all up in his ontological argument for God. It might have been better if he had kept the argument simply the ontological argument.

That ontological argument proper cannot be answered. Its answer is not theoretically possible because to answer it is to prove it.

Once proven, or rather shown, that we cannot even think of anything other than eternally existing being, it is easy to show that such being must possess all possible excellencies (some of which we have shown above).

For an argument rejected by Aquinas, Kant, and a host of formidable philosophers and theologians, to be accepted as virtually axiomatic on my part seems brash, I admit. But the fact remains that in spite of the near-universal consensus there have only been two (puny at that) arguments offered against it. One is Pascal's mentioned above, that the God of the philosopher is not the God of Abraham, Isaac, and Jacob. This we refuted. Merely mentioning it is all it deserves unless the number of names on its petition gives cogency to its argument.

In a sense, the second argument is yet more puny, if possible. It would easily be seen as such if not for the fame and number of those citing it. Existence, they say, is not an attribute, but a mere analytic statement implied in the term itself. If you mention an idea existing as an idea, existence goes along with it and proves nothing in addition to it. But of course Anselm, Descartes, and Leibnitz knew this, as did Malcolm, Hartshorne, and a host of other users of this argument, past and present. But the argument is for an existence beyond the mere idea of the thing. Existence as a part of the concept in no way makes it greater than anything else conceivable (including Gaunilo's ideal island or Kant's imaginary money in his pocket).

Anselm and the others were open to this criticism not because of the argument, but because of the way they stated it, or, rather, didn't state it. It was clear enough in their articulation that the existence they were thinking of was "outside" the mind. It is better stated, I think, that the eternal being cannot be thought of as not existing *outside the mind*. His being must eternally be *outside the mind* because the mind cannot conceive otherwise. It is easy to think of perfect islands and imaginary millions in the pocket existing merely in the mind, but not as necessarily existing outside the mind. It is even easier for me to think of millions not being in my pocket as being in it. But try as I will, I cannot, you cannot, think of being not eternally being. That is the irrefutable ontological argument for eternal being outside the mind.

So eternal being must exist, and that eternal being must be God. Therefore, God must necessarily exist for the best of reasons. God exists because He cannot even be rationally thought of as not existing.

There is no rational creature anywhere who does not have God in his thinking. If one has a mind, God comes in the same package. That man who said, "I'm an atheist, God knows," said a mind full. He couldn't think of being an atheist without being a theist rejecting his God by his feelings, while incapable of doing so with his mind. The atheist cannot even dislike and therefore "disbelieve" in God without believing in Him. One has to know God to hate Him. Be hostile to Him we can; be ignorant of Him we cannot.

## 8. The Nonproblem of Evil

Evil is not the absence of good. It is the presence of good or God, which is the same thing.

Perhaps we do well to begin with a definition of evil. When I pick up the first dictionary I can find near me I read: "Evil (adj.) 1. Morally bad or wrong; wicked. 2. Harmful;

injurious. 3. Unlucky; disastrous—(noun) 1. Wickedness; sin. 2. Anything causing harm, pain, etc."

We are concerned here only with the noun "evil," from which its adjectival attributes derive. Evil is "wickedness" or "sin," which causes "harm, pain, etc."

Let us consider the more familiar religious term "sin." Evil is sin. Now sin is a violation of the commandments of God. So evil is defined as a violation of the commandments of God.

But all violations of the commandments of God are ordained by God. Everything that God ordains is good. So evil is good. It is good that there is evil. It would, by implication, be "evil" if there were no evil; but, evil existing, it is good.

So with "sin." Sin is a violation of the commands of God, but still according to the will of God.

Manifestly there are two kinds of good: "good good" and "evil good." Both good (which is obedience to the commandments of God) and evil (which is disobedience to the commandments of God) are good. Good good is what we mean when we use the word "good." Evil good is what we mean when we use the word "evil."

Our careless or thoughtless use of terms causes good and evil to seem opposites, mutually exclusive. Actually they are identities—only different sides of the same moral coin: the commandments of God. This carelessness comes from not always thinking of God when we use (as dictionaries do) these terms when He is essential to their very meaning. Evil or sin has no meaning apart from the commandments of God any more than good or virtue does.

But in the dictionary we also encounter the term "injury" and "injuriousness" figuring in the definition. Injury, too, must be understood with reference to the deity if it is to have meaning. To be a true injury something would have to be injurious to God, who alone does not deserve to be injured. Now since nothing causes injury to God, evil is not injurious. On the contrary, if injury causes hurt to those who deserve to suffer injury, it is a good thing. And this is always the case. God, who is the only one who never deserves to suffer injury, never suffers injury. All who do suffer injuries deserve to suffer injury. That, too, is good. It would be evil if they did not suffer injury.

Once again our carelessness in thought is evident. We leave God out of our thinking when we think of injury. But with God in our thinking there is no such thing as injury or wrong because all injury is right or deserved and, therefore, not an injury at all. With God in our thinking, there is nothing worthy of the pejorative term "injury."

Likewise, "wickedness" is in the dictionary, but not in life. Wickedness means unrighteousness or out of the line of duty to God. But everything that happens, being commanded or decreed by God, is in the line of duty or what is owed to God. Therefore, there is no such thing as wickedness.

Yet those who do what is called "wickedness" are punished for so doing, not praised. So, on the surface at least, there seems to be wickedness, especially if this punishment is eternal, as it always is in the sinner or his Substitute. Yet, leaving God out of our thinking again, wickedness does appear to exist as such. But since the so called "wickedness" brings no injury to God, but only promotes His glory, it is good that wickedness exists.

But why are doers of wickedness punished rather than praised for their so-called wickedness? That is because they do not intend it as what it is. Their wickedness praises God but they do not so intend by their wickedness. Consequently, they cannot be praised for the good thing because they do not intentionally do it. Good wickedness comes *by* them, but not *from* them. So they are not rewarded.

They are punished for *not* doing something, namely, deliberately aiming at the obedience and glorification of God. Evil is the undone, the *absence* of the good. It does not exist except as the absence of good. It has no positive quality. It is, in fact, just the opposite; it is the *lack* of good.

One can see why the doers of "good evil" are not rewarded because they do not do it deliberately. But why are they punished for what they did not do? Because they were commanded to do it. They sinned in not doing what they were obliged to do. They did not do anything evil, but their sin was not doing the good they ought to have done.

Thus Christ says to these who sinned by not doing, "I was hungry and you fed Me not . . ." (Matthew 25:35). Their sin was in not feeding Christ's "brethren." They were eternally damned for "sins of omission," or sins of not doing what ought to have been done.

But the damned *may* have fed some of Christ's brethren. We can't conclude that they never in their charity fed true Christians or brothers of Christ. But if they did, they did not feed them *as such*. They may have fed them with compassion for the hungry and no consideration of their suffering hunger for Christ's sake. They may have refused to feed them, though hungry, when they learned they were Christ's brethren. One thing is certain. They were damned for what they did not do—feed people who were hungry because they were Christ's "brethren."

It was good that these were damned because that is what they deserved at the hand of a just and holy God. Had they not suffered eternally, that would have been an eternal evil. Likewise, they can never be delivered, but must pay the "last cent" (Matthew 5:26) because the goodness of God, which they refused to do, is a sin for which they must be punished as befits this crime of omission. Hell, from that angle of moral vision, is as good as heaven and worthy of the same eternal praise which will be everlastingly and gladly given by the angels and redeemed in heaven (Revelation 18:9).

A further reason for the punishment of the impenitent in hell will be because even there they refuse to praise God for their righteous judgment as they ought to do. Saints in heaven will see the holiness of God's eternal torment and will, for that reason, bless God for it, even though it be visited on their spouses, children, or parents.

God has no pleasure in the death of the wicked (Ezekiel 33:11). His pleasure, and that of holy angels and saints, will be in the manifest rightness of their suffering. If they had turned and lived, He would have rejoiced in the holiness of rewarding them for their righteousness in Christ Jesus.

God and good creatures ever rejoice in the manifestation of God's glory—in heaven, hell, and in this world. There would be no rejoicing in either the blessedness of saints or the torments of sinners if both did not possess the same excellent quality—expression of the perfect holiness of the God of heaven and earth and hell.

So we have seen that evil is good. It is good that there is evil. Should the word "evil" be eliminated from the dictionary and the Bible? Probably it would be good if "evil" were eliminated from language. Since that is not likely to happen, we must always remember that evil means good. But that "evil good" is somewhat different from "good good."

Let me illustrate by an example at random. "In Adam all sinned" (Romans 5:12). That means that all mankind, represented by Adam, did the "evil good" of disobeying God's commandments. They did not do "good good" as God did in their act. They did "evil good." They died for their "evil good" because they did not disobey God *intending* to do the good that they *unintentionally* did.

This carefulness about the meaning of language will be rewarding. We will then never forget that God's hidden commandment is never violated even when His revealed commandment is. Let me explain "hidden commandment" and "revealed commandment." Revealed commandment is what we usually call commandments such as the Ten Commandments or the Golden Rule. They are "revealed" because God makes them known to us before we act. The hidden commandment is not usually known beforehand. It is known beforehand that sinners will violate the Ten Commandments, but not how or in what circumstances. But

the "how" and "what circumstances" are decreed, or or-
dered, or commanded by God to happen beforehand (from
etemity, in fact) "secretly"; that is, without the creature
being told beforehand. That is a hidden commandment of
God compared to the revealed commandment. Both are revealed, but one is revealed before the deed and the other not
until afterward.

For example, as I write this, you and I know beforehand
that the commandment of God is that I write the truth.
Whether I have obeyed His commandment you and I can
know afterward by comparing what I have written with
God's revelation in Scripture and nature. So we know that
we will be remembering that all that ever happens is at
least "evil good" and gives pleasure to all "good good"
persons. Good persons will always be pleased with all
God's works because they are always good as He does them
and at least "evil good" as creatures do them. God is to be
praised in all His works which are ever "good good" as done
by Him and either "good good" or "evil good" as done by
the creatures.

We know that there never was, is, or will be "evil evil."
Such evil (the dictionary definition) does not exist, and
ought not even to be in the dictionary. In fact, that evil is so
defined in the dictionary is, itself, an "evil good"—an incorrect definition that God has willed against His commandment that all expression should be true and accurate. He
has decreed this inaccurate untruth as an "evil good." It is
evil because the definer did not will his error for good as
God did. He will then be judged and damned to hell unless
he begs for the mercy offered by God in His Son, Jesus
Christ. He, too, received no praise for the good in his evil
good because he did not intend it. God is all the more to be
praised for bringing out the good in spite of the definer's not
intending it. It is "good good" to know that all is good and
that evil evil does not exist. It is sobering to remember how
many suffer because they do not know this. They suffer
justly (and eternally if not redeemed) because they do not

know what they ought to know. The reader must have
noticed that all "sin sin" is "sin sin" of omission. One
cannot "sin sin" except by not doing what is commanded.
How do we come by the incorrect expression "sin of
commission" when there is no such thing?

As I said above, because we commit the "sin sin" of for-
getting God. We forget that God is in every act and that
alone makes it good. Thus, the act is good. And even the
creature who acts, or does the "good good" which is "sin
sin" for him because he fails to will it as God's intention. It
is God's intention, but no thanks to this creature but rather
punishment because of his failure or sin sin of omission. In
other words, the act as committed is "good good," but the
creature-actor is guilty of "sin sin" because of what he does
not do, namely intend the "good good" in his own act.

If this little (but, I hope, partly "good good") explanation
is correct, what becomes of philosophy's and theology's
greatest and dearest problem, the problem of evil? Of
course, it is meaningless. There is no problem of evil. What
is meant in the expression "problem of evil" is "problem of
'evil evil'." We have seen "evil evil" does not exist; it is
merely an inaccurate expression. Those who inaccurately
use the term must mean, to be meaningful, "the problem of
'good evil'." But, of course, if they come to think of what
they are thinking, they should realize that "evil evil" does
not exist, and the "good evil" (which they must have in
mind if they have something in mind) being "good evil" is
not "evil evil" nor a problem. If they use this expression
meaning "evil evil" (because that alone could be a "problem") and do not know or intend that it means "good evil,"
they must be censured for not intending the "good evil"
which they are thinking. Therefore, they are not rewarded
for so thinking, but are punished for not so thinking.

P.S. Someone is asking: What is new in this since
Christian Science? Has it not been saying this for more than
a century? Christian Science has been denying evil's ('evil
evil") existence, and it has been maintaining that "all" (God)

is "good good" (good). Insofar it would seem to be "good good." This is not so, however, for several reasons. One, Christian Science denies sickness, suffering, and death and hell, all of which do exist, though not as "evil evil," but because of the absence of "good good." This amounts to an implied denial of God apart from whom there cannot be any "good good" in the creature. So, second, Christian Science is a denial of the "good good," its "good" being an "evil good" not intended (but the opposite). Christian Science is aiming at the "evil evil" which does not exist because it does not understand its own "good."

Another question may be: How does this fit with biblical Christianity or Calvinism? I think it fits perfectly, but many fellow Calvinists may, especially at first, not agree for several reasons. One, Calvinism was not so expressed by Augustine, Calvin, or Edwards (the greatest of the Calvinists), or any of the lesser ones. I think it would be easy to show that this is in accord with Augustine and Edwards, but also with the less "speculative" Calvin. Too, many Calvinists, especially at first, may think that the absence of "evil evil" entails the absence of punishment, and if that is so, this which I say here must be profoundly erroneous and anti-Calvinistic. This in spite of the fact that evil as the absence of good has been held by Augustine and Edwards, especially, who certainly taught an everlasting torment for the damned, whose evil evil was the absence of good.

Three, some Calvinists, like John Calvin, simply distrust the speculative, and wrongly see it forbidden by Scripture. Calvin once said that hell was made for the overly curious. One can be overly curious, but also underly curious. Remember Deuteronomy 29:29. So, in conclusion, I submit this entire chapter to whomever will read, with little hope of anything but its condemnation as being "evil evil" (at least, at first, while I myself will be consoled that even these attacks are but forms of "evil good" and will trust that most of the attackers mean their attack as such).

P.P.S. To those who will ask after the initial hubbub,

Was it worth the trouble to read? My answer will be: I certainly believe so. It seems to be extremely important for everyone to realize that God is in His heaven and all is well with the world (including the worldlings who are seeing the "good good" purpose of suffering the damnation they deserve, even though they are doing so unwillingly). Praise the Lord: All is truly good, including "evil," which is therefore no problem for apologetics.

## 9. Where Apologetics and the Gospel Leave Us

Apologetics and the Gospel leave us far worse than they found us. They find us as sinners hiding from God our Judge, remove our fig leaves, confirm our fears as infinitely short of the reality of our peril, show us that we must repent if we would avoid perishing, and that though God stands ready to forgive, we are so corrupt that we are incapable even of asking Him for forgiveness. The more light apologetics sheds on God, His Son, His Word, and His Gospel, the more we hate God, His Son, His Word, and His Gospel. In fact, we love nothing but darkness and hate light. The more light, the more hatred. Apologetics is the science of shedding light on God, and thereby stirring up hatred in us human lovers of darkness.

Why apologetics? To make us more damned than we were before it shed its light on our darkness? No, though that is its tendency—not because of its light, but because of our natural love of darkness. It is not the cause of our greater darkness, but only the occasion of it, the cause being our love of darkness made the greater in the presence of light.

The purpose of apologetics is to show us the light and lead into it. If it does not do so it is our fault, and not that of apologetics.

If apologetics does not lead us into the light it is our

fault; but if it does, it's God's grace. The apologist's light stirs up your darkness, but God may shed His light along with His apologist's light. And in His light you see apologetic light and love it.

Why, then, not dispense with apologetics and pray only to God? Because you will never pray truly until the light reaches you. And the Light of God comes only through the lesser light of apologetic witnesses. To be sure, we are not the Light, but only witnesses to the Light. But the Light comes only after the witness. We must decrease, but He must increase. But He only increases after we have appeared and disappeared. Yes, we have appeared and disappeared. Yes, we are only John the Baptists who baptize with words and water. He is the Light of the world who baptizes with fire and the Spirit. But, first, John the Baptist; second, Jesus the Christ, the Son of God.

More people were hardened than convicted by John the Baptizer. But those who were converted by the Christ first learned of Him by John. The Christ does not need the Baptizers, the apologists, or the witnesses, but He makes Himself dependent on them. They *can* do nothing without Him. He *will* do nothing without them.

So you may not be reasoned into the kingdom by this or any other apologist, but you won't be brought into the kingdom without us, either.

Where does apologetics leave us? Worse than we were when it found us? We are left with a possibility of being saved where there once was a certainty of being lost forever. As I said, apart from Christ, we apologists *can* do nothing, but apart from us He *will* do nothing.

So you are now in a position to deal with the One to whom we have introduced you. If you find it in you to accept our (and His) invitation to Him, you are saved forever and ever. He has been pleased to use our candles to illumine the Light of the World. You are now looking in His heavenly beams, and will walk in the Light as He is in the Light and be little lights in the world pointing to its Sun.

However, if you do not find it in your dark souls to come to the Light, you are damned the more for knowing more about that Light and hating Him more. You will wish in hell that you had never heard these arguments and encountered the Light Himself, only to hate Him more. But even if you are repelled by the Light, you may yet be saved if you will but seek to be born again by that Light.

How can you sincerely come to a Light you hate? You can't. How, then, can a hater of the Light be saved by the Light he hates, will not come to, but extinguishes in his heart?

This is where apologetics can help. You know that there is a God who wrote sixty-six books which tell you the way of salvation for light-hating sinners such as yourself. You now know with your mind, however much you may hate it with your heart, that the Light of the World commands you to "strive to enter" His kingdom (Luke 16:23). Many in His day were pressing into it (16:16), though some were not able to enter (16:23). *Few found it* (Matthew 7:14); but, some were enabled to find that narrow way. Those seekers found; those askers received; those knockers had the door opened to them (Matthew 7:7, 8).

It may be ("maybe", 2 Timothy 2:4) so with you. You know that God is not only a God of infinite wrath, but also of infinite sovereign grace. You must not, therefore, presume, but you may not despair. While there is life there is hope, if God has not already rejected you for the unpardonable sin (Matthew 12:31, 32). Your present unbelief is not unpardonable; your present skepticism is not unpardonable; your present sin is not unpardonable; your present guilt is not unpardonable. If God has not allowed you to harden against Him by attributing His work to the unholy spirit rather than the Holy Spirit, for you there is hope. No promise. No certainty. But hope, real hope, hope of eternal life.

Apologetics has brought you near. "Call upon the Lord while He is near."

# A Primer

# on

# Bible

# Inerrancy

# Contents

## Part III

# Introduction

This second of our little primers is on the most fundamental of themes. Bible Inerrancy (or the doctrine that "what the Bible says God says") has been under relentless attack since the Bible was written, but never more so than today. Something new, however, has been added in the modern onslaught. While the old liberal tradition of rejecting vast portions of the Bible still continues, the New Orthodoxy rejects all of it—as the Word of God, that is. John 3:16, no less than the Old Testament command to exterminate the Canaanites, is demoted from the status of Inspiration. The Bible, according to the new view, is the "instrument" (if God wills to make it such) of revelation and not itself revelation. This mentality is back of the proposed *Confession of 1967,* and for that reason we devote a lengthy appendix to it as a typical phenomenon of our time by no means restricted to the United Presbyterian Church in the U.S.A. We have tried briefly and non-technically to present a case for Bible Inerrancy that a serious-minded layman can follow and evaluate. Our critique of various false starts is first given to prepare the reader for what we feel is the correct view. While this little book is not in any way an exhaustive treatment of its divine subject, we trust that it is sound and faithful to the Scriptures of God.

# Part I

## Some Unsound Bases for Sound Doctrine

*1. The Bible's Own Testimony as the Basis for Inerrancy*

We could compose a book many times the size of this one consisting merely of fervent and eloquent evangelical appeals to the Bible itself as the proof of its own inspiration. Some three thousand times the Bible does make this claim for itself. "Thus saith the Lord" is a veritable refrain of the Scriptures. No book in the history of literature has made such frequent and moving assertions of its divine origin. Because of this remarkable characteristic of the Scriptures many have almost unconsciously concluded that the Bible is the Word of God.

This we believe and later shall attempt to prove is the right doctrine. The Bible is the Word of God; the inerrant revelation from above. It is the Word of God indeed, but not because it says so. Rather, it says so because it is.

How, we ask, would anyone prove the Bible is the Word of God simply because it so often says so? There could only be one basis for accepting Scripture for Scripture's sake: assertion for assertion's sake. But what an incredibly naive notion: A thing must be what it says it is. A man must be what he says he is. A book must be what it says it is.

Surely the mere setting forth of such an argument must be its sufficient refutation. An identification of claim with proof of claim is palpable error.

If it is not beating a horse that was born dead, let us point out the absurd consequences of the position we are here considering. If everything is to be believed simply because it says it is to be believed, then Hitler was a Messiah, the devil is an angel of light and antichrist is Christ. As Jesus said: "Then if any man shall say unto you, Lo, here is Christ, or there; believe it not" (Matthew 24:23).

But on the principle under scrutiny we would have to believe everyone who claims to be Christ—here and there, now and then. After all, according to the supposition we first believed in Jesus as the Christ because He said he was the Christ. We would have to be fair with other claimants whose claim is as loud or louder than his. If we would say "You are not the Christ because the Christ says you are not the Christ," anti-Christ could well say, "If you believed this other one because he said he was the Christ; why do you not, on the same principle, believe me when I say that I am the Christ; and if you will not believe that I am the Christ because this other Christ, whom you believe merely because he said what I also say, why not believe me when I say that he is not the Christ?"

There cannot be any answer to this criticism, for even to attempt to answer it is to admit it by retreating from the position being maintained (acceptance on mere assertion without any argument). If, for example, one says to antichrist, "I believe Jesus' claim because He has confirmed it in my experience," then you do not believe Jesus simply because He says He is the Christ. Rather, you believe Him because of something which He does in your heart; your ground has changed. You are no longer believing Him for His mere word's sake, but for His work's sake, specifically, His work in your heart.

Consequently, if you give no answer to the criticism of belief on the mere basis of assertion you are exposed to palpable naiveté and absurdity. But, if you do give an answer you flatly contradict yourself.

Some suppose that the Word of God is a special case to which ordinary rules of evidence do not apply. They admit essentially what has been written above, but take exception to its application to the matter in hand. It is true of men, they say, that their word may be challenged and must be proven to be true. But God's Word cannot be challenged, but must be immediately accepted as true and obeyed as right.

To hesitate when God speaks is to be both foolish and impious, they say.

With all of this we cordially agree, but it misses the point under discussion. We are not here asking whether God should be obeyed when He speaks. We are simply asking whether a being must be acknowledged as God speaking merely because he so claims, or, more particularly, whether the Bible is to be regarded as the Word of God merely because it so claims. It cannot be said too emphatically that when God speaks He is to be instantly believed. Any question whatsoever at that moment is utterly and dangerously out of order. When God the Lord speaks, the devout and intelligent mind can only reply: "Speak, Lord, for Thy servant heareth." But like Samuel, who spoke those words, we must first know that the voice speaking is God's.

It would be just as foolish and impious to accept and obey any voice whatsoever which claimed to be divine, as it would be *not* to accept and obey the divine voice when it is shown to be such. To apply some reasonable test for ascertaining the voice of God and distinguishing it from the voice of men is not presumptuous as many charge, but, on the contrary, is as humble as it is necessary. Humble? Yes, humble because it is using the only means which our Maker has given us whereby we may distinguish between truth and error; God and men; His Word and theirs. To accept any voice which claimed His divine name would be arrogantly to disregard the means God Himself has graciously provided to prevent just such a mistake. The person who professed to believe without evidence would be despising the God who gave us minds, which must have evidence in order to provide a basis for reasonable belief. While God is, of course, infinitely above His creatures it does not follow that if and when He condescends to speak to them He will speak in a manner which is infinitely above them. Manifestly, if He speaks to men He must speak so that men can understand what He says. He must, as Calvin has said, "lisp." If parents must accommodate their language to their infants when they would be understood, surely God must indulge in baby talk when speaking to those infinitely below Him. If He chose to speak to us in a manner which is as infinitely above us, as His being is above ours, He would be, literally, infinitely over our heads. This would not only make comprehension by us infinitely impossible, but it would inevitably reflect on God's infinite intelligence, which would know no better than to attempt to communicate with finite creatures by going infinitely over their heads. It is equally evident that He will make it known that He is speaking—which means He will give some signs of His presence which the human mind can recognize.

In conclusion, then, the fact that the Bible claims its inspiration is not the basis for Inerrancy. If there is a sound basis for believing in Inerrancy, as we shall attempt to show in the second part, the self-testimony of Scripture will be a wonderful confirmation of it. Without the Bible's own claim it would not be impossible, but it would be more difficult, to believe that it is the Word of God. But with such self-attestation the truth of divine Inspiration is gloriously sealed.

## 2. The Holy Spirit's Testimony as the Basis for Bible Inerrancy

One of the precious doctrines of the church is called the "Internal Testimony of the Holy Spirit." Like the self-attestation of Scripture, it is a most gracious gift of God to His church. And like that gift it is sometimes misunderstood and misused even by those who love it most. A case in point is the one before us in which the internal testimony is submitted as proof that the Bible is the inerrant Word of God.

The thinking here may be shown to be wrong, but it does have the merit of being clear. It runs like this: just as the Bible certifies itself by the letter of Scripture, so by the living voice of God the Spirit convinces the hearts of men. Many think that the Bible's witness to itself remains a dead letter until the living Spirit speaks within the soul. But when the

Spirit does thus speak men have the most solid possible basis for knowing that the Bible is the inerrant Word of God. Some, by no means all, of the advocates of this view go on to teach that unless the Spirit testifies, the Bible is not the Word of God; and only when He does is it the Word of God. In any case, the argument at first glance is quite impressive. When God witnesses to His own Word, how can there be any doubt that it is His inerrant Word? If you want evidence, these men assure us, here is the best. What more can any reasonable or spiritual person desire than to have God speaking directly to his own soul?

We agree. As this case is often stated, it leaves nothing to be desired. We would never be so foolish as to question the very voice of God in our souls. Our search for truth would be ended promptly when God opened His mouth and spoke and that to each of us individually and inwardly.

We agree, that is, if the Holy Spirit does actually thus speak to individual souls. But I have never heard the Holy Spirit say to my soul or mind, "The Bible is the Word of God." I have never met anyone who claims to have heard the Holy Spirit say that or anything like that to his soul. In fact, the advocates of the internal testimony as the basis of inerrancy never quite get around to saying it either. Rather, most of them would be inclined to rebuke us at this point for gross misunderstanding, if not outright caricature, of their opinions on this subject. "We do not mean," they will reply, "*testimony* as an audible voice in the soul. Of course the Holy Spirit has not spoken to individual hearts telling them that the Bible is His Word! Of course you cannot find anyone in his right mind who claims any such experience," they may indignantly respond.

Very well," we reply. "We are sorry; we meant no offense and intended no caricature of a brother's doctrine. Nor are we totally ignorant of the history of this doctrine. Indeed, we ourselves believe it in the sense in which Calvin, for example, meant it. But when it is used as the *argument* for inerrancy (which, incidentally, we do not think was Calvin's idea at all), that is something else. It is that something else which we are now considering." If it is so used as proof of inerrancy how is it such unless somehow God's Spirit testifies, tells, signifies to us, reveals in us or the like that the canonical Scriptures are from Him? But very well, we will withdraw our query as we hear our wounded brethren protesting that they mean no such thing. Let it be agreed, then, that the "testimony of the Spirit is not like the testimony of a witness in court speaking to what he did or did not see or hear. The Spirit's testimony is non-verbal, more subtle, more in the nature of an influence on the soul than an audible voice or mystical writing. But, we must insist, how then does the Spirit's witness reveal inerrancy?

If the advocates of this line of thought say that the Spirit confirms our own convictions when we read the Bible; if they say that He makes the Bible student sure that the Bible is what the Bible student feels that it is; then the Spirit does not communicate any new information which the Bible reader receives, but somehow intensifies his experiences as he meditates on Holy Writ. We are inclined to believe that the Holy Spirit does precisely that in the hearts of many. But we do not see that even if He does so that this proves the inspiration of the Bible. All we would now have is this: a man reads his Bible. His feelings are stirred as he reads. He senses, or thinks he senses, that there is some other spirit besides his own at work in his heart as he reads. He cannot be sure that there is another spirit. If he does believe it, he cannot know what spirit it is. Certainly, he has no way of knowing that it is the divine spirit. And, even if he did, all he knows is that the divine Spirit is working in his heart as he reads the Scriptures and not "testifying" or saying that this Scripture is the inerrant Word of God. If it is said, "But the Bible tells us that the Spirit bears witness and therefore it must be true and the Word to which He testifies must truly be God's Word," we are back where we began: accepting the testimony of the Scripture to itself without any (at present) just reason for so doing.

In summary, we must reject the testimony of the Spirit as the basis of inerrancy (not, please note, the testimony of the Spirit) because, first, if His "testimony" is construed as audible or verbal, it simply does not exist; second, if His "testimony" is construed as a spiritual effect intensifying our feelings as we read Scripture, this is not a proving of the inspiration or inerrancy of Scripture.

It may be necessary to show that we are not here opposing the *Westminster Confession of Faith's* view of things, but actually defending it. It teaches that "our full persuasion and assurance of the infallible truth, and divine authority thereof (of the Scriptures) is from the inward work of the Holy Spirit bearing witness by and with the Word in our hearts" (I, 5). But these words teach only that the "testimony of the Holy Spirit" *persuades* us of the inspiration of the Bible. It does not prove the doctrine, but persuades us of the truth of the doctrine. It leads us to acknowledge the evidence for inspiration which, apart from the Holy Spirit's influence, we (as sinful persons, cf. Chapter VI) are prone to resist. This evidence is utterly sufficient to persuade us if we were frank enough to admit evidence when we see it. Thus the *Westminster Confession of Faith* says in full: "We may be moved and induced by the testimony of the Church to an high and reverent esteem of the Holy Scripture; and the heavenliness of the matter, the efficacy of the doctrine, the majesty of the style, the consent all the parts, the scope of the whole (which is to give all glory God), the full discovery it makes of the only way of man's salvation, the many other incomparable excellencies, and the entire perfection thereof, *are arguments whereby it doth abundantly evidence itself to be the Word of God*; yet, not withstanding, our full *persuasion and assurance* of the infallible truth and divine authority thereof is from the inward work of the Holy Spirit bearing witness by and with the Word in our hearts" (Chap. I, 5).

According to this great creed the various characteristics of the Bible "abundantly evidence" (prove) its inspiration, but only the influence of the Holy Spirit (overcoming our sinful dispositions) can "persuade" us to acquiesce in what we clearly see is the Word of God.

The reader may notice a certain difference (not discrepancy) between the approach of the WCF here cited and that of this little monograph. The "arguments" to which Westminster appeals are internal evidences drawn from the nature (not testimony) of the Bible itself, such as its harmony, perfection, etc. That these, in their cumulative effect, are arguments we agree, and have so written elsewhere. We are bypassing them in this monograph only because they take longer to develop, involve more debates with modernity, and are not so directly conclusive as the argumentation developed in Part II. That the approach of this *Primer* was abundantly used by the Westminster divines and seventeenth century Orthodoxy in general could be extensively illustrated, were there any necessity to prove what no one questions.

### 3. The Believer's Testimony as the Basis for Bible Inerrancy

It may not have been obvious that the fallacies of the preceding views lay ultimately in their unconscious elevation of the creature above the Creator who is blessed forever. It seemed to have been quite the opposite. By accepting the authority of the Bible on the basis of its own divine affirmation, or its divine corroboration in the soul, advocates of these positions intended to bow before the majesty of heaven, but, in fact, did not. Since there is no evidence that an avowed Word of God is a genuine Word of God simply because it avows itself to be such, accepting it for no reason is sheer arbitrariness (however reverent the intention). Instead of abiding by the laws of evidence which God has given us, we become laws to ourselves. In other words, the first two unsound bases for sound doctrine, though they appear to be quite objective, are actually only appeals to mere personal feelings. But to this position, in the purity of its expression, we now come.

The view runs something like this: the Bible is inspired because it inspires me. It "finds" me. It rings a bell in my soul. I know that this is God's book because I feel within that this book is God's book. It affects me as no other literature does. It exhibits a power and an energy which speak to me.

This view is not intended by those who favor it to be an appeal to subjectivity. It is, of course, an appeal to the subject's experience. However, it is claimed that the subject experiences something not himself. He senses the presence of a spirit not his own. The argument is not subjective, then, in the sense that the subject himself "existentially" produces the experience. It is not a creation of the human soul, but something that happens to the soul, which is thought to prove that the Bible is the inerrant Word of God.

This experience, then, is offered as the basis for believing that the Bible is the Word of God. In itself, and in it alone, is the argument for inerrancy. No matter how sincere the Christianity of those who reason thus, no matter how truly the Bible of which they speak may indeed be the Word of God, still their argument amounts to this: "My heart is moved when I read the Bible more and/or differently than when I read any other literature. Therefore, this Bible, which is the occasion or cause of this wonderful feeling, must be God's Word." These good men do not phrase their argument that way, or they, too, would immediately recognize its futility as an argument. They imply this, but do not usually express it. Some of them will not even recognize it when someone else expresses it. They may even sincerely resent such a spelling out as saying something which they never intended. And, of course, they may not have meant it. People often imply what they do not intend. "Happy inconsistencies" abound everywhere. Whatever their inner intentions may be we leave to God, the only Searcher of Hearts. We concern ourselves only with their reasoning. Experience is set forth as a case for inspiration, and the only way that it could appear to be such is by supposing that such an inference is valid.

But is it valid to suppose that because I have a certain experience when I read the Bible that the Bible is thereby shown to be the Word of God? Surely not. First, the experience could be a mere coincidence One may have happened to have felt well for some reason when he began to read the Bible. By association he may have attributed this to what he was reading. Thus the Bible reading may have been a mere concomitant, rather than cause, of his experience. Christians do, in fact, testify that often, when they read the Bible, nothing "happens."

Even if something always happened when one read the Bible, that would not prove that the Bible was the cause of what happened. We all have heard of the rooster who thought that his crowing caused the sun to rise each morning until he found it rising one morning when he had a sore throat. But suppose that rooster had never had a sore throat; he would have gone to his death still thinking that his crowing was the cause of the sun's rising. We must have more than succession for a causal argument. There must be necessary succession. But this can never be shown by mere experience. Second, even if the Bible were the cause of these experiences, that would not prove that the Bible was the Word of God. It would prove that it had a unique power, but not a divine power. A unique power is not necessarily a divine power. The devil has power that is unique and, so far as men apart from special revelation know, it could account for such a phenomenon as that we are considering. Of course, that is not the case here. Of course the advocates of this view are correct in saying that this power comes from God. They are right, but they have no basis for being right. Their conclusion may be correct (as we think), but, their premises are incorrect (as we have shown).

No one is likely ever to admit that the Bible is the Word of God apart from the experience here described. Nothing so powerfully affects men's convictions about inspiration as this experience. Nevertheless, precious and valuable as it is, the believer's testimony is not the basis of an argument for

Inerrancy. On the contrary, inerrancy must be the basis of validating Christian experience.

### 4. The Church's Testimony as the Basis for Bible Inerrancy

The very futility of the preceding views has led some to the church's testimony as the basis of inerrancy. Sensing that they cannot prove even to themselves, not to mention others, the inerrancy of Scripture from something within themselves or within the Bible, they succumb to the temptation of appealing to Mother Church. Yet, there is more here than that. It is not simply that many are thought to be able to do what a few cannot accomplish, but that God does in the many what He has not chosen to do in the few. That is, God has promised guidance to the body of the faithful and will lead them into all truth and not permit them to be misled fatally.

Now, where does the Church get the idea that it is the "pillar and ground of the truth"; that it is to "bind and loose" on earth? From the Bible! So it is the Bible which is the basis of the Church's authority, not the Church which is the basis of the Bible's authority. The Bible is the pillar on which the Church rests, not the Church the pillar on which the Bible rests. Incidentally, the expression in 1 Timothy 3:15 that the Church is the pillar and ground of the truth does not point to a pillar on which truth rests, but to a pillar on which truth was posted for public announcement in antiquity. In other words, it refers to the Church as *witness* to the truth, and not the *basis* of it.

But some will say that the Church came into existence before the Bible, and then called everyone's attention to the Bible as the Word of God. This is true in an irrelevant sense and false in a relevant sense. When we say that it is true in an irrelevant sense that the Church existed before the Bible, we mean that granting the Church existed before the written and canonical form of the Bible is no proof of inerrancy. If, for example, the Church is thought of as beginning when the first sinners trusted in the mercy of God, and if sinful Adam and Eve were the first sinners to trust in the mercy of God, then the Church existed centuries before the Bible was probably written, and certainly many centuries before it was gathered into a canon of books recognized as the Bible. If the church is thought of as coming into existence at Pentecost,, then the Bible (the Old Testament) preceded it by centuries. Still, the New Testament Church would have preceded the New Testament Bible because there were New Testament Christians before a word of the New Testament was written.

All of this is obviously true, and just as obviously irrelevant to the matter in hand. First, granted that the Church, in a sense, existed before the Bible in its written form, what does this prove? According to the advocates of the view in question it is supposed to prove that the Church's testimony is the argument for inerrancy. But does the Church's testimony, which preceded the Bible, prove the inerrancy of the Bible? How does the fact that the Church may have preceded the Bible in existence prove that the Bible is inspired and inerrant? How does the fact that the previously existing Church testifies to the subsequently existing Bible prove the Bible to be what the Church says that it is? It is no doubt true that if the Church had not testified, and did not continue to testify, to the Bible as the Word of God, the world might soon forget about the Bible and thus never come to realize its inspiration. The Church is indispensable to the Bible's being considered for what it is. But this fact is in no sense a proof that the Bible is what the Church says it is. The Bible is, we believe, exactly what the Church says that it is, but it is not what the Church says it is because the Church says it is. Rather, in the true order of events, the Church testifies because the Bible is what it is rather than that the Bible is what it is because the Church so testifies.

Perhaps it will become clearer if we outline the order of events:
1. God speaks (revelation).
2. Men respond in faith (church).
3. Revelation is recorded (inerrant Bible).

4. The Church recognizes, receives, and testifies to the inerrant Bible.

The question is: what is the basis of the Church's testimony? Surely it is not the Church's testimony.

Some will still say, "Granted that the Church's testimony is not the basis of inerrancy, but inerrancy is the basis of the Church's testimony. Still, is not the Church's testimony the basis of inerrancy *for us*? That is, granted that the church had good and sufficient reasons for recognizing the Bible for what it is, nevertheless we do not have access to these reasons, or, even if we did, we do not have the infallible divine guidance necessary for correctly perceiving them. So, we must rest on the Church's testimony as the basis for our belief in inerrancy, though the Church herself must have another basis."

We reply that, even if this were so, it grants our main point:, namely that the Church's testimony cannot be the basis for inerrancy. But this point would still be important because it would terminate *our* search for the basis for inerrancy. Our search would have ended in a realization that we should not search anymore, that the answer has been found by another (the Church), and can be found by none other.

If this is so, so be it. But is it so? It is not so, nor could it possibly be so! Why not? For the simple reason that if it is proposed that the Church's testimony must become our argument for inerrancy, we must ask "why?". If the answer is: "Because the Bible says so," it is obvious that we are right back where we began. It is the inerrant Bible itself which alone can tell us that the Church alone can tell us that the Bible is inerrant! So for us to accept the position that we can only know that the Bible is inerrant by the testimony of the church, we must first know that the Bible is inerrant. For example, Rome claims papal authority from Matthew 16:18; but to do so she must first prove the authority of Matthew 16:18. If that church is to establish her authority, she must first establish the inerrancy of the Bible. That is, even according to her own argument, she cannot establish the Bible's authority, but the Bible must establish hers (which, incidentally, it does not do).

This then is another wrong basis for a right answer. We must continue our search. We have not yet found the right basis for accepting the Bible's inerrancy.

# Part II

## A Sound Basis for Sound Doctrine

### 5. *The Testimony of Divinely Commissioned Messengers as the Basis for Bible Inerrancy*

(A) The Argument from Commissioned Messengers to Inspired Bible.

Let us outline the steps of this argument before proceeding to explain it:

1. There is a God.
2. Men were made in his image, rational creatures.
3. As such, they are designed to make their choices on the basis of evidence.
4. The evidence for the Inspiration of the Bible is as follows:
   a. Men have appeared in history with powers which only God could have given them (miracles).
   b. Miracles are God's seal to mark men unmistakably as His messengers.
   c. God's message is indubitably true.
   d. God's message includes the Inspiration of the Bible.
   e. Therefore, the inspiration of the Bible is indubitably true.

1. There is a God. This must be assumed here. This is a small, popular *Primer on Bible Inerrancy*. Time, space, and the nature of the undertaking make certain assumptions inevitable. What is here an assumption (the existence of God) has been proven elsewhere in many, many volumes. If the reader of the *Primer* does not believe in God's existence its argument may interest him, but it cannot possibly convince him. We must believe there is a God before we can consistently believe that there is a special revelation of God in the Bible or anywhere else.

But here we will detour a little, for there are many today who say that we can only know the existence of God from special revelation (such as the Bible). Exactly opposite to what we said in the preceding paragraph, they contend that God is utterly unknown until He supernaturally discloses Himself. We say that God cannot supernaturally reveal Himself until He has naturally made His existence known. They say, "No, His existence cannot be naturally known until He supernaturally reveals Himself."

Let us examine their view. According to it:

First, there is a book, the Bible, claiming the existence and revelation of God.

Second, we are to believe in this God.

Third, apart from this revelation we could not know that there is such a God.

The paucity of this approach is plain to see. First, we would have no possible tests to ascertain whether the deity revealed in the Bible is what He says He is. We do not know, on this view, that there is such a being, nor whether this Biblical being is such. If this is God we can only accept it on His own word. We would not trust a dollar to a human being whose honesty we know only because he claims it. Here we trust our lives to a being whose "Godness" and whose very existence we know only from Himself. Custom inspectors look at a visitor to see whether he resembles the picture in the passport before they admit him to their nation. But here comes a God without passport, a God who wants to rule our lives merely because He says He has a right to do so. If this were not bad enough, we have, second, the further objection that there are many claimants to this role of God. Many books present their candidates. If we worshiped any one of them without credentials we would be out of our mind; if we worshiped all of them we would be multiple-schizophrenic.

No, there must be evidence of the existence of God from the creation, of which we ourselves are the most exalted part, if we are to recognize a further revelation of this glorious being, if and when it comes. So here we assume what most people do quite rightly assume, that God exists. This we can safely assume here only because it is proven elsewhere. Otherwise, the assumption would be gratuitous.

2. Men were made in God's image as rational creatures. This point also we must largely assume because of the limitation of this little book. But this is a very safe assumption, is it not? If we were not rational beings, you would not be reading this (or any other) book in your search for knowledge, nor would we be writing books. Aristotle was quite right that man is a rational animal. If we were not rational beings, no one could prove (for this involves reasoning) that we were not rational beings. We could not even think that we were not. So our rationality must be assumed, for even to deny it is to assume it.

3. As rational beings, men are designed to make their choices on the basis of evidence.

Being rational beings they are not the mere product of natural forces. They choose according to reason (or what appears reason). That is virtually the definition of a rational being. If he were merely the product of external forces, how could his own reason and will be operative; and, if not, how could he be a rational being?

Being rational beings they are not the mere product of supernatural forces. That is, not only does nature not force rational beings, but even supernature, that is God Himself, does not force them. We would go so far as to say that God *cannot* force men. By definition, they have been made (by

God Himself) rational beings. If they were forced, even by God, they would cease to be the kind of beings He had made them, that is, rational beings. So if God forced men they would cease to be men. Or, to put it another way, so long as men remain men they are not forced even by God (in fact,, *least* of all by God, who made them rational in the first place).

Being rational beings they cannot be forced by sin. Granted that man is not what he ought to be. Granted that there is something perverse within him. Granted that he does not always (if ever) think what is true and do what is right. Still, this evil bent of his nature does not actually force him to will against his will. The absurdity of the notion is seen in the last statement: "Still this evil bent of his nature does not actually force him to will against his will." How could he meaningfully be said to will against his will? If he wills against his will, that would be his will, namely, to will against his "will." So his willing against his "will" would not truly be against his will; or, if it were against his will, it could not be his will.

Therefore, man is a rational being. It is his very nature to choose according to the judgments of his mind. Nothing could possibly take that character away from man without taking his humanity away from him.

Consequently, if God is graciously disposed to reveal Himself to His creature, man, God must necessarily reveal Himself according to the rational nature of His human creature. The necessity is self-imposed and, therefore, consistent with the sovereignty of God. God cannot go over or under the "head" of man. He cannot treat him as a God or an animal, but as the creature which He, God, made: a rational being.

4. The evidence for the Inspiration of the Bible is as follows:

   *a. Men have appeared in history with powers which only God could have given them, namely, miracles.*

(The discussion of miracles which follows is reproduced

from the author's *Reasons for Faith*, published by Soli Deo Gloria.)

Concerning miracles there are two important questions to be asked: first, what is the evidence for miracles, and, second, what is their evidential value? If there is to be any argument from miracles, there must first be clear evidence that they actually occur.

Before we proceed to consider the evidence for miracles, let us ask ourselves whether there can be any such evidence. This is a rather absurd question, we grant, but we must consider it. Many persons never face the question at all because they rule out the possibility of miracles before they consider any actual evidence for them. One of the most outstanding Biblical scholars in the country once said publicly, in answer to a question concerning his interpretation of miracles in the Old Testament, "When I meet an alleged miracle, I simply treat it as legend." This scholar no doubt would not bother reading this chapter or anything like it. He knows in advance that any and all alleged miracles are merely legends. But how does he know it? He does not know it; he merely declares it. However, there are more philosophically-minded thinkers who would say that this professor is right in his conclusion, but wrong in the way he arrives at it. They agree that there is no such thing as miracles, and that records of them must be legends of some sort, but these men attempt to prove their statement and not merely to assert it arbitrarily.

Some would offset the evidential power of miracles by claiming that there never could be enough proof of a miracle in the face of the overwhelming evidence of natural law against it. David Hume once argued that there is more evidence for regularity in nature than for irregularity (supernaturalism); therefore, regularity, and not irregularity, must be the truth of the matter. The argument is palpably unsound, indeed irrelevant. Certainly there is more evidence for the regular occurrence of nature than there ever could be for any supernatural occurrence. But the argument for miracles is not meant to be an argument against the regularity of nature. It is merely an argument against the regularity of nature in every particular instance. Indeed, the argument for miracles rests on the regularity of nature generally. There is no such thing as supernatural events except as they are seen in relation to the natural. And they would not be extraordinary if there were nothing ordinary against which background they are seen. They could not be signs of anything if they were not different from the *status quo*. When one argues for the occasional miracle, he is, in the same breath, arguing for the usually non-miraculous. If all nature became supernatural, there would be no room for miracles; nothing would be a miracle because all would be miraculous.

At the same time, all the evidence that there is for the regularity of nature generally is no argument at all against the occasional miracle. Such evidence simply argues for the fact that the normal course of nature is natural. It does not rule out or in, for that matter, the possibility that the irregular may happen. It only proves that as long as there is nothing but nature to take into consideration, there will probably be no deviation from the order with which we have become familiar. If there is a God, all the evidence of an undeviating nature from its creation to the present moment does not provide the slightest certainty that nature will continue the same way another moment. The same God who made it, and preserved it in the present pattern for so long, may have fulfilled His purpose in so doing, and may proceed immediately, this moment, to do otherwise than in the past. Only if the evidence for the regularity of nature were somehow to show that there is no being outside nature who can in any way alter it could there be an argument against the possibility of miracles. But this the evidence does not do, does not purport to do, cannot do. Therefore it can never be regarded as an argument against miracles. In the strictest sense Hume's objection is irrelevant.

What is the relation of unpredictability in modem physics to the notion of miracle? Certainly the universe is no longer thought to be fixed in the sense that it once was. The

quantum theory has satisfied most physicists that there is
such a thing as indeterminism, or unpredictable behavior, in
the laws of nature. As Bertrand Russell has remarked, while
psychology in our time has become more deterministic,
physics has become less so. Some have utilized the concept
of indeterminacy in nature as a wedge for miracle. Having
felt fenced in by the arguments based on the regularity of nature, they have welcomed this apparent avenue of escape by
which they may remain scientific and still affirm miracles.
Indeterminacy runs interference for the power of God, or
more piously we should say, makes it possible to believe that
God may act miraculously inasmuch as he acts indeterminis-
tically in created nature.

So far as we can see, the situation for the credibility of
miracles is neither improved nor worsened by indeterminacy. For one thing, indeterminacy is hardly a proven concept. Or, more precisely, it would seem more likely that man
cannot in every case determine the laws by which nature operates than that she herself is indeterministic. It is conceivable that in the area of quantum physics, no less than elsewhere, nature is deterministic, and what is undetermined are
the laws of her behavior. Nature may be determined, but
man has not determined how. If this is the case, the to-do
about indeterminism is wasted mental effort.

If nature herself is indeterministic, then what? Then it
still would remain highly unlikely that an indeterminism in
nature could explain why once and only once, thousands of
years ago, a man walked on water, but no one else has been
able to do so before or since. Presumably the indeterminism
of nature could never be employed to account for such a
unique phenomenon. Furthermore, if this is the explanation,
Christ Himself was deceived. He should have been surprised
to be around at the one moment when nature was behaving
differently from all previous times. He should have been as
much amazed as the others, unless (and here is the hopeless
supposition) He were a downright, sophisticated fraud who
took advantage of the most unbelievable opportunity that the

world could imagine. Furthermore, there is the matter of His actual predictions, which would be rendered impossible in an indeterministic universe.

Some would affirm the *a priori* impossibility of miracles because of the nonexistence of God. They rightly state that a miracle, to have meaning, must be the work of an intelligent, powerful, and purposive divine being. In this we go along with them. Then they say that since there is no such being as this, there can be no such thing as a miracle. And we agree with that. If it can be shown that there is no God, it will also be shown in the same effort that there is no miracle. But the non-existence of God cannot be proven, while His existence has been.

What is the positive evidence that miracles have occurred? A discussion of this subject with any degree of fullness would require an entire volume itself. We must delimit the field. And so we will consider here only the miracles of Jesus Christ.

Everyone knows that the Gospel narratives (considered only as good historical sources, not necessarily inspired) tell of a large number of miracles that were performed by Christ. A great many more are alluded to, but not related. This is so generally known that I feel perfectly safe in assuming the readers' acquaintance with the accounts of Christ's healing the sick, opening the eyes of the blind, raising the dead, walking on water, multiplying a boy's lunch to feed more than five thousand hungry persons, and a host of other such deeds.

No one disputes the fact that the Gospel accounts tell of Jesus Christ's performing miracles. There have been attempted naturalistic explanations, to be sure, but so far as we know no one has attempted the job of showing that all accounts of the apparently miraculous are merely accounts of natural events which were misconstrued by the writer or reader. For example, who would care to show that John's report of Thomas' placing his fingers in the side of the resurrected Christ to feel his former wounds was not meant to present an essentially supernatural event, namely, physical resurrection? Persons may or may not believe what John says, but how can they doubt that John presents them as happening? As even naturalistic New Testament critics usually say, there is no doubt that the early Christians believed these supernatural things did occur.

If it is granted that the biographers of Christ say He wrought miracles, the only questions remaining are: can these writers be believed (please note again we are not, in a circular fashion, assuming their Inspiration but the well-established historical value of their manuscripts), and, if so, what do the miracles prove?

Can these writers be believed when they relate that Christ wrought supernatural deeds or miracles? Well, why not? People are assumed to be reliable in their relating of events unless there is some reason for thinking that they are not so. What reason is there for thinking that these writers are not reliable? So far as they are known, they have the reputation of honesty. Was there some bias present which would have tended to corrupt their honesty in the case of these miracles? There is no evidence of bribery by money or position. Their reporting of miracles as vindications of Jesus did not bring them into good standing with the powers in their own community. It caused Peter and John to be imprisoned and all the apostles to be brought into disfavor with most of the Jewish community. It stands to reason that a person cannot advance his own worldly interests by championing a person condemned by law and executed as a criminal.

But what about their other-worldly interests? Is it possible that these men believed that by shading the truth and relating what did not occur they would thereby gain an interest in heaven? Did they think that because of their lying about "miracles," Jesus would own them in the next world? Merely to ask this question dispels it. The whole picture of Jesus is that of a teacher of righteousness who required His disciples to make righteous judgments and speak the truth which alone could make free. It would not seem reasonable to believe that they could have thought they would please Jesus by telling lies about Him, and actually earn His praise in the world of perfect righteousness to come.

Or could they have been sentimentalists? That is, could they have supposed that, by telling what they knew to be untrue, they could nevertheless do good? Could they have felt that if people could be persuaded that this Jesus was a supernatural being with supernatural powers, they would then obey Him and walk in paths of righteousness? Could they have supposed that by doing evil this great good would come? Is it possible that they, knowing there were no miracles, were nonetheless willing to follow Christ to the death, but that others would need the help of such superstition?

There is an insuperable objection to this "pious fraud" idea. As we have already mentioned, Christ Himself is depicted as a teacher of strict truth and righteousness. If the disciples had told deliberate and huge falsehoods, their very zeal would have led them into the grossest kind of disobedience. They would also have known that their own souls were in peril, for Christ had said that a good tree brings forth good fruit, and that He would say to liars in the last day, "I never knew you; depart from Me, ye that work iniquity" (Matthew 7:22–23). "If you love Me," Christ had said, "keep My commandments." It seems incredible that the disciples, in their very zeal for Jesus, would zealously disobey His commandments, that in their desire to be with Him and advance His cause they would seal their own doom.

So much for the inherent improbability of such a course on the part of the disciples. But there is equally great difficulty in the external situation. Even if it were conceivable that the disciples so forgot their Master's teachings and their own spiritual interest as to violate this grossly His canons of righteousness, it does not at all follow that those to whom they addressed themselves stood to be deceived. After all, the disciples would have foisted these "pious frauds" upon those among whom they were supposed to have been done. They would have told the very people who were supposed to have been present on the occasion the fiction that Jesus fed five thousand. They would have told the people of Cana themselves that Christ turned water to wine at a feast in their small community, which everybody in that community would immediately deny ever took place there. The "pious fraud" idea, even if it were psychologically thinkable, could be historically thinkable only if it were perpetrated in a different land at a different time. But that in the same generation these things could have been preached as having occurred among the very people who knew that they had not occurred is hardly credible.

Although the witnesses of these events might have gotten away with such reports among highly credulous strangers who knew nothing about the events in question, they could never have deceived the very people among whom the miracles were supposed to have taken place. It would therefore seem impossible to impeach the honesty of the witnesses. All the factors actually favor their honesty, which must be assumed in the first instance unless there is some reason for questioning it. But when we examine any possible reasons, we find none. Candor requires that their record be received as a record of what they thought took place.

But the question still remains whether what they thought took place actually did take place. Granted that they meant to tell the truth, but did they succeed in their honest intention? With the best of intentions men have often been grossly mistaken. Is it not possible that these writers were similarly mistaken? In other words, there remains the question of the competency of the witnesses.

We note, in the first place, that they had the best possible jury to test their competency—their own contemporaries, among whom the events related were said to have taken place. If the writers had been palpably contradicted by the facts, the people to whom they related the facts would have been the very ones to expose them. If they had been misguided zealots, the non-zealots to whom they spoke could have spotted it in a moment and repudiated it as quickly. If they had garbled the actual events, eyewitnesses in quantity could have testified to the contrary. If these historians had actually been bigoted, benighted fanatics with no historical sense, incapable of distinguishing between fact and fancy, between occurrences in external nature and in their own imagination, thousands of Israelites could have made that very clear.

As a matter of fact, their record went unchallenged. No man called them liars; none controverted their story. Those who least believed in Jesus did not dispute the claims to His supernatural power. The apostles were imprisoned for speaking about the resurrection of Christ, not, however, on the ground that what they said was untrue, but that it was unsettling to the people. They were accused of being heretical, deluded, illegal, un-Jewish, but they were not accused of being inaccurate. And that would have been by far the easiest to prove if it had been thought to be true.

Actually, the Israelites of Jesus' own day, so far from denying his miraculous power, admitted it. They not only admitted it, but they used it against Him. Precisely because He did miracles, they condemned Him. That is, they attributed the miracles, which they admitted He did, to the power of the devil (Matthew 12:24). We are not here concerned with the accusation, but with the incidental admission. What we are concerned with here is that hostile, contemporary leaders freely admitted that Jesus' miracles were true, however evil they held their origin to be. The fact they did not dispute, only the interpretation of it. The witness they did not question. The competency of the writers was not doubted by the very generation which alone could have challenged it. It seems highly irrelevant on historical grounds for subsequent generations to raise such questions when the generation in which the events are said to have occurred did not do so. Later generations may object on philosophical grounds, or argue *a priori* that these things could not have happened. Those arguments have to be met on their own grounds, as we have attempted to do. But the historicity of certain events cannot be questioned by people who were not there when they were not questioned by the people who were there. We may or may not agree with the Pharisees' interpretation that Christ did His works by Satan's power, but we are in no position to contest the Pharisees' knowledge of what He did. They were there and we were not.

This corroborative testimony of contemporaries, friends, and, especially, enemies, is the main vindication of the competency of the Gospel witnesses. But there is also the feasibility of the documents themselves. These miracles are not fantastic things such as those recorded in the apocryphal accounts of Jesus. They are of a piece with the character of Jesus Himself—benign, instructive, redemptive. He Himself was a special and unique person; it is not surprising that He had special and unique powers. Indeed, it would be more surprising if He had not had them. Never man so spake, never man so lived, never man so loved, never man so acted. As Karl Adam has said, Jesus' life was a blaze of miracle. Miracles were as natural to Him as they would be unnatural to other men. He was a true man indeed, but He was no ordinary man. Miracles are surprising when attributed to other men; it would appear surprising if they had not been associated with this man.

Some have asked whether the miracles may not be naturally explained as the result of Christ's unusual knowledge and understanding of the laws of nature. May he not have possessed some occult acquaintance with the secrets of nature that enabled Him to unleash certain of her powers in a perfectly natural manner, however supernatural it may have appeared to those unfamiliar with these esoteric laws?

To this there are several negative replies. For one thing there is a moral objection. Jesus Himself referred to His works, or allowed others to refer to them, as evidence of His supernatural power. It would have been palpable dishonesty to do so if He had known all the time that He was merely exerting secret, but natural, power. Thus He asked His disciples, if they could not believe Him for His words' sake, to believe Him for His works' sake (John 14:11). He reassured the doubting John the Baptist of the reality of His Messianic calling by appealing to the miracles He wrought (Matthew 11:2–4). He did not object when Nicodemus said, "We know that thou art a teacher come from God: for no man can do these miracles that thou doest, except God be with him" (John 3:2). The blind man whom He healed believed on Him because of this miracle, and Christ took full advantage of that belief to press His claim to being the Messiah (John 9:35ff.). He refuted the Pharisees who had criticized Him for forgiving a man's sins by pointing out that He was able to do the equally supernatural thing of instantly curing his sickness. "Whether is easier, to say, Thy sins be forgiven thee; or to say, Arise, and walk? But that ye may know that the Son of man hath power on earth to forgive sins (then saith he to the sick of the palsy), Arise, take up thy bed, and go into thine house" (Matthew 9:5–6).

The Messianic prophecies had frequently foreseen the Messiah as a miracle worker. Jesus not only knew this, but obviously pointed to Himself as qualified in this very particular. If He did not believe Himself to be possessed of supernatural powers, He must have known Himself to be engaged in palpable fraud and deliberate deception. So from the moral angle, if Christ wrought what He wrought merely by an unusual knowledge of nature and not by supernatural power, He must have been a lying deceiver. That is more difficult to believe than any miracle with which He has ever been credited.

Second, on the supposition before us, His own argument in His defense would be an argument against Him. That is to say, when the unbelieving Jews claimed that He did His works by the power of Beelzebub, He replied, "How can Satan cast out Satan? And if a kingdom be divided against it-self, that kingdom cannot stand. And if a house be divided against itself, that house cannot stand. And if Satan rise up against himself, and be divided, he cannot stand, but hath an

end" (Mark 3:23 ff.). But if Christ really did not do true miracles, but only took advantage of His superior knowledge to
play on the credulity of His times and later times, then He
would have been perpetrating fraud as the prince of de-
ceivers, and as such He would have been the devil's instrument. For He regarded the devil as the father of lies, and He
would have been his son. Not only is such a thing utterly unthinkable from a moral standpoint, but it is, as His argument
makes it, utterly irrational. For Satan would have been using
lies to destroy his own kingdom. By these frauds of his servant Jesus, he would have been establishing the kingdom of
Jesus, which was founded on truth and which called men to
repent of their sins. Thus Satan's house would have been divided against itself, for Christ, the son of lies, would by His
lies have been destroying His father's kingdom of lies.

Third, if Christ had the kind of knowledge which this
theory attributes to Him, such knowledge would have been
as miraculous as the miracles it attempts to explain away.
For centuries before and for centuries after, no other person
but this solitary, untutored Jew knew how to walk on water.
Modern science has performed many amazing feats in this
century, but it still is nowhere nearer than it was in Jesus'
day to multiplying loaves and fishes by a mere word.
Machines can compare, classify, and do hitherto unbelievable things, but with all their powers they still depend on the
feeble mind of man, their inventor. They cannot even put a
question to themselves, but can only operate with their wonderful efficiency along channels made for them by men.
Certainly none of them can anticipate an historical event tomorrow, much less predict the fall of a city a generation
hence as precisely as Jesus did (Matthew 24:1ff.). This explanation of the miracles of Jesus, therefore, requires as
much, if not more, explanation than the miracles. It would
be the miracle to end all miracles. Intellectually, it would be
straining the gnat and swallowing the camel.

*b. Miracles are God's seal to mark men unmistakably as His messengers.*

If the evidence is convincing that Christ did work miracles, what do these miracles prove? Miracles as such do not prove that Jesus was more than a man. For though men do not have this power as men, they could be enabled by God to perform them in His name. Miraculous power belongs only to the Author of nature, but apparently it is not incommunicable as God's omniscience, omnipotence, or eternality must be. So the power to work miracles is not necessarily proof that the person who has that power is God Himself. But it does prove Him to be sent from God, for only God has this power and can delegate it. This is the very conclusion which Nicodemus drew when he said to Jesus, "We know that thou art a teacher come from God: for no man can do these miracles that thou doest, except God be with him" (John 3:2).

At this point, however, we face another problem or question. Is it not possible that there are other, non-human beings who, though not the Author of nature, are nevertheless able to influence nature in supernatural ways? Apart from revelation, we cannot know there are not such beings; we therefore consider the possibility that Christ's miracles were wrought by a man who had received His power from some supernatural being other than God, whether good or evil. If there are such beings, and they are good, then they are in subjection to God and His servants. If, therefore, they communicated their powers to the man Jesus, they must have done so in obedience to the will of God. Thus their giving of power would be essentially the same thing as God's giving it, for they would give it in accordance with His will.

If these beings are evil beings, what then? Then they are not subservient to God and do not deliberately do His will. In that case they would not necessarily have power over nature, for that would obviously be in the hands of the Author of nature and of those to whom He willingly permits it to pass. If, therefore, these evil spirits possess any such power as we are here supposing, it can only be by the permission of

God. So the question is, is it conceivable that God would permit these evil spirits to possess such power? Maybe we cannot answer that question, but we do not have to. The question that really concerns us here is not whether such spirits could possess such powers, but whether, even if they could, they would be able to communicate them to a human being. But we do not even have to answer that question, for we are dealing with a specific human being, Jesus Christ. So the question precisely is: if there are such evil beings and these beings are permitted by God to have power over nature which could conceivably be communicated to some human being, could they conceivably communicate it to such a human being as Jesus Christ? We have already shown that they could do so only if they wished to destroy themselves. They would be empowering Him to make converts to a kingdom which was set up to destroy the kingdom of evil. They would be giving power to one who would use it only for good when, by definition, evil spirits would want it to be used only for evil. They would be providing an instrument for healing when they wished only to spread sickness and death; they would insure the success of the person best fitted to insure their own failure. If these evil spirits were intelligent spirits, they simply could not do such a thing even if God would permit it. And is it possible that God would communicate His great power to a man after His own heart by spirits utterly alien to Him? So, from the standpoint of the devils themselves or from the standpoint of God Himself, it would seem inconceivable that Christ's supernatural power could have been derived from Satan, if there is such a being. And since there is no other conceivable source from which His power could have come, it must have come, as Nicodemus said, from God.

As observed above, what is shown of Christ in particular would apply in general to all true miracle workers from whom the Bible comes.

*c. God's Message Is Indubitably True.*

There are only two ways by which any person can come to say something that is untrue: either by ignorance or lying. A person may either mean to speak the truth but not know it; or know the truth but not mean to speak it. Thus the error must come from a defect of mind (not knowing enough) or a defect of heart (not loving the truth). God suffers from neither limitation, and therefore cannot speak untruth. His message must be true indubitably.

First, God cannot err from ignorance. His knowledge is infinite. There is nothing which He does not know. All things which exist, exist of His power and will and cannot lie outside the range of His knowledge. If there were anything which God did not know it would lie outside His domain. If so, He would not be infallible, all-powerful, independent; in short, He would not be God.

Second, God cannot err by lying. If God lied as well as told truth, His creatures could never know which was which. Nor would it do any good to ask Him, for if He lied He would tell us that the truth was falsehood and falsehood was the truth. This would be cruel. It would leave the creature in hopeless confusion. It would also be unintelligent on the part of Creator, for His creature would be of no use as He wandered hopelessly in the dark. So, if God lied He could not be God for He would not be good or intelligent

Thus, God's message is indubitably true. He could not lie if He would, nor would He lie if He could. He could not be wrong if He would, and He would not be wrong if He could.

*d. God's Message Includes the Inspiration of the Bible.*

Jesus Christ, the "teacher sent from God," taught that the Bible (Old Testament) was the inspired Word of God. "Scripture," He said, "could not be broken" (John 10:35). Every "jot and tittle" was to be fulfilled (Matthew 5:18). He claimed to be divine (Matthew 11:27; John 10:30; 14:9), and also said that the Scriptures bore witness of Him (John 5:39) which implied their inspiration. He argued from details (John 10:34) and recognized Biblical authority by the formula: "it is written" (Mark 11:17; Luke 18:31). This is admitted by virtually all modern scholars. As one of them put it: Christ's teaching concerning the Old Testament Bible was "fundamentalistic."

Likewise, Christ authenticated the New Testament by promising to send the Spirit to lead the apostles into all truth (John 14:26). This leading the apostles, in turn, claimed (cf. for example, 2 Corinthians 12; 13) as they wrote or sanctioned the writing of the New Testament.

*e. Therefore the Inspiration of the Bible Is Indubitably True.*

One may and must question whether a message is from God, but one cannot question a message which is once shown to be from God. This is the basic point which those who rest the inspiration for the Bible on the Bible's own testimony overlook. They rightly and righteously recognize that the Bible must be instantly accepted as what it says it is; namely, the Word of God. But they overlook the fact that the Bible is not instantly accepted because it says it is the Word of God. They are unconsciously persuaded of the Bible's divinity on other grounds. Consequently each time they hear the Bible referring to its inspiration, they know and accept this as true. Nevertheless they forget, because they never consciously recognize, that the truth of this self-affirmation is established on other grounds and merely confirmed by the self-affirmation.

There can be no higher proof of anything than the *ipse dixit* of God. God speaking is Truth speaking. What God says is so is so. It could not be otherwise. If God could be supposed to have made an error, our world and all worlds are in ruins. Reason, meaning, life and all have perished instantly. We may ask these prior questions about God's existence necessarily assuming the validity of our thinking processes as we do. These lead us to the knowledge of God. He, in turn, verifies the validity of our prior assumptions. But if He did not exist, or if He could err (which are one and the same thing), then the very thinking processes by which we arrive at the conclusion that God does not exist are so many gratuitous assumptions. Therefore if God could err, error would have no meaning, for truth would have no meaning. Nothing would have any meaning. Nothing would even be.

So God who is truth, who cannot err, has inspired the Bible, and the Bible is truth and cannot err.

## 6. The Testimony of Divinely Commissioned Messengers as the Basis for Bible Inerrancy (continued)

(B) The Argument from Inspired Bible to Inerrant Bible.

So far we have shown the inspiration of the Bible. But some will say, "You are supposed to show more than that: namely, the inerrancy of the Bible." They seem to think that it is possible to have an inspired Bible which is yet an errant Bible. Or, to put it another way, they suppose that it is possible to have a partially-inspired Bible. If this were so we would readily grant that we have not proved our point. If the Bible is partially inspired and partially not inspired, there can be no denying the possibility of error in the uninspired part of the Scriptures. So let us attempt to show the movement from inspired to inerrant Bible.

1. An inspired Bible means an inerrant Bible. They are one and the same thing. To put it another way, an inspired Bible is a completely inspired Bible. If it is completely inspired it is, as we have shown above, a completely inerrant Bible, because God cannot err or lie.

Why do we say that for the Bible to be inspired is to be completely inspired? The question should be the other way around. That is, if a message is said to be inspired, why does anyone say that it is only partly inspired? We have said above that God commissioned these Bible writers and that they wrote under His commission. If this is so, why would we not assume that all that they wrote rather than certain parts of it were inspired? We admit that if they said that their message was only partly inspired that would prove that such was the case. But then for those parts they would not be speaking as the divinely commissioned writers, but on their own, as it were. In other words, the burden of proof is on partial inspirationists and not total inspirationists. They must show that these writers who claimed inspiration for the Bible exempted certain parts of it from their claim.

Some have accepted this burden of proof. Let us examine one of the very few texts to which they appeal to show the merely human writing of certain parts of the Bible. Here are Paul's words in 1 Corinthians 7:10: "And unto the married, I command, yet not I, but the Lord . . . ." First, we note that this proves far more than our friends want to prove or can admit. If these words were intended by Paul as this interpretation would have it, then he is uninspired unless he specifically claims to be inspired within the contexts of his writings. "Not I, but the Lord," according to this view, means that it was Paul alone who had been speaking, but at this particular juncture the Lord Himself speaks. That this is not the meaning we have already shown by proving that the Bible writers claimed the authority of Christ in writing. They were commissioned by God to give His message. On the view being considered, Paul would be going back on that and rarely, on occasions such as this one, actually claims inspiration for himself. According to this, then, only a tiny fragment of the Bible is the Word of God. Second, another construction of these words is possible which would fit with Paul's over-all doctrine and appears, therefore, to be his meaning. He may, according to the words themselves, be here distinguishing his particular revelations on the subject of marriage from that which came from the teaching of Jesus Himself. (Jesus, in fact, did teach in Matthew 5:32 that infidelity was a just basis for divorce by the innocent party, but said nothing about separation, which Paul here reveals as another just ground for divorce.)

Paul is also thought to contradict total inspiration doctrine when in 1 Corinthians 1:16 he says he is unable to remember whether he had baptized any others. But how this in any way, directly or indirectly, denies his inspiration at that moment is never shown. It is merely insinuated. The insinuation seems to be that God could not inspire forgetfulness. But God's inspiration guarantees only inerrancy, not necessarily total recall. If Paul remembered wrongly we would have an uninspired Paul; but a Paul who does not remember is a Paul who is inspired to record that very fact for our instruction (presumably, concerning the nature of inspiration, what it does and does not include, what it does and does not exclude) .

2. There are not merely implicit, but also explicit statements that the Bible is completely and not merely partially inspired. The classic text is 2 Timothy 3:16. We cannot in a small work go into a detailed exposition, but can merely say here, as is generally granted, that the correct translation of this text is: "All scripture is inspired by God and profitable for teaching, for reproof, for correction, and for training in righteousness" (RSV) . "Not one jot or one tittle" (the slightest detail, that is) of the law shall pass away until all is fulfilled (Matthew 5:18; cf. also 1 Corinthians 2:13). This could never be said of any partially fallible law. Christ and Paul could not make their arguments rest on single words (John 10:35; Galatians 3:16) if inspiration did not extend to the individual words.

3. If the Bible were merely partially inspired, we would be worse off than if it were totally uninspired, for we would then have the excruciating task of distinguishing the Word of God in the Bible with no means for so doing. No one who has ever advocated the partial-inspiration view has provided us with a means of separating the inspired and uninspired parts. Some think that Luther, for example, used the doctrine of justification by faith alone as the touchstone of inspiration. We do not think that is an accurate understanding of Luther; but, for the moment, let us suppose it is. How could Luther or anyone else know that justification by faith is true, if not on the ground that it is taught by the Word of God? If the Bible is the Word of God because it teaches justification rather than justification being the truth of God because it is taught in the Bible by what means do we know this? We

have shown how we know that the Bible is the Word of God, and how from this we could know that justification is true, but how can anyone prove that justification is true and able to serve as the touchstone to the Word of God? This is a basal fallacy of the "Confession of 1967" (cf. appendix) which virtually makes "Reconciliation" as the mark of the Word of God.

If we pushed this matter to fundamentals we would find ourselves back on one of the wrong bases for the right doctrine which we considered in Part I. This is no doubt the reason that adherents of this view prefer merely to advocate it rather than argue for it, that is, to assume that one can know what part of the Bible is inspired and what part is not (but neglect to tell us how to do this little thing).

We said above that the partial-inspiration doctrine is actually worse than no doctrine of inspiration. With no doctrine of inspiration you would be most unfortunate; however, you would not be doomed to searching for it where it could not be found. On this present view one would have to search without ever knowing whether he had found. By comparison, searching for a needle in a haystack would be child's play, for you know there is the needle and, given sufficient effort and time, it can be found. But on the partial-inspiration theory you know that a great and invaluable mine of divine truth is there, but you also know that, while you must seek for such a treasure, it is impossible that you would ever find it. You could never know that you found it even when you had it in your hands, as it were. You could hold the precious gold of God's Word in your hand and not be sure that it was not human slime, while, on the other hand, you could hold human slime and not be sure that it was not God's precious truth. You must ever be searching, and never coming to the knowledge of the truth.

Thus, we believe that we have shown that the Bible is the Word of God, inspired and inerrant. Not everything that God says, He says in the Bible. We have indicated that He revealed Himself to us before He revealed Himself further and savingly in sacred Scripture. But everything that the Bible says, God says.

# Part III

## Some Objections to Inerrancy and Their Answers

### 7. Objections Allegedly Arising from Science

It is objected to the inerrancy doctrine that the Bible has many errors traceable to the inadequacy of the knowledge of the period during which the Bible was written. This is a major reason for setting aside the Westminster Confession by the drafters of "The Confession of 1967," as may be seen in the Appendix. It is added that these errors do not invalidate the message of the Bible, but merely disprove its inerrancy and inspiration. Adherents of infallibility, it says, are forced into all sorts of unscholarly and obscurantist positions in their necessary defense of the Bible versus the findings of modern science. Admitting the mere humanness of the Bible, and seeking the Word of God elsewhere than in its pages, are presented as truly scientific and, at the same time, truly spiritual.

To this we reply, first, this position overlooks the two kinds of authority in an infallible Bible. There is what is called "historical authority" and "normative authority" (which is discussed more fully in the Appendix). Historical authority applies to every word of an inerrant Bible, and tells us simply that whatever the Bible says was said or done was indeed said or done. Such information does not tell us whether what was said and done ought to have been said or ought to have been done. Only the normative authority of the inerrant Bible answers that question. For a fuller discussion of this difference see the Appendix. Its relevance to the point under question is important. It teaches us that Bible writers themselves may have been laboring under erroneous impressions without this being normative instruction for us. Suppose they did think of a three-storied universe, which was the common opinion in their day, the Bible does not err unless it teaches such as a divine revelation of truth. In fact, by showing that the writers may have personally entertained ideas now antiquated it reveals its own historical authenticity without its normative authenticity suffering.

Second, sometimes the difference between popular and technical or pedantic language is overlooked. "At sunset, Isaac went out to meditate" (Genesis 24:63) does not mean that the Bible teaches the Ptolemaic astronomy. It is not pedantically teaching that the sun rotates about the earth so that there is a literal "sunset." This was and is a common way of speaking and does not necessarily reflect the thinking of those who use such language. Someone has said that if the Bible were to be scientifically exact it would have read: "when the rotation of the solar luminary on its axis was such that its rays impinged horizontally on the retina, Isaac went out to meditate." I once lived in "Sunset Hills," and not one adult in the community believed that the sun ever sets. Likewise the "sun's standing still" (Joshua 10:12) would be the way things would appear, not necessarily the way they would be. While we are referring to this miracle let us add another observation dealing with another criticism. Some object to the accuracy of this particular miracle, arguing that if the sun did appear stationary for so long a period the whole universe would have been thrown out of order in one way and another. The objection is puerile. If God is able to do as much as the narrative relates it would be no more difficult to take care of all the attendant details! For the Creator, any manipulation of the creation whatsoever would be infinitely easy—but it seems infinitely difficult for some to see this.

Third, much unnecessary strain is caused by the hasty judgments of the Bible's friends and foes alike. We cannot examine at all thoroughly all the problems growing out of the creation narrative (Genesis 1–3), for example; but this general statement is true, we believe: If every Bible scholar were careful not to read anything out of the Scripture teachings except what it indubitably teaches, and natural scientists were equally careful to claim nothing as scientifically established but what is indubitably true, the tensions between science and Scripture would be reduced to a negligible minimum. For example, the Bible does not teach that God created the world in 4004 B.C. As Gordon Clark has written, "We defend the inspiration of the Bible, not of Archbishop Ussher."

These are merely a few samples of a few types of objections to the doctrine of inerrancy. There are many more types and there are many more answers. But this would seem to be a sufficient sampling for our purposes. A select and recommended bibliography may be found appended which will serve for further and more extensive investigation. In closing we should like to say only this: in the case of alleged discrepancies, it is not our burden to show how these may be reconciled as we have done above out of the "goodness of our hearts" and not the exigencies of our situation. We have given a case for the inerrancy of the Bible. Unless this case can be shown to be false, then it carries with it the guarantee that there are no discrepancies. We have, in other words, if our case is sound, shown that discrepancies are only apparent and must be reconcilable, even if we say not one word about how this reconciliation is to be shown. It behooves the opponent to prove us wrong by showing his "discrepancies" to be discrepancies incapable of harmonization. We have every reason to anticipate that he can succeed in so doing no better in the future than he has in the past because the Bible, we believe, is the inerrant Word of God.

## 8. Objections Arising from an Alleged "Docetism"

A very modern theological objection to inerrancy is an implied "Docetism." Docetism refers to an early heresy denying the genuineness of Christ's humanity. It maintained that

Christ merely appeared (*dokein*) to be human. Inerrancy does essentially the same thing to the Bible, it is said, that the docetists did to Christ namely, deny its genuine humanness. "To err is human" and to be human is to err. If the Bible has no error it could not really have been written by men. Thus the human authors of the Bible, according to inerrancy, it is charged, only appear to have written the Bible. In brief, the argument runs thus:

1. Inerrancy teaches that the Bible authors could not err.

2. But humans can err.

3. Therefore, inerrancy implicitly teaches that the authors of the Bible were not human.

However, in this neat little syllogism they have neglected to observe a crucial part of the picture. Perhaps it will be clearest if we insert it where it belongs in the otherwise consistent syllogism:

1. Inerrancy teaches that the Bible authors could not err.

2. But humans can err (*unless the omnipotent God preserves them from error without destroying their humanity*).

3. Therefore inerrancy implicitly teaches that the authors of the Bible were human (*but we deny merely that their sinful erring tendencies were in operation during the writing of Holy Scripture*).

Some may think that we here deny a principle we have defended above. There we said that God could not force the will of man without destroying man as man. Here we say that God can suspend the operation of human sinfulness without destroying the humanity of the persons concerned. The difference is this: freedom is essential to the nature of man but sinfulness is not. Remove freedom and man ceases to be; remove sinfulness and he does not cease to be a man (in fact, he is only perfectly human without sin).

Furthermore, there is a rather interesting inconsistency among most of our critics. While they deny that the Bible writers can be truly human while writing without error, they will not deny that Jesus could be truly human while living without error or even sin of any kind.

This criticism has the value of calling even greater attention to inerrancy's insistence on the genuineness and indispensable importance of human participation in the writing of Scripture. While God's part has been insisted on throughout this and most literature on the inspiration of the Bible, this is because it is so often challenged and is of such infinite importance. Sometimes in this stress on the divine, the human is, we regret to say, overlooked. Finally, some critics appear who claim that we deny the human role altogether. This calls forth our reiteration that the Bible is no less the word of man than it is the Word of God. But it is the word of men inspired by God. The Bible, then, is the Word of God expressed in the inspired words of men.

# Appendix on *The Confession of 1967*
## (of the United Presbyterian Church in the USA)

The one position of the *Westminster Confession of Faith* which the "Confession of 1967" avowedly and admittedly changed is that on the Bible. In the "Introductory Comment and Analysis" the Committee says, "This section is an intended revision of the Westminster doctrine, which rested primarily on a view of inspiration and equated the Biblical canon directly with the Word of God. By contrast, the pre-eminent and primary meaning of the word of God in the 'Confession of 1967' is the Word of God incarnate. The function of the Bible is to be the instrument of the revelation of the Word in the living church. It is not a witness among others, but the witness without parallel, the norm of all other witness. At the same time questions of antiquated cosmology, diverse cultural influences and the like, may be dealt with by careful scholarship uninhibited by the doctrine of inerrancy which placed the older Reformed theology at odds with advances in historical and scientific studies" (p. 29; all quotations are from the official "Bluebook" of the General Assembly, May, 1965).

This is flatly contrary to the promise on page 1 of the "Bluebook": "The proposal for amending the *Confession* does not entail revision or deletion (except for the deletion of the Westminster Larger Catechism) . . . ." Here is an admitted revision following on the heels of a denial of such a purpose. But still it is to be admired for its candor. We suppose that it was an unintentional oversight that the committee did not mention this one acknowledged revision as it did the one acknowledged deletion. What is far more serious is that the whole mentality of the new *Confession* is different from that of the old one. Its intention is probably not revision, but rejection. But candor has not reached the point of admitting that. The lack of frankness at this point is an advantage as well as disadvantage, however. It results in an ambiguity which, while it covers the probable intention of the committee, also permits adherents of the *Westminster Confession of Faith* to remain in the church in good conscience. They will be offended by this absence of the very clarity for which the *Westminster Confession of Faith* has always been justly famous. But whatever heresies may lurk in the shadows of vague language all of them have not yet dared to come to the light. Through the obfuscations of the new creed, the light of truth from the old ones will continue to shine unabated to the glory of God and the comfort of those who still believe what they vowed at their ordination.

Let us first examine the preliminary statement (p. 29) before proceeding to the creedal section on the Bible: "...Westminster doctrine which rested primarily on a view of inspiration and equated the Biblical canon directly with the Word of God..." We have no serious quarrel with this statement, but will elaborate a little so as to prevent misunderstanding, especially by the layman. First, Westminster is not unique in resting its doctrines on a view of inspiration. Virtually all Christian creeds have done this either expressedly or impliedly. (It is one of the notable weaknesses of the new creed that it does not do so.) When we say impliedly, we mean that inspiration is assumed even when there is no special article on the Bible. Inspiration is a catholic or universal or ecumenical, if you please, and not an exclusively Presbyterian, doctrine. In other words, in its eagerness to be modern, the new creed would antiquate the Presbyterian Church by reverting to the time before creeds began. As soon as the church did begin to speak about the Bible it testified to its inspiration. Never before has a church spoken of the Bible without bearing witness to its inspiration. So powerful is the pull of the past even on this new creed that it cannot get entirely free of this tradition, as we shall see when we come to consider its testimony that the Bible is the "normative witness." Even that word "normative" did not satisfy the Commissioners to the

General Assembly of 1965.

Second, while Westminster "equated the Biblical canon directly with the Word of God" this does not imply that it admitted of no differences within the Word of God. Obviously, when the Word of God says "And Satan said," that does not mean that God said what Satan said! It means that God said that Satan said it. This is quite another thing. To use a distinction that was acknowledged by the Westminster divines, as well as all other Reformed theologians: the authority of the Bible is complete, but it is of two kinds. The Bible has both descriptive and normative authority (*authentia historica* and *authentia normativa*). Descriptive authority means that everything which the Bible says happened, was spoken, or was thought, did happen, or was spoken, or was thought. It is authentic history, however bad the event may have been which the history records. All of the Word of God, according to Westminster, has this descriptive authority or authenticity. Within this Word of God as authentic record is the Word of God as normative or authoritative for faith and practice. When God said, as noted above, that Satan said, we know that Satan so said; but, we are not to believe and practice as Satan says. But when the Word of God says that God said, then we know both that God so said and that we are so to believe and so to practice.

We must add, also, that although Westminster equated the Biblical canon directly with the Word of God, as thus explained, this does not deny progress within the normative revelation of God anymore than affirming that God is the author of the whole creation is meant to deny that there is a difference between the egg and the chicken which comes from it.

One further and rather technical detail perhaps ought to be added. Westminster did not exactly "equate" the Word of God with the "canon." It identified the Word of God with the *original text* of the canonical books. Furthermore, the Word of God is not quite identified with the canon because the canon is the judgment of men about the Word of God and not the Word of God itself. As B. B. Warfield of old Princeton, who as much as any man since the Westminster standards were formulated shared their mentality, has written that the canon is not an inspired collection of books, but a collection of inspired books.

By contrast, "the pre-eminent and primary meaning of the word of God" in the "Confession of 1967" is "the Word of God incarnate." What have we here? The "word of God" (that is, the Bible, the fallible word of men which incidentally ought not from this viewpoint to be called the word of God but the word to God) means Jesus Christ ("the Word of God incarnate"). We invite any competent and candid interpreter to make of these words something other than nonsense or blasphemy. If the words of men, which we call the Bible, means Jesus Christ, then such statements as we mentioned above ("Satan said") mean Jesus Christ; the statement of Paul that "Demas has forsaken us having loved this present world," means Jesus Christ; "At sunset Isaac went out to meditate" means Jesus Christ; and so on.

To say that sinful actions, incidental details, trivial data severally mean Jesus Christ—well, it is far more charitable to say that this is nonsense rather than blasphemy. But what other construction can fairly be placed on these words? But someone (charging us with a lack of love when we think we are being as charitable as it is possible to be) will say: The statement simply means that the words of the Biblical writers point to Jesus Christ. What words? Some point away from Christ as truly as others point to Him. Reformed theology has shown how to distinguish them, as we indicated above; but, in the new creed no such formula is given. We have only the blanket statement: "the pre-eminent and primary meaning of the word of God . . . is the Word of God incarnate."

But if we should grant that the words of men in the Bible do in fact point to Christ (directly and indirectly, by inference and affirmation, by what is not, as cue to what is) then what is the difference between this and what the

*Westminster Confession of Faith* teaches? Or, do our new
creed writers wish to add slander to neglect when they
write: "By contrast (to the *Westminster Confession of Faith*)
the pre-eminent and primary meaning of the word of God
in the 'Confession of 1967' is the Word of God incarnate"?
Do they suppose for one moment that our fathers in the
faith thought that the Bible as the Word of God had any
other pre-eminent and primary meaning than Jesus Christ?
"Ye search the Scriptures for they bear witness of me"
(John 5:39). 1647 believed this as much as 1967, and in a far
more intelligible manner. What it amounts to is this: the
new creed is saying nothing or something; if something, it
is a slander of our fathers; if nothing, it is an insult to us.

"The function of the Bible is to be the instrument of the
revelation of the Word in the living church." Let us compare this with the classic statement of the *Westminster
Confession of Faith*, Chapter I, Sec. 10: "The Supreme Judge,
by which all controversies of religion are to be determined,
and all decrees of councils, opinions of ancient writers, doctrines of men, and private spirits, are to be examined and in
whose sentence we are to rest, can be no other but the Holy
Spirit speaking in the Scripture." In the Westminster doctrine the Bible is indeed the instrument of the revelation of
the Word (Christ) in the living church. But it is a doctrine
of the Bible as instrument which we can understand. The
Bible was inspired by God, and as such has perpetual authority. The Holy Spirit of Christ still works by means of it
as the permanent expression of His will by which the
Church is to be led. Here is a characteristic reaffirmation of
the famous Calvinistic principle: the Word and the Spirit;
the Word reveals the Spirit and the Spirit illumines the
Word. The Word will not be properly received apart from
the Spirit and the Spirit does not speak apart from the
Word. If our new creedalists meant this we should rejoice;
but, alas, nothing is further from their doctrines. We must
not forget that they have explicitly rejected the Westminster
view of Scripture. What, then, do they mean? This they at-

tempt to explain first, affirmatively and, second, negatively, in the two sentences which immediately follow, to which we now turn.

"It is not a witness among others but witness without parallel, the norm of all other witness." "It" clearly refers to the Bible which is the subject of the preceding sentence. Thus the new creedalists are saying here that the Bible is the witness which is the norm of all other witness. Now a "norm" is a standard by which others of like character are tested. Accordingly, the Bible is the standard or test by which all other witnesses including, for example, this new creed, are tested for their truthfulness. The Bible, mind you, is the norm of all witness to Christ. The Westminster divines could not express it better. In fact, this is what the *Westminster Confession of Faith* is expressing. Why then do the new creedalists take exception to Westminster while expressing the same doctrine? The fact seems to be that they are not using the normal meaning of "norm." Here is an abnormal "norm"; a standard which is not a standard. It is rather embarrassing to say that men are not using language normally and are not saying what they took seven years to formulate. That such is the sorry case is, however, as clear as it is surprising. First, they said, as noted, that their doctrine is other than Westminster. Second, they expressly repudiated the historic doctrine of "inspiration." Third, they call the Bible the "word of God" in sharp contrast to the "Word of God." If the Bible is not inspired and is merely the word of men, then either men are perfect or a norm of the Word of God is not a norm The imperfection of men is taught not only in the other creeds left standing in the new program, but taught in the "new creed" also (Part I, Sect. I, B). So we lamentably say that the new creed is one in which a "norm" is not a "norm", or error is the norm of Truth (the Word of God) .

Fourth, the next, the negative, proposition to which we now come explicitly rejects the Bible as "normative" (in any sense).

"At the same time questions of antiquated cosmology,
diverse cultural influences, and the like, may be dealt
with by careful scholarship uninhibited by the doctrine of inerrancy which placed the older Reformed
theology at odds with advances in historical and scientific studies."

We are certain that every member of the committee
which drew up the new creed would agree that the above
statement means the following: the new creed, rejecting the
doctrine of Inerrancy, leaves its adherents freer to accept
historical and scientific studies which contradict the historical and scientific statements of the Bible. This is not, in fact,
what this inaccurate, pejorative, disrespectful-to-the-fathers
statement actually says; but, since it is undoubtedly what it
intended to say let us address ourselves to the intention and
ignore the unhappy form of expression. The upshot of the
matter is this: We are being told that the scientifically and
historically errant word of God is nonetheless the norm of
all witness to the Word of God! The committee shows wisdom in not seeking to illustrate this.

We turn now to the main treatment of the Bible in the
creed itself, Part I, Section III b. "The Bible."

"The one sufficient revelation of God is Jesus Christ,
the Word of God incarnate, to whom the Holy Spirit
bears witness in many ways. The church has received
the Old and New Testaments as the normative witness
to this revelation and has recognized them as Holy
Scriptures."

We grant that "the one sufficient revelation of God is
Jesus Christ," but why do they not grant that the one sufficient revelation of Jesus Christ is the Bible? Christ did:
"...they (the Scriptures) bear witness of Me" (John 5:39).
Paul did: "The saying is sure and worthy of full acceptance,
that Christ Jesus came into the world to save sinners"
(1 Timothy 1:15; cf. Luke 19:10; Romans 5:8). What God
has joined together (the Word of God incarnate and the

Word of God inscripturated), why does the committee attempt to rend asunder?

"...to whom the Holy Spirit bears witness in many ways": Whatever the word "norm" may mean when applied to the Bible it is here clear that the Bible is not unique. It is not the only "revelation" of its kind as the church from the beginning (the whole church from the very beginning) has confessed. According to the new confession, it is only one among many ways in which the Holy Spirit bears witness to Christ. To be sure, it is the "norm" for others which, however, can only differ from it in degree, not kind. It is becoming clear that the Bible is thought of merely as the first and best of all these witnesses. But assuming this inadequate view for the sake of argument, how do we know that the Bible is the norm of the rest of the witnesses? Answer: "the church has received" it as such. The Bible claims its own inspiration some three thousand times, but this does not prove it. But the church recognizes the Bible as normative; this does prove it. Rome must be amused to hear such sentiments coming from the children of Calvin. They may well anticipate that it should not be long before these seers find the Holy Spirit bearing witness to the Word of God in the papacy, as Romanists have themselves contended for centuries (for critique of this approach cf. Chapter 4 above).

> "The New Testament is the recorded testimony of apostles to the coming of Jesus Christ and the sending of the Holy Spirit to the church. The Old Testament is received in the church as Holy Scripture which bears witness to God's faithfulness to Israel and points the way for fulfillment of his purpose in the Jew, Jesus of Nazareth. The Old Testament is indispensable to understanding the New, and is not itself fully understood without the New."

That the New Testament is the recorded testimony of apostles to Jesus Christ is, of course, true. It is also much more than that—it is the recorded testimony of God to the apostles. The most vital thing for us is not that the apostles testify to God, but that God testifies to or confirms the apostles. There is a vast difference between an infallible witness to an infallible Christ and a fallible witness to an infallible Christ. If it is a fallible witness it may (fortunately) be generally reliable as historical testimony to the major matters, but not absolutely reliable on all matters.

Here, again, in this paragraph we have the church's receiving of the Old Testament and the New Testament as the crucial evidence for its authority—an utterly Romish view, as already shown. Here, again, also, is the selective, discriminating acceptance of the witness of the Bible. It would seem that the committee is normative for the Bible rather than the Bible, as such, for the committee. That is, the Scripture is received as witness to God's faithfulness to Israel. But the Scripture also bears witness to God's rejection of Israel. That witness, nevertheless, seems not to be accepted by the committee, as the Bible teaches it. Hosea, for example, is a favorite Old Testament prophet because of his representation of the longsuffering of Yahweh. But what becomes of Hosea when he says: "...I will no more have pity on the house of Israel, to forgive them at all" (1:6)? Paul is supposedly writing Scripture which the church can accept when he says in 2 Corinthians 5:19: "...God was in Christ reconciling the world to himself, not counting their trespasses against them..." But the same apostle must be uncanonical when he declares in Romans 11:22: "Note then the kindness and the severity of God: severity toward those who have fallen, but God's kindness to you, provided you continue in his kindness; otherwise you too will be cut off."

As soon as we express gratitude for the enunciation of a sound principle, such as the interdependence of the two Testaments, we must immediately remind ourselves that we are reading something into this document which it does not intend. It does not mean that the New Testament is latent in the Old Testament and the Old Testament patent in the New Testament, as this phraseology would normally signify. So to construe it would be to wrench this text of the new creed out of its context. It may seem charitable to do so but it would not be true. But if it is not true neither is it charitable, for charity rejoices in the truth (1 Corinthians 13:6). And the truth, according to this context, must mean: not that the New Testament is latent in the Old Testament, but that some of the New Testament is latent in some of the Old Testament. Nor is the Old Testament patent in the New Testament, but some of the Old Testament is patent in some of the New Testament. And that "some" in each case is that which the church of the new creedalists deigns to receive.

> "God's word is spoken to his church today where the Scriptures are faithfully preached and attentively read in dependence on the guidance of the Holy Spirit and with readiness to receive their truth and direction."

Surely this is the form of sound words, but its meaning is loaded and all in the wrong direction. Faithfully to read and preach the Bible, according to this committee, is to distinguish between the errant husk and cleave to the inerrant but also indefinable Truth. If this seems to be an impossible task, an adequate help is suggested in the Holy Spirit's guidance. But, alas, the Holy Spirit cannot help us either, for we do not know how to recognize his guidance until the committee tells us. If the Holy Spirit guided us into the understanding of inspired Scripture, as the *Westminster Confession of Faith* taught us, this we could understand. Or, if the Spirit led us into an understanding of some definite part of Scripture, this we could understand. But it is only when the Spirit guides us into an understanding in accordance with this or some committee's understanding that we can rely upon him. Having dispensed with the inspiration of the Bible, we must now look to the inspiration of a committee. We are sure that this committee does not think that it is the only inspired committee. There must be other committees also, alas. If anything is likely to awaken the church to its real danger it will be the realization that once we have done away with Holy Scripture-Holy Spirit, in the vacuum thereby created we must have an infinite series of holy committees!

> "The Bible is to be interpreted in the light of its witness to God's work of reconciliation in Christ. The words of the Scriptures are the words of men, conditioned by the language, thought forms, and literary fashions of the places and times at which they were written. They reflect views of life, history and the cosmos which were then current, and the understanding of them requires literary and historical scholarship. The variety of such views found in the Bible shows that God has communicated with men in diverse cultural conditions. This gives the church confidence that He will continue to speak to men in a changing world and in every form of human culture."

The reader will recognize that this has been said before and criticized before. There appears to be no need for repetition. If our earlier words were true then the new creed's climax is untrue. The important thing for the reader of this and all doctrines, for that matter, is to judge righteous judgment (John 7:24). There is an unrighteous judgment of principles as well as a righteous one, and it may be favorable as well as unfavorable. Some seem to think that we do an injustice to a statement only when we draw unfair, incriminating deductions from it. But we also do an injustice when we draw unfair, exonerating deductions from it. To make a righteous judgment, as commanded by our Lord, is to avoid all unfair judgments whether favorable or unfavorable. Because this is the proposed creed of earnest, serious-minded, hard-working Christian persons who are more likely to be unrighteous in our judgments by being too lenient than by being too strict. But we must avoid both if we would render righteous judgments. We must attempt, as we have here attempted (God being our witness), with malice toward none, free of any desire to find anyone at fault for a word, to ascertain what is meant by the proposed "Confession of 1967." With one member of this present committee we are personally and fairly intimately acquainted, and we bear him witness that he appears to be one of the most sincere Christians we have ever had the privilege of knowing. It may be that every other committee member is of such caliber. Nevertheless, notwithstanding the possible soundness of the persons who composed it, this creed is anything but sound. We appeal to them, no less than all others, when we urge them in the name of the Christ, whom we all profess to love, to rescind this confession before it becomes an indelible blemish on the escutcheon of the church.

# Select and Recommended Bibliography

Bruce, Frederick Fyvie. *Are the New Testament Documents Reliable?* London, InterVarsity Fellowship, 1946.

Engelder, Theodore. *Scripture Cannot Be Broken; Six Objections to Verbal Inspiration Examined in the Light of the Scripture.* St. Louis, Concordia Publishing House, 1944.

Gaussen, Francois Samuel Robert Louis. *Theopneustia: The Bible, Its Divine Origin and Inspiration, Deduced from Internal Evidence, and the Testimonies of Nature, History and Science.* Cincinnati, George S. Blanchard, 1859.

Haley, John W. *An Examination of the Alleged Discrepancies of the Bible.* Chicago, W. G. Holmes, 1876.

Henry, Carl Ferdinand Howard (ed). *Revelation and the Bible.* Grand Rapids, Baker Book House, 1958.

Packer, J. I. *"Fundamentalism" and the Word of God; Some Evangelical Principles.* Grand Rapids, Wm. B. Eerdmans Publishing Co., 1958.

Walvoord, John F. (ed.). *Inspiration and Interpretation.* Grand Rapids, Wm. B. Eerdmans Publishing Co., 1957.

*Warfield, Benjamin Breckinridge. *The Inspiration and Authority of the Bible.* Philadelphia, Presbyterian and Reformed Publishing Co., 1948.

*Can I Trust My Bible?* Important questions often asked about the Bible, with some answers by eight evangelical scholars. Chicago, Moody Press, 1963.

*The Infallible Word,* a Symposium by the Members of the Faculty of Westminster Theological Seminary, Philadelphia, The Presbyterian Guardian Publishing Corp., 1946.

*Warfield is the author of other works and articles bearing on our subject. We recommend his writings as best of all, and himself as the ablest Reformed theologian of the twentieth century.

# A Primer

# on

# the Deity

# of Christ

*[This primer, unlike most in this series, is in the form of a dialogue. The dialogue is between "Inquirer," who is an educated, thoughtful person becoming convinced of the truths of the Christian religion (though not yet converted to them), and "Christian," an experienced evangelical minister.]*

I: Among the many Christian doctrines we have discussed so far, we haven't yet taken up the doctrine of Christ Himself, have we?

C: No, not directly, although we did ground our doctrine of Holy Scripture on the teaching of Christ.

I: Yes, I recall. That was after we had demonstrated that Christ was a messenger sent from God. And that, in turn, was proved by the miracles He performed.

C: Exactly. From His "credit as a proposer" of doctrine, we noticed that we had to believe every doctrine He taught. Our primary concern there was with His view of Scripture. We agreed that as an authenticated divine messenger, He was to be believed in what He said about the Bible, specifically that Scripture, Old and New Testaments, was inspired of God.

I: Yes. And on that basis, I agreed that the Bible is indeed the Word of God. From that point on, we've grounded all the doctrines we've discussed on what the Bible says. But we haven't yet focused on what the Bible teaches about Christ Himself, have we?

C: No, not yet, even though that is the central verity of the Christian religion.

I: What do you mean?

C: Well, it is not only an important doctrine of Christianity. but the most important doctrine. Furthermore, it is indispensable to Christianity.

I: You mean that if a person doesn't have a sound doctrine about Christ, he is not a Christian at all?

C: Exactly. You see, many who call themselves Christians should not; their very idea of Christ is unsound.

I: But what if they still regard Him as very important and central in their lives?

C: They still would be at odds with the truth. If Jesus is none other than God incarnate, then to think He is merely a man would be a fatal mistake, would it not?

I: A very serious mistake, I grant you. But can you say that they don't believe in Him or follow Him when they do listen to His teachings and try to do what He teaches?

C: That's precisely the point. If He teaches that He Himself is God, and they follow Him as merely a man, can they meaningfully be said to follow His teaching?

I: I see your point. And yet, could they not follow some of His teachings, or even all of them, without realizing who He is as their Teacher?

C: That seems reasonable. But let's take a specific example of His teaching. As you know, He taught the Golden Rule: "Do unto others as you would that they do to you."

I: That's what I have in mind. I know people who follow the Golden Rule and agree with Christ's teaching about it, and yet they don't think He is God. As a matter of fact, they would be appalled by the idea that Christ is divine. They regard Him as a very godly person who taught very sound maxims, including the Golden Rule. If these people take the Golden Rule seriously and practice it rather admirably, how can you deny that they follow Christ's moral instruction, even if they don't share the church's theological estimate of Him?

C: I would grant that they could understand the Golden Rule and live according to it at least superficially.

I: The people I'm thinking of, however, are anything but superficial. They're very serious people, and they do take the rule very seriously. I can't quite see how, though they don't believe in the divinity of Christ, they are superficial in their observance of His moral commandment.

C: I understand your perplexity. As far as our discussion has gone, you would seem to be reasonableness itself, and I would seem to be way off reality. But let me make an observation we have not yet considered.

I: Please do.

C: Well, as you probably know, Christ taught also that He is the vine, and His disciples are His branches. Are you acquainted with that teaching found in the fifteenth chapter of John?

I: Yes, vaguely. He did say something about His being the vine in which they are the branches, and they bear fruit through Him. I'm beginning to see what you're hinting at. But, spell it out, please.

C: Well, as you sense, He teaches there that He is the source of their life and their fruit-bearing, that is, their morality. In another place He says, "Let your light so shine before men that they may behold your good works and glorify your Father who is in Heaven." Here in John 15 He explains where their good works actually come from, does He not?

I: Yes, I suppose that is the point of the analogy He makes. He, as the vine, is the source of life, which somehow fills His followers, producing in them a moral life. As I ponder this, I see how profound the idea is. Are you saying that Christ not only teaches a morality but also claims that He Himself fulfills that morality in His followers?

C: Yes, that's right. I don't mean to deny that time and again He just issues commandments, as it were. He often sets forth teachings, describes maxims. But occasionally He also talks about the source of power for fulfilling the moral law, as in the vine and branches. In other words, the morality He commands is fulfilled in those who don't simply hear what He says and obey it, but actually look to Him for the necessary strength to fulfill it.

I: I guess my friends who try to follow Christ's morality without acknowledging that He is divine overlook this aspect of Christ's teaching. I can't help wondering if they've ever thought of Jesus' representing Himself as the source for fulfilling His own commandments. I'm not sure they would follow His teaching on that point. I suspect they would not. These people are real moralists. They try to be humble, but they really are proud of their character. They feel it's *their* character, and they don't need outside help to obey these commandments. If you told them that they could not carry out what Jesus taught without His power, they would not buy that. They would, in fact—well, I don't know quite what to say here.

C: What you're thinking, but are hesitant to say, is this, is it not? If they understood Christ to say His moral commandments could not be kept except by His own power, they would simply reject Him. Isn't that really what this whole thing amounts to?

I: I think you're right. It's hard to say, because I doubt they

ever think in these categories. But when you put two and
two together your answer seems inevitable. They think
Christ is admirable as a moral teacher addressing Himself
to moral persons such as themselves. They agree with His
ideas. They join *with* Him in following them. But depend
*upon Him* for the power to do good—you're right, they
would not accept that. I have to conclude that they would
want nothing more to do with Him. They would reject
Him. He would be insulting them.

C: Well, it looks as if we've gotten the answer to our question, doesn't it?

I: It surely does. I'm surprised I didn't even suspect that a
few minutes ago. And yet it's obvious, now that I think
about it. I'm learning about myself, as well as about my
friends. Up until this moment, I myself supposed that
even though Christ was a messenger sent from God,
whose every teaching I must accept, it was *I* who accepted
them, *I* who would perform them (if I am forgiven for the
sins I've already made).

C: Don't be too hard on yourself. Most people think that
way at first. It's only when they realize how deep their depravity is and how little inclined they are to general morality that they begin to look around for help. Once they do
realize they are sinners, as your friends apparently do not,
then they know that they need forgiveness and power as
well.

I: I can see that now.

C: Most people don't think in terms of the parable of the
vine and the branches. If, as sinners, they sense that they
cannot become new people unless they have a new principle of life within them, they may not realize at first that it's
nothing less than Jesus Christ Himself dwelling in them

and moving them to morality. But they learn quickly enough once He teaches them that.

I: I, for one, am catching on fast. I wonder why I took so long? Now that I do see it, it's very plain. I get your point that there is no following the moral teachings of Jesus Christ without recognizing who He is. It's really strange to me that just a few minutes ago it would have seemed self-evident that a person could follow the commandments of Christ, regardless of what he thought about Christ. I guess that's because I thought it similar to following Socrates or the Buddha or any other teacher without believing anything particular about the man himself. But a moment's reflection shows me that Jesus Christ is different from these other teachers.

C: Indeed He is. The others can understand certain moral principles and articulate them excellently and strive to fulfill their own moral ideals. You can join with them in recognizing the ideals and trying to fulfill them also. But once you realize that you're a sinner, you know that you do not have the internal power to make your ethics rise up and walk. That's because you've become acquainted with your own heart and with the Christian doctrine. These other teachers have not and, therefore, remain superficial in both their understanding of commandments and their understanding of their own ability to perform them.

I: That's precisely the case. And it was the case with me, also. Now that I am awakened to this truth, I realize that Christ, even in His moral teaching, implies His very— should I say, deity? That's certainly what you're driving at. But how does that follow? Granted that He presents Himself as the power by which His own morals are realized; how does that prove that He must be divine?

C: I don't suppose it does.

I: You don't'? Well, if not, what's all this about? Aren't we talking about the person of Christ as supernatural?

C: We are.

I: I don't get it. That's what I thought this was proving, that He is divine because He dwells in us to make His morals come alive through us. Yet you say it does not prove that He is divine. I'm confused.

C: It would prove, as you have observed, that He Himself must empower us to fulfill His own laws by somehow in- dwelling us as the vine indwells and energizes the branch to bear fruit. But could you imagine Christ's being used by God in that role?

I: You mean as a spirit of some sort, while God would ulti- mately be the actual source of our morality? I guess that would be a theoretical possibility. Of course, Christ would have to be superhuman. He couldn't dwell in disciples as one person of a finite character.

C: Indeed no. (Remember, we're just trying this idea for size.) If that wouldn't be possible, then He'd have to be a spirit, would He not?

I: Yes. And moreover, He would have to be more than fi- nite, would He not?

C: I would certainly think so.

I: So aren't we back where we started? That is, for Christ to indwell every Christian who bears moral fruit, He would have to be spiritual and not material, and He would have to be infinite. What else would that be except deity itself?

C: I couldn't agree with you more.

I: Well, I thought you said it did *not* prove that He was deity.

C: I meant that it did not at first glance prove it. Theoretically God could have used some agent. But as we have probed that concept, we have realized that the agent Himself would have to be divine. So, at a closer look, it does indeed require what you say, and does vindicate your original supposition.

I: In other words, I'm correct after all?

C: I think so; but, I think you do have to prove it, in the way you have just done.

I: In other words, we must conclude from the teaching of Jesus Christ about morals that He Himself is the fulfiller of them, and that, therefore, He Himself must be the infinite divine spirit.
  We have our first proof, then, that Jesus Christ is God. Although it's an indirect one, it's a very impressive one for me. Let me see if I have this right. He teaches the way of morality and furthermore teaches that He is the way. Even if He said nothing more, that much would imply that to fulfill His own role He would have to be God.

C: I think that's exactly the case. Obviously He may say much more than that. But, as you put it very well, if Christ said nothing other than that, we would have to conclude that this was a veiled allusion to His deity.

I: I find that most interesting, because I'm still thinking of my friends who consider themselves Christians precisely because they follow the morality of Christ. The next time I talk with them, I'm going to start the conversation right along that line and see if I can't get them to see that the very moralism they regard as Christian would lead them inevitably to the conclusion that Jesus Christ is God, contrary to what they now think.

C: I wish you well. That is a fine approach to mere moralists who think they can be Christian without believing that Christ is God.

I: You did say that there were other, more direct indications of the deity of Christ?

C: Yes, many others. Christ says directly that He is God.

I: Directly? I don't know the New Testament as well as you do. But I can't remember ever hearing Christ say, "I am God." And that's the sort of thing I don't forget. Where does He say that?

C: Nowhere to my knowledge does He say in so many words, "I am God." But He says the obvious equivalent of it. For example, He says to His apostles, "He who has seen Me has seen the Father." There's no question in anybody's mind that the word "Father" there refers to the Deity. So when He says those words to Philip, His obvious meaning is, "He who has seen Me has seen God." That's the same thing, is it not, as saying, "I am God"?

I: Yes. It could hardly be plainer. I don't know why I didn't notice that before. Strange, isn't it, how we can read the New Testament and not notice things. We can look at certain words and not see them. I must at some time or other, though I don't remember when, have read, "He who has seen Me has seen the Father." Yet it never struck me as "He who has seen Me has seen God." If Jesus had put it that way, I think it would have shocked me the first time I read it, and I'd never have forgotten it. Yet, until this moment, I didn't realize what He actually said.

Now that I've gotten over that shock, there's something

else that puzzles me.

C: I have an idea what that is, but tell me anyway.

I: It's just that Jesus of Nazareth was the one speaking those words, "He who has seen Me has seen the Father." The first thing one would think is that God is a man. After all, there talking to Philip was this man, maybe six feet tall, 165 pounds perhaps, and thirty years of age. I guess that's why I didn't see it the first time I read it. It sounds so absurd to say a six-foot-tall, 165-pound, thirty-year-old man is God. Yet, "He who has seen Me has seen the Father." What are we to make of this? The more I reflect on my past, the more I suppose that I simply must have shaken my head when I read that. I must have thought, "I don't know what He means, but He can't mean what He seems to mean"—and let it go at that. Now that you make me stop and look more carefully at it, I have to admit that Jesus is seriously and unmistakably saying that to see Him is to see God. But what does that mean, if it can't possibly mean that God is six feet tall, 30 years old, weighing 165 pounds?

C: You're quite right that Jesus didn't identify deity with His human nature or any other human being.

I: I'm relieved at that, but I still don't know what He does mean.

C: Well, what else can He mean except that, in uttering those words, He is in union with God? In other words, we have here Christ's own reference to the Christian doctrine of the incarnation.

I: Incarnation, meaning "in the flesh." God in the flesh, Immanuel. I remember that is one of His names, and the Bible itself interprets that as "God with us." What we have is "God in Jesus," I take it you are saying.

C: That would certainly seem to be His meaning, would it not? If so, that would be coherent.

I: I see what you are saying. That man who says, "He who has seen me has seen God," is in union with God. Seeing that man is seeing God, though not with literal eyes, but with the eyes of the mind. Am I right?

C: I think so.

I: Isn't there a sense, though, in which everybody has God dwelling in him. Could I not say in that sense, "He who has seen Me has seen the Father"? I tremble even at the utterance of those words because frankly they sound blasphemous. But if Jesus alludes only to being in union with God, would there be anything but a difference of degree between Jesus and His followers in whom He dwells?

C: As you say, you would feel blasphemous in saying. "He who has seen Me has seen the Father." I too would feel blasphemous. Why is that?

I: Well, in my case, and I suppose yours also, it's because I know I am not God. Even if I were sure, which I am not, that God dwells in me, I am absolutely certain that I am not God. So whatever Jesus Christ means by that statement, I know I couldn't say it with anything other than a feeling of abhorrence. You'll have to speak for yourself.

C: I couldn't say those words any more than you could, and for the same reason. I know I am not God. It would be a blasphemous falsehood. So we are really answering our question, are we not?

I: Yes, we are. You and I and others like us simply could not say, "He who has seen Me has seen the Father," because we know we are not God. Which drives us to the conclusion that when Jesus calmly makes such an utterance, He really is God. The only way to make sense of that claim coming from the lips of a visible human being is that He, Jesus of Nazareth, is actually in a unique unity with God. It is so different from the way any other human being is related to God that He alone can say that to see Him is to see the Father. Yes, I think you've proved your point. That statement is, on reflection, a clear claim of deity and simultaneously of incarnation.

C: On another occasion, Jesus said something similar and yet significantly different.

I: What was that?

C: He said, "I and the Father are one." Surely that sounds like, "He who has seen Me has seen the Father." But there is this difference: In the statement we've been discussing, Jesus claims a one-to-one identification between Himself and the Father. But in saying, "I and the Father are one," He indicates not a one-to-one identity, but a two-in-one identity, if I may use that expression. He has in mind two persons when He says, "I *and* the Father are one." Referring obviously to Himself in distinction from the Father, He emphasizes at the same time that He is one with the Father: "I and the Father *are one*."

I: I think I see the subtle, wonderful difference here. The statement, "He who has seen Me has seen the Father," stresses His identity with God. But, "I and the Father are one" speaks of both identity and diversity.

C: So we have here a reference to two persons in one Godhead, do we not?

I: Two persons in one Godhead? I hadn't thought of it that way, but I guess that's true. The two persons, "I" and the

"Father," are "one," that is, one Godhead. I see what you're saying. But what does that mean?

C: Does that not indicate the doctrine of the Trinity in principle? In other words we have here a reassertion of the oneness of God or "monotheism," the unity of the divine essence or being. At the same time, we see that Christ is distinct from the Father. So we have, in the phraseology of the traditional Trinitarian doctrine, a reference to two of the three persons in the Godhead. The Son and the Father are one in the same divine essence.

Though our discussion does not focus on the Trinity, but on the deity of Christ, His being a member of the Trinity clearly underlines the full deity of Jesus Christ.

I: That is certainly true.

C: Before we leave the Gospel of John, let's take one other assertion that occurs there. In the eighth chapter, Jesus carries on a dialogue with certain "Jews who believed on Him." That phrase occurs in verse 31, but before the chapter is over, those Jews who believed in Him were seen not to believe in Him.

I: How is that?

C: When Christ claimed to be deity, these professed believers realized they did not in fact believe in Him. They believed in the person they *thought* Jesus was. When they learned who Jesus claimed to be, they were outraged at Him.

It was in the course of the dialogue with these "believing" Jews that Jesus indicated that He came from the Father and indeed was one with the Father. These "disciples" were getting the message and not liking it.

I: What happened then?

C: Well, as the chapter unfolds, the more these "believers" learn about Jesus and His claims to deity, the more they become hostile and outraged. Finally, they recognize that Christ unmistakably claims to be God. In their book, that is blasphemy, because Jesus was a human being, and it is blasphemy for a human being to claim to be God. When they put two and two together and came to the inevitable conclusion they picked up stones to kill Him because, as they said, "You being a man make yourself to be God."

You see, that other statement, "He who has seen Me has seen the Father," was made to His believing disciples. They accepted it. But this statement about Christ's deity was made to professed believers who really did not believe. So here we have the testimony of unbelievers to Christ's own self-opinion as we have in the other chapter the testimony of believers to His belief about Himself. Both groups are confronted with the same Christ. One group accepts Him as divine and worships. The other group rejects Him as a blasphemer and endeavors to execute Him.

I: Different reactions to the same proposition of Jesus that He was indeed God incarnate.

C: Correct. John's Gospel concentrates on this theme, but we could also find evidence for Christ's deity elsewhere. Before we go to a direct statement of Christ's that clearly indicates His deity, let's notice a feature of the Sermon on the Mount in Matthew and Luke that, while not mentioning deity directly, unmistakably implies it.

I: You're referring to the famous sermon-lecture of Jesus on morals, where we have the Lord's Prayer and the Golden Rule and so on?

C: Yes.

I: Are you saying that the Sermon on the Mount teaches the

divinity of Jesus?

C: Indirectly, yes.

I: That's the first time I have ever heard that. In fact, it is to the Sermon on the Mount that my friends, who do *not* believe in the deity of Christ, appeal.

C: I hope so. It may make believers out of them.

I: Show me.

C: The Sermon on the Mount in Matthew is found in chapters 5 through 7. Here Christ says the type of thing that leaves no doubt He assumes His own deity. For example, consider the Beatitudes in general. We're all familiar with these. Many of us have memorized them: "Blessed are the poor in spirit, for theirs is the kingdom of heaven." "Blessed are the peacemakers, for they shall be called the children of God." And so on. I'll not cite them all, but just note that Jesus utters them with absolute finality and on His own authority alone. You know how the prophets would constantly say, "Thus saith the Lord." They would always ground the authority of their message not on themselves but on its source in God, who had revealed His message to them. They make it very clear that they are the servants and He is the Lord.

I: Doesn't Jesus call Himself the servant of the Lord?

C: True, He does say, "I came to do the Father's will." He was a man and He was subordinate to the divine will. He says so on a number of occasions. Nevertheless, on other occasions He appeals to nothing and relies on nothing. The authority of His message does not depend upon a source outside Himself.

I: How so?

C: In the Beatitudes, for example, on His own authority, He tells us who will inherit the kingdom of God, who will be the children of God, who will inherit the earth, and so on. No mere human being can say that on His own authority. He can give educated guesses. Or, if he is commissioned by God, he can say it in God's name, but not of himself. Yet this man Jesus spoke these things very calmly with a supreme and serene authority appropriate only to deity itself. Is that not so?

I: I suppose you're right. I had never thought of it that way before. As you say, I've known those Beatitudes for a long, long time. I've even memorized a good many of them. But since Jesus doesn't say so in so many words that He's God, I guess I never noticed that He was really doing something even more impressive than that—just tacitly assuming it. That's what it amounts to. He talks as if He is God, even when He doesn't say so directly. A person might not notice that fact.

C: Maybe that's a tribute to Jesus: that these things sound so natural coming from His lips that we don't notice extraordinary implications.

I: It is as if we have a tacit, unconscious realization of His deity. It doesn't seem strange to hear *Jesus* speak that way. It certainly wouldn't be appropriate for anyone to speak that way unless He were divine.

C: I had never thought of it that way myself. You have a very fine point there. I thank you for it. I myself never realized that the reason people reading the Beatitudes miss their implicit argument for Jesus' deity is that it seems so natural coming from His lips. They almost instinctively realized that this was no mere preacher, that this was a divine preacher. Thank you, my friend, for that observation.

I: I'm glad to return a favor for all you have done me. What other things in the Sermon on the Mount imply the deity of that preacher?

C: Notice the last beatitude especially. Christ says there. as you know, "Blessed are you when men shall revile you and say all manner of evil against you falsely for My sake. Rejoice and be exceeding glad for so persecuted they the prophets that were before you."

I: Wait a minute. Don't tell me. I see for myself what you are about to say. Jesus is saying that the prophets suffered for Him. And the prophets lived hundreds of years before Jesus, did they not?

C: Indeed. Some lived thousands of years before Him. The prophets proper, those whom He may well have meant, were as early as a thousand years before Him. The latest before John the Baptist would have been several hundred years before Him.

I: In other words, people who lived a thousand years before Him suffered for His sake. That implies that He was preexistent, a supernatural being. If He lived hundreds of years before that sermon, and people suffered for Him a millennium before He was born, then He existed in another form before taking upon Himself a human form. Is that it?

C: It would seem an inescapable conclusion that He was preexistent, but not necessarily that He was eternal.

I: Is there not an implication of eternality here?

C: How so?

I: Well, if a person suffered for His sake, that would suggest deity because people don't suffer humiliation and slander and so on for anything other than what they regard as their God, or at least His representative.

C: That seems reasonable. They're willing to suffer for this preexistent person, and such a willingness is almost always reserved for God, or as you say, one who represents God. So, I guess you're right. There *is* an implication of more than the preexistence. The preacher's words suggest *eternal* preexistence.

I: It's strange how you can read a statement and not notice its significance the first time around. I've read that more than once and been impressed with what Jesus says about people rejoicing in suffering for Him. Yet I never thought that in mentioning the prophets' suffering for Him, He must be far more than a mere man preaching on the mount. How blind I was.

C: The point is even more plain if you imagine an ordinary person making the kind of statement He does. Suppose, for example, I stood behind a pulpit and said, "Blessed are John Calvin and Martin Luther and John Wesley and Jonathan Edwards because they suffered for my sake." It would not only be *false*, because, of course, they never knew me, or suffered for me, or would even think of suffering for me had they known me; it would also be absolutely *absurd*. I would have to be out of my mind to say a thing like that. But Christ says it as a simple matter of fact. In perfect calmness and secure rationality He casually remarks that men hundreds and thousands of years before suffered for His sake.

I: When you think of it, you realize what an overwhelming assertion of His deity that is. The fact that it comes in this veiled form (once the veil is penetrated) makes it all the more impressive.

C: The same thing is noticeable when Christ comments directly on the Bible. He says, "It is said by them of old time, 'Thou shalt not kill,' but I say unto you..." or "It is said by them of old time, 'Thou shalt not commit adultery,' but I say unto you..." Do you realize the significance of that?

I: You mean that He's putting Himself on a level with Old Testament Scripture?

C: Yes. For Him and His audience the Old Testament was the Word of God. Granted that some of His comments were not directly aimed at the Old Testament, but at contemporary misinterpretations of the Old Testament; nevertheless, in the same breath that He cites what His audience regarded as the inspired Word of God, He calmly says, "But *I* say to you."

I: In other words, by putting His word on a level with what was revered as the Word of God, Christ puts Himself on a divine level.

C: It certainly seems so. Again, I think we can get the impact of this all the better by comparing it with *our* saying such a thing. Suppose I, from the pulpit, said to a worshipping congregation, "Now, the Word of God says so and so. But *I* say unto you." You know what that congregation would say to me. "Who do you think you are?" How dare I put my word on a level with what I and my listeners consider to be the Word of God. Only one person may properly do such a thing: God Himself. The only one equal to God is God. And Jesus Christ certainly sounds as if He is making God His equal. If He were not God. then, of course. He would be just as impertinent and blasphemous as I to say such a thing. His being a perfect man doesn't change the fact that He'd be infinitely beneath the infinite God. Moreover, a perfect man would never utter such blasphemy.

I: Therefore, Jesus Christ is claiming to be God. I hear the argument.

C: There is more in the Sermon on the Mount, but let's move to its conclusion to see what intimations of deity we have there. Notice, that is where Jesus tells the well-known parable of the two men who built their houses on differing foundations. One man built on a rock; the other on sand. One of the houses, you remember, collapsed during a storm; the other stood. Do you recall what Christ was driving at in that story?

I: I do remember that story. It's even sung by kids in a simple chorus. The point of it is that the man who built his house on a rock really was building on Christ, is it not? And the man who built on sand did not build on Christ or His teaching. Am I right?

C: Yes, and you can see the implication.

I: I can indeed. Jesus is saying that if an individual believes in Him and His teaching and obeys Him, he will be able to go through the storms of life, and no doubt the storms of final judgment. If a person does not believe, he will be ruined in this world and the world to come. Knowing Jesus, that's the sort of point He's always making, is it not?

C: Yes. The people, no doubt, got that insinuation. This speaker was divine because no one other than God can assure that a person who does not follow Him will be ruined, and that a person who does will be saved. For anyone else to say that would be consummate arrogance and, again, blasphemy. And yet, what is more natural than for a divine person to say such a thing. If Christ is divine, you could never understand His *not* saying it; and if He were not divine, you could never understand His saying it. It's that simple.

Probably the most definitive utterance of all in this sermon is at its very end.

I: What is that?

C: Christ ends the Sermon on the Mount by describing the final judgment: "In that day, men shall come before *Me* and say, 'Lord, Lord. Have we not prophesied in Thy name? Have we not cast out devils in Thy name? Have we not done mighty works in Thy name?' And I shall say unto them, 'Depart from Me ye workers of iniquity. I never knew you.'"

I: In other words, Jesus is saying He's going to be the judge of the last day. He is going to reject some people at His judgment seat. I get the point. The inference is clear. How can anybody miss it? The judge of the last day, who will determine the destinies of men, must be God. Is that what you deduce from this teaching?

C: I can't deduce anything else. There's only one judge of the last day: God Himself. Christ says He's the judge of the last day. Therefore, He is saying unmistakably that He is God.

I: I certainly see that. But something in what He says at the last judgment puzzles me.

C: I think I know what it is. It's that He denies at the day of judgment people who say they were His servants in this world. He even calls them evil-workers, doesn't He?

I: But why?

C: I could give you a flip answer here and say He calls them that because that's what they are. You yourself know that whatever He calls them, that's what they are. But what you're really asking is how could they be what they are. Is that not the question?

I: Yes.

C: Well, let's see if we can get to His point. These people before the judgment seat of Christ are saying that they prophesied in His name and did many great things. Can we be
sure they're telling the truth? They wouldn't try to deceive
that Judge. So, let's assume they really were prophets of
Christ or preachers of the Word of God. They were even
successful at casting out devils. We are assuming they did
*many* mighty works, because they wouldn't dare lie about a
matter like that before the judgment seat. They may have
been liars in this world, but not before the all-wise God in
the next world.

I: You're fixing the noose ever tighter by making my question all the more difficult to answer, aren't you?

C: It would seem so, wouldn't it? By my saying that they
must have spoken the truth about having done mighty
works in the name of Jesus Christ, the question is indeed
sharpened. Why would Christ reject such persons? But,
don't you see, that's the very point. They did these things
in the name of Christ, no doubt. But they didn't, apparently,
do them in the Spirit of Christ. They could be preachers of
the Word as, for example, I am one. They could declare the
gospel, the true gospel, as I believe I do. They could even
thereby deliver people out of darkness and into light, doing
many other mighty works. Is that not so?

I: I guess it is. But, wouldn't the Spirit of Christ be what
motivates them when they do preach the gospel and are
blessed by conversions?

C: Not necessarily. And according to Christ, apparently not.

I: You're saying that people can preach Christ without loving Christ?

C: That seems to be the case, does it not? These people are witnesses of Christ and are even successful. Yet He disowns them. He never "knew" them. Now what can that mean except that they didn't have communion with Him. They didn't love Him and He was not in love with them. For some reason or other, they went about His business, maybe for gain or fame or a half-dozen other reasons.

I: But how could they be successful when they didn't love what they were doing?

C: Well, you see, it's the Word of God that the Spirit uses as His sword—not necessarily the one who voices the Word of God. Christ says His Word will not return to Him void. So when the Word goes out, even from an insincere heart and from lying lips, it's nonetheless the Word. God may see fit to honor His Word regardless of the source through which it comes.

I: I see. And that must be what happened. It's a very sobering thought, of course, even frightening. A person's success would be no proof that God is pleased with him.

C: Yes. It means we must very carefully search our motives. If we do what's right for the wrong reason, we're up against what we call "bad good works." The works are good, and God honors those works by benefiting others. The worker, however, is bad. And God gives him the punishment *he* deserves.

I: I see what I was missing before. And I thank you, though I must admit that I'm still reeling a bit from that observation.

C: Imagine the effect the Sermon on the Mount had on the hearers.

I: If they were anything like me, they must have been overwhelmed.

C: They were. Their response was most significant. The text says that the people marveled because He spoke "as one having authority and not as the scribes." Considering the themes on which He was speaking and the manner in which He spoke about them, they realized that His was an inherent authority. In other words, Christ was God. The very comparison they made between Christ's teaching and that of the scribes and Pharisees confirms this.

I: How so?

C: The Jews of that day had a very great veneration for their scribes and Pharisees. The scribes and Pharisees were the main teachers and champions of the law. The Jewish people venerated the law of God as the divine thing it actually is. They didn't always understand it, and they seldom obeyed it, but they always recognized it for what it is. They were like a good many Christian people who keep the Holy Bible in their houses and revere it as inspired, only to dust it off occasionally for lack of use. That is how the Jews reverenced their Scriptures and those who were the official interpreters of them.

I: I see. And they recognized that Jesus spoke with an authority that was different from the scribes' authority. The scribes had authority as the expounders of the authoritative Word. Jesus had authority in and of Himself. The people knew that a scribe's authority was outside himself. But Christ's authority resided in Himself. He did not need to appeal to another authority.

C: Well said. And so we have seen that in a sermon on morals, Jesus has a great deal to say about His own person, even when He is not talking directly about that subject. He assumes His deity here, as in other places He asserts it. Having noticed this tacit assumption of deity in the sermon, let us turn to a direct assertion of it in Matthew 11.

I: Granted I'm no expert on Matthew, but I don't remember Jesus' saying anything like "I and the Father" in that Gospel. As I recall, Matthew is more preoccupied with Christ as the Messiah and the fulfillment of Old Testament prophecy, and so on. Is it not?

C: You're quite right. That makes any direct statement by Christ about His deity in that Gospel all the more outstanding. In chapter 11, He makes a very significant declaration: "No one knows the Father save the Son, and He to whomsoever He reveals Him. No one knows the Son except the Father, and He to whom He reveals Him." Do you get the point?

I: I get two points, as a matter of fact. The first one is that Christ claims a unique knowledge of God. That is striking, because, really, all men know there is a God. So it's puzzling that Jesus says no one knows the Father except the Son.

C: Yes. His statement implies that He has a *unique* knowledge of God.

I: The implication of that is unmistakable. Jesus Christ is saying that He is God, once again. This time it is obliquely stated. There is no unique way of knowing God except as *God* knows God. But is it possible that Christ would be an incarnate angel and have a knowledge of God different from what human beings have?

C: That's theoretically possible. On the other hand, He

refers to Himself in the singular. No one knows the Father save the Son. That would not be true if He was referring to an angel because there are many other angels. On the supposition, they would all know God. So that uniqueness of His knowledge seems to preclude the possibility of its being some angelic knowledge of God. Though such angelic knowledge would be different from men's knowledge, it would not be unique: it would belong to another order of beings.

I: Furthermore, there is the additional statement that no one knows the Son save the Father. Here angels are clearly ruled out. If He were referring to Himself as an angel, He could never say that only God knew Him, because certainly the other angels would know Him, as would human beings who came in contact with Him. Though angels are superior, they are not entirely different from men. After all, men and angels alike are creatures. Presumably they could know fellow rational creatures, however different they may be in some respects.

C: So, any way you look at it, this unique knowledge, which the Son has of the Father and the Father has of the Son, spells the deity of the Son.

I: Yes. I'm especially impressed by the latter statement, "No one knows the Son save the Father." As you have said, creatures can know other creatures, especially of their own kind. Presumably other creatures, because they are finite, have limited knowledge. So when this creature, the man Jesus of Nazareth, says no one knows the Son save the Father. He must be referring not to human nature, but to divine nature. Only divine nature is known exclusively by God. It takes a God to know God (uniquely).

C: This is a relatively clear and direct assertion of Christ's deity and His oneness with the Father. They are joined in this case by unique knowledge of each other. Therefore they must each be persons in the Godhead. Again, we have an allusion to at least two persons in the Holy Trinity.

Let us take one other reference in the Gospel according to Matthew that clearly indicates the deity of Jesus Christ. That is the Great Commission, which occurs at the very end of Matthew. Here we have the ascended Lord Jesus Christ, after His resurrection, saying to His apostles, "Go into all the world, making disciples of all nations, baptizing in the name of the Father, the Son, and the Holy Spirit; and teaching people to observe whatsoever I have commanded you; and lo I am with you to the end of the age."

I: This is a supernatural context to begin with, is it not? Christ has risen from the dead, has ascended into heaven, and is claiming that all authority in heaven and earth is given to Him. All these supernatural things certainly indicate Jesus to be a supernatural being. At the same time, they of themselves would not prove Him to be a divine being.

C: True He could still be another exalted creature who has been given all authority in heaven and earth. He, in turn, gives His apostles a commission to go into the world and make disciples for Him. But there is more here than that, which makes the exalted-creature interpretation an impossibility.

I: What is that?

C: The Trinitarian formula. You'll notice that Christ commands His apostles to baptize disciples in the name of the Father, the Son, and the Holy Spirit. They would have known from Jesus' teaching that He was the Son of God, as we have seen. They would know that the baptismal formula referred to not only God the Father, and the Holy Spirit, but also the Son of God standing before them in His resurrected and ascended human form.

I: So Jesus is bracketing Himself with the divine Father and with the divine Holy Spirit.

C: Yes. Here you have the doctrine of the Trinity. It is inconceivable that Christ as a mere creature would be mentioned in the same breath with two divine beings and associated with them as if they were one. We know indeed they are one according to the overall teaching of the Bible. "Hear, O Israel, the Lord thy God is *one* God." So this formula would indicate that Jesus Christ is on a level with these other persons and constitutes with them one God. He must, therefore, be a person in the Godhead, judging from the baptismal formula. That is another proof of the deity of Jesus Christ; indirect but unmistakable. Christ does not say, "I am God"; He just brackets Himself with divine beings. That amounts to saying, "He who has seen Me has seen the Father," or God.

I: I can't help but note in passing that the deity of Christ would be implied in other aspects of the Great Commission as well.

C: What are they?

I: For one thing, He commands the apostles to teach people to observe whatever He has commanded them. Certainly, it's that same "arrogance" we noticed elsewhere if He were merely a creature, however exalted. Only God really has the right to demand that people follow His teaching. A mere servant such as you can only claim that his teaching should be followed insofar as it expresses the divine teaching. I think you will admit as a minister of Christ that you cannot properly say to me, "You must follow my teaching."

C: You are right. Was there something else as well?

I: Yes. It's the way the commission ends: "Lo, I am with you always to the end of the age."

C: You seem to be going ahead of me at this point. Wouldn't it be possible for Christ just to be a divine *agent* who is with the church until the end of the age?

I: I guess, theoretically. But in His saying on His own authority that He will be with them to the end of the age, that would imply His omnipresence. To be with the whole church, or even those eleven apostles only, would require more than being a creature. Otherwise He couldn't be with all of them all the time. We assume, as the church always has, that Christ's promise applies to the whole church, which seeks to carry out His mission to this day. If Christ was to be with the apostles through all their days, and with the entire church until the end of the age, He'd have to be divine, eternal, and infinite.

C: You've shown me something, which in turn has brought to mind another argument for Christ's deity I had not noticed before. Don't ask me why I didn't. It's plain enough when you point it out to me.

I: In other words, you're admitting that a non-Christian may understand some points of Christianity better than a Christian?

C: I readily admit that. I know non-Christians who know aspects of Christian truth better than I do. I suspect you know many more things than the few we've so far discovered better than I do, while you have not yet professed the Christian faith. Your point is gladly, though humbly, granted.

I: Thank you.

C: Now let me turn to what is the thinnest of the Gospels, Christologically speaking. I refer to Mark, which most people think has very little developed theology, especially Christology, or theology about Christ.

I: You mean that there is less reference to the deity of Christ in Mark than in the other Gospels, just as there is much more in John than in any of the other Gospels?

C: Yes. That's the general view. As you may know, there was a time when many scholars thought that the deity of Christ was lacking in all the Synoptics and developed only by John.

I: Yes. When I was in school, they felt that John was much later than the others. Did they not?

C: They did indeed. In fact, many of them thought the apostle John was not the author. It was once thought to be a late second-century writing, so exalted was its Christology.

I: But as we have seen, John is clearly in the generation of Jesus. Didn't you mention that some scholars today think it's the earliest of the four Gospels and certainly before the fall of Jerusalem?

C: Yes. What an amazing shift in critical opinion that's occurred in this century! Getting back to Mark, it's interesting to note that at the turn of the century, some radical critics recognized that Mark taught the deity of Christ as truly as John did.

I: How was that?

C: Well, one of the early form critics, a man named Wrede, made the remark that "Mark is as bad as John."

I: Whatever did that mean?

C: It meant that Mark was as good as John. Mark taught the deity of Christ as truly as John did.

I: So some unbelieving critics were reversing themselves? They were, at least this man Wrede, saying that the earliest Gospel and the earliest records represented Christ as God. Is that the point?

C: Correct. You can see it in the very opening verse of Mark's Gospel. There we read: "The beginning of the gospel of Jesus Christ, the *Son of God...*"

I: That was the statement of Mark and not of Jesus, was it not?

C: Yes. Consequently, we cannot say that it was a self-disclosure of Jesus Himself. Nevertheless, the very fact that Mark, a follower of Jesus, attributed deity to Him must, we suppose, have come from Christ Himself. You remember that the reason the statements in John affirming His deity were supposed to be later was the supposed late date of John. The notion was that there were no claims for deity early in His career and in the following years; only after a century and a half did the church attribute to Jesus a deity He never claimed for Himself. But here in what the critics consider the earliest Gospel, and at the very first verse, we have a statement by Mark that Jesus is the Son of God. It's hard to believe he could have gotten such a notion from anyone but Jesus. There certainly was no time for an elaborate evolutionary development of this doctrine from something not found in the sources at all.

I: I see your point. You say this man, Wrede, was a critic. Does that mean that the critics had changed their minds by the beginning of this century and recognized that Jesus was thought to be and taught to be divine at the very beginning of His ministry?

C: Not all of them. But at least some critics believed it; form criticism and Wrede and Schweitzer definitely acknowledged that it was in the record and not a later importation.

I: Then, there was a sudden influx of higher critics into the church at the turn of the century?

C: No. Sorry to say, there was not.

I: I don't understand. You said they did recognize that Jesus was indeed divine, did you not?

C: They recognized that some of the sources said Christ was divine. Some of them even recognized that Christ Himself said He was divine. But most critics themselves did not believe He was divine. You see, some of the more liberal scholars, who did not believe Jesus was divine, claimed that *He* didn't either. Yet radical scholars were beginning to acknowledge the clear evidence that both Jesus and the early church believed Him to be God. Those who denied that had to admit that they were no longer loyal to Christ and the early church, though they once claimed to be.

I: This interests me very much, as you can well suppose. These critics were like me, were they not?

C: You mean that they knew that Christ is God, but had not yet been converted?

I: Yes. Are they not in exactly the same situation?

C: No. Not quite as hopeful a situation as yours. You see, they simply acknowledged that Christ and the early church believed He was divine. They didn't believe it themselves. You do believe it. You are persuaded not only that Christ taught His deity and the early church believed it, but that it is true. Unlike these critics, you think that He is God, though you are not certain you have a saving faith in Jesus Christ. Recognizing the same facts as you, they made no pretense of personal belief in them. You do, though you have not come to trust in Christ as your Savior.

I: Yes. That's my situation. I am persuaded He is divine and that if I believe in Him, He would be my Savior. Yet, I'm not convinced that I have that kind of saving belief. I see the difference. Why don't these critics believe what Christ Himself claimed? The early church, which comprised witnesses of Him, believed it. I think I know the answer to my own question.

C: I think you do. too.

I: Was it the old naturalistic bias?

C: I think so. Why would people note that Christ said He was God, and that the people closest to Him believed it, and that there was evidence of miraculous power, which showed He was sent from God, and not believe it themselves? Why would they disbelieve unless they simply rejected sound theistic thinking and evidence of a revelation from God? That wasn't always clear in their writings. Though they didn't always say why, I suspect that common to their unbelief was their naturalistic bias against the supernatural.

I: Maybe you and I should talk with people like that today.

C: Indeed we must. Let us now turn to the Gospel of Luke for a verse or two there on the deity of Christ. It might be well to start with a statement of Jesus that suggests to many people a denial of His deity.

I: A denial?

C: Yes. That is what the famous British scholar H. G. Wells thought it to be. He wrote an article years ago entitled "Man among Men," intending to show that Christ was merely a human being. Others too have claimed that when Jesus says to the rich young ruler, "Why do you call Me good? Only God is good," He denies that He is God.

I: That does seem to be what He's saying.

C: The question is whether that is what He is intending by those words.

I: What's this distinction between what He's saying and what He's intending?

C: Well, we earlier mentioned that He said He was the vine and we are the branches. When He said that literally, His *intention* was that He is the life-principle of Christians, who bear fruit by His indwelling presence. The form of words may convey a deeper meaning than the words themselves. In the present instance, there is no parable or figure of speech. Christ is using plain speech. But is it not possible that He means something other than those words normally convey?

I: I would have to admit that it's possible. Just as I suppose you will admit the burden of proof is on the person who seeks some meaning other than the obvious one H. G. Wells took from it.

C: Yes, I must shoulder this burden because I am arguing for an interpretation other than the obvious one. Are we agreed it is not out of the question that Christ may mean something other than what the words normally mean?

I: Agreed.

C: The first thing that alerts us is that this remark is a question rather than a statement. Christ does not say that He is not God. He simply asks the young man why he calls Him good inasmuch as only God is good. That is certainly not the same thing as denying that He is God.

I: Still, He does go on to assert that only God is good, does He not?

C: Yes, He does say, "Why do you call Me good? None is good save God." The way we usually read that, and even enunciate it, is that Christ is denying that He is God because He's denying that He is properly called good. Nevertheless, strictly speaking, that is not what it says. Christ is simply addressed as good master, and He quizzes the addresser on why *he* calls Him good. By pointing out that only God is good, He could be saying that the reason He is good is that He is God. Could that not be the meaning of the words?

I: Yes. I guess that is a possible construction. Nevertheless, you yourself admit that's not the first thing that comes to mind.

C: Granted, but we have also seen, time and again, that the first thing that comes into one's mind is not always the last thing to stay there.

I: Yes, I know, and I admit that could be the case here. At first glance, Christ is denying His deity. At subsequent glances, He may not be doing that. In fact, one has to grant that Christ is *not* denying His deity. He may actually be asserting it in the form of a question. He may be saying to the rich young ruler, "Since you call me good, do you realize I am God, inasmuch as only God is good?" That interpretation is possible. It remains to you to show its feasibility and probability.

C: Of course we already have clear evidence from other places that Jesus is God. He knows that He's God, and He tells people that He is God: "He who has seen Me has seen the Father." When we remember that this is the same person who says, "Why do you call Me good? None is good save God," that does put a different light on that question, does it not?

I: Yes, it does. Admitting that Jesus Christ is God, we would have to say that this question actually probes the ruler's mind to see if he recognizes that fact, rather than implying a denial of it. That is a cogent argument, given the other data we have about Jesus Christ. The more I reflect on it, the more I like that interpretation. I realize now that it can be the only legitimate one, given the identity of the questioner.

C: On the other hand, if we didn't know that Jesus Christ is God, we would not think He was intending a subtle assertion of His deity by that question. It would be more naturally taken as an implicit denial. Knowing that Jesus elsewhere plainly says He is God, we realize His question must be a subtle way of bringing the rich young ruler to a recognition of implied deity.

I: At least it would be a gentle rebuke advising the young man not to be careless in his use of language. That is, the only proper use of the word "good" belongs to God. Did you say there's something else in the passage that seems to suggest the deity of Christ?

C: Yes, in the very conversation Christ had with this rich

young ruler.

I: Reading it again. I see no other indication that Christ says He is God incarnate.

C: Christ tells the young ruler that if he wants to be perfect (reach his goal of eternal life), he must sell everything, give to the poor, and follow Him.

I: That shows that Christ is the determiner of eternal life.

C: And only God is the determiner of eternal life.

I: But can't you, as a minister, tell me or anyone what is necessary for eternal life without being divine? Can you not advise us what God requires without being God?

C: Yes.

I: Are you claiming deity for yourself?

C: No.

I: What am I missing here?

C: As a minister, I can tell the *general*, not *individual*, terms of eternal life.

I: Please explain.

C: I can tell you, or anyone, that it is difficult to be rich and a Christian. I can advise you that it is harder for a rich man to enter the kingdom than for a camel to go through a needle's eye. What I cannot do is tell you that *you* are worshipping mammon, and you must give up all of it if *you* would be saved. Only God can do that.

I: In other words, only God can see into the hidden heart of men?

C: That is the difference between Christ and the servants of Christ.

I: I am convinced about the deity of Christ. I know there is much more in the Bible that you could cite in proof, but you have given me enough. Except—

C: Except?

I: I can't help wondering whether other religious leaders don't claim deity, too.

C: Claiming and proving are two different things. But they don't even claim it. Occasionally some of their followers have attributed deity to them. But, you name a great religious leader, and you will find that he did not present himself as divine.

I: You mean that only Jesus of Nazareth ever said, "He who has seen Me has seen the Father," or anything like it?

C: Compare Confucius, who, as you know, was really a skeptic. He took one world at a time. He was very sagacious about laws of conduct for this world, but dubious about the future world. He was satisfied to be a moral legislator for this sphere in which we live.

I: What about the "Enlightened One," Buddha?

C: Gautama, the Buddha, was an atheist.

I: Yes, I suspected that.

C: It is easy to demonstrate that Buddha was further from

theism than was Confucius. While Confucius was insecure about the future, Buddha didn't even entertain a belief in a personal deity. He was a pantheist in the pure sense of the word. He certainly was not laying claim to being God when he didn't believe there is one. The same is true of other Eastern religious leaders such as Mahavira, Zoroaster, and so on. None of them ever laid claim to being deity.

I: The greatest religious influence in the world today, next to Christ, is Mohammed. His followers seem utterly devoted to him

C: He categorically repudiated deity. As you know, the great creed of Islam is there is *one* God, Allah, and Mohammed is his prophet. The Muslims are rigid monotheists. While Mohammed is, for them, the greatest prophet, he is *merely* a prophet and in no way deity.

I: As a matter of fact, I understand that the Muslims have a high view of Jesus. They believe He was virgin born, was sinless, did miracles, and is coming again. But they certainly do not believe that Christ is God. Nor do they believe Mohammed is God.

C: In fact, they consider belief in the deity of Jesus Christ, whom they admire as a prophet, to be the greatest blasphemy of the Christian church. I'm even told that, because Christians worship Christ, Muslims do not like to be called Mohammedans for fear people will think they worship Mohammed. They admit that Christians worship Christ, which they consider our worst sin. They do not want people to suppose they worship Mohammed. Neither Mohammed nor his followers have claimed deity for him.

I: Likewise the Jews don't think that their Moses was God, or that Moses Maimonides of the Middle Ages, their second great Moses, was God either. They, too, would regard the

Christian notion that Jesus Christ is God as a form of blasphemy.

C: Yes. In John's Gospel they accused Jesus of blasphemy because, being a man, He made Himself to be God.

I: I get the point. And I'm going to be ready the next time I hear students confidently remark that all religious leaders lay claim to being deity. To be told that Jesus made a unique claim should have quite an impact on them. I can only hope it makes them think more seriously about Christ.

C: It's real irony, isn't it, that this unique event, the incarnation of God in human flesh, should be made out to be a commonplace, as if all religious leaders taught such doctrine.

I: What do you do when sophisticated people such as George Bernard Shaw, for example, say things like, "Yes, Jesus did think of Himself as God. We have to admit that He suffered from megalomania." In some ways, that's the most devastating criticism of Christ one can hear. It patronizingly grants that Christ made this claim. Then on the basis of that assertion, Shaw, Bunby, and others go on to question Christ's sanity. I hope you'll forgive me, my good Christian friend, for raising a question like this. I know how much it must hurt you to hear anybody questioning the sanity of the Lord and Savior of mankind. You must consider that blasphemy and suffer from merely hearing such speech. At the same time, as you know, probably better than I, that sort of thing is said and comes from some very influential sources. What do you say to such a thing?

C: Don't apologize for mentioning it to me. You're perfectly right. It's hard speech, and I detest it. I do consider it blasphemy. At the same time, it comes from responsible sources and must be faced responsibly. From where

George Bernard Shaw stood, it was an almost inevitable rational conclusion. And I often cite Shaw precisely because he admits Christ's claim to deity. There are plenty of people who try to ignore that or turn it aside or denature it. Shaw is to be commended, as others, for "telling it like it is." I'm sure Shaw himself would have been much more comfortable with a Christ who didn't make such claims. He must have been tempted, as were other liberals, like H. G. Wells, to say that Christ was merely a man among men, never entertaining any grandiose illusions about Himself. Shaw knew better than that. Don't ever apologize for raising any kind of blasphemy that takes the form of an argument against the Christian religion. Such things cannot be turned off. Though horrible, they have to be dealt with squarely, in honor and integrity.

I: Thank you. How do you do that?

C: Well, what I say is simple enough. I agree with the Shaws of the world. If this man Jesus were merely a man, and laid claim to deity, He would be sick, and probably worse than sick. He would not be worthy of a following. He would be out of his mind. I suppose I would ridicule Him more than Shaw does if I were standing where Shaw stood. But Shaw's mistake is that he just gratuitously assumes that Jesus Christ is not God.

I: That's true. He takes it for granted that Christ is merely a man, just as most people take it for granted that any man is just a man. Hardly anybody can imagine God's actually becoming man. The almost inevitable assumption is that any man claiming to be God has to be out of his mind. What other conclusion could you draw? I think you're on target with respect to Shaw's mentality. It is virtually the mentality of the human race. I plead guilty to it myself. Until I started to talk seriously about these matters, I would have assumed as self-evident that Jesus Christ was merely a man. If you had proved to me then that He *claimed* to be God, I would have turned Him over to a psychiatrist.

C: I agree. We, on the other hand, know that of course there isn't any rational objection to the proposition that God could take upon Himself a human nature. Where we agree with Shaw is that we will assume a man is merely a man until there is evidence to the contrary. Short of that evidence, we will agree with Shaw that any person claiming to be deity is a "liar or a lunatic." Shaw will have to listen to us at this point, will he not? He will have to give some proof that it's impossible for God to take upon Himself human nature and remain God. Yet Shaw doesn't do that, He doesn't even attempt to. And I'm confident he never could if he did try.

I: But he must try. You're perfectly right. He has no right simply to say something that is not demonstrative. It is *not* self-evident that God cannot take human nature upon Himself. It is self-evident that a man is merely a man *unless* there's conclusive evidence to the contrary.

C: Until a person examines the evidence of Christ's claim and shows that evidence to be false, he has no right to say that Jesus is not actually God.

I: We have found the very opposite. The evidence is in and it shows that, first, Jesus Christ *claimed* to be God, and, second, Jesus Christ proved Himself to be God. But yet—

C: What's that?

I: I hate to bring this up at this late date.

C: If it is relevant, it's never too late.

I: That's the problem—I don't know whether it's relevant.

C: Maybe we had better hear what is on your mind and judge together whether it's relevant.

I: Well, just the other day a Jehovah's Witness came to my door...

C: And argued against the deity of Christ?

I: Yes Most of what he said was characteristically puerile. But one thing disturbed me.

C: What was that?

I: He reminded me that Christ is called "Son" in the Bible and even in Christian churches.

C: I can guess what else he said that disturbed you.

I: Go ahead.

C: My guess is that this Witness went on to say that Christ's being called "Son" means He was *born* and therefore could *not be eternal*, and therefore could *not be divine*.

I: Exactly. I didn't—and frankly, don't—know how to answer that.

C: That is not surprising. At first glance, it is very puzzling. As we use the word *son* it always means someone born in time and not eternal.

I: You say, "As we use the word *son*." Is there some special meaning when the word is used of Christ?

C: Right on the surface, there is. For example, when Jesus (or John referring to Jesus) says: "*God* so loved the world that He gave *His only Son*..." (3:16), this is not a typical reference to a human son, but to the Son of God.

I: Granted, but still He is a *Son*.

C: Yes, but a Son *of God*.

I: I don't get what you are driving at. Son of God or son of man, does the word *son* not mean "born" and therefore temporal?

C: It means "born," but does it need to mean "temporal"?

I: I'm beginning to see the light. If Christ or the Word is the Son *of God*, He is born of God (Son), but eternally born (of God)?

C: If that were not so, the Word would not be *His only* (unique) Son. God is the Creator of all men, who in that sense are "sons" born in time.

I: But "His only Son" must be as eternal as He is?

C: That is the reason the church all throughout her history has adoringly referred to the Word as "the eternally begotten Son of God."

I: The Witnesses will never believe that.

C: They should—

I: Why?

C: Because, first they agree that Christ is called the *Son* of the Father. Second, they agree that the *Father* refers to the *eternal* God. Third, they agree that the word *Father* has *no meaning* without an offspring (Son). For example, I, like some Witnesses, existed forty years before my first child was born. Only then did I *become a father*. There cannot be a father, or a Father, without offspring. Therefore—

I: Let me interrupt and see if I cannot state the inevitable conclusion (just as a Jehovah's Witness should). Therefore, since the Father is admittedly eternal, *His Son must also be eternal* because the very term *Father* is meaningless or false apart from *Son*.

C: Amen.

I: How could I have failed to see that? How could that Witness fail to see that?

C: The question is, How does anyone ever fail to "see" the deity of Christ?

I: Yes, how?

C: It is not because the deity of Christ is not plain enough.

I: How is it, then?

C: Suppose we let Christ tell us how one *does come* to see the obvious deity of Christ.

I: Does He?

C: He does precisely in the dialogue with Peter (Matthew 16:13ff).

I: What does He say there?

C: First, He asks the apostles, "Who do you say that the *son of man* is?"

I: I do remember And Peter answers, "Thou are the Christ,

the Son of the living God."

C: Correct, and it is Christ's comment on that confession that gives us our answer to how one comes to "see" the deity of Christ.

I: Which is...?

C: "Blessed are you, Simon bar Jonah, flesh and blood has not revealed this to you, *but my Father who is in heaven.*"

I: In other words, it is the Father who reveals the Son.

C: Just as we had noticed earlier when Christ said that no one knows Him "save the Father and he to whom He reveals Him."

I: Where does that leave me? Or you? Are you telling me that we have spent an hour talking about the deity of Christ and I will never understand what you are saying unless God "reveals" it to me?

C: Exactly.

I: Then what is the point of our talking?

C: If God ever does reveal it to you, it will come out of dialogue such as this, just as it was revealed to Peter only after Jesus had explained it to him. You see, the true witness paints the picture. God gives the eyes to perceive it. God does not paint the picture, and we painters cannot provide eyes to see.

I: What am I to do?

C: Ask God to give you the eyes to see and the heart to confess: "Thou art the Christ, the Son of the living God."

# A

# Primer

# on

# Predestination

# Contents

# 1. Definitions

Let us try to clarify our subject by a few definitions. Many of the objections to predestination are based on simple misunderstanding. While I do not mean that all the difficulties will be eliminated if we do some defining at the beginning, I do suggest that our discussion will be greatly simplified, and many problems will never arise, if we can get some clear definitions before we begin to discuss this matter.

Now you will have to brace yourselves, because definitions are not exactly exciting pursuits. As a matter of fact, they are usually very dull, especially when the definitions are made before the discussion begins. Nevertheless, definition, as you realize, is probably the ultimate form of knowledge. The dictionary and lexicon is the basal structure of the whole body of learning. I think you will find the same to be true here with respect to our discussion. What I am about to launch into will be, admittedly, rather dull, and I am forewarning you to set yourselves for a fairly tedious discussion here. I can only comfort you with the assurance that if you do master these terms, dull as that process may be, you will, before the discussion is over, be grateful for it. While it may seem to delay the discussion and keep us from getting on with the job, as it were, I think we shall realize that it is a way of making haste slowly.

Coming to some of the actual definitions, let me mention, first of all, that the most comprehensive word in this whole area of discourse is the term "foreordination." (Before reading this section, you may wish to consult the diagram in Appendix 3.) "Foreordination" means God's ordaining, or decreeing, or determining, or appointing, from eternity *whatsoever* is to come to pass. We have italicized the word "whatsoever" because that is the distinguishing peculiarity of the word "foreordination." That is what sets this term off from other words which are used in this sphere of discourse. "Foreordination" is the comprehensive, all-inclusive term. This informs us that there is nothing at all in the whole universe which is exempt from this pre-ordinating of the Eternal God. Thus, if it is a stone or an animal, if it is a man or an angel, if it is in this world or some other, if it is in the past or the future, if it is in heaven or in hell, it makes no difference what it is, where it is, when it is— "foreordination" teaches that it is the outworking of the eternal decree of God.

Now when we come to the doctrine of predestination, we come to consider a part, and only a part, of "foreordination." As we said, "foreordination" pertains to everything, but predestination pertains only to a part of the total whole—a very small part of the total whole. As far as importance is concerned, however, and especially importance for us, it is incomparably more significant than anything else which falls within the foreordination of God. Predestination is that part of foreordination which deals with the actions of free moral agents, be they angels, men, or devils. This doctrine teaches that God foreordains specifically the actions of free moral agents.

Thus, when I drop a piece of chalk, foreordination generally and predestination specifically are being carried out. The chalk's dropping is an instance of foreordination proper. It is a part of that totality of things which have been eternally decreed by God. But since the chalk is inanimate and not a free moral agent, it does not belong to the domain of predestination, properly speaking, but rather to foreordination, properly speaking. It does not will to fall. It does not choose to drop. It is acted upon and not acting. It therefore does not pertain to predestination, but is a part of foreordination merely.

When, however, we consider my dropping the chalk, we have an instance of predestination. Unlike the chalk, which does not decide to fall, I am a free moral agent who does decide to cause the chalk to fall. Being a free moral agent I come within the domain of predestination. Thus, when we speak of the chalk's falling, we speak of foreordination; and when we speak of my dropping the chalk, we speak of predestination.

Please note, we are here dealing strictly with definition, and nothing more or less than definition. Thus, for example, if any of you are presently saying to yourselves, "I don't believe that Dr. Gerstner is a free moral agent if what he does has been eternally predestined," you are not thinking to the point. We are not now discussing the truth of the doctrine of predestination. We are merely discussing the meaning of the doctrine of predestination. Whether predestination is true or false it means this: that when I drop the chalk I give an illustration of the outworking of predestination. You may think to yourselves that if I have been predestined I am not a free moral agent. You may be right in your thinking. Later on, when we come to discuss the subject, your thinking will be relevant, and if you can justify your thinking you are entitled to say, "Predestination is an erroneous doctrine." But before we can discuss the validity of the concept or the invalidity of the concept, we must first of all fix carefully the meaning of the concept. So, I repeat, the meaning is that God foreordains, foreappoints, foredecrees, foredetermines the actions of free moral agents. Therefore, my dropping the chalk is an illustration of what is meant by a predestined act. You keep in the back of your minds, you reserve until later, the discussion whether or not such a predestined act can be truly free, or, if it is truly free, whether it could have been predestined.

Now, with our eye on that subdivision of foreordination called predestination, let us notice two subdivisions of predestination. Predestination, remember, refers to the foreordination of the acts of free agents. Now, one part of predestination is called "election," and another part of predestination is called "reprobation." "Election" is that part of predestination which pertains to the saving acts of free moral agents. Election teaches that God from all eternity predestinated those acts of free moral agents which would lead to their eternal salvation. "Reprobation," on the other hand, pertains to the free acts of moral agents which lead to their damnation. Reprobation, therefore, means that part of predestination which pertains to God's ordaining the evil acts of evil beings which lead to an evil end.

Although election and reprobation are, both of them, divisions of predestination, they differ from each other in one very important particular. Election is what is called "a positive decree," and reprobation is usually regarded as "a permissive decree." This is what is meant by these two terms: by saying that election is a positive decree we mean to indicate that God from all eternity foreordains that some actions should be unto eternal life by actually initiating, or instigating, or energizing, or empowering these actions. Thus, when God chooses from eternity to save a person who has fallen into sin and is unable to save himself, or even to reach out to be saved, He must actually empower this person to accept the salvation which God proffers to him. This is called "positive" because God actually does do something. He actually effects the act in the person. Though the act remains the person's act, God provides the basis or the impetus or the empowerment for that act of faith in the Savior.

Now, then, we call reprobation a permissive decree. What is meant is this? According to this decree God predestinates the acts of sinful men by ordaining all the circumstances which lead to the sinner's choice of evil without actually inclining or disposing or energizing the sinner to do the evil deed. God simply permits the reprobate of himself and his own instigation or inclination to do that which is evil. God has predestinated that it should come to pass; and He effectuates it, or He brings it to pass, by ordaining the circumstances which a sinner, left to himself, will wickedly use to his own eternal damnation. God, in this instance, refrains from positive action. He does not change the heart of the individual, or enable or incline the individual to do the virtuous and saving act, but, on the contrary, leaves the individual to himself. This individual then inclines toward the evil and does the wicked deed which brings about his damnation.

Let us illustrate the difference between election and reprobation. Consider Jesus' words in John 14:6: "No man cometh unto the Father, but by Me." Now there, in that teaching Jesus sets forth two truths, one of which pertains to election and the other to reprobation. He says something negative and something positive. The negative thing is that no man comes unto Him. That is the same as to say that no man, left to himself as a man in his present condition, actually comes to Jesus Christ. Christ has said a similar thing earlier in the words: "This is the condemnation, that light has come into the world and men love the darkness rather than the light." That is, men left to themselves prefer darkness to light. Before conversion, they prefer *not* coming to Jesus to coming to Jesus. If a person, therefore, does not come to Jesus Christ, it will be because of his own indisposition. And if his own indisposition prevails, that will indicate that God has not seen fit to overcome that indisposition He has rather chosen, for reasons known only to Himself, to leave this individual to himself, to his present fallen humanity, to his indisposition to light and faith. And thus left to himself, that person does not come to Christ that he may be saved. If God decides not to change a particular individual, but rather to leave that person to himself, we call that decree "reprobation."

Now notice the other part of this passage, "No man cometh unto Me except the Father draw him." There it is taught that if the Father draws a particular individual he will indeed come to Jesus Christ. In other words, for a person to come to Jesus Christ there must be a prior divine action in that person's heart. That action is here called "drawing" the person. In John 3 it is called "being born again," or making the person over again by a power from above, a power which is identified as the Holy Spirit. But, you see, in this instance, where we are dealing with a person's coming to

Jesus Christ, God is active in drawing that individual so that he is inclined to come to Jesus Christ. God is not merely standing by and leaving the individual to himself, but, on the contrary, is actually taking what the theologians call a "divine initiative." That is, He is instigating a change in the person's heart. He is drawing that person so that the person now feels an inclination to come to Jesus Christ and, as everyone *always* does, he acts according to his inclination.

The same truth is stated in John 1:12–13. Here it is said that "He came unto His own, and His own received Him not." (It is Christ's coming to the Jews to which the Evangelist is referring.) "But as many as received Him, to them gave He power to become the sons of God . . . which were born, not of blood, nor of the flesh, nor of the will of man, but of God." The passage teaches that though Jesus did come to people who were called His own, that is, who were prepared through the oracles and the prophecies to expect the Messiah, and of whose line He was Himself born, the mass of these people did not receive Him. Of themselves they were not believing, but, on the contrary, they "received Him not." On the other hand, those persons who did believe in Him were born, not of the flesh nor of the will of man, but of God. You see, here again we find God active. He has made these persons over again. That is the meaning of the expression "were born of God"; they were given a new principle of life. God does not do anything at all with the one group except to urge them and invite them to come to Jesus; otherwise, He leaves them to themselves. They, of themselves, choose not to come to Jesus, whereas, those choose to come to Jesus in whose heart God has effected a prior change.

We must not get the notion that people come to Jesus, and as a result of that they are "born again" by God. On the contrary, we see what people do when they are left to themselves: they do not believe; they do not come to Jesus. Those who do come to Jesus are not therefore born again, but, on the contrary, indicate that they have been born again. In other words, they are not born again because they come to Jesus, but they come to Jesus because they have been born again.

Perhaps we have taken enough time to show not only the difference between reprobation and election, but also the general difference between a permissive decree and a positive decree. I repeat, election is that part of predestination which teaches that the acts of some men from all eternity are ordained to salvation, whereas the acts of some other men from all eternity are ordained to damnation. However, the decree of election is a positive decree because it is brought to pass by means of an active, divine initiative; whereas, on the contrary, the decree of reprobation is a permissive decree because it is brought to pass by God's simply permitting persons to do as they are of themselves inclined to do.

Another definition which is not immediately a part of the subject of predestination, but which is so intimately related to it that we must consider it, is "total depravity." This is the doctrine which teaches that man, in his present condition since the Fall, is so polluted with a principle of evil that all aspects of his being are affected thereby. The word "depravity" refers to this inclination toward evil or disinclination toward good. It is a principle of pollution and corruption which disposes a man away from righteousness and toward wickedness. The term "total" reminds us of the fact that this vicious principle is not restricted to the area of the body, or to the area of the mind, or to a particular area of the mind, such as the intellect proper in distinction from the will. Rather, it teaches that all areas are affected by this principle so that every time a person acts his action is defective and positively evil in the realm of thought, feeling, and volition. He is totally and not partially depraved in that sense of the word. He is not, however, totally depraved in the sense that he is as depraved as he possibly can become. In other words, total depravity does not mean utter and ex-

treme and ultimate depravity—rather, depravity in the total
personality.

But there is another question which is precipitated by
the definition of total depravity. We refer to the origin of sin.
One cannot mention that man's present condition is depraved without a person asking, "How did he come to be
this way?" We know that God did not create man evil, not
only because the Bible teaches otherwise directly, but because the very nature of God as a good Being would make
Him incapable of actually doing or creating evil. But if God
did not make man this way, who did? That is a very great
question indeed. As a matter of fact, it is probable that there
is no really satisfactory answer to it. However, we have
some light on the question from Biblical sources. The Bible
teaches that God created man in His own image, good and
holy. He was not merely free of evil; he was not merely innocent and void of sin, but he was positively good. He possessed what the theologians call "original righteousness."
At the same time, he was also endowed with a unique ability to sin. Thus he was good and able not to sin, but at the
same time, though he was not evil in nature, he was able to
sin. In the immortal words of Augustine, he was *posse non
peccare* (able not to sin), but also *posse peccare* (able to
sin). Perhaps it would be helpful to contrast the condition
of man as he was first made by God and as he is in heaven
redeemed by God. In heaven he is only *posse non peccare*.
That is, in heaven he is able only not to sin. He is no longer
*posse peccare*, or able to sin.

The very great question is, of course, how was a good
being, endowed with original righteousness, so made that
he was capable of sin? I, for one, do not know the answer to
that question. Furthermore, I have never heard or read
anyone who gives a satisfactory answer to that question. It
seems to me that we must leave the matter at this point.
We have evidence that God created man good and yet *posse
peccare*, but we do not know how such a creation was
possible. This is a profound mystery and we must leave it

so. In other words, we have evidence *that* man fell into sin from a condition of holiness, not *how* he was able to do it. We will find in many cases of theological reflection that we are confronted with the same situation. That is, often we know that something is so without being able to explain how it is so. With respect to this question of the origin of sin, for example, we cannot say that because man was *posse peccare* that he therefore had a sinful inclination. We have evidence that such is not the case. He had a good inclination and dispositon and nature, but nevertheless was made mutably or changeably good and was able to choose the evil in a particular instance. How this could be we may not understand, but, on the other hand, no one knows enough to say that it could not have been so.

Returning to total depravity, or the condition which resulted from Adam's sin, let me indicate the extreme importance of keeping in mind this concept of total depravity while we are discussing the subject of predestination. In my own opinion, most of the problems which people have with the doctrine of predestination really are not problems concerning predestination, but problems concerning total depravity. It all reminds me of something I read in a medical book years ago. In this book it was observed that frequently an ache or pain in the shoulder was an indication of gall bladder trouble. Of course, a shoulder ache does not always mean gall bladder trouble, but it is sometimes a symptom of gall bladder trouble. Now suppose a person does have an ache in the shoulder and does not know the possible significance of the symptom. He will invariably think that he has something wrong with his shoulder. He does not suspect that that is symptomatic of a trouble elsewhere, namely, in his gall bladder.

So it seems to me in our area of discussion many people are really plagued by a trouble with the doctrine of predestination. However, the problem of predestination in many cases is merely symptomatic of a real problem located elsewhere, namely in the area of sin. A person supposing that man in his present condition is not totally depraved thinks that he does have, of course, an ability or a disposition which enables him to repent, believe, and be saved if he so chooses. Consequently this person thinking of man's condition in such terms sees no reason whatever for a predestination of his acts or an election of him to salvation. This person whom we are considering thinks the issues are much simpler than they actually are. He supposes that all one needs to do is present the gospel to an individual. This individual will understand it and he will take it or leave it as he pleases. He may be pleased to take it just as he may be pleased to reject it. However, this naive view does not take into account the doctrine of total depravity. If that doctrine is true, man will by no means be inclined to take the gospel or leave it. On the contrary, he will be inclined always to leave it. By definition he is a totally depraved person, which means that he is utterly indisposed to all that is good and right and holy, and will, of course, express himself in accordance with his disposition. Left to himself, a totally depraved person every time, necessarily, inevitably, and certainly will reject the gospel of Jesus Christ. The mere provision and proclamation of the gospel to such a person as that will do him no saving good whatsoever. But when a person does not realize the condition of sinners, he does not realize the necessity of the doctrine of election.

Again I remind you I am not arguing the case. I am simply stating the meaning of the traditional doctrine. Persons who believe in election believe in it as the election of totally depraved sinners to life in Christ Jesus, and that election was necessary because apart from it the totally depraved person would choose death intead of life. So election is absolutely necessary in this pattern of thought. Anyone who sees and believes that man is totally depraved and yet is saved would necessarily believe that he was elected to salvation. On the other hand, if the person does not believe election is necessary, he invariably believes it is not necessary because man apart from election is able to believe and be saved. Therefore, the doubter's trouble is not with the doctrine of election, but with the doctrine of sin. He is rejecting the doctrine of election, to be sure, but the reason he rejects the doctrine of election is not because he is opposed to it fundamentally, but because he rejects the doctrine on which it rests, namely total depravity.

# 2. Total Depravity

Now having spent a considerable amount of time in what we deem to be absolutely essential definitions, we are in a position to discuss the subject before us with, I hope, maximum efficiency and fruitfulness. First, a word is necessary about the general procedure we will follow. Our handling will be somewhat different from the usual way by which this doctrine is taught. Normally, expositors begin with express statements of Scripture on the topics of predestination, election, and so forth. This is a perfectly valid procedure. We are not implying any criticisms of it when we choose another method of approach. But we, instead of beginning with the predestinarian passages, will begin rather with man as he now is so that we may see what must happen to him in order to effect his salvation, and then come, not first but last, to predestinarianism. We follow this procedure because we feel it is far easier for us to understand this doctrine in the context of our condition than to understand our condition in the context of this doctrine. As I said above, many people have trouble with predestination because they have a prior trouble with depravity. If, therefore, we face the problem of man as he now is in the first instance, and then see the way in which his salvation or his damnation is brought about, we shall be in a far better position, I believe, to understand predestination, and also are likely to be far more sympathetic with it.

Furthermore, there is another basic defense of this particular type of approach. The doctrine of predestination rests far more on the overall system of truth taught in the Bible than on individual statements of the doctrine found in the Bible. We do not need to depreciate for a moment the absolutely authoritative character of the texts of the Sacred Word. We simply mean to say that the overall teaching of the Bible, its system of truth, is even more profoundly significant and understandable than the individual doctrinal propositions found in its pages. So in a sense we will be following the Biblical lead better in this procedure than by actually considering individual verses in the first instance.

We shall trace four steps to predestination. First, there is the total depravity of mankind. The second step is the resultant inability. This necessitates the third step, the divine initiative in the soul. And that brings us to the fourth and last step, predestination itself.

The very first step toward predestination is the Bible teaching that man is utterly corrupt, exposed to the wrath of God, unable to save himself, and due to perish forever unless he is saved. Consider, for example, the very opening pages of the Bible. Does not the third chapter of Genesis, for example, teach us very plainly that man, who was made in the image of God, was placed on probation and that when he failed that probation he died? Not only the express words of the probation which says, "The day thou eatest thereof (referring to the forbidden fruit) thou shalt surely die," but the whole context of the episode in the Garden indicates the same thing. As soon as Adam and Eve ate of this tree which was forbidden, they became conscious of their nakedness, they were ashamed, and they hid from God. Previously they had been in perfect harmony with one another, they had enjoyed their life in the Garden, and they had had natural and blessed fellowship with the living God, their Creator. But as soon as this transgression was committed everything was changed. Now, instead of coming to the voice of God as it walked in the cool of the Garden, they fled from it. Instead of being happy and joyous in His presence, they were ashamed to appear before Him. His voice, instead of a voice of fellowship, becomes a voice of searching and condemnation. The curse which comes upon the human race in the context of this original transgression drives them out of the Garden and places the angels with flaming swords to prevent their return. The murder, which follows very shortly in their history, is just a grim evidence of the utter change in the nature of man and human society. We are told, therefore, at the very outset of the Bible, that man is not what he was made to be. On the contrary, instead of being in communion with God, he is at enmity with Him; instead of enjoying the divine favor he is exposed to the wrath of the Almighty.

In the sixth chapter of Genesis, the fifth verse, we read these words: "And God saw that the wickedness of man was great in the earth and that every imagination of the thoughts of his heart was only evil continually." Here we have an indication of total depravity indeed. Not only are man's works evil but according to this passage the very thoughts and intents of his heart are evil. Not only are the thoughts and intents of his heart evil, but they are evil continually. Not only are the thoughts and intents of his heart evil continually, but they are only evil, that is, they are unmixed with good. They are unalloyed evil. This certainly tells us in the most ultimate terms that man's nature has been thoroughly corrupted, or that he is totally depraved.

Likewise we find in Job in the fourteenth chapter, verses 1 and following, that "Man that is born of a woman is of few days, and full of trouble . . . Who can bring a clean thing out of an unclean?" Job is arguing that anyone who is born of a woman by natural procreation is evil, and that there is no more possibility of a man, born of woman, being good than there is of dirty water being clean.

The Psalms have much to say about the depravity of mankind, but we will restrict ourselves just to one familiar verse. After David had committed his dreadful sins and had occasion to look deep into his soul, he was persuaded that the evil of his acts had proceeded from the evil of his nature.

The most significant thing about the confession in the fifty-first Psalm is not that it is a confession of gross outward sinfulness, but that it is a confession to God of the depravity of nature. In David's own words: "I was born in sin, and in iniquity did my mother conceive me." Here he traces the crimes which he committed back to their source in his very birth. This is what we call "original sin," or a corruption of the very nature from which evil deeds originate. So deep is the depravity of the soul, according to David's confession, that nothing but the creating of a new spirit within him would be adequate to deal with it, as he indicates in verse 10. He wants to be purged with hyssop that he may be clean in the inward parts. Here is David, therefore, acknowledging on the one hand that as to his own condition he is depraved and corrupt through and through, and on the other hand he fervently prays that he may be made, by divine grace, pure through and through.

Jeremiah, by divine inspiration, gives us the well-known words: "Can the Ethiopian change his skin, or the leopard his spots? then may ye also do good, that are accustomed to do evil" (Jeremiah 13:23). Here Jeremiah is indicating to us that the corruption of our nature is so fundamental to us that there is no more possibility of our changing our ways than there is of an Ethiopian changing the color of his skin or a leopard ridding itself of its spots.

As you will notice, different aspects of human sinfulness and depravity are indicated in these various passages. While they have many things in common, and indeed a common strand indicating the totality of depravity and the depth of sinfulness, still each one of these verses has its own peculiar angle of vision. Thus in the passage which we have just previously observed in the fifty-first Psalm, the aspect of this grim truth which King David is impressed with particularly is the depth of his depravity, the fact that it goes back to his very birth, and indeed before his birth, to the depravity of his parents. In the Jeremiah statement of the same doctrine, another point of vision is in focus. The prophet is noticing especially what the theologians would call "inability," that is, the fact that this depravity is so profound that man cannot, of himself, possibly overcome it. He is no more capable of coping with this problem than the leopard who might prefer not to have spots is able to alter his appearance.

In the New Testament this doctrine is made all the more explicit. Notice, for example, how our Lord teaches the same thing. He has his own point of emphasis just as the various teachers of the Old Testament do. Thus Jesus shows the inability and the depravity of men not so much by direct statements as by indicating the predicament in which they are because of their sin. He warns them that "except ye repent ye shall also perish." That is, man as he now is, is exposed to the dreadful judgment of God. In the twenty-third chapter of Matthew, the thirty-third verse, he says, "Ye serpents, ye generation of vipers, how can ye escape the damnation of hell?" Jesus is saying that this is a generation of evil men represented by the characteristic symbol of evil, namely, serpents. Precisely because they are of a serpentine nature there is no possibility of their escaping the damnation which is due to sin, namely the damnation of hell. Here, you see, Jesus is not so much emphasizing the depravity of their nature as He is showing what the consequences of it will be. But the very fact that the damnation of hell is inevitable for such a generation underlines in red the fact that this generation in indeed depraved that such dreadful punishment should be necessary. Likewise our Lord positively teaches that a man must be born again. Compare especially the third chapter of John. If a person cannot see the kingdom of God or enter the kingdom of God unless he be born again by the Spirit of God, surely the inference is that his condition is one of bondage to evil. Jesus is not saying this directly here, but he is certainly indirectly and unmistakably implying it.

So the rest of the New Testament, especially Paul, teaches very plainly that man is in bondage to his corruption. To take but one example, there probably is no portion of the entire Bible which emphasizes the undone condition of mankind more than the first three chapters of the Book of the Romans, and no part of Romans more than Romans 3:10–20. After surveying the human race, Gentiles and Jews, Paul comes to an awesome conclusion in chapter 3, verses 10–20. As you read these words which summarize the whole mighty argument of the opening chapters of this great Epistle, please note that the words themselves are nothing other than a quotation from the Old Testament. Thus here, as it were, we have the verdict of the entire Bible, Old Testament and New Testament, to the effect that man is as described in the following verses: "As it is written, There is none righteous, no, not one: There is none that understandeth, there is none that seeketh after God. They are all gone out of the way, they are together become unprofitable; there is none that doeth good, no, not one. Their throat is an open sepulchre; with their tongues they have used deceit; the poison of asps is under their lips: Whose mouth is full of cursing and bitterness; Their feet are swift to shed blood: Destruction and misery are in their ways: And the way of peace have they not known: There is no fear of God before their eyes. Now we know that what things soever the law saith, it saith to them who are under the law: that every mouth may be stopped, and all the world may become guilty before God. Therefore by the deeds of the law there shall no flesh be justified in his sight: for by the law is the knowledge of sin."

# 3. Inability

Very well, then, we are now ready for the second step, inability. Let us ask ourselves this question: What is the possibility of the salvation of sinful man? It is manifest, is it not, that of himself there is no possibility whatever of salvation. There is no possibility that he can escape his damnation. That is self-evident. Salvation by works is an absurdity, is it not? There is no conceivable way by which an evil tree can bring forth good fruit, and if it does not bring forth good fruit, certainly it is not going to be justified by its evil. This is what we mean by the "inability" of fallen man. But we mean more than that, and to that "more" we now come.

Admitting that no man can possibly save himself, we now must face the question: but if Christ offers him a way of salvation, may he not avail himself of it? That is, granted that if left to himself he is unable to work out his own salvation, but, still, if Christ dies to save him from his sins and offers him redemption upon his acceptance of it, may he not then be saved? That is, though he is sick unto death and cannot possibly heal himself, if the Great Physician should come and offer him a healing remedy, can he not at least reach out and take it, and thus, by relying upon the Great Physician, heal himself? This is actually what Arminians think man can do. They suppose that he is "too far gone" to save himself, but he is not "too far gone" to co-operate with the Savior. He cannot provide the medicine which is necessary to heal him, but he still has enough strength left to take that medicine if someone else offers it to him. In other words, he is sick, dreadfully sick, fatally sick, but he is not dead; and as long as there is a spark of life in him, as long as he can move at all, he is able to reach out and take the healing which is offered to him by the Great Physician. That is the theory of the Arminians, and whether that is true is precisely the question before us right now.

There are at least two basic reasons for a negative answer to the question of whether man is able to reach out and take the salvation which Christ offers him or not. First of all, the Bible explicitly says that man is not just sick, but that he is actually dead. "You hath he quickened, who were dead in trespasses and sins" (Ephesians 2:1). Now, admittedly, a dead man cannot cooperate with an offer of healing even if healing had any meaning for a person who is already dead and gone. It is not only that the Bible uses that particular metaphor of death, but it teaches the undone condition of man in many other ways also. Thus we have noticed that the Book of Genesis says that the thoughts and intents of his heart are only evil continually, that is, that he has no disposition toward goodness or holiness or God, so that even if he had any supposed strength left he would have no disposition whatever to use it because he is utterly hostile to God. Likewise, we notice in the teaching of the Book of Romans that "there is none that seeketh God. No, not one." It is not only, you see, that there are none that do good, as the Apostle says, but he also insists that there are none that even seek God. It is not only that men do not do good themselves, but they do not even seek God in order that He may enable them to do what is good. If this person actually reached out to accept the salvation which is in Christ Jesus, that would certainly be doing good, would it not? If Christ attracts anybody so that that person is disposed to accept Him, well, then, surely there is something left in that man to which goodness and holiness may yet appeal, is there not? But the Bible says very plainly that such is not the case. On the contrary, the thoughts and intents of the heart are only evil continually. Man is the bondservant of sin. He will not have God in his thinking.

Second, the Bible says that when a person does come to God and Christ, God has inclined him so to do. Thus we read in Scripture that in the day of God's power, the people shall be willing. And Jesus says in John 6:45, "It is written in the prophets, 'And they shall be all taught of God.' Every man therefore that hath heard, and hath learned of the Father, cometh unto Me." Thus, according to the Bible, even if salvation were wrought out for men and offered to them very freely, they would not—unless something happened to them that changed their condition—reach out and take the salvation which is offered. John Ruskin has said that man is determined to merit salvation rather than receive it.

All the religions of the world are autosoteric (that is, do-it-yourself-religions); only Christianity is heterosoteric (that is, "Jesus paid it all").

So, then, here is our dilemma, is it not? (We are leaving predestination utterly out of our thoughts at the moment.) We find man, as he presently, is totally undone, so completely hostile to God and good that even if salvation were offered to him he would reject it. As Jesus says, this is the condemnation, that light is come into the world and men love the darkness rather than the light. A famous evangelist of the eighteenth century, the British preacher George Whitefield, described the spiritual condition of man in terms of Lazarus, the physically dead person. I ask you, as you read the following statement from Whitefield, if it is not a true description of man in his present condition according to the Scripture:

> Come, ye dead, Christ-less, unconverted sinners, come and see the place where they laid the body of the deceased Lazarus; behold him laid out, bound hand and foot with grave-cloths, locked up and stinking in a dark cave, with a great stone placed on the top of it. View him again and again; go nearer to him; be not afraid; smell him. Ah! how he stinketh. Stop there now, pause a while; and whilst thou art gazing upon the corpse of Lazarus, give me leave to tell thee with great plainness, but greater love, that this dead, bound entombed, stinking carcase, is but a faint representation of thy poor soul in its natural state: for, whether thou believest or not, thy spirit which thou bearest about with thee, sepulchred in flesh and blood, is as literally dead to God, and as truly dead in trespasses and sins, as the body of Lazarus was in the cave. Was he bound hand and foot with grave-cloths? So art thou bound hand and foot with thy corruptions: and as a stone was laid on the sepulchre so is there a stone of unbelief upon thy stupid heart. Perhaps thou hast lain in this state, not only four days, but many years stinking in God's nostrils. And, what is still more effecting, thou art as unable to raise thyself out of this loathsome, dead state, to a life of righteousness and

true holiness, as ever Lazarus was to raise himself from the cave in which he lay so long. Thou mayest try the power of thy own boasted free-will, and the force and energy of moral persuasion and rational arguments (which, without all doubt, have their proper place in religion); but all thy efforts, exerted with never so much vigor, will prove quite fruitless and abortive, till that same Jesus, who said "Take away the stone"; and cried, "Lazarus, come forth," also quickens you.

# 4. The Divine Initiative

We come now to the third step: the divine initiative. We have found that man in his present condition is totally undone, and unable to save himself, even if the Savior were offered to him. In and of himself there is no hope whatever. He is dead in his trespasses and sins. We come now, then, to our third fundamental observation: that those who are saved, who do believe in Jesus Christ, are those who have benefited from what is called the "divine initiative." The divine initiative refers to the fact that a desperately undone sinner must, if he is ever to be rescued, have God take the initiative in his salvation. This initiative is of a particular kind. It is an initiative on God's part which really copes with man's desperate problem. Since man's desperate problem is how to get a new heart when he is dead in trespasses and sins, God actually instills a new heart. He gives him a new principle of life. He makes him over again. By the Spirit of God this sinner is born again, born from above.

Now this is the fulfillment of those words: "in the day of the Lord's power the people shall be willing." In other words, when God reveals His right arm and displays His mighty strength in changing the soul, the spirit, the principle of a sinner, is then by this new nature willing and disposed and believing in Jesus Christ. Thus the man comes pressing into the kingdom of God. He becomes a man of violence who takes the kingdom of heaven by force. He is so determined to have this Christ—whom he now sees in all His loveliness and whom he loves with all his heart—that he will permit nothing to stand in his way. This is the way the divine initiative works out. We choose God. Indeed, we choose God. But "ye have chosen Me," says Jesus, "because I have first chosen you" (John 15:16). We love Him indeed, but we love Him because He first loved us (1 John 4:19). As the Psalmist puts it: "When thou saidst, 'Seek ye My face'; my heart said unto Thee, 'Thy face, Lord, will I seek' " (Psalm 27:8). When God says "Seek ye My face," then we do indeed seek His face. And that saying is no mere command to do it; that is speaking to the soul so that we are actually disposed to do what we are told. This is not the outward calling of a mere invitation to the gospel; this is an inner call by which Christ's sheep hear His voice.

But speaking of that simile which Jesus uses about the sheep and the shepherd leads us to an observation. Christ teaches us that it is the sheep who hear the shepherd's voice. And just as plainly He says to the Pharisees that they do not hear His voice because they are not His sheep. But who makes a person a sheep of Jesus Christ but Christ Himself? So that when the gospel comes to us and we hear it as the voice of our beloved Shepherd, and come very happily and docilely in obedience to His command, this in itself is an evidence that we are sheep and we have been made such by Christ just as truly as some others, such as the Pharisees, may at the moment, at least, not be sheep because Christ has not yet, at least, made them such.

# 5. Predestination

We come now to the fourth and last step of our journey into predestination. If man is dead and has no inclination or concern or ability to help himself therefore, and if when he does become alive it is because God has sovereignly planted a new life in him, then God must have previously decided to do so. Why do we say this? Is it not obvious why this is certainly true? You are a rational creature yourself. Do you, as a rational creature, do things without going through some sort of a previous thought process? When you do something do you not say you do it "because"? If you behave in a way that someone else does not understand and he says "Why are you doing that?" do you not say "Well, for several reasons"? In other words, does a finite rational creature not always have some sort of reason for doing what he does?

If you as a rational creature do not do anything without first having some reason for it, it is not reasonable to suppose, is it, that God, in whose image you are made, who is a Logos or a rational Being, would do anything without previous deliberation? If, therefore, He changes persons, He must have decided to change persons. He is no machine who does things without any reason. He is a rational Being who has a reason in Himself. Therefore, He had some reason or some previous decision to effect this change which He has now effected.

Very well, then, when did God make up His mind? How long before the event would He have decided to effect this change of heart? He would have decided as soon as He had, as it were, all the data before Him, would He not? That is, as soon as God knew all the factors which were involved, and His wisdom could settle on which was the best course, at that particular time presumably He would have made up His mind, would He not?

Well, what was that time? Was it not from all eternity? Did He not always know all the factors which are involved and what is the infinitely wise course to follow? Did He not always have all the data before Him as a present fact no matter how present, past, and future it may be in our experience? Since there is nothing new to God, but all things are known to Him from the beginning, He would have known from all eternity what was the wise thing to do, and what was the thing He was going to do. Therefore, God had from all eternity decided to change the hearts of those whose hearts are actually changed. Now this is nothing more or less than eternal predestination, is it? This is eternal election, is it not?

So, then, by these four simple steps, we have arrived at our eternal predestination. Let us very briefly retrace these steps to show how we have come to our destination. First, we have seen that man is dead in trespasses and sins, and is unable to take steps to save himself. Second, we found that he was unable even to take salvation when it was offered. Third, we noticed, therefore, the manifest truthfulness of the Scriptural teaching that it is only when God takes the initiative that man responds in faith, believing. And so, in the fourth place, we reflected that since God would always know the wise course of action He would, from eternity, have made up His mind about everything which He was going to do. Therefore, God from all eternity, chose to change certain persons who were of themselves unable to change and turn to Him, and He did not choose to change certain other persons. Thus, we have seen in a very simple way the profound truth of predestination and election (and reprobation) as the Bible teaches it to us.

# 6. Objections to Predestination

Let us now observe some of the questions or objections which are raised concerning this doctrine of predestination. I should like to suggest this to the reader. After I have stated the question or objection, why do you not try to answer this question or resolve this difficulty from your own understanding of the doctrine as it has already been developed here? These questions or problems connected with the doctrine are real tests of whether a person understands. His ability to answer these is a test of whether a person understands the doctrine of predestination. So why not test yourself before you read the discussion which follows the questions in this booklet? See what you can do with them yourself.

OBJECTION 1. If predestination is true, man cannot be free.

The first question which arises is whether predestination does not destroy human freedom. If God predestinates all the actions of all moral agents, the question runs: "Can there be any meaning to the statement that man wills? Can man meaningfully will if God from all eternity—before man was even created—decreed everything which man was going to do?"

This is an exceedingly common question. I have heard it hundreds of times myself. I presume everybody has heard it or raised it at one time or another. Its frequency of occurrence is some indication of the vitality of its nature. Nevertheless, I am surprised at how rarely the question itself is analyzed. Usually the person just says, "If God does predestinate, can man be free?"

The answer to that is a simple and blunt "Yes." Nevertheless, that will not satisfy the questioner because he does not really want you to tell him "Yes" or "No." He wants you to say "Yes," and then overcome his objection. He wants you to show him how it is possible that God predestinates, and yet leaves man genuinely free. In other words, this question is more than a question. It is an objection implied. The questioner is virtually saying that if God predestinates, man simply cannot be free because . . . . But this is where we must demur. We must ask the objector to present a reason for his objection. Just as he would not be satisfied by a blunt "Yes" or "No" on our part, and we do not blame him for that, so we feel he should not expect us to be satisfied with a mere blunt statement that these two propositions cannot be true. Unless his mere statement that these two things cannot be simultaneously true is to be accepted as a divinely inspired declaration, we have every right to insist that he must make good his charge. He must give us some reason for his statement that these two things cannot co-exist.

We think that almost every objector would admit that our request is a legitimate one. He will admit that an objection cannot be sustained simply because he made it. That is, he will grant that he has some obligation to advance a reason why we should acknowledge the cogency of his objection. Very well. He will attempt to do so. And what will he say?

Now, suppose he says, "If God predestinates something to come to pass, in order to guarantee that it will, He must *force* human agents to do what He has predestinated." We will admit that if that statement is true it surely establishes the objection. But, we must ask, what proof is there that if God predestinates something to come to pass then He has to *force* someone else, some free or some moral agent, to do it? Is that way of stating the matter anything other than a repetition of the original objection in other words? In the first place, you see, he says, "Predestination and freedom cannot co-exist."

"Well," we say, "what proof do you have of that?"

He says, "If God predestines, He must *force* somebody to do what he has predestinated." That is the same thing as saying that if God predestinates somebody to do something He must take away his free will and treat him as a machine of some kind. But that is not telling us why this must be so. It is a mere declaration that it must be so. As such it is just a repetition of the earlier declaration that predestination and freedom cannot co-exist. So we must insist here, now just why is it that, if God predestinates, man can not be free and must be forced? Then what will our objector say to substantiate his objection?

Suppose he says, "Why, this is self-evident. It is perfectly plain to every candid mind that if God predestinates a certain action He must force a human creature to do that particular action. We admit there are such things as the self-evident. Furthermore, we admit that when something is truly self-evident that is the same thing as saying it is self-proving, and therefore it is a cogent contention. We would grant that if this objection is self-evident that establishes the objection. But, we say, ourselves and a few million other people insist that this is not at all self-evident We do not see that because God predestinates that a certain action is going to come to pass that that act must violate human freedom. We do not see that it is impossible for God to pre-destinate an act to come to pass by means of the deliberate choice of specific individuals We admit that a good many people do say this cannot be. We admit that a great many people think that it is self-evident that it cannot be. But as long as there are so many people who say that it is by no means self-evident, we are afraid that there can be no appeal (by either side) to an argument from self-evidence here.

So, once again, our objector is challenged to make his objection stick. What will he say then if we ask him to prove to us that God's predestination of an act takes that act out of the realm of human freedom? Well, he may say something like this, namely that if God predestinates an act He makes that act certain. If He makes the act certain, then there is no possibility that men will act otherwise. If there is no possibility that men will act otherwise than in a par-ticular manner, then they are not really free. When our ob-jector gives this defense of his objection he is talking reason, admittedly. He is advancing an argument, this we grant. We do not for a moment admit that this argument is a sound one or that it will stand up under analysis, but we do admit that it is a relevant observation and deserves our attention.

So let us give our attention to this particular contention that if God predestinates He renders an act certain; and if He renders an act certain there is no possibility that man will choose otherwise; and if there is no possibility that man will choose otherwise man cannot be free. You see that this point rests on the last part of the statement, that is, if man is certain to will a particular act, and there is no possibility of his willing another act, he is not free. But is this statement true? Is it a fact that if it is certain that a person will choose a particular act and impossible that he will choose another act he cannot be free? Is not the raising of this question an exposure of the fallacy of the contention?

Let me put it in another way. This contention is saying that if a person is certain to will an act, a particular act, there is no possibility of his being free in willing that particular act. Now that is clearly untrue, is it not? That is, anybody will grant immediately that it may be absolutely certain that a person will choose a particular act without that individual being in the slightest bit constrained by any force outside himself. That is, in any given instance, when I see a particular course of action as appealing to me, as having the strongest arguments in its favor, I will certainly choose that course of action. There is no possibility in the world that I will do what does not seem good to me. There is no possibility in the world that I will not choose what does seem good to me, for if I did choose what did not seem good to me that would be the same thing as choosing what I did not want, what I was not inclined to. But choosing is inclining to, it is preferring, and if I do choose or incline to or prefer a certain course of action it is surely because the reasons for this course of action appeal to me more powerfully than any other reasons or any other course of action appealed to me.

On the other hand, if the reasons for this particular course of action appeal to me more than any other reasons or considerations for any other course of action then I certainly will follow this particular course of action and there is absolutely no possibility that I will choose another course of action. But no one is forcing me to choose this particular course of action. It is absolutely certain, you see, that I will do such and such but it is equally evident that nobody is pushing me to do it. On the contrary, I myself incline, prefer, choose this course of action. I certainly choose this

course of action. There is no possibility that I will choose
any other course of action because this is the course of action which appeals most cogently to me. So we have all the
certainty in the direction of this action and all the impossibility of choosing in another direction without the slightest
bit of constraint or lack of freedom on my part.

Let us take an illustration of the point before us. You are
now reading this little book on predestination. Very well, let
me ask you a personal question. Why are you reading this
book on predestination? I do not know the exact reasons,
the precise reasons, why you are reading this. I do not even
know you. But this I know, that you do have reasons for
reading it. And this also I know: You have more reasons, or
at least stronger reasons, for reading it than for not reading
it. Shall I guess at some of your reasons? Well, you are
reading this book because you are interested in the subject
of predestination. The matter haunts you. You recognize
the extreme importance of the subject. Or, you may be
reading this particular treatment because your girl is reading it. You want to impress her by knowing something
about the subjects which interest her. Or you may feel that
you can help her understand something. It may not interest you in the slightest, but on the other hand it may interest her very greatly, and anything that interests her interests you because it interests her. Again, you may be reading this book because your mother has begged you to read
it or your father has commanded you to read it. So you may
be reading it because you are interested in the subject or
somebody else is interested in the subject for direct reasons
or indirect reasons, for motives concerning the subject itself
or ulterior motives. I do not know who you are or what
you are, or what it is that is affecting you, but this I know:
you are now reading this discussion because you have
your reasons for so doing. This also I know, that if you saw
more reasons for not reading this at this particular moment
than for reading it, you would not have this particular book
in your hand at this particular time. In other words, you

are reading it because you choose to read it. And when you choose something you do so because there are more and stronger reasons in favor of doing it than not doing it. And when there are stronger reasons for doing something than not doing it, you always do it, you certainly do it. You cannot possibly choose something other. To choose something other would be to choose what you do not choose, to prefer what you do not prefer. That is a sheer psychological impossibility.

In the last analysis, it is impossible for you to be forced to choose anything. It may seem that you can be forced, but I think if we investigate this matter we will see that that is an optical illusion. There is absolutely no possibility of anyone, you or anyone else, ever being forced to choose. For example, suppose the author of this booklet was standing right by you at the moment with a pistol in his hand, its barrel pointed at your temple, and saying to you meanwhile, "You read this writing of mine or else!" Now suppose under those conditions you proceeded to read. You may be tempted to think that you are being forced in such a situation as that.

Now, to be sure, you have a delicate instrument of persuasion aimed at your temple, but that gun does not actually force you to choose to read what I have written. You choose to read what I have written because it seems good to you to do so. Now, admittedly, the reason it seems good to you to do so under these circumstances is that it seems preferable to you to read even this to having your brains splattered all over the desk. But if for some strange reason it would seem better to you to have your brains splattered all over the desk than read this particular book, you would not be reading this particular book. So the reason you are reading this particular writing under these circumstances is that you prefer to read it than to depart this earthly existence in this particular manner at this particular time. This would come as close to being the type of situation in which the will would actually be forced as any kind of situation can be. And yet, as we see when we look at it, we are not really forced to choose even with a gun pointed at our head. It is still within our power to choose to have the gun go off. There is no power with which we are acquainted in this world which can actually force our will. It can force our body. A person can tie us, rope us, and carry us if we do not choose to go. He can take our life away from us when we do not want to relinquish it. The powers of this world can do virtually anything they want to but this one area is invulnerable and impervious to anybody and anything, namely, the sovereignty of our own will. I choose, in the last analysis, what seems good to me, and there is no such thing as my choosing anything other than that. Not even Almighty God, once He has given me this faculty of choice, can make me, coerce me, force me to choose. If God forced the will it would no longer be a will. Just as if He squared the circle it would no longer be a circle.

I may remind the reader that though the above illustration is quite bizarre and fantastic, it illustrates something which is by no means far-fetched. After all, emperors have sat before Christians and said, "You rescind your faith or we will kill you." These persons have chosen to be killed rather than recant their faith. A threat of death itself does not determine the will. Our will is determined by one thing only: what seems best to us.

So this rather extended analysis tends to show us one thing, namely that when we choose anything it is absolutely certain that we will so choose and there is no possibility of our choosing otherwise, and yet so far from destroying our freedom it is virtually a definition of our freedom! Remember, the objector has been saying that predestination renders an act certain and makes it impossible that the actor will do otherwise. Therefore, it makes the actor a machine, taking away his freedom. Our analysis of human choice and action shows, however, that a thing being certain and the alternative being impossible as a matter of choice, so far from taking away our freedom is that wherein our freedom actually consists. So that this argument has boomeranged and, instead of its cutting down predestination, it has destroyed the objector.

But the objector may continue and insist that we have altered his original situation somewhat. Or he may say that we are talking about something which is certain to a man because the course of action seems good to him. But according to predestination the thing comes to pass because it seems good to God. If it is God who has His reasons for decreeing what is going to come to pass, then that is what determines what is going to come to pass and not what seems good to a man. But, please notice: If God predestinates what comes to pass in the life of man, and has made man such a type of creature that he always chooses only what seems good to him, then God has actually predestinated things to come to pass in the life of man in accordance with human freedom. Granted that what has been predestined has been predestined according to what seems good to God—that is admitted—but we deny the deduction which the objector is making that because predestination represents what seems good to God it therefore does not represent what seems good to man and his true choice. On the contrary, if God predestinates the actions of free agents, and free agents operate in such a way that they choose what seems good to them, then manifestly, in predestinating the actions of free agents, God has taken the choices of men for granted. And in some profoundly mysterious way, what God decrees is what seems good to a man. No one can say that this is not so, that it could not be. According to the concept of predestination and the nature of man, which we are now considering, this must be exactly the way predestination operates. In other words, the closer we look at it, the more clearly we see that predestination is the great Magna Charta of human liberty. God's predetermination of every act of men is the same thing as predetermination of the freedom of men. That is, it is the acts of free agents which are predestined!

Another point ought to be made about this matter of the certainty of men's actions as a supposed hindrance to their freedom. We have already shown the fundamental reason why we cannot say that because an action is certain it is not free. Now we want to give a second reason for the same point. The reason is this: the generally admitted doctrine of divine foreknowledge involves the certainty of free actions. People often think they object to predestination who, at the same time, think they have no objection to foreknowledge. But they object to predestination because it implies that the acts of men are certain and do not object to foreknowledge, although it also implies that these acts are certain. If a person really does believe that the certainty that particular free acts will come to pass rules out the possibility of their freedom, he must not only object to predestination but to foreknowledge as well. On the other hand, if he does not object to foreknowledge then his supposed objection to certainty must be insincere, and he has no right to object to predestination on that ground.

Perhaps we need to explain, however, what is meant by saying that the foreknowledge of God indicates the certainty of the actions of mankind. Foreknowledge means that God knows before the event precisely what the event will be, or before the choice of man precisely what the choice of man will be. If God did not know the acts of man beforehand He simply would not have foreknowledge. But, if He does have foreknowledge, then that means that He knows what the actions of men will be before the actions are taken or before the man himself is actually born. That is the same thing as saying that if foreknowledge is true the absolute certainty of all the actions of free agents is certain from all eternity; because, if they were not certain then God could not foreknow them as such. If there were a possibility that a man would choose B rather than A, then God could not know from all eternity that he would choose A. Or else, if God did, such foreknowledge would prove to be fallacious. But if God has a true and reliable foreknowledge that man will do A, then it is absolutely certain that man will do A, and there is no possibility at all that man will choose B.

Thus, for example, Judas' betrayal of Jesus is declared to be an item of God's foreknowledge, according to Acts 2:23: "Him, being delivered by the determinate counsel and foreknowledge of God, ye have taken, and by wicked hands have crucified and slain." God had foreknowledge that Jesus Christ would be delivered up and crucified by wicked hands. But if God had that knowledge from all eternity that Jesus Christ was to be crucified by wicked hands, the wicked hands of Judas Iscariot, then there was no possibility whatever that Judas Iscariot would not betray Jesus Christ by wicked hands. It was absolutely certain an eternity before Judas Iscariot was born that he would be born at a particular time and place and would enter into the apostolic circle and would betray Jesus Christ to be crucified. All of that absolute certainty, and complete rejection of alternative possibilities, is involved in the statement, "I believe God possesses foreknowledge."

Either, therefore, we reject God's foreknowledge or we accept the fact that the actions of men are certain from all eternity and yet are the free acts of men. If we should reject the foreknowledge of God we must recognize that this is tantamount to a rejection of God. If, for example, God does not possess foreknowledge and does not know everything that is going to come to pass, He cannot be said to be all-wise. He has created the universe, to be sure, but if He does not know what is going to come to pass He may be in for surprises. There is no way of assuming that the creature, left to himself, will work out a pattern of wisdom. It would be a mere accident if he did. And God certainly cannot be called the all-wise ordainer of everything that comes to pass according to His own will and glory. Again, God could not possibly be sovereign if He did not possess foreknowledge. If He did not know in advance everything that was going to come to pass and if He were in for surprises, it would be manifest, would it not, that He did not control the situation?

If He controlled or sovereignly determined what was to come to pass, He would know what He had controlled and sovereignly disposed. If He does not know, then He does not control and sovereignly dispose. The events are determined by someone, some thing, other than Himself. Still further, God cannot be an all-loving God. If He does not know what is to come to pass and He is in for surprises, then anything can happen. Foolish things may happen which are destructive of the well-being of the universe. We do not know. God does not know. These things are uncertain, and are in the hands of someone other than an all-wise God. But, if He does not know what is going to come to pass, then He cannot be certain that the things which do come to pass will be for the good of the creature or even for the good of God Himself. So, on this supposition, we could not say that a loving hand is behind all that is and that God's mercy is over all His works.

To mention only one other attribute, if God does not have foreknowledge, neither does He possess truthfulness. He declares in His Word that such and such things are going to come to pass, and through His prophets He makes predictions of the future. He indicates that there will be a final judgment, that Jesus Christ will return again, that some will believe and some will not believe, and some will be saved and some will be lost. But if He does not really know, He is making so many rash statements. The event may prove Him to be mistaken. He should not be saying that things are going to happen when He Himself does not know that they are going to happen. He would be untruthful even in making the assertions as if He knew, when, according to the hypothesis, He does not know.

This is just the briefest indication of the fact that the denial of foreknowledge is a denial of God. And again we remind the reader that the denial of certainty is the denial of foreknowledge, so that we can say the denial of certainty is the denial of God. The denial that man's actions are certain from all eternity is nothing more nor less than atheism. We

know full well that many people, who like to think that
perhaps God does not know everything in advance, wish to
be reverent and not to demean the character of God. But,
whatever their intentions may be, they should be conscious of the implication of their statements

The implication of a statement that God does not know
in advance what men's actions will be is that God does not
know in advance; and if God does not know in advance, God
is not. So, there is no escaping for the serious Christian
thinker. If he denies the certainty of men's acts, he is, in the
same breath, denying the reality of God's very being. The
gravity of this matter can hardly be seen in a sharper light
than at the point of veritable atheism.

OBJECTION 2. If predestination is true, it makes no
difference what a person does.

Let us consider now a closely related objection which is
nevertheless different from this first one. Some will say, "If
predestination is true, it makes no difference what a person
does. If he is predestined to sin, he will sin; if he is predestined to repent, he will repent; if he is predestined to be
saved, he will be saved; if he is predestined to be lost, he
will be lost. So there is no point to his doing anything
inasmuch as the outcome is already certain. Predestination
insures (the critic continues) that the outcome is certain regardless of what I do or whether I do."

Our answer to that objection is a flat denial of its understanding of predestination. The doctrine of predestination
does not teach that certain events will come to pass regardless of whether certain other events take place. Rather, one
predestinated event is to issue from another event—predestinated, to be sure. Predestination refers not only to
ends, but to means as well. It simply is not true that Judas
would have been damned whether he betrayed Christ or
not. It simply is not true that Peter would have been saved
whether he repented or not. If Judas had repented he would
have been saved, whereas if Peter had not repented he

would not have been saved. Of course, predestination rules
out these "if's" and "whereas's." It does not rule them out,
however, in a way that does any violence to the will either
of Judas or Peter, as we have already shown. One thing
predestination does not rule out is the connection between
ends and means.

OBJECTION 3. If predestination is true, there is no
incentive to preach the gospel.

Another question which is raised concerning predestination is this: If the doctrine is true, what incentive is there
to preach the gospel to other persons? If they are predestined, they will be saved; if they are not predestined, they
will not be saved. Therefore, why bother? Why endeavor to
save persons by offering the gospel to them?

Remember now, salvation is through faith in Jesus
Christ. There is none other name given under heaven
whereby we must be saved than the name of Jesus. The
doctrine of predestination, or here, more specifically, of election to everlasting life, teaches that some are chosen to be
saved, it being understood, to be saved through Jesus
Christ. In other words, election means that some persons
are predestinated to believe in Jesus Christ and be saved.
Now this question is raised with reference to the matter of
predestination: Why preach the gospel? It is the same thing
as asking: Why, since people are predestinated (elected) to
be saved by the preaching of the gospel, preach the gospel?
In that light, is this question not really rather foolish? Why
preach the gospel since some people are predestined to be
saved by the preaching of the gospel? You see where the error lies, do you not? The objector is unconsciously thinking
that predestination to life is independent of the gospel. But it
is not independent of the gospel. There is no salvation, no
eternal life, that is independent of the gospel. There is no
other way by which anybody is saved than by the gospel.
Therefore, the gospel must be preached if anybody is going
to be saved. Predestination does not deny that. On the con-

trary, predestination operates by means of that. That is to say, since some persons are predestined to eternal life through the gospel, it is an integral part of predestination that the gospel be presented. Predestination cannot be carried out unless the gospel is presented. Or, to put it another way, the preaching of the gospel itself is predestinated as much as the believing of the gospel and the salvation of the elect are predestinated. Or, again, to put it still another way, in a somewhat more technical phrasing, God predestinates not only the end but the means. That is, He not only predestinates the end (the salvation of the elect), but also the means by which their salvation comes (namely, the preaching of the gospel).

Again, let me illustrate this point. The writer believes in predestination, and he therefore writes this little book. He speaks about sin and grace, the way of redemption, and God's relation to the whole process. Why does he do so? Well, in the first instance, he does so because he is requested to do so. However, there is a far more fundamental reason why he does so. He proclaims this message with evangelistic hope precisely because he believes so firmly in the Biblical doctrine of predestination. That doctrine assures him that that proclamation of the Christian message is essential to the salvation of souls. Furthermore, it assures him that his proclamation will be effectual. God's Word will not return unto Him void. God has predestined that some will be saved by the message of the evangel (which includes predestination). So he believes that his teaching and preaching of this doctrine will be integral to the salvation of those who read or hear. As a matter of fact, if he did not believe in predestination he would not get much joy out of preaching. That is, he realizes the only reason anyone is ever going to be saved by his preaching (or writing) is that God has eternally chosen through preaching and writing to save some. If God had not so chosen, and he were to continue to preach, his preaching would be in vain. Why? Well, because, as we have shown, men are dead in trespasses and sins. They have no disposition to life at all and are indisposed to the gospel of redeeming grace. The writer knows, therefore, that if men are left to themselves they will perish, while he pleads with them to believe and be saved. But when he knows that God has predestinated to life and life comes by means of the Word, then he knows that as the Word of God is preached it will be the instrument of salvation to those whom God has chosen. So he preaches with confidence and assurance and optimism and hope because of predestination. So far, in other words, from predestination's being a deterrent to preaching it is probably the most powerful incentive conceivable.

Nevertheless, you will still ask, is it not true that if a person is not predestinated he never can be saved? No, that is not exactly true. It is almost exactly true, but there is one word there which is at least misleading and perhaps, depending on what is in your mind, erroneous. It is not true that men *cannot* be saved unless they have been predestinated to salvation. If you mean by "cannot" that they are unable to even though they *want* to be saved; if you get the impression that an individual may be convicted of sin and repent and decide to believe in Jesus Christ and be saved but be prevented from doing so or be rejected by Jesus Christ as an unelect person; if you think that, you are laboring under a very serious misunderstanding of the doctrine of predestination There is no "cannot," you see, of that character involved in this matter The word is not "cannot" but "will not." If a person has not been predestinated to eternal life and has been left to himself in his sin, that person *will not* believe and be saved. There is no possibility that he will choose Christ against his disposition, against his disinclinaton. It is an absolute certainty that he will reject Jesus Christ and perish in his sins. But it is not because he *cannot* do otherwise in one sense of the word, but because, ultimately, he *will not*. The immediate cause, therefore, in his damnation is his own sin and unbelief. We must not get the impression that the nonelect are to be pitied because, even though they long for salvation, God has denied it to them. That is not the case. It is *because* they hate Christ and the way of salvation that God denies it to them. If *anybody* ever does repent of his sins and does believe in Jesus Christ, that individual will have salvation. But, of course, that individual, by definition, is a predestinated person.

OBJECTION 4. If predestination is true, God is insincere in inviting all men to salvation!

Again, you will ask, Why, if a man is not elected or predestinated to eternal life, but is actually passed over in the decrees of God, does God proceed to strive with him nonetheless? Why does God send His gospel to a person who has been predestinated to be left to himself and perish? Or, in the form of an objection, it is said: If predestination is true, God is insincere in inviting all men to salvation.

Now before we come to grips with this question in its fundamental nature, let me call attention incidentally to a significant fact. The situation which is before us at the moment is in no sense different from the situation we would have if there were no such thing as predestination. That is, if there were merely foreknowledge and no predestination of events, God would know from all eternity that certain persons were going to disbelieve and to perish in their sins. He has perfect knowledge of all things, and therefore knows who will believe and who will not believe. The question can still be raised, just as legitimately as in the predestination context, why does God strive and work and present the gospel and its means of grace to persons whom He knows are going to reject every overture which He makes? We know that God knows the outcome, and we also know that God works strenuously for the salvation of people whose unbelief He has known from all eternity. This is just to remind you once again that as long as there is such a thing as foreknowledge we have problems like this regardless of the doctrine of predestination. Predestination, in other words, does not bring a problem like this into existence; it exists independently of predestination and is made neither better nor worse, that is, more or less severe, by the doctrine of predestination.

Otherwise it is a perfectly legitimate question to ask why God strives with men whom He knows and has predestined should perish. Again, incidentally, before coming to this question, let me notice another significant point. This question really does concern God and not us. What I mean is this: we may wonder why God, who knows all things, including the fact that certain persons will in spite of all efforts reject and disbelieve, continues to work with them to persuade them to believe; but we cannot ask why *we* would do so with all men. We do not know the outcome. To us there is always a possibility that anybody with whom we work and for whom we pray may be an object of the divine mercy and may be predestinated to eternal life and may actually believe and be saved. God knows, in a given instance, that such is not going to happen, but we never know it. Therefore, we cannot only work in obedience preaching the gospel, but we can work in hope that our preaching will be successful in the salvation of the persons with whom we strive. It does not affect our evangelistic endeavors or zeal in the slightest, but nevertheless it is a question which we may ask concerning God himself.

What reason, then, are we able to discover why God, who knows the futility of certain endeavors to convert certain persons, proceeds to make these endeavors which He knows are going to be futile? There appear to be several reasons. First, God, by this means, shows the hardness of the sinful heart. As we have said, it is only the wickedness of the human heart, and not the decree of God, which causes men to reject the overtures of God and His gospel. What more clearly reveals the depths of depravity than the rejection of such invitations from a glorious God? Second, this hardness of the human heart apart from the converting presence of the Holy Spirit shows that God is essential to goodness. Third, God's sincerity is evident in that if any person whosoever accepts the gospel, God will accept him. Fourth, the elect see, in the invitations of God and their rejection by men, how hard their own hearts were apart from the grace of God, and what they would have done apart from that grace. They may say now and through all eternity, as they contemplate the righteous judgments of God against the wicked, "There but for the grace of God go we."

# 7. Am I Predestinated to Eternal Life?

In conclusion, let us ask this personally most vital of all questions. Am I predestinated? Am I an elect person? Have I been chosen before the foundation of the world? The answer to this question, "Yes" or "No," will be the greatest answer you ever know, for good or for ill. It is awesome; the decree of God is awe-inspiring. It is the most important thing about you or me or any person by virtually inconceivable odds. But, what of the answer to the question, Have I been elected by Almighty God? How do you find the answer? Where do you find it?

The answer is to be found in your heart and your life. God knows from all eternity. He has written the names of the chosen in the Book of Life. But you cannot know directly the mind of God, nor can you read, as it were, the Lamb's Book of Life. You can only know indirectly. You know the way in which predestination to life operates, and you can see whether or not this operation is taking place in you. Predestination is to life through faith in Jesus Christ. You are confronted with the gospel. You believe it or you do not. You can know whether you believe it or whether you do or not. If in your heart you love the Lord Jesus Christ, and in your life of obedience to His commandments you are demonstrating that you sincerely trust Him and love Him, then you have life. "This is life eternal, that they may know Thee the only true God, and Jesus Christ, whom Thou hast sent." If you know Christ and God His Father, you have eternal life. And if you have eternal life it is because you have been eternally predestinated to it. If you have life in Christ Jesus you have been predestinated thereto and are elect persons chosen before the foundation of the world. You have in that instance the greatest of all grounds for rejoicing, because you are the objects of the eternal mercy of God and Christ Jesus our Lord.

On the other hand, if you do not at this moment have faith in Jesus Christ and give evidence of the genuineness of it by love and obedience to Him, you are not in a position to conclude that you are not elected persons. In other words, you may have evidence that you *are* elected, but it is impossible for you to be sure that you *are not* elected. The Lord may not yet have shown you saving mercy, but it does not follow that He never will show you saving mercy. The salvation of the dying thief on the cross is a wonderful reminder of the possibility of mercy at the last moment.

There is a word of caution which must be given at this point. We dare not presume on our predestination to life, but neither, on the other hand, dare we presume that we have not been predestinated to life. We do not know, at the moment, possibly. But precisely because we do not know, we dare not assume a negative answer. Even if we did we would be presumptuous still further to despise the means of grace, the work of the Holy Spirit, the proffer of the gospel, on the arrogant assumption that none of these things will do us any good. We do not know. As long as there is life there is hope. And while God is pleading with us to believe and be saved, while Jesus Christ is standing at the door of our hearts and knocking for admittance, it is a dreadful thing indeed for us to return negative answers to the gracious invitation of God on the presumptuous ground that we have not been chosen. It would be a wicked thing for us to do even if we knew our reprobation to be the case; but it is doubly wicked if we do not know. Let everyone of us, therefore, be solemnly warned against taking this doctrine and perverting it to a form of fatalism, and bringing damnation upon himself because he despises the truth of God and turns His Word into lasciviousness. There may be some profound mystery connected with the doctrine of predestination, but there is no mystery here that justifies our presuming to know what we do not know and to act wrongly therefore.

On the other hand, even for anyone who at this moment may not be sure of his salvation, there is a word of very great encouragement. I cannot presume to say, nor can anyone else, that you are an elect person. Nevertheless, the very fact that you are concerned about your soul is a healthy sign. Seek God while He may be found. When you find him you will know that He found you an eternity earlier.

You must not allow any notion of predestination to lead you into despair and inactivity. I shall never forget talking with a high school girl about this great subject concerning which she had many problems. Finally she said to me "I was never so close to not being a Christian."

I replied: "You were never so close to being a Christian." You see, the true God is a sovereign God. And this is life eternal that you know the only true (that is, sovereign) God and Jesus Christ whom He has sent.

We hope that we have said enough to fulfill our promise of writing a primer on predestination. For those who want to know more we heartily recommend Loraine Boettner's, *The Reformed Doctrine of Predestination* (Phillipsburg, New Jersey: Presbyterian & Reformed Publishing Company, 1981).

# Appendix 1

## Some Bible Verses Dealing with Predestination

### Foreordination

Nehemiah 9:6: "Thou, even thou, art Lord alone; thou hast made heaven, the heaven of heavens, with all their host, the earth, and all things that are therein, the seas, and all that is therein, and thou preservest them all; and the host of heaven worshippeth thee."

Psalm 33:11: "The counsel of the Lord standeth for ever, the thoughts of his heart to all generations."

Psalm 104:24: "O Lord, how manifold are thy works! in wisdom hast thou made them all: the earth is full of thy riches."

Proverbs 16:33: "The lot is cast into the lap; but the whole disposing thereof is of the Lord."

Isaiah 40:26: "Lift up your eyes on high, and behold who hath created these things, that bringeth out their host by number: he calleth them all by names by the greatness of his might, for that he is strong in power; not one faileth."

Isaiah 46:10–11: "Declaring the end from the beginning, and from ancient times the things that are not yet done, saying, My counsel shall stand, and I will do all my pleasure: Calling a ravenous bird from the east, the man that executeth my counsel from a far country: yea, I have spoken it, I will also bring it to pass; I have purposed it, I will also do it."

Matthew 10:30: "But the very hairs of your head are all numbered."

Acts 15:18: "Known unto God are all his works from the beginning of the world."

Romans 11:36: "For of him, and through him, and to him, are all things: to whom be glory for ever."

Ephesians 1:11: "In whom also we have obtained an inheritance, being predestinated according to the purpose of him who worketh all things after the counsel of his own will."

Hebrews 1:3: "Who being the brightness of his glory, and the express image of his person, and upholding all things by the word of his power, when he had by himself purged our sins, sat down on the right hand of the Majesty on high."

Revelation 4:11: "Thou art worthy, O Lord, to receive glory and honour and power; for thou hast created all things, and for thy pleasure they are and were created."

## Predestination

Job 14:5: "Seeing his days are determined, the number of his months are with thee, thou hast appointed his bounds that he cannot pass."

Psalm 139:16: "Thine eyes did see my substance, yet being unperfect: and in thy book all my members were written, which in continuance were fashioned, when as yet there was none of them."

Jeremiah 15:2: "And it shall come to pass, if they say unto thee, Whither shall we go forth? then thou shalt tell them, Thus saith the Lord; Such as are for death, to death; and such as are for the sword, to the sword; and such as are for the famine, to the famine; and such as are for the captivity, to the captivity."

Daniel 4:35: "And all the inhabitants of the earth are reputed as nothing; and he doeth according to his will in the army of heaven, and among the inhabitants of the earth; and none can stay his hand, or say unto him, What doest thou?"

Luke 21:24: "And they shall fall by the edge of the sword, and shall be led captive into all nations: and Jerusalem shall be trodden down of the Gentiles, until the times of the Gentiles be fulfilled."

Ephesians 1:5: "Having predestinated us unto the adoption of children by Jesus Christ to himself, according to the good pleasure of his will."

## Election

Matthew 25:34: "Then shall the King say unto them on his right hand, Come, ye blessed of my Father, inherit the kingdom prepared for you from the foundation of the world."

John 17:6: "I have manifested thy name unto the men which thou gavest me out of the world: thine they were, and thou gavest them me; and they have kept thy word."

Acts 13:48: "And when the Gentiles heard this, they were glad, and glorified the word of the Lord: and as many as were ordained to eternal life believed."

Acts 18:9–10: "Then spake the Lord to Paul in the night by a vision, Be not afraid, but speak, and hold not thy peace: For I am with thee, and no man shall set on thee to hurt thee: for I have much people in this city."

Romans 9:23: "And that he might make known the riches of his glory on the vessels of mercy, which he had afore prepared unto glory."

1 Corinthians 2:7: "But we speak the wisdom of God in a mystery, even the hidden wisdom, which God ordained before the world unto our glory."

Ephesians 1:4: "According as he hath chosen us in him before the foundation of the world, that we should be holy and without blame before him in love."

2 Thessalonians 2:13: "But we are bound to give thanks alway to God for you, brethren beloved of the Lord, because God hath from the beginning chosen you to salvation through sanctification of the Spirit and belief of the truth."

2 Timothy 1:9: "Who hath saved us, and called us with an holy calling, not according to our works, but according to his own purpose and grace, which was given us in Christ Jesus before the world began."

Titus 1:2: "In hope of eternal life, which God, that cannot lie, promised before the world began."

*Reprobation*
Matthew 20:18–19: "Behold, we go up to Jerusalem; and the Son of man shall be betrayed unto the chief priests and unto the scribes, and they shall condemn him to death. And shall deliver him to the Gentiles to mock, and to scourge, and to crucify him: and the third day he shall rise again."

John 6:64: "But there are some of you that believe not. For Jesus knew from the beginning who they were that believed not, and who should betray him."

Acts 2:23: "Him, being delivered by the determinate counsel and foreknowledge of God, ye have taken, and by wicked hands have crucified and slain."

Acts 4:27–28: "For of a truth against thy holy child Jesus, whom thou hast anointed, both Herod, and Pontius Pilate, with the Gentiles, and the people of Israel, were gathered together, For to do whatsoever thy hand and thy counsel determined before to be done."

Romans 9:11–13: "For the children being not yet born, neither having done any good or evil, that the purpose of God according to election might stand, not of works, but of him that calleth; It was said unto her, The elder shall serve the younger. As it is written, Jacob have I loved but Esau have I hated."

1 Peter 2:8: "And a stone of stumbling, and a rock of offense, even to them which stumble at the word, being disobedient: whereunto also they were appointed."

Jude 4: "For there are certain men crept in unawares, who were before of old ordained to this condemnation, ungodly men, turning the grace of our God into lasciviousness, and denying the only Lord God, and our Lord Jesus Christ."

# Appendix 2

## The Westminster Confession and Larger Catechism Statements Concerning Predestination

### I. The Westminster Confession

*Of God's Eternal Decree*

1. God from all eternity did by the most wise and holy counsel of his own free will freely and unchangeably ordain whatsoever comes to pass: yet so as thereby neither is God the author of sin, nor is violence offered to the will of the creatures, nor is the liberty or contingency of second causes taken away, but rather established.

2. Although God knows whatsoever may or can come to pass upon all supposed conditions, yet hath he not decreed any thing because he foresaw it as future, or as that which would come to pass upon such conditions.

3. By the decree of God, for the manifestation of his glory, some men and angels are predestinated unto everlasting life, and others foreordained to everlasting death.

4. These angels and men, thus predestinated and foreordained, are particularly and unchangeably designed; and their number is so certain and definite that it cannot be either increased or diminished.

5. Those of mankind that are predestinated unto life, God, before the foundation of the world was laid, according to his eternal and immutable purpose, and the secret counsel and good pleasure of his will, hath chosen in Christ, unto everlasting glory, out of his free grace and love alone, without any foresight of faith or good works, or perseverance in either of them, or any other thing in the creature, as conditions, or causes moving him thereunto; and all to the

praise of his glorious grace.

6. As God hath appointed the elect unto glory, so hath he, by the eternal and most free purpose of his will, foreordained all the means thereunto. Wherefore they who are elected, being fallen in Adam, are redeemed by Christ; are effectually called unto faith in Christ by his Spirit working in due season; are justified, adopted, sanctified, and kept by his power through faith unto salvation. Neither are any other redeemed and kept by his power through faith unto salvation. Neither are any other redeemed by Christ, effectually called, justified, adopted, sanctified, and saved, but the elect only.

7. The rest of mankind God was pleased, according to the unsearchable counsel of his own will, whereby he extendeth or withholdest mercy as he pleaseth, for the glory of his sovereign power over his creatures, to pass by, and to ordain them to dishonor and wrath for their sin, to the praise of his glorious justice

8. The doctrine of this high mystery of predestination is to be handled with special prudence and care, that men attending the will of God revealed in his Word, and yielding obedience thereunto, may, from the certainty of their effectual vocation, be assured of their eternal election. So shall this doctrine afford matter of praise, reverence, and admiration of God; and of humility, diligence, and abundant consolation, to all that sincerely obey the gospel.

## Of Providence

1. God, the great Creator of all things, doth uphold, direct, dispose, and govern all creatures, actions, and things, from the greatest even to the least, by his most wise and holy providence, according to his infallible foreknowledge, and the free and immutable counsel of his own will, to the praise of the glory of his wisdom, power, justice, goodness, and mercy.

2. Although, in relation to the foreknowledge, and decree of God, the first cause, all things come to pass immutably

and infallibly, yet, by the same providence, he ordereth them to fall out according to the nature of second causes, either necessarily, freely, or contingently.

3. God, in his ordinary providence, maketh use of means, yet is free to work without, above, and against them, at his pleasure.

4. The Almighty power, unsearchable wisdom, and infinite goodness of God so far manifest themselves in his providence that it extendeth itself even to the first Fall and all other sins of angels and men, and that not by a bare permission, but such as hath joined with it a most wise and powerful bounding, and otherwise ordering and governing of them, in a manifold dispensation, to his own holy ends; yet so, as the sinfulness thereof proceedeth only from the creature, and not from God, who being most holy and righteous, neither is nor can be the author or approver of sin.

5 The most wise, righteous, and gracious God doth oftentimes leave for a season his own children to manifold temptations, and the corruption of their own hearts, to chastise them for their former sins, or to discover unto them the hidden strength of corruption and deceitfulness of their hearts, that they may be humbled; and to raise them to a more close and constant dependence for their support upon himself, and to make them more watchful against all future occasions of sin, and for sundry other just and holy ends.

6. As for those wicked and ungodly men, whom God as a righteous judge, for former sins, doth blind and harden, from them he not only withholdeth his grace, whereby they might have been enlightened in their understandings, and wrought upon in their hearts; but sometimes also withdraweth the gifts which they had, and exposeth them to such objects as their corruption makes occasion of sin; and withal, gives them over to their own lusts, the temptations of the world, and the power of Satan; whereby it comes to pass that they harden themselves, even under

those means which God useth for the softening of others.

7. As the providence of God doth, in general, reach to all creatures, so, after a most special manner, it taketh care of his Church, and disposeth all things to the good thereof.

## Of Free Will

1. God hath endued the will of man with that natural liberty, that it is neither forced, nor, by any absolute necessity of nature, determined to good or evil.

2. Man, in his state of innocency, had freedom and power to will and to do that which is good and well-pleasing to God; but yet mutably, so that he might fall from it.

3. Man, by his fall into a state of sin, hath wholly lost all ability of will to any spiritual good accompanying salvation; so as a natural man, being altogether averse from that good, and dead in sin, is not able, by his own strength, to convert himself, or to prepare himself thereunto.

4. When God converts a sinner, and translates him into the state of grace, he freeth him from his natural bondage under sin, and, by his grace alone, enables him freely to will and to do that which is spiritually good, yet so as that, by reason of his remaining corruption, he doth not perfectly, nor only, will that which is good, but doth also will that which is evil.

5. The will of man is made perfectly and immutably free to good alone, in the state of glory only.

## Of Effectual Calling

1. All those whom God hath predestinated unto life, and those only, he is pleased, in his appointed and accepted time, effectually to call, by his Word and Spirit, out of that state of sin and death, in which they are by nature, to grace and salvation by Jesus Christ; enlightening their minds spiritually and savingly, to understand the things of God; taking away their heart of stone, and giving unto them an heart of flesh; renewing their wills, and by his almighty power determining them to that which is good; and effec-

tually drawing them to Jesus Christ, yet so as they come most freely, being made willing by his grace.

2. This effectual call is of God's free and special grace alone, not from any thing at all foreseen in man, who is altogether passive therein, until, being quickened and renewed by the Holy Spirit, he is thereby enabled to answer this call, and to embrace the grace offered and conveyed in it.

3. Elect infants, dying in infancy, are regenerated and saved by Christ through the Spirit, who worketh when, and where, and how he pleaseth. So also are all other elect persons, who are incapable of being outwardly called by the ministry of the Word.

4. Others, not elected, although they may be called by the ministry of the Word, and may have some common operations of the Spirit, yet they never truly come to Christ, and therefore cannot be saved; much less can men, not professing the Christian religion, be saved in any other way whatsoever than by Christ, be they never so diligent to frame their lives according to the light of nature, and the law of that religion they do profess; and to assert and maintain that they may is without warrant of the Word of God.

## II. The Larger Catechism

*Q. 12. What are the decrees of God?*
A. God's decrees are the wise, free, and holy acts of the counsel of his will, whereby, from all eternity, he hath, for his own glory, unchangeably foreordained whatsoever comes to pass in time, especially concerning angels and men.

*Q. 13. What hath God especially decreed concerning angels and men?*
A. God, by an eternal and immutable decree, out of his mere love, for the praise of his glorious grace, to be manifested in due time, hath elected some angels to glory and in Christ

hath chosen some men to eternal life, and the means thereof; and also according to his sovereign power, and the unsearchable counsel of his own will (whereby he extendeth or withholdeth favor as he pleaseth), hath passed by, and foreordained the rest to dishonor and wrath, to be for their sin inflicted, to the praise of the glory of his justice.

*Q. 14. How doth God execute his decrees?*
A. God executeth his decrees in the works of creation and providence, according to his infallible foreknowledge and the free and immutable counsel of his own will.

*Q. 17. How did God create man?*
A. After God had made all other creatures, he created man, male and female; formed the body of the man of the dust of the ground, and the woman of the rib of the man; endued them with living, reasonable, and immortal souls; made them after his own image, in knowledge, righteousness, and holiness, having the law of God written in their hearts and power to fulfill it, with dominion over the creatures; yet subject to fall.

*Q. 18. What are God's works of providence?*
A. God's works of providence are his most holy, wise, and powerful preserving and governing all his creatures; ordering them, and all their actions, to his own glory.

*Q. 30. Doth God leave all mankind to perish in the estate of sin and misery?*
A. God doth not leave all men to perish in the estate of sin and misery, into which they fell by the breach of the first covenant, commonly called the covenant of works; but of his mere love and mercy delivereth his elect out of it, and bringeth them into an estate of salvation by the second covenant, commonly called the covenant of grace.

*Q. 31. With whom was the covenant of grace made?*

A. The covenant of grace was made with Christ as the second Adam, and in him with all the elect as his seed.

Q. 32. *How is the grace of God manifested in the second covenant?*
A. The grace of God is manifested in the second covenant, in that he freely provided and offereth to sinners a mediator, and life and salvation by him; and, requiring faith as the condition to interest them in him, promiseth and giveth his Holy Spirit to all his elect, to work in them that faith, with all other saving graces; and to enable them unto all holy obedience, as the evidence of the truth of their faith, and thankfulness to God, and as the way which he hath appointed them to salvation.

Q. 58. *How do we come to be made partakers of the benefits which Christ hath procured?*
A. We are made partakers of the benefits which Christ hath procured by the application of them unto us, which is the work especially of God the Holy Ghost.

Q. 59. *Who are made partakers of redemption through Christ?*
A. Redemption is certainly applied, and effectually communicated, to all those for whom Christ hath purchased it; who are in time by the Holy Ghost enabled to believe in Christ, according to the gospel.

Q. 67. *What is effectual calling?*
A. Effectual calling is the work of God's almighty power and grace, whereby (out of his free and especial love to his elect, and from nothing in them moving him thereunto) he doth in his accepted time invite and draw them to Jesus Christ, by his Word and Spirit; savingly enlightening their minds, renewing and powerfully determining their wills, so as they (although in themselves dead in sin) are hereby made willing and able freely to answer his call, and to accept and embrace the grace offered and conveyed therein.

*Q. 68. Are the elect only effectually called?*
A. All the elect, and they only, are effectually called; although others may be and often are outwardly called by the ministry of the Word, and have some common operations of the Spirit; who, for their willful neglect and contempt of the grace offered to them, being justly left in their unbelief, do never truly come to Jesus Christ.

*Q. 80. Can true believers be infallibly assured that they are in the estate of grace, and that they shall persevere therein unto salvation?*
A. Such as truly believe in Christ, and endeavor to walk in all good conscience before him, may, without extraordinary revelation, by faith grounded upon the truth of God's promises, and by the Spirit enabling them to discern in themselves those graces to which the promises of life are made, and bearing witness with their spirits that they are the children of God, be infallibly assured that they are in the estate of grace and shall persevere therein unto salvation.

*Q. 81 Are all true believers at all times assured of their present being in the estate of grace, and that they shall be saved?*
A. Assurance of grace and salvation not being of the essence of faith, true believers may wait long before they obtain it, and, after the enjoyment thereof, may have it weakened and intermitted, through manifold distempers, sins, temptations, and desertions; yet are they never left without such a presence and support of the Spirit of God as keeps them from sinking into utter despair.

# A

# Primer

# on

# Free Will

Dear reader, you have in your hands a booklet entitled *A Primer on Free Will*. I don't know you, but I know a good deal about you. One thing I know is that you did not pick up this book of your own free will. You have picked it up and have started to read it, and now continue to read it, because you must do so. There is absolutely no possibility, you being the kind of person you are, that you would not be reading this book at this time.

Still, you have not already put down the little book in indignation. If you had, you would not have read that sentence. A few of you may smilingly know how right I am. But some of you are angry because you think what I have said about you is foolish and absolutely false. You insist, "It was of my own free will that I picked up this book and am reading it now. And you, author, are not telling the truth when you say it was otherwise and that I actually have to be reading this at the present moment."

Then there are others of you who are simply puzzled by my statement. It sounds positively absurd to you, but you are puzzled, rather than being angry, because you think that there must be more here than meets the eye. You say to yourself, "The man has written a book that somebody believed ought to go into print. So, there must be some strain of sanity in the author that this thing is in fact in print." At the same time, it taxes your credulity to believe that the author is, after all, sane, because you are fully convinced that you have picked up this book and are reading it of your own free will. You strongly suspect that anyone who would say otherwise, if sane, can't be very intelligent. But, being puzzled, you continue to read in what you fear is a vain hope that some sense might come out of this whole business.

Then, as I say, there are those among you who smilingly know what I mean and how right it is. You agree with me instantly that you did not pick up this book of your own free will. You did it very much the way others who are either puzzled or angry did. But, you are neither puzzled nor angry. You recognize the truth of what I have said. You

know what I am getting at and what I am going to say, and
that it will become clear, even to those who may not have
agreed with me, that it's anything but a silly notion that
they didn't pick up this book of their own free will.

Now, I say to those who are doubtful, and especially to
those who are angry, please do not put down the book, but
hear me out. I shall try to prove my case.

I take it that when you say, "I picked up this book and
am reading it of my own free will," this is what you mean:
"Spontaneously, without anything forcing me to make this
choice, I did, of myself alone, arbitrarily if you please,
choose to pick up this book and read it." At least that is
what 95 percent of the persons who use that term, "free
will," mean by it. They mean their choices are free of any
factors in the background influencing them, let alone compelling them.

Applying that understanding of free will to your
choosing to read this book, it means that, of yourself alone,
simply because you chose to do so, you have picked up
this book and started to read. It includes the idea that no
desire on your part or on your spouse's part that you read
the book, or no idle time on your hands, which reading anything would help to fill, or no real, philosophical interest in
the subject, or no religious concern has in any way made it
necessary for you to pick up this book and read it. You
could never accept my original proposition that it was impossible for you not to read this book. "No," you say by
reply, "I could most certainly have chosen not to read it,
just as easily as I could have chosen what I did, in fact,
choose, to read the book and continue doing so (if my pa-
tience doesn't run out before I get to the next page)."

Let me show you that no matter how sincerely and
earnestly, and even passionately, you say what you have
just said, you are not speaking the truth about yourself.
That is actually not the way you came to make this choice
at all. I know it sounds presumptuous for me to be telling
you that I know more about you than you know about

yourself. I can almost hear you muttering in protest, "What kind of a man is this who thinks that he understands what goes on in my mind better than I do?" But if you will bear with me a little longer, I think we can see together that, even though you are closest to yourself, you aren't as well acquainted with yourself as this stranger who is speaking through these pages. I propose that what led you to the reading of the book is a series of considerations, such as the following: You have an interest in the subject of free will. It does happen to be the most discussed topic in all of philosophy and it's a part of religion. So it would be very surprising to find anybody who is totally uninterested in the subject of this book. Although I think I may safely assume that you had a native interest in the subject, and you have thought about it, and you have opinions on the subject, and, consequently, that the ideas that the author of this book may have would have interested you naturally, I feel certain, too, that you have some free time which allows you to read, and that you have no pressing duty that precludes the possibility of your reading this book at this time. I mention a factor like that because if there were other considerations that demanded your time more than this book does, they would have prevented you from choosing to read this book at this time. It's a negative consideration, but it is a reminder of the fact that the freedom you think you possess would not have operated arbitrarily if there had been other factors making it necessary for you to choose other than you did.

Getting back to positive considerations or motives, I mention this also: You may very well have had a little free time, and not knowing what to do, your eye fell upon this booklet with the interesting title, and you may have thought it a pleasant way to spend a few minutes or an hour or so. So, diversion from what you were or were not doing may have played a part in your choice also. Again, it could very well have been the case that someone else in your family had read this book or thought about it, found it sound, and thought it would interest you. So, perhaps, to satisfy them more than your own natural curiosity, you may have felt constrained to read this book at this time. Again, the fact that it is a small book could have appealed to you as well. If this thing were five or six hundred pages rather than 30 or so pages, you may very well have been turned off by the overwhelming amount of material before you. But you may well have said to yourself, "Ah, I can skim this book pretty quickly and don't have to spend too much time with it, and, obviously, it can't be too difficult, or the person would have written a more substantial and impressive volume than this little booklet." That consideration may have been a factor in your buying the book in the first place, because it's small and, therefore, inexpensive and doesn't involve a major investment of your money, either. Again, it is possible that you may know me, the author, personally. You may have heard me speak, or you may have read something else that I wrote that seemed congenial to you. Or, you find this subject of free will an entrancing subject, and you might think that I would take a viewpoint that would be congenial to you because you have favorably received other things that I have said or written. You may have been taken aback by my first statement, that you did not pick this up of your free will. But you may have been able to continue, in spite of that statement, because you have heard me say some sane things on other occasions, and you think that, maybe, if you stick with this book a little longer, I'll return to my right mind and say some sensible things before the book is finished.

You see what I mean. I don't have to go on mentioning all the motives that may conceivably have been in your mind when you chose to pick up this book. What I am saying is that motives like that not only figured in your choice to pick up this little book and continue reading it, but they actually *determined* your choice to do so. That is, those considerations outweighed any considerations to the contrary. For example, you may have been in a hurry; you may not have had time, and you may have preferred to do something else (maybe play ping-pong, or something like that). You would have resisted, momentarily at least, giving any time to this booklet. I am sure there were arguments against reading this book at this time. But I can conclude by the fact that you have chosen to read it, and are continuing to read it, that those considerations, however potent they were, were not as strong as the consideration that led you to pick up this book and read it. That being the case, since I know you are a rational person, you found it necessary to pick up this book and read it; you just had to choose to peruse these pages. It was impossible that you would have chosen not to read the book. It was absolutely necessary that you pick up the book, and it is absolutely necessary, as of this very moment, that you continue at this moment reading this book.

If you say to yourself, "Well, that does it! I am going to show this author that I am a free-willed individual, and I am going to close the pages right now and put it down," then, of course, I am going to go on talking without your listening until, later on, perhaps, your curiosity might overcome your indignation and you might resume reading. If and when you do, this is what you will see me writing here: You are continuing to read because the motives for reading it are outweighing those against it. If you did, at that particular time mentioned, put it down in indignation, it was because the reasons for putting it down outweighed other considerations to continue reading. And now that you are with us again, I know also that you did not resume reading of your own "free will." On the contrary, what has persuaded you to read these words right now is the overwhelming consideration that you want to read these words right now. If the arguments against it were prevailing, you would not be reading these words at this moment. You would be, as maybe you are about to be, slamming the book closed, throwing it down on the table, and going out to mow the grass, or shovel the snow, or play ping-pong.

You see what I am getting at, surely. Your choices, as a rational person, are always based on various considerations or motives that are before you at the time. Those motives have a certain weight with you, and the motives for and against reading a book are weighed in the balance of your mind; the motives which outweigh all others are what you, indeed, choose to follow. You, being a rational person, will always choose what seems to you to be the right thing, the wise thing, the advisable thing to do. If you chose not to do the right thing, the advisable thing, the thing that you are inclined to do, you would, of course, be insane. You would be choosing something which you didn't choose. You would find something preferable which you didn't prefer. But you, being a rational and sane person, choose something because it seems to you to be the right, proper, good, advantageous thing to do. If I came into your room right now and saw you reading this book, or any other book, or painting the wall, or cooking a meal, or chatting with your spouse, or playing with the kids, or whatever I saw you doing, I would know that it seemed good for you so to do. And what you were not doing at that particular moment, you were not doing because it did not seem good to do, or as good as the things you actually are doing at the moment. That is an awfully matter-of-fact observation. It's a simple description of sanity. When people don't choose according to what seems to them to be the thing to choose, we consider them to be demented. They are not acting as proper, rational human beings. Something has disturbed their minds, and they are not functioning in the normal human way of choosing according to what seems good.

Now, you see, that sort of thing—choosing regardless of considerations, or choosing without considerations, or choosing against considerations—is precisely what 95 percent of the people mean when they talk about "free will." What I have been describing they would call an *enslaved* will. When I say that they must choose according to what seems good to them, that very word "must" drives them up the wall. When I tell them that when they choose to read this book, they could not *not* choose to read this book, they feel that they are in bondage. They think that I have taken their freedom away from them when I say, "You must choose according to what seems good to you." It is the end of all freedom when it is said that they *must* do something, and they cannot do something else, and it is impossible for them to do such and such a thing, and it's necessary for them to do such a thing. That's where they raise their banner and say, "I believe in free will," and "when I choose, I choose freely of myself alone." But, you see, you don't choose freely in that sense, and you don't choose of your own free will alone in that sense. Your choice is based on intelligent considerations, if you're a rational human being. Intelligent considerations are what *determine* the behavior of rational human beings. As a rational human being, you don't have a freedom to deny those considerations. You must, necessarily, act according to what you think is the right way, the proper way, the good way, the advantageous way to act.

Notice, when we use the word "arbitrarily" we mean of the *arbitrium*, or will. We act willfully, not rationally. We act in spite of our rational judgment when we act willfully. We are not complimenting people when we say, "You are willful in your behavior." What we mean is that they are acting against their own better judgment. They are allowing willful, stubborn determination to override their judgment. You see, when we say a person is willful in that sense, we are censoring the person, we are not congratulating him.

But even that matter requires closer scrutiny. Even there, a person is not being willful or arbitrary in the sense in which the free willers mean the term. When someone is being willful or stubborn, what the critic means is that he is allowing his selfish prejudices to cloud his judgment and to give things he favors an undue weight in determining his choice. While he may not be using what the critic considers "wisdom" in his choices, he is still being determined by what he, in his stubborn way, considers the advisable thing to do. I hope you get this point. Even "the willful" person is not operating "willfully" or arbitrarily, without any reference to his judgment. He is still making a choice according to what seems good to him. But he is not weighing carefully what should seem good to him, in as detached and objective a manner as he ought to do. In other words, he is allowing some rather frothy considerations to have undue weight. Be that as it may, it's their weight as motives which determines his choice. Even when it is a foolish choice, it is still a choice based on motives. It may be the wrong kind of choice, but one thing it is not and cannot be (in a sane person) is a choice without any constraining motives or considerations. This normal person, good or bad, is always choosing according to what seems good to him. Maybe what seems good to him (in the opinion of the critic) ought not to seem good to him. There is a question about his very motives, but there is absolutely no doubt that the strongest motive triggers his will into motion. The will, even in that case, is not really, technically, willful or arbitrary, or acting independently of considerations. That type of thing can never happen in a rational human being. A rational human being never makes a choice of his mere, bare "free will."

So I put it to you, dear reader. Am I not right in saying that you did not pick up this book and are now reading it because of your free will? Am I not justified in saying that you had to pick up this book, and you now have to continue reading exactly where you are at this time? My only assumption is that you are a rational human being acting on your own choices without somebody literally thrusting the book in your hand, rigidly holding your eyes open, and turning the pages so that you must see them whether you want to or not. Apart from some such absurd limitation as that, am I not quite justified in saying that you have, of yourself, chosen to read because, everything considered, it seemed better to you to read than not to read; and, consequently, you were not "free" in your choice but were constrained by your own motives? And, is it not true that to talk about acting of your own free will without any considerations whatever being determinative is to talk irrationally about an insane person rather than rationally about a sane, normal human being? When a person chooses of his own free will without any reason whatever, that is a mark of insanity, not of humanity.

Now let me, hopefully, anticipate that I have made some sense for my silent readers. Let me, perhaps wistfully, believe that you are now saying, "Yes, I guess you do have a point there. When you put it that way, it is true that I have reasons for picking up this book, and those reasons prevailing, it is not rational, or normal, or human, or anything else, for me not to read it. If that's what you mean by your denial of free will, then I have to admit that denial is justified. I am *not* free in the sense of scot-free. I do *not* choose regardless of all considerations by some presumed power of a spontaneous generation of choices. Okay, I think I'm prepared to grant (even though I must admit that that's the way I had thought of choices) that my idea of free will does not stand up under analysis. However reluctantly, I think I must grant your point that I do not have that kind of free will, and I did not exercise that kind of free will when I picked up the book, nor do I exercise it now as I am reading the book.

"But now I have a problem to put to you, Mr. Author. If you are right, and I am inclined to think you are, what has become of my freedom? All my life I have been talking about freedom and fighting for it, contending for it, and insisting that I am willing to die for it, and here I am tamely admitting that I don't possess it! What have I been talking about all my life? Surely, there is some meaning to this term *free will* or *freedom*. But, what I am hearing so far is making me wonder if it exists at all."

Let me address that question. I put it in this form: Are our choices free, responsible, valid, even though inevitably, certainly, and necessarily in accord with the motives which seem good to us and are most powerfully before our minds? My reply is they are not free in that other sense (which is the common and unfortunate sense in which the term is usually used), but they are free in a couple of important senses. Our choices are free in the sense that they belong to us and not to somebody or something else. That is, it isn't my glands that determine my choice. It isn't my environment that makes me choose a certain way. It isn't my fellow human friends or enemies who necessitate my choosing a certain way. These choices are of me and of my will, and not somebody else's will. In a real sense, they are not even God's will, but mine. When I choose something, it isn't that God is choosing that something. The role He plays does not preclude my role as a choice-maker. So, while the word "free" may be a bit dubious here, it certainly is *my* choice. It is not imposed on me by something or somebody else.

Putting the matter positively, my choices are my will. I am conscious that I have chosen to pick up this book and read it. My wife's desire may have influenced me, but it was I who chose to read the book. God may have some role in this; I know He does. After all, He is my Creator and my Preserver. That much is certain, and obviously He has had something to do with everything. However, if I can rely on my consciousness, this is my choice and that cannot be denied. We must rely on our consciousness. If we could not rely on our consciousness, there would be nothing on which we could rely. We could not even rely on God's revelation of Himself to us without relying on our consciousness because it is by our consciousness that we become aware of His revelation to us. If we couldn't trust our awareness and our consciousness, we couldn't trust Him who reveals Himself through our consciousness. We are so built that that is the only means by which we can apprehend anything or anybody. So the fact that I am conscious of making my own choices, whatever may have been the considerations which led me to do so, persuades me that these are my choices and that I have made them in that sense freely. The motives that constrained me have seemed good to me.

Another consideration which shows the sense in which I am free and proves that I am free is the fact that I feel responsible for these choices. You say, "I have a problem with drink. And when I take a drink, which starts me on the road to drunkenness, I know very well that that's exactly what could happen, and in my case, almost certainly will happen. Consequently, precisely because I know that choice is my choice and am fully aware of the inevitably bad consequences that will follow it, I feel highly blameworthy. The very fact that I am conscious of blame when I make choices, and that I can't blame it on the alcohol or on the temptation of my friends, or on the loneliness which leads me to forget myself for awhile, shows that I am making these choices; otherwise, there would be no point to my feeling responsible for them and, in this case, ashamed of them."

Let's put the whole matter this way: Free will, in the sense of a will, or faculty, in us that produces our choices out of thin air, out of nothing, based on no controlling factors, is a will-o'-the-wisp. It's a nonentity. It makes no sense at all. We simply do not exercise our will that way. We do, as a matter of fact, choose, but we always have reason for choosing the way we actually do choose. We must get rid of that fanciful illusion, haunting so many people, that we have this phony kind of free will which, under examination, has no meaning whatsoever. On the other hand, there is a meaningful sense in which we make responsible choices. If you want to call them "free" choices in the sense of your personal choices, for which you are solely responsible and for which you alone are to be blamed or to be praised, then, of course, that is true. They are our choices, even though they are not "free" in the sense of uninfluenced and undetermined by considerations.

On the contrary, they are determined by influences and considerations which we find attractive or repulsive, as the case may be. And, obviously, we are good persons if we find good considerations attractive, and bad persons if we find bad considerations attractive. This would be the definition of a virtuous person: one who inclines to the virtuous. This would be the definition of a vicious or criminal character: a person who inclines to what is vicious or criminal.

If he is inclined to criminal acts, it is impossible for him not to choose criminal acts. But he is not irresponsibly in bondage, so that he can say, "I couldn't help it." He couldn't help it only because he was so wickedly disposed. The fact that he is disposed to criminality is the very definition of a criminal personality, not an excuse for it. The fact that being of such a disposition as that he could not find virtue attractive and could not find vice unattractive is his sin. You cannot say, "Since I find vice attractive I cannot resist vice and cannot be blamed for it." The point is, why do you find vice attractive? Don't you realize that you have to be a vicious person or you would not be disposed to viciousness?

Even your vicious acts, in themselves, wouldn't be vicious if they weren't coming from your vicious disposition. That is, if you did an act, a criminal act such as killing someone, it wouldn't be a criminal act if it were done accidentally. If you, for example, shot a person, honestly not knowing that the gun was loaded, you would not be a murderer, though the person would be just as dead as if you were. But you wouldn't be a murderer because you would not have had the murderous intention. You would not have had the vicious disposition. You would not have been criminally inclined. You could have been a virtuous person who, in this case, was careless and killed a person unintentionally. Our point is that there is no such thing as a vicious act considered in and of itself. An act has character only in terms of the person who perpetrates it. If he chooses it because he is inclined to it, then and only then is he a vicious person. What we are saying is that one cannot excuse himself for vicious deeds because he is a vicious person. That's the very locus of responsibility.

By the same token, the virtuous deed in itself does not exist. If I accidentally, for example, saved a person from being shot, I would not be a saint. If I happened to fall against a would-be murderer and knocked the pistol out of his hand, so that the victim was thereby spared, I wouldn't be considered a hero or a person who had done anything at all commendable in itself. It was a pure accident. I stumbled on the person and, fortunately for the victim, I knocked the gun out of the criminal's hand, so that the man whose life was spared was able to run away safely. It's not like risking my own life in order, deliberately, to prevent a crime and succeeding in doing it. If I did succeed, of course, the person would be no more saved than if I had saved him by the accident. However, I would have been, in that case, the perpetrator of a good deed because I was inclined and intending to do that deed. It didn't just happen without any respect to my choice.

So everything that we are really concerned about, by this will-o'-the wisp called "free will," is actually guaranteed to us in a proper conception of the will. That is, when we realize the will is our choice, according to our disposition, that's really all we are concerned about. It's not somebody else's choice; it is our choice. It's not according to something else; it's according to our own disposition. It can, therefore, be called our choice, and we can be praised for it or blamed for it, as the case may be. That is really all we are concerned about when we speak of our free will. So let us pull down that banner of free will, which is a false symbol of a non-existent entity, and raise the proper banner (call it *free agency*, or whatever you please) to indicate that *our* choices are *our* choices. Then we have accomplished what we are really concerned about. We are fighting for real principles under a proper banner and not for illusionary principles under a false banner.

"All right," you say, "I guess I can buy this, that the

general notion of a free will is an illusion. While I have in-
dulged that illusion for a long time, I am glad that I am
aware that it is an illusion, and I'll henceforth treat it as such
and have no further respect for this nonsensical idea about
something that does not exist.

"But where does all this lead us, with respect to the
things that really matter, such as our relationship to Jesus
Christ? After all, what we have been talking about so far
has had to do with trivia, like reading this book or not
reading this book, mowing the lawn or shoveling the snow,
or playing ping-pong. What about the things that matter
most, like our relationship to God and to Christ, and to
eternal life? Does this all mean that I don't have any 'free
will' in that area either? I am persuaded now that when I
picked up this book and continued to read it, I did not do so
of my free will, but of my will acting according to reasons.
But when I am confronted with Jesus Christ offering me
salvation through His blood and through His name, am I
not free to choose or refuse Him as I please? Do I not even
have a free will with respect to the gospel offer?"

Will you notice the two different ways in which you put
that question about your relationship to Christ? You ask,
"Am I not free to choose Him or reject Him? Do I not have
free will with respect to Him?" You see they are not identical questions. When you ask, "Am I not free to choose Him
or to reject Him," the answer is definitely that you are. It is
your decision to accept Him or reject Him. It is no one else's
decision at this particular point, not even God's decision. It
is your decision, as we have said before. But your second
way of putting the question is, "Is it not of my own free
will? " No, it is not of your own free will. We already have
shown that there is no such thing as a free will. That's a
will-o'-the-wisp. You never make choices without reasons,
not as a responsible or a rational person. And if you don't
make choices without reasons or considerations, even in a
trivial thing such as reading this little book, you certainly
are not going to make choices without reasons in the most

momentous choice you will ever have to make, namely about your relationship with Jesus Christ. If it's nonsense in these small matters, it's got to be absolute absurdity in the big matters.

How then does the will actually work? Well, it's quite obvious, is it not? When Jesus Christ puts the question to you, "Whom do you say that I, the Son of Man, am?" He's putting the question to you. He's asking you what your verdict is about Him. He gives you all the evidence. You're a rational person who can ponder the evidence and see whether, indeed, it does justify His own claim to being the divine Son of God. You should, therefore, answer Him when you have pondered the evidence and weighed it properly and say, "Indeed, Thou art the Christ, the Son of the living God." When you say that, and the Son of God says to you, "Come unto me all you that labor and are heavy laden and I will give you rest," you should come running at His invitation. Indeed, you will if you find that invitation attractive. Likewise, if you find it unattractive, you will not come running. If you find it repulsive, you will be repelled by it. It's impossible that you will come to Him when you are disposed not to come to Him. It's impossible that you will choose Him when you do not choose Him. You will not prefer Him when you do not prefer Him. On the other hand, if He is attractive to you, you will most certainly be attracted by Him. It is not possible that you will run *from* Him when you are attracted *to* Him, any more than it's possible for you to run *to* Him when you are repelled *by* Him.

All we have said about this little thing of reading this book applies to the big things about coming to or fleeing from the Lord Jesus Christ. You will choose according to what seems good to you. If He is, as Isaiah puts it, one from whom you hide your face, that's a reflection of the way you actually feel about Him. He is repulsive to you, you are ashamed of Him, and His gospel insults you. So you turn away from Him. On the other hand, if He's the fairest

among ten thousand, the bright and morning star, the
Savior of your soul, then, of course, nothing will keep you
from Him. You are a man of violence who takes the kingdom of Heaven by force. You have found the pearl of great
price. You sell everything for Him whom you are seeking.

It's all as simple and wonderful as that. Nothing at all
mysterious about it. In the great things as well as the small
things you choose according to what seems good to you,
and your choice is going to determine whether you are a
good or bad person. If the perfect Son of God is unattractive
to you, then obviously you are an unattractive person. If
the perfect Son of God is irresistible to you, then you are a
good person, because a good person, by definition, is a person who is inclined to the good, and the good is Jesus
Christ, the divine and perfect Son of God. If you are repelled
by Him, you are a bad person because you are repelled by
the quintessence of the good. What attracts you must be
the rejection of what is good. A person who is attracted by
that which is evil and repelled by that which is good is an
evil person.

But I hear you asking at this point, "Well, if I am a
wicked person, then I can't come to Christ."

And I say, "Yes, that is true. If you are a wicked person,
you cannot come because you will not come. You find
Christ repulsive rather than attractive. That's what being a
wicked person means."

But you say, "Even if I wanted to come to Christ, being
a sinful person, I couldn't come to Him."

No, I didn't say that even if you wanted to come to Him,
you couldn't come to Him. I say exactly the opposite. If you
want to come to Him, nothing could keep you from Him.
You are then a person who is virtuous and is inclined to the
good, and you most certainly can come to Him; you are ir-
resistibly drawn to Him. If you do want to come to Him,
then you are no longer the wicked person you were talking
about. A wicked person is a person who doesn't want to
come to Christ. He wants to flee from Christ. He is not at-

tracted by Christ. He is repelled by Christ.

When you talk about being a wicked person who wants to come to Christ, you are talking about a condition contrary to fact. A wicked person does not want to come to Christ; otherwise, he would not be a wicked person. If he wants to come to Christ, he is a virtuous person. He is a new creature. He is a person who loves righteousness and truth. You always choose according to what seems good to you or what you want to choose, and, if you want to choose Christ, you most certainly can choose Christ. Indeed, you have chosen Christ.

"Okay, I get that," you say. "If I want to come to Christ, I can come to Christ, and I have already come to Christ; is that what you are saying?" Yes, that is what I am saying.

"If, on the other hand, I am a sinner who loves sin, I will not find Christ attractive, and, consequently, I will not be able to come to Him, because I will not find Him at all attractive?" Yes, that is correct.

"And you say that I am to blame for that because I shouldn't find a virtuous person unattractive?" You are right again. You should not find virtue unattractive. It proves you to be a vicious person, if you are repelled by virtue, just as it proves you to be a virtuous person if you are attracted by virtue.

"Then," you continue, "in what sense am I free?" You are free in this sense, that if and when you find Jesus Christ attractive, you may and do, indeed, come to Him. If you are in a state where you don't find Him attractive, you freely reject Him—that is, in and of yourself because you are the type of person you are; namely, one who loves the evil and hates the good.

Suppose we continue this in direct dialogue. I will represent the Christian and you be the inquirer:

I: I think I get the point clearly enough. I, in my present sinful state, am not attracted by Christ, but on the contrary, repelled. So, even though He invites me to come to

Him and be saved from my sins, I cannot come. That is, I simply will never choose to come to him while I am not inclined to come to Him. And, if I understand you correctly, I am to blame for being disinclined. My inability to respond to His invitation shows me to be a sinner. As you say, a sinner (by definition) is a person who hates what is good and loves what is bad. And I show by my preference to flee from Christ that I am a sinful person. I can't excuse myself because of what actually accuses me. The very fact that I am so set against Christ that I can't possibly come to Him is the very thing which condemns me.

C: Yes, that is what (I believe) the Bible teaches very clearly.

I: Well, then, I don't have a free will. It is freely bound to sin. I choose of myself alone, not forced by any other factors, but I always choose what is wrong because that is the kind of person I am. That is, I freely choose, to be sure, but I always freely choose what is evil, and, being of the kind of disposition I am, I always will. Regardless of the promises or threatenings of Jesus Christ, I will always choose what is against His will. The thing I want to know is what in the world do I do in a situation such as this?

C: Well, if you recognize, as apparently you do, that you are a sinner, that in the depth of your heart you love sin and hate virtue and, therefore, you love your own selfish ways and hate Jesus Christ—if you recognize all that, then what you should do is confess to God that you are a sinner and ask Him to forgive you. That is precisely what Christ is calling upon you to do. Repent and believe the gospel. Now, if you are persuaded that, indeed, you are a sinner and that your only hope is salvation by grace, why don't you instead of merely recognizing that (as you apparently do) confess it to God and ask Him to give you what He promised He will if you but ask for it?

I: The problem is that I love my sins, as you say. That is what being a sinner means. I do love sin. I am bent toward sin. I always choose sin. I always will choose sin. Now you are asking me to hate sin, to repent of sin, to turn away from sin. But that is exactly what I love and am not at all disposed to turn away from.

C: You asked me what to do. If you recognize that you are a sinner, then why don't you confess it to God? Ask Him for forgiveness.

I: This is rather strange advice, coming for you. You are virtually asking me, or telling me, to ask God to forgive me for something I love and do not want to give up. As we both agree, I love sin. Are you advising me to tell God that I hate sin?

C: No, I am not advising you to tell God you hate sin, when you love sin. That would be a lie and hypocrisy. I would never advise you to lie and play the hypocrite. On the contrary, I would advise you not to lie or be hypocritical. What I did say was, if you do recognize that you are a sinner and that you need salvation, why don't you say that to God?

I: That's a good question. Why don't I confess to God what I admit to you? That's a very good question. Why do I not confess it to God and receive the forgiveness He has promised? It doesn't make any sense, does it? Why in the world would I admit to you that I am a sinner and not acknowledge it to God?

C: That's exactly what I'm asking you.

I: You must know the answer better than I do. But, I can see that you are not going to give me the answer, but prod me into producing the answer myself. Is that it?

C: That's precisely so. I ask you once again, why do you acknowledge to me, or say to me, that you are a sinner and not confess to God the same thing and ask Him for His pardon?

I: Once again I realize that you are better acquainted with me than I am with myself. I guess the answer is this, isn't it, that I don't really believe that I am a sinner? Because if I really believed it, I would, indeed, go immediately to the foot of the cross, which I am not at all disposed to do! I should be asking for forgiveness of this sin. So, in spite of my saying to you that I admit that I am a sinner, I don't really believe what I am saying. Is that it?

C: That seems to be the case, doesn't it?

I: Let me go over again why I say that I believe I am a sinner. I believe the Bible is the revelation of God. I believe it teaches that all of us, outside of Christ, are sinners. So, since I know I am out of Christ, I draw the conclusion that I am a sinner. I think I believe those things. Yet, you are virtually saying to me that I don't believe them. Or I would be on my knees at the foot of the cross. I can't help but think you are right about that matter. It looks as if I believe and yet don't believe.

What is my situation? I am not asking that as a question of anybody except of myself right now. But I am asking myself what is the truth about me and my beliefs in the doctrine of sin as applied to me? I simply must not believe it, because I don't have any genuine desire to ask God for the forgiveness of it. That has to be a fixed principle with me.

But, then, I ask myself the question, What is this belief I have in the Bible and the conviction I have that it teaches sin and that applies to me? I really do believe that! Yet my actions show that I don't believe that! How is this possible? If I really believed the doctrine I would feel it, and I would actually be acting according to it. But I don't *feel* it. That's the reason I am not acting according to it. My mind is saying that the authoritative Word of God teaches that I am a sinner. I don't *really* believe either that the Bible is authoritative or that it teaches that I am a sinner. When I ask myself the question, What do I think about the authority of the Bible?, I feel definitely convinced of that point, but I guess what I am hoping here is that it is not authoritative everywhere. I just can't quite believe that we are the enslaved sinners it says we are. There are other things in it which seem to be very congenial, but as I reflect on my general appraisal of the Bible, I am beginning to realize that I am not constrained by the authority of the Bible; only certain aspects of the Bible. If I really believed the Bible's authority, I would believe everything it teaches, and it is obvious that I do not.

C: Keep on going.

I: So I am learning the hard way that, in spite of my previous avowals, I really am not convinced of the total authority of the Bible. In fact, I am not really convinced of *anything* it says. It cuts against the grain of my preferred thinking. That's the reason I don't accept the doctrine (even though I have a sneaking suspicion that the Bible teaches it) of sin. I wouldn't dare say a thing like that if I thought I was contradicting God. So I am realizing slowly that I really don't believe that the Bible is the Word of God. And I am thinking and hoping that what it teaches is in error.

C: It would seem so.

I: Furthermore, I realize, too, that I am not sure that I have to believe that the Bible does teach uniformly the doctrine of sin. I have read books in my life, and I guess they have reached me more than I realize. They have denied that the doctrine of depravity, universal sinfulness, and such things are indeed biblical doctrines. I know that Judaism, for example, which professes to believe in the Old Testament doesn't find the doctrine of the fall and universal depravity, and the hopelessness of men before God. I guess I am hoping it is right. I know there are Christian teachers who construe the New Testament the same way. I guess I have been hoping that they, too, are right. When it comes right down to where I cast my vote, I guess in spite of my earlier superficial thinking, my vote is with those who interpret the Bible that way. In the last analysis, I don't accept the absolute authority of the Bible; and even if I did, I wouldn't admit that it teaches this awful doctrine of sin and slavery. So, it all adds up to this: I don't really believe I am a sinner. I have been saying that, but the fact that I am not down on my knees is the real evidence. This has led me to reexamine my thinking and realize what my failure to bow proves. I don't really believe that I am a sinner! Where do we go from here?

C: Well, I would say that we go back to square one. If you are willing to listen, I will try to persuade you that the Bible is the absolute Word of God; and, secondly, that it teaches the doctrine of your sinfulness. Where shall we start?

I: We can't go back to square one. I know full well that you have far better arguments for the authority of the Bible than I can ever offer against it. We have gone over this before. This is the reason I have been saying all along that I do believe in the authority of the Bible. Because when I talk with people who are knowledgeable about the matter, they answer my objections, and they mount so many defenses of the doctrine of inspiration to which I can't possibly really respond, that I have to admit that the case is closed. I do know that the Bible is the Word of God.

C: Well, then, let's go on to its teaching about sin. Let me attempt to prove to you that the authoritative Word of God teaches that this is a fallen race and that you, as a member of it, are full of sin.

I: Here again, I admit that is unnecessary. We have been all over this before. You have established, time and time again, that the authoritative Word of God does teach that there's none good, no, not one, and that I am among those whose thoughts and intents of heart are only evil continually. I have to admit that this is the doctrine which is taught and that, therefore, I know that I am a sinner convicted by the Word of God. Where does that leave us now?

C: It leaves us with a question. Why are you not on your knees asking God to forgive you? When I put that question to you before, you analyzed your thought and realized that you didn't really believe that the Bible is the Word of God and that it does teach, indeed, that you are a sinner. When we went through that analysis, you came to the conclusion you really do believe the Bible is the Word of God and that you are a sinner. So that route of escape is blocked. You cannot account for your not being on your knees now because of the fact that you doubt the authority of the Word of God, or because you doubt that you are a sinner. What excuse do you have then for not being on your knees? Why are you not asking God to forgive you for your sins? You know that you are a sinner. Why are you not repenting?

I: I give up. Why am I not on my knees? I have to admit, once again, if you can answer that question, you know me better than I know myself. Tell me, Christian, why, with the convictions I have, am I not on my knees asking God for the forgiveness of my sins?

C: I would say that there is never a real discrepancy between what a man really thinks and what he actually chooses. In spite of the fact that you do think that I have satisfied you and all your objections against the authority of

the Bible and its teaching on sin, you, in your heart, are still
not persuaded. You still at least *hope* that the Bible is not
authoritative and *hope* that if it is, it does not teach this doctrine. You don't want to express that hope because you
know I will refute it and you will have nothing to say in defense of it. But you, nevertheless, are hugging it to your bosom, and you are not about to part with it. Consequently,
you are not willing to enter into a free debate on the matter
because you know it would lead you to where you are not
willing to go.

I: Reluctant as I am, I admit the truth of your accusation.
What you say is precisely true. My mind consents to what
I find repulsive; namely, that the Bible is the Word of God
and it points me out as a sinner. I don't like to admit that,
but I cannot deny it. As you say, hidden in my bosom
somewhere, I have this deep desire, without any reasons
whatever, just a sheer preference for what is attractive to
me; namely, to continue in my sins rather than give them
up.

C: I am afraid you do know yourself now.

I: Let me see now if I understand my predicament.
However reluctant I am to admit it, I do know, at least with
my conscious intelligence, that I am a sinner under the
judgment of God. Perhaps, in my deepest heart, I don't really admit that. I can't actually face it, as we say. I know it's
true, but I won't even admit to myself that it is actually
true, because it is so very damning. I keep hoping against
hope that what I know to be true is not true. That is, that I
am a sinner and because I am a sinner I find the invitation
of Jesus Christ to be the Savior from my sins actually repugnant rather than inviting. I am a sinner, and I know I
am a sinner, and as such, I need a Savior.
  Yet, because I am a sinner I really love my sin and,
therefore, hate a person who would separate me from it,

which is precisely what Christ intends to do—to separate me from the guilt of it, and from the power of it, and from the practice of it. And that practice is what I am not willing to be separated from. I wouldn't mind being free from the guilt of it and maybe even, in a sense, from the power of it. But, I certainly refuse to give up the practice of it because this is what I really love.

This is where I am. And Christ is asking me to "deny *myself*"—not deny this, that, or the other thing, but deny *me*. As long as I love myself, I'm not going to deny myself. If Christ insists that I do, then I am going to deny Him. I am going to reject Him. That's going to be the status of affairs and that is, indeed, where I am at the moment. Is that right?

C: I think so, and do you see what all this has to do with free will?

I: What does all this have to do with my free will? It just shows that I don't have any so-called free will! Doesn't it? If I had such a power as that, I might conceivably come to Jesus Christ by a sheer act of the will in spite of my absolute slavish love of the sin which Christ requires me to leave. But sin has a fatal grip on me. I love it so much I will not part with it. I am proving that my so-called free will, my so-called power of "contrary choice," simply does not exist. As long as I love sin, and only sin, I am simply not going to part with it. There is literally no power in me, no inclination, no desire in me to leave my sins. As long as that is the case, I literally cannot leave my sins. This is all my choice. I realize that I am the one who finds sin attractive. I am the one who chooses to remain with my sins. I am the one who chooses to reject Jesus Christ (precisely because He would be the Savior from my sins). I simply don't want (will) to be saved from my sins! I don't want (will) to be rescued from my filth! I don't want (will) to be separated from the evil which I hold to my bosom!

lute slavish love of the sin which Christ requires me to leave. But sin has a fatal grip on me. I love it so much I will not part with it. I am proving that my so-called free will, my so-called power of "contrary choice," simply does not exist. As long as I love sin, and only sin, I am simply not going to part with it. There is literally no power in me, no inclination, no desire in me to leave my sins. As long as that is the case, I literally cannot leave my sins. This is all my choice. I realize that I am the one who finds sin attractive. I am the one who chooses to remain with my sins. I am the one who chooses to reject Jesus Christ (precisely because He would be the Savior from my sins). I simply don't want (will) to be saved from my sins! I don't want (will) to be rescued from my filth! I don't want (will) to be separated from the evil which I hold to my bosom!
C: Does this bondage make you feel free of guilt?

I: So far from finding myself innocent because I am unable to leave my sins I realize my inability to leave my sins shows how sinful, how guilty, I am. The only reason I can't leave my sins is that I love them. *I* love them, not somebody else or something else, or some decree. I love my sin, and as long as I love my sin I am going to choose to stay with my sin, and I am going to choose to reject anyone who would separate me from my sin. That is *my* choice. I am responsible for it and no one else. I admit, in my head at least, that I am fully to blame, and that the wrath which the Bible threatens me with is indeed deserved. I can't be surprised if it does come upon me. I am afraid it will!

Is that, Mr. Christian, a true statement about me? Tell me, do I now know myself?

C: I would say that you now know yourself.

I: The I whom I now know is not a very nice person, is he?

sinner and cleave to my sin and reject my Savior I can't anticipate anything except the impending wrath of God. Didn't you say that?

C: Yes, I said that, and I say that. If you *remain* as you now are, as you yourself say you are, you are in imminent danger of the eternal wrath of God which is, even now, upon you and will remain forever if you are not changed from your present condition.

I: That's what I thought you were saying all along. That's the reason I am so surprised that you now say there is *hope* for me. What possible hope can there be for such a person as I am?

C: Let me say this emphatically—that hope doesn't grow out of any imaginary free will. I think we are both satisfied now that free will does not exist. You do not have some mysterious faculty in your heart somewhere called free will, which *at will* can produce a love for Christ that is not there at the present time.

I: I see that very plainly, but what I don't see is what hope there is for me. Won't all my choices proceed from that sinful inclination?

C: That is true. I am glad you recognize that now. As long as you are the kind of person you say you are, you will make a sinful choice. You will not be saved by your activities. And yet, there are certain activities which promise some hope, great hope, for you.

I: Tell me more, I can hardly believe my ears.

C: Well, look, for one thing, you know the Bible, and you remember the statement, "Faith comes by hearing"?

I: Yes, I remember that passage very well, but I thought you said that I won't listen. How is faith ever going to come by hearing if a person won't hear?

C: That's keen thinking on your part. It is a pleasure to work with a person who thinks so clearly and so honestly about himself. It is perfectly true that faith comes by hearing, and if you will not hear, you are not going to have faith. What the passage means is this: that when faith comes (if it comes) it will come by hearing the Word of the gospel. You can listen! You hear the Word every time you read the Bible, every time you hear an evangelical sermon. In this whole dialogue you have been hearing it constantly from me, and you have been saying it sometimes yourself. In that sense of the word you know what the gospel is, you hear what the offer is. You don't yet hear the Shepherd calling you by name. This is what the theologians call the "inner call." That you do not hear yet. But the "outer call" you have heard, and do hear, and even now are hearing.

I: Yes, I understand that. But, as you say, that's not the call that saves. It's the inner calling, which I do not have. So what good will this outer call do me, unless I hear the Shepherd call me by name?

C: Well, the Scripture also teaches this, that you never do receive the inner call without first of all having the outer call. "Many are called but few are chosen," says Jesus. But the few who are chosen are first of all called. In other words, not everybody who is called outwardly is called inwardly; but, everyone who is called inwardly is first called outwardly. You see the point?

I: Not quite. Explain further, please.

C: What I am saying here is that you can and do hear the gospel and you hear it very clearly. You are at least willing to listen to the outer call. The more you hear it, the greater the possibility, presumably, of your hearing the inner call also. As I say, you never hear the inner call without listening to the outer call. Manifestly, the more you listen, seriously, desperately, if you please, to the outer call of Christ, the greater the possibility that you will hear His voice calling you by name. When you do, you will come running at His call!

I: I see your point. As long as I do hear and am willing to hear the gospel, not only through my ears, but through my eyes, and so on, the more possibility exists that I may yet hear the Shepherd calling me by name. But I still have a problem.

C: What is the problem?

I: How can I possibly hear this inner call if, as you say, when I hear Jesus, I turn Him off. I don't want to hear this inner call. That's a call that separates me from my sins. I have already confessed myself that I will never be parted willingly from them!

C: Do you not see that, if that inner voice comes calling you by name, you will hear the Shepherd calling you, and you will be glad to come? Don't you see that when you hear that inner voice you will be another person?

I: What do you mean by that?

C: In your present condition, you don't welcome the voice of Jesus at all. It's repugnant to you. You turn away from it even as you listen to it. When we talk about hearing the inner call, you see, that's different. When you hear that voice, it is with the heart, not merely with the ear. You are attracted by it, and what would that mean except that you are a new person? You then are not the same person you at this moment are—the person who rejects the call of Christ and does not want to hear the call of Christ. But, when you actually, with the heart, hear the call of Jesus calling you by name, you will come running at that bidding. Then you will be a new creature.

I: Oh, I see. That's just another word for my conversion.

C: Essentially.

I: In other words, if I continue to listen to the outer call of the gospel, through reading the Word, through pondering its meaning, through hearing its preaching, and so on, it may please God to open my heart and to change me from the sinner I now am to a person who hates sin and loves the Savior from sin. Is that what you are saying?

C: That is exactly what I am saying. That may happen to you, and the more you listen, with your outer ear, as it were, the more likely it is that it will happen. That's what I mean by saying there is great hope for you, my friend, not as you now are, but that you may be changed by divine grace from what you now are to what you ought to be.

I: But I have a problem even here.

C: What is that?

I: I don't even want to hear the gospel now. It's repugnant to me as it is. As you say, it calls me out of my sins to the Savior for salvation. As we both know, I don't want to be called from my sins, and I don't want to come to Christ! So how can I willingly listen to His Word when I now hate it?

C: Again, a very fine penetrating question on your part. If I may say so, in passing, if you ever are converted, as I hope to God will be His pleasure, you certainly will know what has taken place! You will, by divine grace, be a wonderful witness because you do understand so very clearly what the transactions of grace actually are. But to come to your question, how does a person willingly listen to something which he hates? The answer to that is fairly simple. How does a person come to take medicine which he hates? He takes it because he believes it may do him good. In other words, he doesn't take it because he likes it. He takes it in spite of his distaste because it may have a good effect; it may actually help his ailment, whatever that may be. It's bitter medicine, perhaps, but nevertheless he chooses it with all its bitterness because of the good which he hopes to get by it.

I: You are saying that I may listen to a word that I find bitter, indeed, because it may actually do me real, saving good?

C: Yes, that's what I mean. Not only that. If you are ever going to receive the good which you need (the saving grace of God), this is the way it is going to come. The situation is very much like the medical situation where you are taking a medicine that you don't know will help you, but you know so well that if it doesn't help you, nothing else will, and that it may help you. So, no matter how bitter it may be, you will certainly take it under those circumstances. So the gospel is for you, at this time, a bitter pill. Undoubtedly, you detest it; nevertheless, you know your only hope is there. Consequently, in this mere hope you do listen to the gospel.

I: But wouldn't I be hypocritical in pretending to be interested in something that really disinterests me and alienates me?

C: You would be if you *pretended!* You are perfectly right: You would be a liar if you said that you liked hearing the gospel. You hate it. It's not going to help your cause with

God to provoke Him with lies. But, you don't have to lie about the matter. You should, as a matter of fact, tell the truth to God—that you hate Him; you hate His son, Jesus; and you love the sins from which they are trying to separate you. But at the same time, you are miserable, and you know you are in danger of far greater misery. Out of a mere calculated self-interest, and not because of any love of the gospel, you are listening to the gospel.

I: Isn't that a sinful thing to say to God?

C: Admittedly—a very sinful deed on your part. You are not pretending that it's a virtuous deed. The point is that it is less offensive than sinfully *not* listening to the gospel. After all, God has called on all men everywhere to repent, as you know from the Bible. You don't have it in your heart to repent. But, if you are ever going to get it in your heart to repent, that gift is going to come through the hearing of the Word. Consequently, in listening to that Word (even though you do so merely out of self-interest and without any real love for the Word at all) you may be saved. That is certainly far less objectionable to God than spurning His Word, disregarding His Word, refusing to read His Word, never attending the preaching of His Word. You are a sinner, in any case. But you are now doing something outwardly, which is in accord with the divine command, even though it is not in the spirit of the divine command, which is to love God with all your heart, soul, mind, and strength. Still, you are not pretending hypocritically that it is so. You are simply putting yourself where God will work if the sovereign God chooses to work savingly.

I: This is a pretty refined form of selfishness, is it not?

C: Yes, it is. It is a form of selfishness, if you want to put it that way. You are doing it only out of self-interest. You don't have any concern really for the glory of God, which is the only thing you ought to be concerned with. All I can say is it is less selfish than disregarding God outright, and trampling under foot His Word. I am glad we are getting this point very clearly. You won't be under any temptation, if you continue to listen to the Word, of thinking that kind of hearing has any merit in it. You know full well you are doing it only out of self-interest. You are not going to provoke God further by pretending piety, which is not there. You are just simply putting yourself where God may be pleased to work, and you are doing that out of a feeling of misery. Even while you love your sins and are not parting from them, you are aware of the fact that they are going to ruin you eternally. You don't want to be ruined eternally. You are putting yourself in a place where you might be given a new heart and where you might be saved from everlasting damnation. That is selfishness; but, it is not as aggravated and provoking as the kind of selfishness which would be a lazy indulgence in your sins—with no concern whatsoever to put yourself where God may be working. Manifestly, that is far more obnoxious to God than doing what I am advising you to do. At the same time, it does not in any way contribute to your goodness. You are still a sinner adding to the number of sins everyday that you read your Bible and listen to preaching, and are in the sphere of salvation without being converted.

I: Thank you, Mr. Christian. This is a great hope, I admit, but you have spelled out very plainly that there is no piety in me; there is no virtue in me; and I have no reason to praise myself that I have suddenly become a good person just because I am doing some good things. At the same time, I would like to ask what this has to do with this question of free will. If God converts me, does He give me a free will? Is that where the free will really comes into being, if it comes at all? We have already seen that (as I am at the present time, and as most people are in the present condition) I don't have anything that meets the definition of free will. If and when we become converted, are we given a free will? Do only Christians have a free will? Is that the point of the whole matter?

C: No, that is not the situation at all. We have shown that there is no meaning to the concept of free will. There isn't any in God, or the angels, or the devils, or man in heaven or in hell. The concept is just a meaningless statement. We simply don't make choices without motives that determine them. We always have an inclination toward something when we express a choice. It doesn't make any difference whether we are unregenerate as you are at this time, or whether we are regenerate persons; our choices are always according to what seems good to us, and the strongest motives always determine our choices.

I: What can I hope will happen to me with respect to my will, if I am by divine grace converted?

C: You see, what will happen is this: You will be given a new heart, a new disposition, a new inclination. You will be made a new creature, other than what you are at the present time in your fallen condition.

I: What does that mean?

C: What it means is that instead of being the type of person you now are, finding only the evil attractive and virtue repulsive, you will be a new person, made over again. As Christ would say, born again. You will love virtue and hate vice.

I: I think I see what you mean. Because I will be made over again and have this new heart or disposition, then the motives which will appeal to me will be different motives than appeal to me at the present moment. As you put it, I will find virtue attractive. If I do find it attractive, then, of course,

I will freely, naturally, choose it. I can almost hear you say that it will be impossible for me to refuse virtue as it is now impossible for me to refuse vice. My heart would be fixed on virtue then as it is now fixed on vice.

C: Exactly! Your will will be no freer after your conversion than now. Your will will still be the same type of faculty it presently is. The mind will still choose what seems good to it. But the mind will now choose virtue, because virtue now seems good to you. Theologians call this experience "irresistible grace." A person isn't drawn against his will. It isn't irresistible in the sense that a person is drawn *against* his will. It is irresistible in the sense that the person is a new person, and it's as *natural* for him to come to virtue as it is for an eagle to fly. That's his new nature. No person acts contrary to his nature. Virtue is attractive in the sense that it is natural to the person in that condition. That's the reason Christ says that for that to happen, nothing less than a born-again experience must occur. "That which is flesh is flesh and that which is spirit is spirit." What He means by that is as long as yours is a fleshly nature you will, naturally, chose your fleshly, sinful goals. If you are born of His Spirit, you will naturally choose the goals of the Spirit. It will really be irresistible. It will be impossible for you to reject virtue utterly. It will be impossible for you to love vice utterly, if and when God pleases and gives you a new heart.

I: So, no free will. I understand that. My will will choose what is right because my heart will be inclined in that direction. That's what you are saying, and that's the kind of will we should have—one that inclines to Christ and virtue.

C: Yes, the great theologian Augustine once said that we have a "free will" (in the sense of unforced will) before we are converted. He meant what we are talking about here—choice according to one's own inclination. After conversion, he said, we have a "freed will." I don't exactly like his language because it doesn't get clear of this confusing phraseology about a "free will," but you see what he means. You will be "freed," in the sense of liberated from sin, because you have a new heart. You're always free. As a sinner you are free. In heaven or hell you are free, in the sense that you make choices according to what seems good to you. But when those choices are always the choices of evil, then of course you are in a bondage to the evil consequences of those evil choices. As long as you make those evil choices, there is no such thing as escaping the inevitable punishment which follows. This is what our Lord meant when he said, "He who commits sins is the slave of sin" (John 8:34). Luther's greatest work was *The Bondage of the Will*. But when you have a new heart from above, when you are born from above, when you are born by the Spirit, then you are, in a really wonderful sense, freed. Then you really choose the good because the good is naturally attractive to your new heart. That is all that Augustine, Luther, and our Lord Jesus Christ Himself meant.

So may God bless you, my dear friend. I urge you to continue to seek the Lord while He may be found. There is great hope that as you do that, He will be pleased to visit you with saving grace.

I: Please pray for me, my Christian friend, that I may be given a new heart.

C; I most certainly will beseech the sovereign God constantly to give you the new heart as you seek it.

I: Before you leave, may I ask one other question, please?

C: Of course.

I: One thing has been bothering me through this whole discussion about my will and especially my will in relationship to Jesus Christ and salvation.

C: What is that?

I: What about those statements in the Bible which say, "Whosoever will may come," and the like? You know that these texts do give an invitation and make it very plain that anyone who wants to come to Christ shall receive salvation. I think I know what you are going to say and I think I am beginning to understand the answer to my own question; but, just the same, I would like to hear it from you, please.

C: I think you do understand very well. Christ is saying exactly what He means there when He invites anyone who wills to come. But, you see, the unregenerate person, as long as he is unregenerate, never will come because he hates Jesus Christ. He simply spurns and detests His invitation. The invitation is standing and any time his heart is changed, his attitude is different, he will want to claim the promises which the Savior offers, and he shall most certainly have them.

Let me ask you a question now, my friend: If the sinner does respond in faith to the invitation of the Savior, what will that prove?

I: I understand exactly what you mean—he has been born again. In other words, when he comes to the Savior, the Savior has already come to him. I see now what Jesus meant when He said to His apostles, "You haven't chosen me, but I have chosen you." They chose Him indeed, but He first chose them. They loved Him indeed, but He first loved them.

C: Yes. You see, in the first instance, He is the one who does the choosing, and our response is the choosing of Him. We are conscious, of course, first of our choosing Him and only afterwards do we realize that we chose Him because He has first chosen us.

I: So many Christian evangelists seem to be citing these "whosoever will" passages all the time, as if they thought that everybody does have this so-called free will. Yet, as we realize from our dialogue here, the Bible does not teach any such notion as that. It teaches the very opposite. It teaches the bondage of the human heart to sin. Only if a person is born again *can* he enter the kingdom of God. How do you account for so much misunderstanding and misrepresentation of the gospel?

C: They don't obey the Word of God, which teaches that men are "*dead* in trespasses and sins" (Ephesians 2:1). Spiritually dead people do not will to come to Christ. They must be given a new heart. These evangelists should continue to invite (as Christ does) without neglecting to teach the *divine initiative!*

I: *Christ* is the Author as well as the *Finisher* of our salvation?

C: *Amen, and amen.*

# A

# Primer

# on

# Justification

Martin Luther called justification the doctrine by which "the church either stands or falls." Calvin declared it the "hinge of the Reformation." The Roman Catholic Church, at the Council of Trent (1546–63), where it dealt with the Protestant Reformation, recognized justification as the central doctrine at issue. This doctrine is the core of the gospel; it is indispensable. The Reformed church of the sixteenth century was purified by reaffirming clearly this doctrine, while Roman Catholicism was destroyed by denying it. There is a difference of opinion as to its precise meaning, but there is no difference of opinion at all concerning its indispensability to evangelism.

Not only does the church stand or fall by this doctrine, but the individual also. That is, dear reader, this doctrine is the doctrine by which you stand or fall before God. Nothing can be more important to you than to understand, believe, trust in, and spread this core doctrine of the Christian religion.

So far are we today from understanding the importance of this doctrine that we hardly ever hear it mentioned. When it is mentioned, it sounds very strange to us. The doctrine that is essential to salvation should not sound strange to people who profess to be saved Christians.

To illustrate how far our twentieth century is from what the sixteenth century considered the heart of the gospel, let me relate a true, though almost unbelievable, incident. I was once speaking to a group of business people on justification, and there was a journalist representing a local newspaper in attendance. I preached justification emphatically, clearly, earnestly, and, I hoped, persuasively. It was, therefore, rather discouraging to learn from the newspaper account that I had spoken the night before on the theme of "Just a vacation by faith!" Fly now, pay later! That's what the journalist heard as the central truth of the Christian religion! Now, a journalist can never be totally devoid of intelligence, nor can I be absolutely meaningless in a presentation. A strange event such as this could happen only because the word *justification* is so strange to the ears of modern Christians. This would be less tragic if one's eternal life did not depend on a correct understanding and sincere belief in justification by faith alone. Though the Bible teaches justification, and only one way of justification, there are many different and conflicting views of this vital doctrine. This primer presents five different and conflicting current understandings of this doctrine, only one of which can possibly be the true biblical and saving doctrine. These competing interpretations may be diagrammed as follows:

1. Liberalism: Works → Justification – Faith

2. Neoorthodoxy: *Faith* → *Justification* – Works

3. Antinomianism: Faith → Justification – Works

4. Roman Catholicism: Faith + Works → Justification

5. Evangelicalism: Faith → Justification + Works

## 1. The Liberal View of Justification:

## Works → Justification – Faith

Liberalism believes justification is earned by works. The liberal believes that by acting virtuously while abstaining from sin, he may make himself acceptable to God, that is, be justified or be considered by God a just or righteous person. For him, justification means being made just by his own efforts. His is a do-it-yourself religion. Its golden text is, "Do this and thou shalt live." The liberal believes that he can earn his own salvation by his own efforts. The gospel or good news for a liberal is the discovery of his own potentialities, and he is perfectly confident that he can make it on his own without any help from anybody, including

God. He does not need Jesus Christ as a Savior. He needs no Savior because he is quite able to cope, thank you. He may or may not think that *you* are okay, but he has no doubt that you *may be* okay and that he *is* okay. Give him the light and he will find his own way. This is the gospel of self-esteem.

The diagram pictures that works (good deeds) bring justification minus faith. I had better explain the "minus" or the liberal view will be misunderstood. The liberal, who thinks he can save himself by his own endeavors, is not opposed to faith, in every sense of that word. He has faith that good food, for example, will nourish his body; that honesty pays in business; that if he posts a letter it is likely to reach its destination. He also has faith that everything will come out all right in the end, and that all's well that ends well. It is strange in a sense, therefore, and unfair on the surface of it, to represent him as minus or hostile to faith. As a matter of fact, he is a practitioner of faith in many, many areas. His greatest faith, of course, is in himself and in his fellow man, whom he considers quite able to meet the demands of an all-holy and perfect God. Some of us would call this kind of faith "presumption"; but, in his own opinion, it is a well-grounded belief in his own ability. So, in a sense, he is far from being without faith. He is almost "plus" faith with a vengeance.

But the liberal is minus or devoid of faith in the sense that he does not trust in the redemption of Jesus Christ for his salvation. He does not have faith in the shed blood of the Redeemer. He does not trust for his salvation in what someone else has done on his behalf. He does not need that kind of help, he thinks, and will not call upon it. In fact, he is insulted by such an offer. He feels that faith is a crutch for the people who cannot get along without it. As a healthy, upright, moral being, he does not need such a crutch as the work of Jesus Christ.

Christ speaks to the liberal when He says, "I did not come to call the righteous to repentance, but sinners." The liberal virtually says, "You can say that again. That is perfectly true, I can achieve righteousness on my own. In fact, I have. I don't need to repent of my sins and trust in salvation from any other source." Liberals in the Gospels were the Pharisees, who trusted in themselves for righteousness. The modern liberal does the same; consequently, far from accepting the death of Christ as the basis of his salvation, he puts Christ to death for insulting him with the offer of salvation.

In that sense, "minus" faith is something of an understatement. If I gave the impression that the liberal was minus any kind of faith, it would be unfair to him who trusts in many other areas. But in the sense of the redemption offered by Jesus Christ, the liberal's minus faith is too fair to him. Far more than lacking in faith, he is positively hostile to it. He takes mortal offense at the suggestion that he needs it. It is precisely because he has faith in himself that he will not have faith in Christ and is insulted by the merest hint that he needs it. So the presence of faith of his kind is what makes him minus, or violently opposed to, faith in the biblical and saving sense.

Liberalism, as I am using the word here, refers to persons who trust in themselves, and who, because they do, feel no need for special salvation. Consequently, they oppose the very claim of Christianity to be a revealed religion. The liberals, in the sense in which I'm using the word, deny the miraculous—the miraculous birth of Christ; the miraculous activities of Christ; the miraculous resurrection of Christ; the miraculous ascension of Christ; the miraculous intercession of Christ—and, of course, they do not expect the miraculous return of Christ in the clouds of glory. J. Gresham Machen, in his classic volume, *Christianity and Liberalism*, which even the liberals admit is a masterpiece, noted that liberalism is another religion, not Christianity. Liberalism and Christianity are not to be confused. They are in direct opposition to one another. Everything that Christianity maintains, such as the fall of man, the sin of man, and the necessity of redemption by grace and justification by faith, is repudiated by liberalism, making it, therefore, another religion altogether. It is indeed salvation by good views rather than by good news (the gospel). One of these religions is based on a high view of man's own character; the other is based on a confidence that man is a sinner who can be saved only by grace. These are two diametrically opposed ways of salvation.

We are grateful when liberals acknowledge this and do not pretend to be Christians. Some years ago I was giving a course on the cults at Pittsburgh Theological Seminary. Representatives of the different sects presented their viewpoints to my class. When I had the liberal pastor of the First Unitarian Church, the Rev. Mr. Cahill, present his views, he began in a very refreshing manner. He said bluntly at the outset of his lecture, after thanking me for the opportunity to address this class: "Dr. Gerstner is a Christian. I am not a Christian. Christianity is a religion of redemption, and your professor believes in it and is entitled to the name Christian. I don't believe in the supernatural events of divine salvation through Jesus Christ, which I admit is the definition of Christianity. I am, frankly, not a Christian. I am a liberal, and I have a religion which is quite different from your professor's, as he understands and I also understand."

Most liberals do not admit they follow another religion. On the contrary, they claim to be authentic Christians. One can see why orthodox Christians are profoundly distressed by this. When somebody who denies Christ is the way of salvation passes himself off as a Christian, that is a dreadfully dangerous business. We must warn people constantly that liberalism is another gospel that is not a gospel at all. While a liberal propagates this religion as the truth, he owes it to everybody not to claim to be Christian and to admit that his views are diametrically opposed to the Christian position.

However, very few liberals actually acknowledge the

truth of their divergence from the evangelical, historic Christian faith. Please note again, dear reader, that I am using the word liberal in a very precise sense of the word. I am not saying that *any* deviation whatsoever from the orthodox consensus constitutes liberalism. A person may be liberally inclined at certain points while nevertheless adhering to essential Christianity. I myself have been called a liberal on occasion because I believe in biblical criticism. Some orthodox Christians think the Bible ought not to be subject to any kind of criticism. They regard persons who think it should be as liberals, whether they are believers in its inspiration or not. I do not consider myself or others liberal because we believe in biblical criticism. We don't consider other persons as liberal (in the sense that we are using it here) simply because they take a different view on predestination or baptism or church order, or a number of other doctrines on which orthodox Christians, who believe the supernatural gospel of Jesus Christ, vary from one another. Please remember, I am speaking here about liberalism as another religion, which opposes supernatural Christianity and denies its essential doctrines (while still claiming to be Christianity).

Liberalism has been with us from the beginning. In the early church it took the name of *Pelagianism*. At the time of the Reformation it was known as *Socinianism*. Today, in the Roman Catholic Church, it is usually called *modernism*. In Protestant churches it is designated by the term *liberalism*. As mentioned, we do not consider it a form of Christianity. In my own book on the cults [*Theology of the Major Sects,* Baker Book House, 1960], I class it with the non-Christian sects. When discussing the sects, I mention that it is far more of a threat to the Christian church than are the Mormons, Jehovah's Witnesses, and Christian Scientists put together. Anybody who is at all knowledgeable about those and other cults is immediately aware that they are not orthodox Christian bodies. But liberalism, flying at a "low level of visibility," is often not seen as a cult or sect, which in fact it is. Consequently, it probably leads more Christian people astray than all the recognized cults combined, precisely because it is not recognized as a cult. On the contrary, it falsely represents itself as, and frequently is thought by its victims to be, a bona fide expression of the Christian religion.

We can see, however, that it is categorically opposed to Christianity at its heart. The way of salvation taught by the Christian religion (the liberal Mr. Cahill very correctly observed) is by faith in Jesus Christ; whereas, according to liberalism, a person is justified by his own efforts. He thinks he is justified by faith in *himself*.

## 2. The Neoorthodox Way of Justification:

### *Faith* → *Justification* – Works

In the diagram presented at the beginning of this essay, you will notice that, after the liberal formula, the other four formulae all begin not with works, but with faith. That shows that they are all at least *possibly* Christian, whereas liberalism, on the very surface of it, cannot be. One cannot conceivably believe that salvation is by his own efforts and be a believer in Jesus Christ. All of these other views, the right one and the three other deviations, have this in common: they begin where they ought to begin, not with works, but with faith. From here on out we are dealing with people who have a right to be considered tentatively, at least, as Christian. I must phrase myself very carefully here. I consider that three of these remaining four ways are not soundly Christian, but are fatally deviant from it. By saying they may be tentatively considered as Christian, I mean this: at least they *start* out right. They do *profess* faith in Jesus Christ, as a Christian (if he is to bear that name) must do. Whether they are consistent in their affirmation or not remains to be seen. By contrast, liberalism is fatally wrong from the very beginning because it begins not with

Christ's salvation, but with man's own achievement.

In the outline of the neoorthodox view of justification, the *faith* that leads to justification followed by "minus works" is in italics. "*Justification*" itself is also printed in italicized letters. The word "works" is in regular print. Neoorthodox theologians, though they vary among themselves as do all schools of thought, do not have the same concept of faith that orthodox Christians teach. They profess faith that, under closer analysis, turns out not to be the genuine article. They differ from the liberals who do not even profess saving faith. When, however, neoorthodox "faith" is examined, it turns out to be incompatible with the orthodox meaning of the word and, indeed, devoid of meaning. By representing faith in italics I mean that the neoorthodox concept of faith in Christ is profoundly different from what is ordinarily in mind.

What we today call neo-orthodoxy is usually thought of as beginning in earnest in Europe with a second edition of Karl Barth's commentary on the Book of Romans. That was in the early twenties, and the movement had an immediate, profound effect on Europe. Its effect began to be felt in the States in the late thirties and early forties.

In the early forties I was doing my graduate work at liberal Harvard, which had reluctantly begun to admit the existence of anti-liberal neoorthodoxy. Harvard was urbanely liberal and had buried orthodoxy a century before, except as an historical phenomenon. It was not about to take it seriously in the present. But the impact of the new form of orthodoxy was not to be denied. Harvard did in time at least take notice of it and invited Reinhold Niebuhr, who was one of the early and powerful American advocates of this style of Christian thinking, to lecture at Harvard.

The liberal professor Julius Seelye Bixler, who introduced Reinhold Niebuhr, then a professor at Union Seminary in New York, presented an interesting contrast to Niebuhr. Bixler, in a characteristically relaxed mood, calmly smoking his Meerschaum pipe and rocking in his chair, was the picture of complacent liberalism. Niebuhr, standing tall and vigorous in the prime of his life, like Elijah on Mt. Carmel, pronounced denunciations on Harvard and other forms of liberalism in no uncertain accents.

Neibuhr said emphatically and repeatedly that Jesus Christ is no mere man. Ninety-five percent of that audience was confident that Jesus was nothing more than a man. They were told time and again in that hour's address that Jesus Christ was God, no mere man. This early champion of neoorthodoxy, who had himself come out of liberalism, was denouncing liberalism in terms that sounded like pure, historic orthodoxy.

If one left after that address, he would have thought that John Calvin *redivivus* had been heard on Harvard campus that morning

If, however, one remained for the question period, he would have known otherwise. A student immediately arose and said, "Professor Niebuhr, you repudiated the liberal notion that Jesus was merely a man. You said that he was God. What do you mean by calling Jesus Christ God?" Niebuhr explained that he did not mean "ontic deity." Christ was not eternal. He was not a member of the everlasting Trinity.

Niebuhr was now repudiating orthodoxy as sharply as he had repudiated liberalism in the address. Definitely, he did not believe that Christ was mere man and, equally certainly, he did not believe that Christ was God in the proper meaning of that word. The Council of Chalcedon in A.D. 451 had declared that Christ was "truly God and truly man." Niebuhr expressly disagreed with Chalcedon by name.

Liberalism we can understand and orthodoxy we can understand. Niebuhr had rejected both. How were we to understand him? That is precisely what the next questioner asked: "What do *you* mean by 'God'?" Niebuhr answered with a word he often used later in print—"symbol." The word "God" did not mean "God," it meant "symbol." The word "man" meant "man." The word "God" meant "sym-

bol." If anyone at that address understood the meaning of
"symbol," it was not I. The term as used that morning, and
on later occasions, defies understanding. We know what it
does *not* mean. It does not mean "man" and does not mean
"God." What it does mean I doubt that Reinhold Niebuhr
knew. This is what I mean by putting "faith" and "justification" in italics. There is no way of knowing what is the
object of faith or the basis of justification.

Of course, the question that wasn't raised that morning
(because there was no point to raising it) was, "What do
you mean by 'symbol'?" I'm sure that if someone had asked
the question there would have been no answer, unless
"symbol" was a symbol for symbol. But no one asked. One
sensed that we were at the end of the line. Niebuhr had gone
as far as he would. He had clearly repudiated liberalism. He
had clearly repudiated orthodoxy. He had unclearly and
utterly ambiguously affirmed neoorthodoxy. John Murray
once called neoorthodoxy "The Theology of Ambiguity."

Obviously, these theologians mean to say something,
but the something they are meaning to say eludes us. Not
only with respect to Christ, but obviously with respect to
faith in Christ. If one has no clear idea of who Christ, the
object of faith, is, how can one have any clear idea of what
faith is? The essence of this school of thought has been the
"paradox." Gordon Clark has referred to paradox as a
"charley-horse between the ears." Whether neoorthodox
theologians are suffering from that kind of mental paralysis
or not, the concept itself does indeed produce a charley-
horse between the ears of anybody who tries to compre-
hend its meaning. He simply cannot make heads or tails of
anything expressed as an absolute paradox. If Niebuhr did
understand what he meant, certainly no one else could.

I know there are some readers who would say immediately you cannot call Paul Tillich a neoorthodox theologian.
But his myths are not essentially different from the para-
doxes and pointers of others. His concept of justification is
pure paradox.

The formula which he and others use is a quotation from Martin Luther, *Simul justus, simul peccator.* Martin Luther, however, meant something quite different. For the Reformer, when a person was justified by faith, he still remained in a certain sense a *peccator,* or sinner. That is, he was not perfectly sanctified, and he never could entirely escape the power of sin during his entire life. But Luther did believe in the vicarious sacrifice of Christ, which removed the guilt of the believer's sin, and in the in-dwelling of the Holy Spirit by regeneration, which broke the back of sin, even though it did not eradicate it fully. In Luther's understanding, while the justified person remained a sinner and imperfect, he was not a sinner in the same way that he was before his conversion. He was acquitted of his guilt, endued with Christ's righteousness, and empowered by the Spirit to pursue righteousness, not perfectly but genuinely, as he never did prior to his conversion. So he was not the identical *peccator* after his being declared just that he was before But in the neoorthodox connotation, that's precisely the case.

The way Tillich shows this is in his essay, "The Shaking of the Foundations," when he talks about the woman of the streets who washed the Savior's feet with her tears and dried them with her hair. Tillich does not say in so many words what he means by the justification of that woman. It is clear, however, that her faith in Christ made her *justus,* even though she remained the same *peccator* (in this case prostitute) that she was before. According to Martin Luther, this interpretation would be the heresy of antinomianism against which he wrote two vehement tracts. When Christ forgave the prostitute of John 8 (as He will forgive any prostitute as soon as she repents), He said to her, "Neither do I condemn thee, go and sin no more." If she continues in her prostitution, she is no forgiven Christian. She is not justified. It is obvious from this essay that Tillich has no such understanding in mind. While he cannot bring himself to say that the woman continued in her prostitution (just as multitudes of others may continue in that and other recognized sins that the Bible denounces, practitioners of which the Bible says shall never inherit the kingdom of God), in Tillich's opinion this woman, even though she continued in her prostitution, was nevertheless just or righteous before God and an heir to eternal life.

That is the reason I put "justification" in italics. It is not the biblical doctrine. It is not a meaningful doctrine. It is an absolutely paradoxical *simul justus simul peccator,* which does not convey the meaning of the Bible at all. So we must say about neoorthodox theology at this very crucial point, that, though it has the form of sound words, it lacks the truth and the power of them.

The "minus works" in the formula needs some explanation, lest I do a very great injustice to the neo-orthodox proponents. Many of them, such as Barth and Tillich, have exhibited real courage and devotion to the Christian religion. Both of them virtually laid their lives on the line in their resistance to Adolph Hitler. Both of them were driven out of Germany because of their opposition to the Fuehrer.

Nevertheless, in their teaching and thinking, works are not necessary. They are advisable, and many of the adherents of this school practice them and exhibit them sometimes in heroic dimensions. Notwithstanding, they are not essential. This was Tillich's point in respect to the prostitute. Paul Tillich did not, of course, recommend prostitution. Tillich would believe that the woman would have done better if she had given up her prostitution. He would maintain, however, that she was justified whether she continued in it or not. That is what we mean by the "minus." The works are not necessary. A person may be justified while being without them. Not *necessarily* lacking in them, he may nevertheless *possibly* lack them without his justification being questioned for a moment.

An illustration of this point I take from an autobiographical story of a minister in the Netherlands, whose name I have forgotten, whose action is a true expression of the neoorthodox mentality. He was approached by a prostitute on his way home one night. He relates that he refused her invitation and went on home. His comment was, "It would not have made any difference if I had gone with her. My relation to Jesus Christ is between Him and me, and not affected by my relation to any other person."

The neo-orthodox doctrine of justification by faith is no sound view of this indispensable doctrine. While it honors the formula of justification by faith, and even emphasizes it, and considers itself biblical in its position, nevertheless its conception of justification plus its conception of faith is quite unbiblical. That is not to say a neo-orthodox theologian or person was never saved, but no person will ever be saved on the basis of such a formula. Furthermore, the antinomian strain in the doctrine, even if it were orthodox, would vitiate it also. This is truly a strange theological movement, and this particular formula is utterly characteristic in its oddity. There is a formal emphasis on the doctrines of the Reformation, coupled with a strange eviscerating of their content.

## 3. The Antinomian Way of Justification:

### Faith → Justification – Works

In the antinomian view of justification, the formula is the same as the preceding, except that the italics have disappeared. Faith brings justification minus works.

We are dealing now with a group of people who, apart from this doctrine, are genuinely orthodox. They have no doubt whatever that justification is by faith alone. And when they speak of justification, they mean the remission of sins by the shed blood of Jesus Christ, the incarnate second person of the Godhead, who was born of the Virgin Mary, fulfilled the law on our behalf, was delivered up for our offenses, and rose again bodily for our justification.

Likewise, faith in Him is of the orthodox variety. One must truly believe that He is the divine Son of God and Savior of the world. This is an orthodox faith, which professes Christ alone as the sole basis of salvation. These people preach Christ and Him crucified. There can be no doubt of it, and we are happy to give them full credit for their unwavering allegiance to the inspiration of Holy Scripture and to the supernaturalism of biblical redemption.

Their "minus" is not against the person of Christ directly, or the nature of justifying faith directly, it has to do with the works that must follow a justified state.

Antinomians, unlike the liberals, stress that Christ is indispensable for salvation. They are not do-it-yourself theologians by any means. They insist that faith is absolutely necessary for salvation. And they mean by "faith," faith in the merits of Jesus Christ, the divine Son of God, the vicarious sacrifice for the sins of the world.

Insistent as they are on the proper conception of faith, they recognize that that is not itself sufficient. One must know more than what faith is; one must actually exercise it. These people usually stress the difference between a mere theoretical knowledge of the Lord and awareness of who He is. They know that faith must have the element Martin Luther stressed so much: the *fiducial*. Faith must be actual trust.

Theologians of this school often use an analogy that shows the difference between an awareness of the reliability of something and an actual commitment of oneself to it. A person may recognize a certain chair as sturdily built and quite capable of holding his weight; but until the person sits in that chair he cannot be said to have truly proper and thorough faith in the chair. A person may believe that he can walk across Niagara Falls on a tightrope. Until he starts walking, say these antinomians, his faith in his ability and the trustworthiness of the rope is not demonstrated. So they will insist that no amount of orthodox Christology can save anybody. No amount of historical faith can justify anybody. A person must indeed know who Christ is and even believe that He is able to save. Until, however, that person commits himself to Christ alone for his salvation, he is not, according to this school of thought, truly a justified person. So, in that matter, they are surely biblical and evangelical.

The same may be said of their doctrine of justification. Again, no italics. They are as far removed from neo-orthodoxy as they are from the self-justification of liberalism. They insist that Christ is a vicarious sacrifice, who by His mediatorial death provided satisfaction for God's righteousness. He bestows on the person who really trusts in Him the cancellation of all his guilt and, to the same, His acquired righteousness.

It is a minor defect in these antinomians that they do not adequately stress the positive element in justification. There is a one-sided, heavy emphasis on the negative remission quality of justification. They are fond of their expression of justification: "just as if I had never sinned." They recognize the full cancellation of the guilt of sin, but are not quite so aware that the righteousness of Jesus Christ is equally essential as a part of justification. They do not deny it. Indeed they teach it. They simply do not adequately appreciate and stress it. But this is a minor criticism at most. On the whole, antinomians are quite biblical, evangelical, orthodox, and Reformational in respect to faith and justification up to a certain point.

That "up to a certain point" has to do with the "minus works." Why do I say "up to a certain point"? I did not mean by that expression that antinomians are thoroughly sound up to the point of works, but rather that their soundness with respect to faith and justification goes *as far as possible with a defective view of works*. That defective view of works has a retroactive effect on the nature of the faith and, ultimately, of the justification. In fact, it utterly vitiates both. So while I am endorsing the antinomian's affirmation of an essentially evangelical view of faith and justification, I

am here qualifying it in anticipation of the defective view of
works. Though I praise the antinomians for these first two
parts of the formula, it is in a qualified sense of taking them
at face value. Not even at this point am I saying that their
affirmation will stand up under an analysis of their view of
justification by faith as a whole.

What, then, is the meaning of the "minus works"? As
in the neo-orthodox formula, it does not mean that the
adherents of this school are opposed to good works. It does
not mean that it encourages people to do bad works or to
regard works as something that they can casually neglect.
On the contrary, they themselves are often zealots for good
works. They always stress the advisability of good works.
Good works are absolutely necessary for rewards. These
preachers mightily urge people to abound in good works so
that they may have an abundant reward in the world to
come. Abounding in the works of the Lord, they teach,
promotes a sense of blessedness and joy in the Lord even
in this world. The absence of good works will disturb our
fellowship with God. As long as they are lacking fellowship
with the Savior, it is impossible to have peace, joy, or
fruitfulness. If this continues, there will be embarrassment
at the *bema* (judgment seat of Christ). In other words,
antinomians usually enthusiastically urge Christians to do
many, many, many good works in the service of the Lord
Jesus Christ, and confidently promise them that they will
receive a heavenly reward for every one of them, as well as
present overflowing joy in the Lord. "Minus" here does not
mean a negative attitude toward works. These antinomians
are often quite positive in their emphasis and their practice.

If antinomians are so enthusiastic about doing good
works, why do I put a "minus" before the works in their
formula? It seems totally out of place and profoundly misleading—even unfair—on the surface of it. It is not out of
place and it is not misleading, but it does have to be understood accurately. What I mean is that the antinomian defends the proposition that there can be a justification by

faith without any works whatsoever. They do not recommend such a life, but they do defend its possibility. Just as I diagrammed it here, so they think that it is possible for a person to be justified by faith, even though, alas, he does no good works at all (in spite of all of their exhortations to the contrary). Some antinomians sing:

> Free from the Law, O blessed condition,
> I can sin as I please and still have remission.

This meets with a very dim reception from many of these teachers. But they cannot deny the proposition any more than they can encourage that way of stating their convictions. They do believe that the Christian is free from the law, and if he does sin as he pleases he still will have remission of his sins, if he does indeed trust in Jesus Christ. They are prepared to die for that proposition. In other words, a "minus" here is utterly indispensable to their way of thinking.

A few summers ago I was teaching a church history survey course to Campus Crusade staffers at Ft. Collins, Colorado. Several times in that survey, antinomianism was mentioned. After class one morning a student brought me a copy of Dr. Charles Ryrie's book on discipleship. He asked me to read a particular chapter and tell the class if that taught antinomianism. Knowing the tendency of Scofieldian dispensationalism to antinomianism, I was still disappointed to find that my friend, Dr. Ryrie, one of the soundest of the dispensationalists, was guilty of antinomianism.

Incidentally, in that chapter, Dr. Ryrie mentions in a footnote that he had some discussion with Dr. James Packer and Dr. John Stott on this matter of the role of works. Packer and Stott take the orthodox Reformational position that faith *must be* accompanied by works. If Jesus Christ is to be one's Savior, He must also, and at the same time, be one's Lord. Dr. Ryrie heartily recommends that when a person accepts Christ as Savior he also accept Him

as Lord, but he defends the possibility of Christ's being
Savior without being Lord. Consequently, in that footnote,
Dr. Ryrie refers to Packer and Stott as "lordship" teachers
(as if "saviorhood" teachers were sound). So if the antinomian is not going to insist that works are indispensable,
then he comes under the indictment of a formula with
"minus works," and that is a fatal fault.

I later met Dr. Ryrie and we talked for about 15 minutes,
which was all we could spare at the time. He convinced me,
even in that brief conversation, that he never meant to be
antinomian. He seems to realize how fatal this doctrine is.
We agreed at that time to have further correspondence.
When I returned home shortly afterwards, I received from
Dr. Ryrie a copy of his book on grace, in which he had underlined a number of sentences emphasizing the importance of the law in the Christian life. I wrote him a five-page
letter expressing my deep appreciation for the parts he had
underlined. I told him that I understood why he felt those
statements freed him from the charge of antinomianism. At
the same time, I pointed out that they did not do that because, enthusiastic as he was, he did not make the works of
obedience necessary. They were highly advisable and very
profitable. They were still, after all Dr. Ryrie's statements
orally and in writing, optional acts. He did not remove the
"minus." I pled with him to do so, but though that letter
was written years ago, I have not yet received a response. I
draw no conclusion from the silence, but neither does the
silence answer my charges, which I have to repeat here
about a dear friend who represents a whole school of
thought. While proponents of that school do not want to be
antinomian, they are, succeeding without trying.

If they will show that the person to be justified by faith
*must* have his faith accompanied by good works, then I
should be very happy to go immediately into print and indicate my personal gratification and endorsement of their
view of justification. Until that time, I can only say of Dr.
Ryrie (and of all dispensationalists, because he is certainly

one of the finest of them), and of the Scofield Bible in its 1909 version, and even in its 1967 revision, that their doctrine is antinomian. It is noticeable that the revision addresses the problem more, and in a certain sense tones down the harshness of the earlier form of statement, but it does not remove the antinomianism of Scofieldian dispensationalism.

I also mention this episode in my *Primer on Dispensationalism*. I use it here because not only does it show antinomianism in an outstanding Bible teacher of great influence, but it is characteristic of the whole dispensational theology from J. N. Darby to Zane Hodges. Dr. Hodges' recent *Gospel Under Siege* should be entitled *Antinomianism Under Siege*. In my *Wrongly Dividing the Word of Truth* [Wolgemuth and Hyatt, 1991, but currently out of print] I demonstrate more thoroughly that dispensationalism, past and present, teaches antinomianism, and therein denies justification by faith alone.

Until dispensationalism repudiates its antinomianism, it is going to have to labor under that awful indictment of cutting out the heart of Christianity by a fatally defective view of justification, which is the article by which the church or theology or the individual must stand or fall. No amount of other excellencies can compensate for it. Just as a human being may be healthy in some ways except one fatal ailment, so it takes a lack of only one essential to destroy a theology.

My favorite illustration of this mentality I heard from a well-known American evangelical who died some years ago. I trust that before he died he saw the fallacy in this episode. This story is true, and it illustrates antinomianism very pointedly because of the relative triviality of the offense involved.

The story is this: this man, before he was converted, was a hobo. After his conversion, he was so conscientious that he wrote to the various train lines on which he had, as a hobo, stolen rides, asking if he could reimburse them for his thefts of free passage. They invariably responded by saying they had no established rates for such travel and forgave him. That shows how seriously he took his Christian life. He got a job, after his conversion, in an electric light company in Akron, Ohio. One time while working for that company, he stole an electric light bulb, took it home, and screwed it up in the ceiling of his room. At night, when he would get down on his knees and pray, he would often look toward heaven and see that stolen light bulb. Finally, it pained him so much that he simply could stand it no longer. He unscrewed the bulb and returned it to its owner. This was his final comment on that episode: "If I had not returned that light bulb, I would have gone to heaven anyway, but I would not have been happy along the way."

There is your "minus works." Minus very, very little work. Minus a five-cent electric light bulb. Minus next to nothing. But, nevertheless, minus a good work of doing what is a manifest duty of a Christian person: providing things honestly in the sight of all, not being a thief. A man who steals a five-cent light bulb, or embezzles $5 million from a bank, if he does not return it, is a thief. One is a bigger thief than the other, but both are thieves. If one takes property that does not belong to him and does not return it while it is in his power to do so, he is a thief.

What is the standing of thieves? The Bible is utterly unambiguous on that subject. Thieves, it says, shall not inherit the kingdom of God. When the rich young ruler asked Jesus what he must do to inherit eternal life, Christ told him in no uncertain terms, "You know the commandments." Christ then mentioned some of the decalogue, including the eighth commandment. A person could not inherit eternal life unless he was about the business of keeping the commandments. Christ was not saying that he would be saved by any merit in keeping the commandments. He simply answered a question as to how a person would inherit eternal life, and made it clear that there was no inheriting eternal life without keeping the commandments. Christ makes no exceptions. "Thou shalt not steal" is one of those commandments, and a person who is a thief is a breaker, not a keeper, of that commandment.

You say, "Yes, but the man may repent." Yes, I grant you that he may repent, and if he repents then he is no longer a thief. If he is a Christian who was overtaken in a fault, he can be restored. But one option is not open. He cannot continue in his thievery and be an heir of eternal life. Thieves cannot inherit the kingdom of God. So our friend was utterly out of line with Holy Scripture when he said that though he was a thief he would have gone to heaven anyway. He would not have been happy on the way, but neither would he have been on the way. Thieves are not going to be happy along the way. He was correct about that. But thieves are not going to heaven either. About that he was fatally mistaken.

Even a favorite hymn can be misleading. It is true that "there's no other way to be *happy* in Jesus, but to trust and obey." It is also true that there is no other way to be *in* Jesus but to trust and obey.

The light bulb is an extreme example cited to make the point most obviously that, however refined, antinomianism is still antinomianism, and a fatal error. Often much more glaring cases are offered. We hear some antinomians saying that a true believer dying drunk in bed with a prostitute and a pot of stolen gold under the bed would be immediately escorted to heaven by holy angels. They are not referring to a godly person who had suddenly, on a single occasion, lapsed into such delinquency. They mean that a true believer who lived his whole life that way would go—without reward, of course—to heaven. And he would have been "unhappy along the way" there. But to heaven he would go. I heard one evangelist tell of a man like that whom no amount of divine chastening could correct. Did that prove he was not a Christian? Not at all! What happened? God took him home to remove the scandal!

What most clearly shows that the absence of works is utterly impossible for a justified person is the relationship of works to faith. That faith which justifies is a *working* faith. If justification is by faith, it must be a real, genuine faith. Everybody who reads this knows we are talking about real, not about counterfeit, faith. The fact that the hat in the window can be bought for $20 does not mean that it can be bought with a *counterfeit* $20 bill. The fact that justification may be by *faith* does not mean that it can be bought by a *counterfeit* faith. A non-working faith is no faith at all, a counterfeit faith indeed. It is conclusive evidence that the person is not a believer that he does not pursue holiness, without which no one shall see the Lord. Those who are Christians take up their crosses daily and follow Him. Only those who *abide* in His Word are His disciples (John 8:31). If a person does not take up his cross, does not abide in God's Word, and does not deny himself, then he simply is not following Jesus Christ. He is not a true believer; he is not an heir to eternal life; he is not going to inherit the kingdom of God.

The classic passage is James 2:21: "Faith without works is dead." James does not say that faith without works is sick. He does not say that faith without works is not very healthy. He does not say that faith without works is dying. He says bluntly that faith without works is *dead*. It simply does not exist. Christ said the same thing in the parable of the vine and the branches. That which does not bear fruit does not abide in Him. It is not in Christ, the vine, if it is not bearing the fruits of good works.

So we sadly conclude that antinomianism is another gospel, which is not the gospel. It is an implicit denial of justification by faith because it does not *require* the working faith that alone brings justification. Without a true faith, there is no union with Christ, and without Christ there is no justification. Faith without works is dead, and justification without faith is dead. If there are any "antinomians" who truly believe in justification by faith alone, then let them deny their antinomianism and join with all true evangelicals.

## 4. Roman Catholicism:

## Faith + Works → Justification

This was the great issue of the Reformation. Romanism and Protestantism were agreed on the other great essentials of faith: the Trinity, deity of Christ, His vicarious death, even the necessity of faith in Christ. The great and crucial difference came in answer to the question, "How is the sinner justified by Christ?" Romanism said, "By our *works* which flow from faith in Christ." Protestantism said, "By faith in Christ *alone*."

As you can see from the formula, Rome has all the right ingredients of justification: faith, works, justification. No italics. No minuses.

Note the "faith." This means that the sinner must believe in the Christ who was incarnate by the Virgin Mary and was a sacrifice for our sins. Rome is quite orthodox here. Though her faith is too purely intellectualistic, and not clearly fiducial, it is, as liberalism's is not and neoorthodoxy's is not, directed to the one and only true object.

Rome's "works," too, are essentially sound. They include obedience to the Ten Commandments and the new commandment of Christ as well. There is no essential error in this area. To be sure, Rome adds duties not in the Bible, such as confession to a priest, conforming to a penitential system, observance of holy days; but what the Bible does require, she, too, apart from Sabbath observance, also requires. Rome's "justification" ("second justification") is fatally faulty. The Bible's justification is a reckoning or imputing of the righteousness of Christ to the believer. Rome's justification is an infusing of righteousness into the believing worker who thereby becomes righteous. It was the desperate, but futile, effort of the monk Martin Luther to achieve justification this way that led him to realize that justification is a gift from God and not an achievement of man. He realized that no one could ever achieve the justification that Romanism mistakenly taught as Christian doctrine. Rome's most obvious error, implicit in her false doctrine of justification, is the position of the works before and not after justification. There is no "minus" before works; that is good. But there are works before justification, and that is fatally bad. Works have become the foundation of justification. How so? Justification is by faith, says Rome, attempting to be loyal to Scripture. Faith is the radix or root of justification according to her Council of Trent. That means that true faith leads to good works (which is a correction of the antinomian error); but, alas, the good works become the title to eternal life.

In other words, through Christ the believer is enabled to achieve his own justification. That teaching is absolutely false in two ways. First, it depreciates the perfection of the atonement. By insisting on our works as the title to justification, it denies it to Christ's work alone. Second, supposing that our works could ever entitle us to eternal life grossly overestimates our most perfect works—if we could do such, which we cannot. Christ, in the parable of the worker in the field who then serves his master in the house (Luke 17:7ff.), accentuates this point. If a man served his heavenly Master perfectly all the time he should say, "I am an unprofitable servant. I have only done my duty." Man's obligation is to be perfect. For so being, he would not even deserve thanks, much less a reward, not to mention an eternal reward. Yet Rome, turning her back on the all-sufficiency of the work of Christ for everlasting felicity, trusts in the works of men who could not earn thanks if they were perfect. (Incidentally, if he as a person thought he were perfect, he would, as John said, deceive himself and could not pray, as his Lord tells him, "Forgive us our debts.")

So all Rome's error is in putting works before justification, but how fatal the error! The theological cart is hopelessly before the theological horse. Neither works nor justification can function. Meritorious works are no works and an achieved justification is no justification.

"Evangelical Catholic" (that contemporary expression) is a contradiction in terms. If evangelical, one cannot be (Roman) Catholic; if Catholic, one cannot be evangelical. Is a Catholic evangelical a happy inconsistency? It is an inconsistency, but not a happy one. A person never has a right to be inconsistent. If a Roman Catholic who is evangelical sees that he is inconsistent, then he must, of course, stop his inconsistency. An inconsistent person is a dishonest person. He is saying one thing and doing another thing. In this particular case, a Roman Catholic, by virtue of his affiliation, says that he believes justification is brought about by the works he does. At the same time, he professes to be an evangelical, which means that he believes justification is not brought about by works, but purely by the work of Jesus Chris and is received by faith alone. So an evangelical Catholic is a dishonest Catholic or a dishonest evangelical. Either his evangelicalism is true and his Catholicism is false, or his Catholicism is true and his evangelicalism is false. He must make up his mind. He cannot say both of those things at the same time. Let him decide whether he is indeed Roman Catholic and repudiate his evangelicalism, which may God forbid, or let him decide that he is truly evangelical and repudiate his Catholicism, which may God grant. A Benedictine monk heard me deliver a half-hour address on justification following the formulae of this booklet. After the address, he said, "Dr. Gerstner, I'd like you to know that I agree with everything you said." I was delighted and asked if that included my critique of his own church's doctrine and defense of the evangelical. He said that it did.

"Good," I replied. "Then you will join with us."

'No," he surprisingly answered.

"Then," said I, "you really don't agree that your church

is in error and evangelicalism is the true gospel, do you?"

"Yes, I do," was his even more surprising reply, "but we have changed!"

That surprised me even more, and I reminded him that Roman Catholicism was supposed to be "semper idem" (always the same) and her dogmas "infallible" and "irreformable." He responded simply, but apparently puzzled, "I will have to think about that."

Every "evangelical Catholic" will have to think about that. If he does, he will have to be one or the other. He cannot honestly be both. May he come with evangelicalism saying, "The just shall live by faith."

## 5. Evangelicalism:

### Faith → Justification + Works

There is the gospel in its glory, or rather in His (Christ's) glory. Strictly speaking, you see, justification is not even by faith alone—it is by Christ alone. What is meant by saying *sola fide* (by faith alone) is not that our God-given faith can save (where works cannot), but that faith unites with Christ who alone saves. *Sola fide = solo Christo*! The faith, because it unites with Christ, justifies immediately by virtue of that union. Though works operate at the same time that faith does (the plus sign refers to distinction, not separation), they are placed after justification because they contribute nothing to justification. It is Rome's placing works before justification that destroys justification and makes it even impossible.

When my daughter was 13, I was discussing justification with her. I told her that I taught a course at the seminary on Catholicism and the Council of Trent. It was very technical at points, and some of the debates were very close-grained and academic. A 13-year-old could easily get lost in them, I told her. But, I said to her (and to you), the issue is at heart extremely simple. It could be stated this way:

Who saves Judy? Is it Judy and Jesus? Or is it Jesus only?

I said to her (and I say to you), Judy, if you get in on the act you will be lost. It is Jesus only or there is no justification for Judy—or you.

But you ask, isn't Judy supposed to be "in on the act," that is, doing good works? Indeed she must be, or she is an antinomian and all is lost that way. One can lose justification many ways, but there is only one way he can have it. I told my daughter that she must be following in Christ's footsteps, seeking to obey Him from the heart in all things without ever for a moment thinking there is any merit in anything she does.

> And He also told this parable to certain ones who trusted in themselves that they were righteous, and viewed others with contempt "Two men went up into the temple to pray, one a Pharisee and the other a tax-gatherer. The Pharisee stood and was praying thus to himself, 'God, I thank thee that I am not like other men, swindlers, unjust, adulterers, or even like this tax-gatherer. I fast twice a week; I pay tithes of all that I get." But the tax-gather, standing some distance away, was even unwilling to lift up his eyes to heaven, but was beating his breast, saying, 'God, be merciful me, the sinner!" I tell you, this man went down to his house justified rather than the other (Luke 18:9–14).

The publican of whom Christ spoke could only cry out for mercy, but he "went down to his house justified." Suppose he was 30 when he went down to his house justified, and lived, after returning all that he had stolen, another 50 years of exemplary Christian service. Suppose he went up to that temple and prayed again. It would be the same prayer: "God, be merciful to me, the sinner!"

Dear reader, I have briefly discussed the most important issue in the world today—or any day. How can a man be right with God? Every religion except Christianity teaches justification by works (of one kind or another). Only Christianity teaches justification by faith alone. Alas, many professed teachers of Christianity preach another gospel of justification, which is not another and will never justify anyone.

It is a matter of eternal life or eternal death that you know the truth that can make you free of sin. You cannot be saved without it. But you can be lost with it. That is, if you know but do not believe (with a working faith), you will be like the servant who knew the master's will but did not do it. Therefore, he was beaten with "many stripes."

Truth is a dangerous possession. If you do not cleave to it, it will abhor you. Only the orthodox are saved, but none are so deep in hell as the orthodox (who have the truth when the truth does not have them). You are either the better or much the worse for having read this little book. If it only convinces you of your false ways and one true way, you are the wiser but none the better, and, therefore, are much the worse. If, however, you from the heart cry out, "God be merciful to me, the sinner!" you will put down this tract justified. And we shall rejoice together forever that

> to the one who does not work, but believes in Him who justifies the ungodly, his faith is reckoned as righteousness (Rom. 4:5).

*Amen and amen!*

# A Primer

## on

## Roman

## Catholicism

# Contents

[EDITOR'S NOTE: This primer is intended to give an overview of the significant theological differences between historic Protestantism and historic Roman Catholicism. In a primer of this size, it is not possible to give a thorough examination of a theology that has been controverted for centuries. For a fuller treatment of the *main* difference between Catholicism and Protestantism—justification by faith alone—please see our book *Justification by Faith ALONE: Affirming the Doctrine by Which the Church and the Individual Stands or Falls* (1995)]

Recently, a Presbyterian-turned-Romanist wrote a book detailing his journey to "Rome Sweet Home." I maintain, "Rome is *Not* Home." Let me explain.

Rome affirms the Bible and its account of the creation of Adam and Eve, their temptation, and the fall of mankind by the disobedience of Adam. So Rome agrees with most Protestants that this is a fallen world and that it needs redeeming, which can only be done by God through His Son Jesus Christ. Unfortunately, the document *Evangelicals and Catholics Together: The Christian Mission in the Third Millennium* pretends that agreement on the deity of Christ and His bodily resurrection is an adequate foundation for Christian unity. As a matter of fact, there *has never been* any disagreement on those doctrines. Rome separated from the true church in the 16th century because she rejected Christ's *way of salvation!*

Let me now sketch the basic differences between Evangelicalism and Romanism. Let us begin with the lost person's becoming acquainted with the way home. He gets information about a way out of his wilderness. Here Rome and Protestantism agree. Both know that a person must hear the gospel of Christ and its divinely appointed way. So Rome is involved in propagating her message, just as all Protestant churches are. Rome has a different road map from the Protestant one. Both agree, however, that unless a person gets on the Christian road he cannot find his way home to God. The views of the road may differ crucially, but there is a concurrence on the fact that the Christian road is the necessary road out of the wilderness and into God's celestial home.

From that point on, the two descriptions of the one way differ fundamentally. Both these theologies, the Roman and the Reformational, believe that lost man can grasp the meaning of salvation, of Christ, and of the atonement. When lost man does grasp the Christian message, his next step is diversely viewed by Rome and Geneva. Rome thinks that he can be persuaded of the truth of the Christian religion centering on an infallible papacy. Reformed theology believes that the Reformed pastor can prove that is not the true way, but that the Protestant, Reformational way is the biblical way.

## 1. BAPTISM

If the lost person is persuaded that the Roman way is the Christian way, his first duty is to be baptized. The Calvinist, however, says that once the person understands that the Christian way is the true way which he ought to accept, he neverthelesss is *incapable* of accepting it. Rome differs drastically there. She maintains that the enlightened unconverted person can see the truth of the Roman way and can decide to be baptized. The Protestant says the person can see the truth of the Reformed way and the need of baptism; but he can also see that "seeing the way" does not qualify him for baptism. According to Rome, seeing the truth of the Roman way does qualify him for baptism. According to Reformed doctrine, seeing the truth of the Reformed doctrine, including the necessity of water baptism, does not of itself alone qualify that person to be baptized.

What is the essential difference here? You see the two traditions are viewing the sinner as lost, but one of them says he is able to save himself by submitting to baptism. The other says he is *not* able to save himself by submitting to baptism. Rome says to the person, "Be baptized and you will be born again into the kingdom of God." The Calvinist says to the person, "Be baptized at this time and you will be bringing yourself under additional judgment of God by taking a sacrament you are not yet qualified to receive." Rome thinks a person even in his unregenerate state is qualified to receive baptism. Reformed Protestantism says that, in his unregenerate state, he dare not take the sign of baptism.

Do we Reformed charge Rome with heresy at this point? We certainly say she is wrong. But do we charge her with deep heresy for urging the unregenerate to be baptized in the name of the Trinity? We certainly do, because we claim that baptism is a *sign* of sin having been washed away, and that this person has not had his sin washed away because he has not yet had saving faith. Rome replies to that by saying he has not had the forgiveness of his sins as yet— that is true—but if he will receive baptism he will be born again and thus receive the forgiveness of sins by faith.

So for Rome, the baptism of an adult is not the sign of his sins having been forgiven, but the way by which his sins are to be washed away. The Reformed faith is saying, in contrast, that baptism can be administered to an adult person only if that person has professed faith and received the forgiveness of sins. Rome is saying that baptism is not a sign of the forgiveness of sins but a means to it. We are saying it is not a means to it but is only a sign when other means to salvation have occurred.

Now what are these other means of salvation to which we refer that Rome denies at this stage? The other means of salvation, and indeed the only means of salvation which we Protestants find in Holy Scripture, is the converting or re-generating work of the Spirit of God. When God has regen-erated a person, and thus brought that person by the new birth into adoption into the family of God, then and only then is he to receive the baptismal sign of such member-ship. It is appropriate then, and only then, to be baptized. Prior to that experience, it is hypocritical for him to claim the cleansing of sins symbolically when he does not claim them actually or experientially.

Rome thinks of the candidate for baptism as an unregenerate son of the devil at the moment he receives baptism. She does not always make this clear to those whom she baptizes. But doctrinally speaking, that candidate for baptism, even though he has had a long catechumenate, is still an unregenerate child of the devil. It is that servant of Satan who is being baptized in the name of the Father, Son, and Holy Spirit at a Roman font. Such baptism does not signify that he is God's child, but assumes, in fact, that he is a child of the devil, at that point in time.

However, Rome says, the moment the water is applied in the name of the Father, Son, and Holy Spirit that person is transformed into a child of God. We admit that is *theoretically* possible. A person could be an unregenerate child of the devil and yet it could be God's plan to persuade him to come to baptism and thus become (by the Holy Spirit's regenerating work at the time of baptism) a child of God. There are Protestants who believe that as well as Roman Catholics. Why do the Reformed differ with it? We do differ with it drastically. The question right now is, what right do we have to differ with it? I will not now ask what right Rome has to teach and practice it. I rather ask the question, How can we Calvinists and Evangelicals be sure that the Roman way of bringing a person into the kingdom of God is erroneous?

There are several arguments we present to demonstrate the error of the Roman view of baptism. The first is this: If a person is a child of the devil, loves the darkness and hates the light, and hates the Christ who is the light of the world, he cannot gladly accept baptism. In truth, he wants nothing to do with the God he hates as a sinner against Him. He is a bondservant of sin. He will not go happily to something God is supposed to have established which is actually going to make him something he does not want to be.

Second, it misrepresents God's attitude toward the sinner. According to the Scripture, as even Rome admits, men are fallen and under the wrath of God. If they are not delivered, they must go eternally to suffer the torments of the damned at the hand of God. So God wants nothing to do with this person except to give him the wages of his sin, which is eternal death. But in the Roman picture of things, he is coming voluntarily and even gladly anticipating the presence of the God he hates. Meanwhile, God, who hates him with a wrath which will destroy him forever, is presumably standing there ready to convert him against his spiritual desires. That is, the sinner wants nothing to do with God. And yet here he is virtually standing and saying, "Baptize me, God, make me the kind of person who loves and serves You." That is simple hypocrisy on the part of an unregenerate sinner. Rome is playing the role of promoting hypocrisy by urging this person to come to baptism, and simultaneously suggesting that God is pleased with him even as he sinfully comes before he is regenerated.

Rome can't have it both ways. She can't say that men are fallen servants of the devil under the wrath of God who is going to punish them eternally, then at the same time say that God is well disposed to them and pleased to have them come as hypocritical sinners into His presence and receive His sacrament of baptism.

By contrast, in the Reformed view the person has been born again. He is a child of God. He is coming to Christ for the symbolic cleansing of his guilt. God has regenerated him and forgiven him and is now giving him the sign of the washing away of his sin. That is very appropriate and suitable and compatible with the doctrine of Holy Scripture and Protestantism (and even of Catholicism, if it were consistent with its view of unregenerate man).

A third indictment of Rome for this practice is that she has no ground for believing that every time baptism is administered to someone that person is born again. She does champion the doctrine of baptismal regeneration. She does teach that the sacraments "work" *ex opere operato* in their very administration.

The Bible does not teach any such doctrine. It nowhere says that everyone who is baptized is born again. It does teach that the born again should be baptized. It nowhere teaches that adults not born again should be baptized, or that, being baptized, they will be born again.

Rome tries to counter this with the contention that in Titus 3:5 baptism is represented as the washing of regeneration. "He saved us, not because of righteous things we have done, but because of His mercy. He saved us through the washing of rebirth and renewal by the Holy Spirit, whom He poured out on us generously through Jesus Christ our Savior." That text refers to the washing of rebirth or the washing of regeneration and renewal by the Holy Spirit, to be sure. It does *not* say that the washing of baptism is the washing of rebirth. Rome reads that into it. The text simply says, "He [God] saved us through the washing of rebirth and renewal by the Holy Spirit." Now the washing of rebirth and renewal by the Holy Spirit is by no means the same thing as baptism with water in the name of the Father and the Son and the Holy Spirit.

Rome will say, "Granted, it is not the same thing, but is the text not saying, when it refers to washing, that the Holy Spirit *through baptism* creates the new birth and renewal?" We say, "No, not at all." It simply says that God saves us by the washing of rebirth and renewal by the Holy Spirit. We admit that the word washing does sometimes suggest the rite of baptism. But it does not say it. Washing and baptism are not necessarily identical. It is true that baptism is a kind of washing. But every washing is not necessarily baptism. Every water baptism is not necessarily washing. The washing in Titus 3:5 is qualified by rebirth and renewal by the Holy Spirit. Even Roman Catholics admit that baptism can occur without rebirth and renewal by the Holy Spirit, and that rebirth and renewal can occur without baptism. That is the reason they say a person (be he a priest or some other person in an emergency) must have a sincere intention when he administers baptism. Presumably, if he does baptize in the triune name with a serious intention, then it "works." God regenerates. Without a sincere intention, baptism presumably does not work.

What I am observing here is that Rome admits that the baptism could occur without a sincere intention and no change would happen. As soon as you add a human factor, such as intention, you are adding something to the Titus text. Titus simply says we are saved by washing of rebirth and renewal by the Holy Spirit. It says nothing about baptism. It says nothing about intention. It says nothing about the trinitarian formula. It says nothing about water. It simply refers to the washing. It simply refers to rebirth and renewal.

Rome appeals to John 3:5: "No one can enter the kingdom of God unless he is born of water and the Spirit." This, Rome falsely teaches, is baptismal regeneration, by means of which a person is translated out of the kingdom of darkness into the kingdom of God's dear Son. But John 3:5 says this no more than does Titus 3:5. It simply says that one is born of water and the Spirit, obviously meaning born of water as well as the Spirit. John 3:3 had already said it was necessary to be born of the Spirit to enter the kingdom of God. One can be born of the Spirit. It is meaningless to say that washing with water creates a new spirit. Even those who teach the error of baptismal regeneration do not believe that. They deny any "magic" in the water. So new birth is a work of the Spirit, not of water. Why then is water mentioned in John 3:5? Obviously, baptism is associated with being born of the Spirit. It does not regenerate but is inseparable from it. How? One born of Christ professes Christ. His first confession is receiving the *sign* (baptism) of being a Christian. If he does not confess Christ he is not a Christian (Romans 10:9).

## 2. CONFIRMATION, OR COMMUNICANT CHURCH MEMBERSHIP

Let us now see what Rome does with a person who is deeper in the pit now than he was before he met Roman dogma and practice. She teaches seven sacraments. The first of these is baptism. Five of them have to do with the way of salvation *a la* Rome. The other two are for some members of the Roman communion, but not for all. The five salvation sacraments are baptism, confirmation, eucharist, penance, and extreme unction. The two special sacraments are ordination and matrimony. No Roman Catholic needs to be married, nor does he or she need to go into orders and become what they call "religious." But all Roman Catholics are to be baptized, to be confirmed, to receive the Mass, to observe confession and penance, and finally to have forgiveness at the time of death. We will consider only the five sacraments which deal with the way of life as they see it. Baptism has been discussed. Then comes confirmation.

Confirmation is normally administered to a baptized infant when he or she reaches 12 years of age. In the case of an unbaptized adult, it can occur any time that he is ready to profess the faith of Rome. Confirmation is based on accepting the explicit and implicit teaching of Rome.

If our criticism of baptism has been sound, the reader can see that confirmation would be a confirmation of death. It could not be a confirmation of life when no life takes place in so-called "baptismal regeneration." We have shown that baptismal regeneration is a fiction that even Rome does not hold consistently, but contradicts at various points. The point here is that if a person is not regenerated at the time of baptism, there cannot be any confirmation of an event which never took place. Rome would have administered the baptism contrary to the Lord's command, and now wrongly but consistently sees the person as ready for confirmation.

Such a "regenerate" person accepts the truth of God as represented by the Roman Catholic church. So the church instructs this person more thoroughly in the faith, which he or she affirms. As he understands more he will affirm more. Because he cannot ever understand all, he will be asked to exercise "implicit faith." Implicit faith is in the Roman Catholic teaching hierarchy. It maintains that that hierarchy, ordained and guided by God, will teach the truth of God. Though the person does not know all that the church has taught in the past, not to mention all that she may teach in the future, he simply accepts the church as appointed by God to be the infallible interpreter of truth. Therefore, whatever she says, he will believe.

That is in and of itself a very consistent view. If Rome did have the role which she claims, I too would place implicit faith in everything she teaches.

We Protestants ascribe ultimate authority to the Word of God while Roman Catholic parishioners ascribe that to the Roman church. That is, we believe that the Bible is the Word of God. We acknowledge that we have never begun to know all the teachings of the Bible. We do know that anything it does teach is true. We do not have to hear what it is before we accept it. We accept it because of its source. Its authority is its being the Word of God. God cannot err. Therefore His Word cannot err. Therefore anything it teaches is true. Whether we at the present moment know what it teaches in a given area or not, we know this: What it teaches in a given area is true. We also know that the moment we know what it teaches in that area, we know the truth in that area. We are full of implicit faith. I, for one, know that I have far more implicit faith than explicit faith. That is, I know far less about the teachings of the Bible than I am ignorant of the teachings of the Bible. Though over 80 years of age, I am far, far from ever exhausting all the truths and have only minimal knowledge. But I do know that whatever you discover and can show me is the teaching of the Bible, that is not only your truth but it is my truth.

We have Protestant debates, but the debates are simply as to whether we are correctly interpreting the Bible or not. We do not debate about the truthfulness of what the Bible says. We may debate one another as to whether he or she correctly understands the Bible. Debate ends the moment we have become persuaded of the Bible's teaching. We have implicit faith in everything it teaches from today to eternity.

Rome claims all that for her magisterium, the hierarchical church. Excuse me for laughing. This is an awful comedown from the Protestant parallel to it. It is one thing to believe that God cannot err. It is another thing to believe that the Pope cannot err when he speaks *ex cathedra*. But that is what all Romanists have to believe. The hierarchy cannot err. Whatever a synod of the church has ever ascertained (the Pope assenting or confirming or agreeing or really establishing it), that is the truth of God. If you do not believe that, you cannot be confirmed as a Roman Catholic. If you do believe that, I am sorry to say, you confirm yourself as an unbeliever. You cannot believe in God and believe that any present human beings have the authority of God. But that is what you have to believe if you want to be confirmed as a Roman Catholic!

Let me remind the reader that confirmation rests on the parishioner's accepting all that the Roman church teaches, including her fatally wrong doctrine of justification.

In the 400-plus-year controversy on justification, it is usually said that Rome teaches justification by works and Protestantism justification by faith. That description is true and false. It is true and false depending entirely on whether one understands the meaning of justification by works in Romanism and the meaning of justification by faith in Protestantism. (See section 7 of this primer.)

Most of the persons who comment on justification do not understand either the Roman view of justification by works or the Protestant view of justification by faith. So on the "article by which the church stands or falls," there is a singular, widespread, almost omnipresent misunderstanding. Persons engaged in the Reformation debate usually did understand the issue. John Calvin certainly understood it, though he used some rather imprecise language at times. Cardinal Bellarmine understood it as a defender of the Roman doctrine. But that cannot be said of all the Roman theologians at the Council of Trent (1546–63).

Speaking generally about Trent, I would say that while it correctly stated some parts of the doctrine, comprehensively speaking, it did not articulate soundly the doctrine which it anathematized. If that is so, it means that after the Reformation had maintained clearly the central doctrine at issue, the Roman church rejected the Protestant position without fully understanding or articulating it. If that is so, it is sad indeed.

It is impossible to overestimate the importance of understanding this extremely critical doctrine. If many of those who waged war concerning it did not know whereof they spoke and thought, that is a warning to all who come today to consider this crucial teaching.

If one understands the way the proponents advocated these positions, he can accurately say that Rome teaches justification by works and Protestantism teaches justification by faith alone. According to the Council of Trent's "infallible" definition of justification, the "root" of it is faith. This faith, informed by love, produces good deeds as its fruit. When a perfect measure of good works is achieved, the person enters heaven. "Saints" actually inherit the kingdom of God or go to paradise as soon as they die. Those Romanists who have not achieved that degree of perfection in this world must suffer further punishment for their remaining sins in purgatory. When they have suffered sufficiently, they will, by the merit of the works which they did, go to heaven. That is justification *by* works, *on the basis of* works, on the *merit* of works (even though Rome formally attributes all "merit" to Christ). In that sense, the Roman Catholic church teaches that justification before God is an achievement of the human being who does the works of righteousness perfectly.

This teaching of Rome is misunderstood and virtually caricatured when it is represented as teaching justification by works *alone*. According to Rome, faith is the "root" of these works. One cannot do works pleasing to God apart from faith in Jesus Christ. No wonder many Roman Catholics become enraged with Protestants who accuse them of teaching justification by works apart from any faith whatever.

Romanists believe that faith is essential, just as Protestants believe that faith is essential. They do not think it is *sufficient* for justification, but they do not believe justification can come about *apart from faith*.

It is true that Rome teaches that ultimate justification is by the works or good activities of the baptized person. They will accept that attribution. They think it is true and infallibly defined by the Holy See itself. But do not tell a Roman Catholic that he is opposed to faith or does not believe in faith or does not realize the necessity of faith. He does indeed. The Council of Trent stressed the fact that faith is necessary as the root of the good works which we do for justification. *Roman Catholicism teaches justification by works alone, but not by the works that are alone.*

The reader can see that I am playing with the Reformation formula. The Reformation insisted that *justification is by faith alone, but not by the faith that is alone.* Justifying faith is working faith. Faith produces good works. Those works do not contribute to the justification, but they are inseparable from the faith which does justify. Likewise, Rome is saying, "Justification is by works alone, indeed, but not by the works that are alone. Works are dependent on faith. Faith leads to the works. So yes, we Romanists believe in justification by works alone, but not by works that are alone."

Now that we are seeing the two positions properly and comparing them properly, let us evaluate the Roman position and, later, the Protestant position. Understanding

Rome to teach justification by works in the manner just explained, is that doctrine the sound, biblical, saving doctrine of justification? Rome says it is. What does the Protestant say? As we know, Protestants in general, and the Reformed in particular, say it is not the true doctrine. It is not the saving justification of Holy Scripture.

So the question before us now is why do Protestants say that, and can such a contention be proven? We prove it this way. First, after a person is regenerated, he is still not fully sanctified. His corrupt nature is crucified and dying, but it is not yet dead. That is the reason Scripture is urging the saint to put to death the old man, and to clothe himself with the new man, to put away the works of darkness and to put on the works of light. The Lord's Prayer teaches us to confess our sins. As long as a man is required to confess his sins, he must have sins to confess.

Rome seems to feel that her "religious" are like that servant who did not only what he was required to do in the field, but did what he didn't need to do—serving his master in his spare time at home (Luke 17:7ff). But there are no works of supererogation. Every man and woman is required to be perfect as the Father in heaven is perfect (Matthew 5:48). They are to serve God with all their heart, soul, mind, and strength, loving Him and their neighbor as themselves. That is minimal duty for every person. If, therefore, a man is *able* to serve the Lord in a ministry by being celibate, he has the *obligation* to serve the Lord in that ministry by being celibate. It is perfectly true that marriage is legitimate for any man or woman, but not true for that man or woman who thinks that he or she can serve God more fully in the celibate state. If that person has the gift to live the celibate life, he or she has the duty to do so. Such persons are not going beyond the standard of perfection, they are only conforming to it.

Our Lord indicates that not everyone has that gift (Matthew 19:11–12). Those who do not have the gift for living a continent, celibate life have no obligation to avoid marriage. On the contrary, it is better to marry than to burn (1 Corinthians 7:9). Perfection is the standard and the goal for every person. If a person has "celibacility," and concludes that they can love God with all their heart, soul, mind, and strength, and love their neighbor as themselves better as a celibate than as a married person, they have no option to marry. Rome sins in making something mandatory for religious orders which God does not make mandatory. God does require every person to serve God perfectly, and to do so by the celibate life if and only if he has the gift to live continently in such a condition. Rome requires everyone who would be an ordained minister of the Word to forego marriage, whether he has the gift or not. The history of the church is full of the lapses from that model and terrible sins which men and women have brought upon themselves and others by endeavoring to do something they had no gift from God to do, but only a command from the church, countermanding God, which Rome is wont to do.

The Roman church's salvation does not begin where she says it does, with baptism. Nor can it continue, as she says it does, in sanctification. And if there were sanctification, it would achieve no merit, which she claims. Certainly, if there were any merit in it, the most meritorious of all individuals is told by Scripture to say, "I am an unprofitable servant" (Luke 17:10). Unprofitable servants do not aspire to heaven on the basis of their perfection.

So Rome has not begun on the way, and even if she had she has not continued on that way. Her way to heaven is merit, and the Bible makes it perfectly plain that no mere human ever achieved justification by his merit. Our duty here is perfection. By divine grace it will be achieved in heaven. It will not be achieved in this world even by the truly regenerate, though they must ever strive for it.

So we see that the Roman Catholic way of justification is not the way of justification but of damnation. Why do I say damnation? Is the implication not obvious? If justification is the way by which a person is made just and acceptable to

God, and the person is not justified, does he not remain in the state of condemnation from which justification alone could deliver him? That is to say, if Rome does not achieve justification, as I have shown she could not possibly do on her principles, she leaves the person in the state of condemnation in which he was born. Only now there is an aggravated guilt. Rome gives him the impression, falsely, that he is no longer in a state of condemnation, but actually is in a way of salvation. His last condition is far worse than his first when he entered the Roman church, by which he is made twofold more a child of hell (Matthew 23:15).

So the author of the book *Rome Sweet Home* denies the only way of justification, and yet fancies, by false Roman doctrine, that he is on his way to justification. If he really understands and believes the Roman Catholic way of salvation, he is in a state of condemnation worse than the one when he first believed this false gospel! How I pray that he and his followers may see that his last condition is worse than his first, and seek the Lord, who alone justifies, while He may be found.

Rome teaches different methods of sanctification. She believes in prayer, for example. One would be inclined to say that anyone who prays would surely be blessed by a prayer-hearing and a prayer-answering God. So whatever other error she may have in her scheme of salvation, certainly calling upon her people to pray regularly the Lord's Prayer and other prayers, and leading them in prayer in worship services and so on, is an unmitigated good. However false their system may be, certainly this is a redeeming element: prayer.

But is it? Scripture says that the prayer of the wicked is an abomination to the Lord (Proverbs 15:9; 21:27; 28:9). Prayers like that would be better unmade. God is alienated by such rather than cultivated. He is angered rather than inclined to bless. Someone might say, "But look, He is a prayer-hearing and a prayer-answering God." Yes, He is, but He is not an abomination-hearing God. The prayer of the wicked is not a prayer, it is an abomination. The way we would write that particular proverb would be by putting prayer in quotes, and reading it like this—"prayer" is an abomination. It is not prayer, it is a parody of prayer; it is a takeoff on prayer, a counterfeit of prayer, a mockery of prayer. An abomination is better left unuttered. Peter tells us that is the way pagans live who choose "living in debauchery, lust, drunkenness, orgies, carousing and detestable idolatry" (1 Peter 4:3). The prophecy of Amos has a section in which he represents wicked, unbelieving people offering sacrifices and singing and praying to God. God's response is to cover His eyes, stop His ears, and hold His nose as the incense ascends. That incense is putrid when offered by the wicked. The hypocrites make worship into a crime against the Most High. He will by no means clear the guilty of such "prayer."

The indictment of prayer in the Roman system may be the hardest one for the reader to bear. But you can see that once a person starts on the wrong road, then everything he does on that road is going to bring him closer to final destruction. Rome has started on the wrong road, and even if she does some things which are externally right, she still is on the wrong road and is moving closer all the while to destruction. People must recognize and remember this fact; otherwise they will be easily deceived into thinking that they are on the right road because they are doing some right things along the wrong road.

I call these "bad good works." I mean by that that they are bad in their motivation because the person is wrongly related to God in the first place, even though the things themselves, such as giving money in church or kneeling to pray or going the second mile with someone who has misused you, are good in themselves. They are corrupted by the source from which they come. They are, as we say, poisoned springs. Even good things are poisoned when they come from a poisonous source. Mafia members often pray about their "hits."

Manifestly, if one confuses this matter, he is prone to think he is an acceptable individual because a particular thing he is doing is in itself acceptable. As long as he is an unacceptable person, all that he does is unacceptable.

As a matter of fact, it becomes more offensive than ordinary evil deeds. An evil *person* always does evil deeds, even though they may appear to be good—grapes among thorns. When one seems to be doing what is good, and purports to be doing what is good, and claims to be doing what is good, and is considered by people as doing what is good, he is playing the role of hypocrite in all these circumstances. Hypocrisy makes a seeming good work worse than an obviously bad work for the simple reason that it seems to be what it is not. Evil as evil is at least seen as what it really is. Evil seen as good is a compounded evil. So none can sin like the saint. That is, none can sin like a person who seems to be a saint while actually being a sinner in false clothes. He is a wolf in sheep's clothing. None can blaspheme like the pious. "As it is written, 'God's name is blasphemed among the Gentiles because of you' " Romans 2:24. You are a devil appearing as an angel of light. And the devil is never more devilish than when he appears as an angel of light.

I will not go on with this theme any longer because it ought to be apparent to everyone. But let me mention just one other matter before I proceed. Take the matter of a Roman Catholic observing the Lord's Supper, which they call the Mass. Let's right now overlook the fact that the Roman church wrongly deprives the people of the cup of communion, restricting that to the clergy. Also let us overlook the error of their doctrine of transubstantiation. That is, let us overlook any faults there may be in communion as administered by the Roman Catholic church. Let us simply consider it as an act of purported obedience to Christ who commands us to observe the Lord's Supper until He comes again. Is it not clear that even when a group of falsely professed Christian people profess to do this communion in remembrance of Him they are sinning most profoundly? Yes, the communion is commanded by Christ. Yes, it is a duty of Christian people. Yes, it is a moment of greatest fellowship with God if it is done properly. But it is not right if the participant is himself not reconciled to God. If we have correctly shown that the Roman way of reconciliation is non-reconciling and actually alienates more than does making no such profession at all, then manifestly this person has no right to come to the Lord's Supper at all. So while it is a duty of true Christian people to come, it is a duty of unconverted persons not to come, unless they choose to eat and drink damnation, as Paul says.

You shrink from this, but the conclusion is inevitable that when an unreconciled Roman Catholic comes to the Lord's table, he eats damnation. At this particular point, you cannot help but observe rather sardonically that the Roman error of depriving the people of the cup turns out to be a benefit to her people, preventing them there-by from drinking condemnation and confining them solely to eating condemnation. The priest, of course, by participating in both the bread and the cup, brings upon himself a double condemnation.

So that which virtually every Catholic considers a high point in his journey toward heaven, namely communion, is where he touches spiritual bottom. There is no place at which a person can be more sacrilegious than when he eats and drinks condemnation to himself by participating in a communion to which he has no right.

## 3. THE MASS

Let us now consider the Roman Catholic eucharist in itself. I have been considering sacraments as received by a person who is not qualified to receive. Now let us look at the doctrine itself as Rome promulgates it before the world. It is not only that it may be abused by people who use it unqualifiedly. What I will now show is that it is intrinisically and in itself, as understood and taught by the Roman church, a travesty of that which the Lord Himself established.

Everyone knows that the Roman church teaches transubstantiation. Virtually everyone knows what that means. Somehow the bread becomes the body of Christ. The substance of the bread is changed into the substance of the body of Christ. The result is that when a person communes properly he actually eats the body of Jesus Christ miraculously present now in the transubstantiated bread. When the priest drinks the cup, he drinks the very blood of Jesus Christ now miraculously, corporeally, and substantially present in the cup.

I will ignore here the contention of Rome that the person does not taste what tastes like flesh, and he does not drink what tastes like blood, because of the nature of "substance." The teaching is that it is the "accidents" of anything which a person actually encounters in an experience with it and not the "substance." So a person actually devours the substance of the body of Christ. Because it is the substance and not the accidents of His body, it does not taste as if the person were actually masticating the body of Christ and drinking the blood of Christ. It is a fact even though it does not seem to be a fact. It is a fact because it is a transubstantiation of the substance but not a transubstantiation of the accidents of the substance.

This is just by way of reminding the reader what the doctrine is. My concern here is to show that there is no biblical warrant for such teaching. The first thing we observe is that to say Christ's body is literally present in the bread is a meaningless proposition. When we were considering baptism, we noticed that even though Jesus says (John 3:5) that we cannot enter the kingdom of God except by *water* and the Spirit, we know that He does not mean, and could not mean, that the water itself has the power to convert. There is no magic in the water, nor does God use it miraculously. While Christ is making it very clear that

baptism is necessary, it is also obvious that it is not necessary as being power-water when actually all the power is in
God.

Here too we have a situation like baptism. One cannot
entertain a conception of bread being *literally* the body of
anyone, not to mention the body of Jesus Christ. Bread is
bread and it cannot be something other than that as long as
it remains bread. Roman Catholics will say I am being rationalistic here. They will say that I am not being truly humble, accepting the teaching of the Bible which has Jesus
saying, "You must eat My flesh," and "This is My body
which is given for you," in the Lord's Supper. "That is
what the Lord says and, whether you can understand it or
not, you'd better believe it!"

I am not trying to be wiser than God, nor do I have the
colossal audacity to reject His teaching and substitute my
own. What I am saying, as a child of God trying to grasp
the words of God, is that there is no meaning for the human intellect in saying that bread is the body of Jesus
Christ. The resurrected body of Jesus Christ is at the right
hand of God the Father in heaven right now, and will remain there until He comes again in His body to "judge the
quick and the dead." He is not in this piece of bread, nor is
His blood in the cup we drink.

When we contradict the Roman Catholic testimony of
people (in their great exuberation and jubilation when they
receive the wafer in their mouth), we are not denying their
*experience*. They usually reply to our criticism by accusing
us of consummate arrogance. They say, "You claim to
know that we do not have an experience which we say we
have? Aren't you being very, very presumptuous? How
can *you* know what we do experience or what we do not experience? How are you qualified to say we do not actually
have this immense transforming satisfaction in participating in the Mass?"

I am not denying anybody's experience. As long as I believe as I do, that they are honest persons, I am sure that

they are testifying to feelings which they truly have. Nor do I deny that they are having those feelings when they are actually eating that wafer which the priest puts on their tongue. Nor do I deny that when they eat that wafer they think they are devouring the body of Jesus Christ. Nor do I question them when they say that "we have this experience because we are eating the very body of our Savior who died to save us." I do not doubt that they *think* that is the case. But I do not only doubt, but I am certain that is not the case, and that I can prove it.

You see, there are two points at issue, not only one. These people are saying two things: (1) we have this wonderful experience; and (2) this experience comes from our masticating the body of Jesus Christ. Now I am not questioning that they have this experience. I am not questioning, in other words, the first part of their affirmation. What I am questioning is the second part of their statement, that this experience comes from the masticating of the body of Jesus Christ. They believe that as firmly as they testify to the experience they have based on that belief. But the *experience* is one thing, the *basis* for it is another. The experience can be theirs, without doubt. But the masticating of the body of Jesus Christ, which they think is the source of it, is utterly impossible, I say.

There is nothing arrogant about making that statement. I am not presuming even to know their feelings except as they reveal them to me. But is it any presumption for me to question whether they can have ever masticated the body of Jesus Christ? If I can show that they could not have, that it is *impossible* to have, masticated the body of Jesus Christ in the Mass, then have I not demonstrated the second part of their testimony is absolutely false, even though they *believe* it to be true, and feel joyful for so believing?

I do not have to do this because I have already shown that there is no warrant for believing in transubstantiation. It is not taught by the Bible, nor is it even rational to the human mind. A finite body can only be in one place at one time. It is a doctrine of Roman Catholic orthodoxy as well as Protestant orthodoxy that the body of Jesus Christ is a finite body. It is also a part of Roman orthodoxy as well as ours that Christ is corporeally present at the right hand of God in heaven right now. So if a finite body has to be at one place at one time, and the body of Jesus Christ is in heaven now and not on earth, then it follows immediately that His body is not on earth anywhere. Christ's body is not in the wafer nor any place else, not to mention on thousands of different altars. Christ's body is only in heaven.

If we have proven that, we have proven those to be false witnesses who claim that their exhilaration at eating the wafer comes from actually masticating the body of Christ. That is impossible. The body of Jesus Christ is in heaven. You cannot see it or touch it, much less eat it. Your experience may be real, but the basis on which you rest it is nonexistent. It is nonreal.

I do not presume to say where these people get their feelings, but I do presume to say as a sane human being, along with the rest of the human race, that there is no way of conceiving that the body of Jesus Christ is in that wafer that Romanists eat at the Mass. I beg Romanists to realize that, though they may have a wonderful feeling, it does not come from the so-called sacrifice of the Mass.

If it cannot possibly come from that source, and if they realize that, then they can ask themselves, "How do I come to feel so exhilarated and joyous when I participate in the Mass?" They will know the nonanswer is that they have masticated the body of Christ. It is *not* that, whatever else it may be. An intelligent person will realize that if it is not what he *thinks* it is, he will become extremely dubious about the experience based on it. It is based on he knows not what, because what he thought it was based on it could not possibly be based on.

It is a sad fact that people can have exhilarated feelings about something they believe which is later demonstrated to be nonexistent. People hear at times that they are inheriting fortunes, and of course they are delighted at the prospect of having so much cash suddenly. As soon as they realize that was a false report and they do not have the cash, then exhilaration collapses and they wish they never had had it. This is what I think would happen to any Roman Catholic who sits down and deliberately thinks through this matter. It ought to lead to his conversion to realize that all his joy is resting on a non-existent fact, and that he is involved in perpetuating a fundamental fraud to the whole world, namely, that he is happy because of an experience which he could not possibly have had.

Romanists (and some Protestants) will charge me with rationalism for denying that a body can be at many different places at the same time. I am being rational (as the Bible is), not rationalistic. Christ has *one* body, not many bodies as transubstantionism affirms. Every Sunday, He is supposed to have different bodies all around the world. That would not be a thousand miracles, it would be a thousand lies. Christ miraculously *multiplied* one boy's lunch. He does not *multiply* His one body. The very utterance of such an absurd error involves a half-dozen Christological and hermeneutical errors.

## 4. PENANCE

Another one of the seven sacraments of the Roman Catholic church which we want to look at briefly is the penitential system. This system begins with a contradiction in terms. The Roman church teaches that when a person is born again and repents, he is forgiven. The guilt of his original sin is canceled. The remaining sin (which Rome calls concupiscence) is not sin at all. I say this is a contradiction at the very beginning of the penitential system. It says the sin has been forgiven and is no longer sin but is now concupiscence. Nevertheless, it has to be repented of and it has to be punished.

The nonsensical character of this teaching may be seen more evidently by contrasting it with the understandable Protestant view. Even a person who may not believe the Protestant view will see that it is comprehensible, while the Roman view, even if he does believe it, is not comprehensible. So I am requesting all of you, whether you are Protestant or Roman or secularist, to read carefully as I try to show that the Roman view is actually a contradiction in terms. That is to say, the Roman church teaches that original sin is really remitted and the remaining sin is not sin at all, but they treat it as if it were. Manifestly, as soon as you treat something as if it existed when, according to your teaching, it does not exist, you are communicating incomprehensibles. It would have to be one or the other. Either it is sin or it is not sin. Either it is punishable or it is not punishable. You cannot have something which is sin and yet not sin, punishable and yet not punishable. Yet this is the heart of the penitential system which in many ways is the heart of the Roman Catholic lifestyle.

To make matters more absurd still, the punishment of non-sin actually continues into purgatory. Persons who go to purgatory are persons whose sins in this world have not been adequately punished in this world. We have already indicated that, according to Roman theory, these things are being punished in this world, not to mention punished further in the world to come, are not sins at all! But that is the oxymoronic Roman Catholic penitential system. The penitential system which is what is occupying most Roman Catholic minds most of the time is, strictly speaking, a nonexistent system, an incomprehensible system.

Someone is very inclined to say at this juncture, "Gerstner, you are the one who is talking in contradictory terms. You are telling millions of people who are living in this system that they are living in a nonsystem. Now who is the idiot around here, they or you? Aren't you like a person saying to a flesh-eating animal that flesh-eating animals cannot eat flesh?" Yes, if you wish to put it that way. This doctrine is as absurd as saying that a certain creature is a flesh-eating animal who cannot eat flesh. Man is a person who has no sins, but whose sins must nevertheless be punished in this world and in the world to come. When you ask how I can be sane when I contradict something that millions of people testify to, my answer ought to be very evident. Crazy as it may sound, they are testifying to something which does not and cannot exist. They must have some sort of coherent concept in their own minds if penitence is meaningful to them. What they must have in their own minds which is meaningful is, however, not what the Roman Catholic church teaches which is unmeaningful, nonmeaningful, impossible to be understood meaningfully.

I will now point out the Protestant way to show the absurdity of the Roman view in contrast to a comprehensible view. Protestantism, I would say, is a meaningful teaching, that a person can understand who nevertheless may deplore it, hate it, and reject it. But he can know what it is. Even though he rejects it, he knows what he is rejecting. If he accepts it, he knows what he is accepting. The Roman view, by contrast, is something which a person cannot know, whether he says he believes or disbelieves it.

The Protestant doctrine teaches that all the *guilt* of a person's sin (past, present, and future) is eternally forgiven the moment he receives justification by the imputation of Christ's perfect righteousness. Also, the *power* of his remaining sinfulness and sins remains but does not reign. These remaining sins bring chastening (not wrath or punishment), by his Father who loves him and for that reason chastens him so he becomes more and more like the One who died for him. That is understandable doctrine, and the Bible proves it true.

## 5. LAST RITES

This last of the five common sacraments requires only brief comment. It represents no new principle. It is only the final transition before death to the next world of purgatory or paradise. Since Vatican II, it is not restricted to "Last Rites" (extreme unction), but is more commonly related to anointing for serious sickness.

These sacraments and theological principles which I refer to briefly here are more fully treated elsewhere in the book *Justification by Faith ALONE,* published by Soli Deo Gloria in 1995. I append this discussion only to show how far *away from* home these sacraments and principles will carry all who sincerely adopt them.

I don't fear the Roman theologians who will simply reject what I have written. All they can do is reject, not refute. For slaves of men that is all that is necessary, alas! The next event on the divine calendar, however, is to appear before the Judgment Seat of the Lord Jesus Christ (2 Corinthians 5:10).

The ones I do fear (because they are so pervasive, though even less persuasive) are those who raise the banner of freedom of religion. They take the *legal* right to believe whatever one pleases to be a *moral* right. Our government allows all sorts of hell-deserving religions to flourish and carry millions with them to perdition. These "religious" people hate argument, detest debate, and refuse even to listen to friends who would save them from ruin. They consider it a crime even to try to prove error and save souls.

But to all who are seeking "Home," I dedicate this essay, hoping that they may come to realize and believe that only the way of the cross leads home. Perhaps the best way to show these people the true way to true *home* is to point them again to the only divinely inspired map, *Holy Scripture.*

## 6. THE BIBLE

There are two fundamental points at which Rome deviates concerning the Bible on the Bible's view of itself:

First, Rome denies that the Bible is a self-interpreting revelation. The Bible declares itself to be self-explanatory. This is called the doctrine of the perspicuity of the Scriptures (the see-through-ableness of the Scripture). It may be understood in its own light. What is obscure in one passage will be clearer in another. What is incomplete here is completed there. What is a figure in one place is a commentary in another.

Rome has substituted for the doctrine of the perspicuity of the Scriptures the doctrine of the audacity of the Church. The Bible says that those who run may read; Rome says that those who run to *her* may read. The Bible says of the Bereans who searched the Scriptures that they were noble; Rome says of the Reformers who searched the Scriptures that they were heretics. The Scriptures say, "Study to show thyself approved unto God, a workman that needeth not to be ashamed, rightly dividing the word of truth," 2 Timothy 2:15. Rome says, "Study to show thyself a slave obediently accepting the word of Rome."

"But," the Roman Catholic church maintains, "the Word of God needs an interpreter."

"If so," replies the Protestant church, "the word of the pope also requires an interpreter." If the Bible must be interpreted by the Church in order to render its meaning certain, then the interpretation of the Church will have to be interpreted by another authority to make its meaning certain, and then there will need to be an interpreter of the interpreter, and so on *ad infinitum*.

Now if the Romanist replies, "Where there are divergent views on the Bible teaching there must be some authoritative decision," we will agree. Nor do we only agree. Our various Protestant church courts actually provide authoritative interpretations on most points when such decisions are necessary. But there is a difference between authoritative and infallible decisions. Compare, for example, the necessity for an authoritative interpretation of the Constitution. A Supreme Court performs that task. Yet what American believes the Supreme Court is infallible? Still, its decisions prevail as a matter of necessity. On occasions the Court may be "stacked" and its interpretations biased. In the long run, however, the people of this land believe an authoritative interpreter necessary, but never do they regard it as infallible. The Constitution remains the law of the land, not the Supreme Court. Likewise, the Bible remains the law of the Christian, not the Church.

The Roman Catholic church proclaims itself to be "the pillar and ground of the truth," since 1 Timothy 3:15 says that the church is the pillar and ground of the truth. But that verse does *not* say that the Roman Catholic church is the pillar and ground of the truth; in fact, the Roman Catholic church did not even exist when this verse was penned. Additionally, where did the Church get the idea that it is the pillar and ground of the truth? From the Bible! It is the Bible which is the basis of the church's authority, not the church which is the basis for the Bible's authority. The Bible is the pillar on which the church rests; the church is not the pillar on which the Bible rests. Incidentally, the expression that the church is the pillar and ground of the truth does not point to a pillar on which truth rests, but to a pillar on which truth was posted for public announcement in antiquity. In other words, it refers to the church as witness to the truth and not the basis of it.

The Protestant church has provided for authority so that decisions can be rendered when necessary, but has avoided the error of investing this authority with infallibility. The Protestant church, not being infallible, can err, has erred, will err. There is one error, however, which it has not made and that is the greatest of them all—the error of thinking it cannot err.

Having considered Rome's first great denial, namely,

that the Scripture is self-interpreting, we will consider her second great denial: that the Scripture is a complete revelation.

"Wherein is the Scripture incomplete?" we ask. No infallible answer has been given to that question, but there are a dozen or more doctrines which the majority of Roman theologians agree are only imperfectly revealed in the Bible, or merely implied, or entirely omitted.

Let us examine one of each of these classes. The Trinity, for example, Rome regards as imperfectly revealed in the Scripture. What, then, has the Church added? That God is one as to substance and three as to person. We agree. But still our philosophical interpretation of the simple Bible teaching may turn out to be quite wrong. And besides, the important thing is *that* God is one God and yet three persons, not *how* He thus exists. Yes, something new has been added (that the substance and personality of God are distinguishable) but it may be wrong. Furthermore, the explanation is not necessary to a knowledge of the Trinity. And finally, what is necessary and certain is already contained in the Bible.

Note as an example of the second group, doctrines merely implied, infant baptism. Church practice sanctions this rite. Well and good. But how did the Church come to sanction it? Undoubtedly because the Church believed that infant baptism was clearly implied in the Scripture! So the very Church tradition that is supposed to add force to the Bible rests on the Bible and has no more validity than the biblical implication.

Note finally as an example of the third class, doctrines entirely omitted in the Bible, purgatory. Here Rome is creating her doctrine out of whole cloth. Purgatory is not only omitted by the Bible, it is utterly precluded by the constant biblical teaching of two and only two possible destinies which face every man.

In order to harmonize such doctrines as purgatory, the immaculate conception of Mary, the infallibility of the pope's official declarations, etc., Rome is obliged to wrest the Scriptures. She is no more able to serve the two masters, tradition and the Scriptures, than were the Pharisees. She has had to cleave to one and abhor the other. Unfortunately, it has been the word of man rather than the Word of God which has been the preferred master.

This reminds me of the art collector who had a painting of the Leaning Tower of Pisa in his office. Each morning when he came in he would notice that the painting was hanging askew. Finally, his bewilderment drove him to ask the maid if she knew how it happened that every morning the painting was askew. She had a ready explanation: "I have to fix it that way in order to make the tower hang straight." Rome, likewise, is obliged to wrest the Scriptures in order to allow her tradition to hang straight.

## 7. JUSTIFICATION BY FAITH ALONE

Martin Luther, the great reformer, while still a Roman Catholic, had an experience which was the cue to his whole career. It occurred, according to his son, Paul, when, mounting the holy staircase of Rome on his knees in penance, he realized in a sudden flash of understanding the meaning of these words: "The just shall live by faith," Romans 1:17. Immediately he rose from his knees and walked down the steps. This was the prelude to the Reformation. Was Luther right? Are men justified before God by faith alone? Let us see.

According to the Bible, justification is by faith in Christ; according to Rome, justification is by faith plus works. According to the Bible, justification produces good works; according to Rome, good works produce justification. According to the Bible, justification is by Christ alone; according to Rome, it is by Christ and the sinner. It would appear that the word of Rome and the Word of God are two different things. The following is a formula I have used for over 50 years when explaining this point:

*Roman Catholic Teaching:*

Faith + Works → Justification

*Biblical Doctrine:*

Faith → Justification + Works

It can be seen from the diagram that works are necessary for justification in both systems; but in the Roman system they are necessary as a prerequisite; in the biblical system they are necessary as a postrequisite. (For a much fuller treatment of this entire issue, see the book *Justification by Faith ALONE,* by John MacArthur, R. C. Sproul, John Armstrong, Joel Beeke, and myself, and published by Soli Deo Gloria in 1995.)

But someone will ask, does the Bible not also state that "faith without works is dead" (James 2:20)? Does it not go on to say that such a faith cannot justify? Does it not imply that faith must be supplemented by works in order to avail? Is the Catholic doctrine not right after all: justification is by faith plus works? The answer is simple—justification is by a living and active faith (this is understood everywhere in the Bible; it is made explicit in James). Now, a living faith leads to good works. So justification, which is by a living faith, is by a full-of-the-promise-of-good-works faith. "Justification is by faith alone, but not by the faith that is alone."

Let us endeavor to illustrate what James is teaching here about faith. He is not questioning the ability of genuine faith to justify, but he is simply insisting that it has to be genuine and not "dead" faith. Suppose a man were fortunate enough to have $35 to spend on a hat and went to a store to purchase one. Having selected the one he wished, he hands the salesman his currency only to be told that it is counterfeit and cannot be accepted for payment. Is the dealer saying that the hat cannot be bought for $35? That something

more is needed? Is he reflecting on the previously adver-
tised ability of $35 to buy the hat in question? Certainly not.
He is only insisting that it be genuine currency. That is all
that is necessary, but it is necessary. In the same way,
James is saying that justification is not by a counterfeit
faith. He is not saying that it is not by genuine faith.

"Justification by faith" is really not the precise statement
of this doctrine. Justification is by CHRIST ALONE
(received by faith). We are not justified by our acceptance of
the redeeming mercy of Jesus Christ crucified, but by
Christ's mercy (ours by acceptance).

This is the heart of our doctrine—that Christ alone was
sufficient for all our sins, that He is able to save to the uttermost those who come to Him in faith. And, conversely,
the most serious part of the Roman heresy on this whole
doctrine is at this point. By denying justification by faith
alone she also denies the sufficiency of Christ's atonement.

We have observed that justification is by faith in *Christ*.
Now let us note that justification is by *faith* in Christ.
Christ is the ground of justification; faith is the instrument.
Christ saves; faith is the means by which Christ's salvation is received. There is no other name than His whereby
we must be saved; but there is no other way than by faith.
A. H. Strong has likened faith to the coupling which con-
nects a locomotive with its train of cars. It is the locomotive
and not the coupling that pulls the train. But without the
coupling even the locomotive could not pull the train. It is
Christ and not faith that saves the soul. But without faith in
Him not even Christ is able to save. (And remember, faith
in Christ is the gift of Christ.)

Some fancy that biblical justification is a process rather
than an act because it is mentioned at different times in a
justified person's life. But its being stated at different times
is because different "works" illustrate its continuing activity. It is cited in connection with Abraham's later offering of
Isaac, not because he did not possess it earlier, but because
that great "work" demonstrated Abraham's faith (which

alone justified him, and not that or any other work). As James said, the work justified (vindicated) the faith (which justified the person).

One concluding word on the fruits of justification. Rome has always charged that this Protestant doctrine leads to immorality. Being justified by faith, Rome says, we have a presumptuous peace with God; we have access into a grace from which we will constantly fall; and we are conceitedly assured of heaven and can find no purpose in tribulation and discipline. But Paul says, "Being justified by faith, we have peace with God through our Lord Jesus Christ: by whom also we have access by faith into this grace wherein we stand, and rejoice in the hope of the glory of God. And not only so, but we glory in tribulation also," Romans 5:1–3. Rome, of course, is thinking of a "counterfeit" grace while the Bible speaks of the genuine product. History shows that where the doctrine of justification by faith alone has been preached in its purity, morals have been most rigorous, Christianity most abiding, and good works most abundant. And why should it not be so, seeing we have been redeemed by the precious blood of Christ?

Furthermore, "faith without works is dead." No works, no faith. No faith, no justification. Protestantism has always been *anti*-antinomian.

And so, when we realize that Jesus has purchased our redemption by His blood, we say with Paul, 2 Corinthians 5:14–15, "We thus judge that if one died for all then were all dead ... that they which live should not henceforth live unto themselves, but unto Him which died for them and rose again."

## 8. CONCLUSION

In a short primer of this kind, it is impossible to deal with the entire Roman system of doctrine. The new Catholic catechism contains over 700 pages of doctrinal teaching of the Catholic church. But perhaps this little primer has helped Protestants and Catholics alike to think through their beliefs. I shall conclude this brief examination of Roman Catholicism by asking three questions:

1. What is the fundamental defect of Roman Catholicism?
2. What are the consequent errors?
3. What should be our attitude towards the Roman Catholic church?

QUESTION 1. What is the fundamental defect of Roman Catholicism?

ANSWER. The fundamental error of Rome is two-fold. It consists in a denial of the authority of God, on the one hand, and a deification of human authority, on the other. Rome rejects the supremacy of God as He has spoken in the Bible. Rather than subject herself to His Word, she subjects His Word to her. Rather than criticize herself in its light, she construes it in her light. On the other hand, she exalts herself to infallibility and would have all men bow down and blindly worship her upon pain of bodily death in the world (if she has the power to enforce it) and spiritual death in the world to come. Not without reason has the Church of Rome been called the greatest tyrant the world has ever seen.

QUESTION 2. What are the consequent errors?

ANSWER. The consequent errors deriving from this original sin of unbounded arrogance are legion. Most important of all, Rome closes the divine way of salvation. She has taken Christ from us and we know not where she has laid Him. All His promises of being the Savior from our sins, the ransom for our souls, the refuge of our weariness, are gone. The just no longer live by faith. Our freedom is over, we are in bondage again, we are yet in our sins. In the place of His invitation, her sacraments; in the place of His mediation, her Virgin, saints, and endless priests; in the place of Him who was made sin for us that we might be made the righteousness of God in Him, her righteousness that leaves us still in our sins. She may warn, threaten, and excommunicate us, but we reply with the inspired words of the Apostle Paul, "If any man preach any other gospel unto you than that ye have received, let him be anathema," Galatians 1:9.

QUESTION 3. But finally, what should be our attitude and policy toward Rome?

May I make a few suggestions? First, our attitude should be one of humility in judging Rome, not because of her arrogance but because of our sin. It must be confessed that Protestantism is greatly divided in organization, and more divided still in testimony. We have lost the salt of the Reformation to such a degree that we are almost good for nothing but to be cast out and trodden under foot of Rome. No longer does the Protestant church ring with the great themes of salvation by grace, the authority and genuine inspiration of the Bible, a divine Christ, and a final judgment. We must humbly confess that to a great degree we have been false to our true gospel and that Rome has been true to her false gospel. Let us, therefore, set our own house in order.

Second, Protestants should not intermarry with Romanists. The fact that there are many conscientious and well-meaning Protestants who have done this and appear to live happily ever afterwards does not make the policy right. The Catholic contract is inimical to Protestantism and cannot be signed by a Protestant without violating evangelical principles. For example, the contract requires the persons to be married by a priest with the understanding that such a marriage alone is valid; it requires the Protestant to promise not to endeavor to win his mate to his faith, which is a violation of his duty as a Christian. Again, it requires the Catholic training of the children, which is detrimental, of course, to the Protestant faith and witness; and it precludes the greatest marital bliss which is based on harmony of religious faith and practice.

Third, Rome should be opposed, but only spiritually.

We repudiate the externalistic view of religion and should therefore repudiate all carnal opposition and persecution. Without being either complacent about her, or satisfied with her doctrine, we should nevertheless oppose her kindly. We must fight her, but only with spiritual weapons.

Fourth, we should recognize Roman merits. This series lacks mention of them only because we have been dealing exclusively with fundamentals; on these we feel she errs. We do not mean to suggest that there is not much that is commendable about Rome.

Fifth, we should cooperate wherever possible. In worship it is impossible, in joint moral enterprises it is sometimes possible, and in general social welfare movements it is possible and often imperative.

Sixth, we should bid our Roman Catholic friends to come to the true church. She, in error, invites us. Surely we, in truth, ought to invite her. We bear the Catholics witness that they have a zeal, but not according to knowledge. We pray God that they might all come to an understanding of Christ's all-sufficient sacrifice and be saved.

# A Primer

# on

# the

# Atonement

CHRISTIAN: The atonement may well be the most important doctrine in the Christian religion.

INQUIRER: Why do you say that?

C: I should qualify that statement. The atonement is the most important doctrine *for us*. In and of itself, it would not be as important as the doctrines of the Trinity and the person of the Lord Jesus Christ.

I: What do you mean, "for us"?

C: The atonement is the way of salvation. If it were not for the atonement, we would not be here at all, not to mention calmly discussing truth about God and man and the world to come.

I: I see what you mean. At the same time, I do not profess to understand the doctrine of the atonement enough to feel the weight of what you are saying. So, if I might, let me ask you some questions.

C: Please do.

I: To begin with the simplest of all questions, what is the meaning of the word "atonement"? Not that I have no idea, but I want to see if my idea is on target.

C: The atonement has sometimes been defined as the "at-one-ment." But that is not so much a definition as a description of the effect of the atonement.

I: The effect?

C: Yes. As a result of the atonement, the previously estranged sinner and God are brought to "at-one-ment."

I: I see. But if that is the effect of the atonement, what is the atonement itself?

C: It has to do with the mercy seat of the Old Testament tabernacle, where the blood of the sacrifice was sprinkled once a year at the Day of Atonement. In Old Testament ritual, that sacrifice was made by the high priest for the people of Israel and taken by him into the Holy of Holies. By the blood of the sacrificial victim, Israel was made acceptable to the holy Divine Being.

I: Are you saying that the atonement was a bloody sacrifice of an animal?

C: Well, you and I know (along with the ancient Jews) that the blood of goats and bulls would not wash away human sin.

I: Then this sacrifice symbolized something other than itself.

C: Obviously so.

I: What did it signify?

C: It signified what John the Baptist, the greatest of all Jews before the coming of Jesus Christ, said of Jesus: "The Lamb of God who takes away the sin of the world."

I: In other words, the animal was the symbol of another victim?

C: Yes. Christ was called a "lamb" because, like the sacrificial lambs, He was slain and was a victim. Yet He was infinitely more than even a human victim.

I: But if Christ is God incarnate, are you saying that *God* was slain for the sins of Israel?

C: In a sense, yes. In a sense, no.

I: I can understand the "in a sense, yes." As you say, He was the Lamb of God who was slain. And, as you also have said, He was God incarnate. So are you saying that God was slain as a victim for the sins of His people?

C: No, although admittedly it looks as if I am saying that.

I: You puzzle me. You say that Jesus Christ is the God-man. Correct?

C: Absolutely.

I: And the God-man died. Is that not so?

C: It is.

I: Then on the other hand, you say that God did not die.

C: True.

I: I thought we had established long ago that orthodoxy is not neo-orthodoxy and therefore does not glory in theological contradictions. What you are saying here sounds as contradictory and as paradoxical as anything I have ever heard. How can you say in one breath that God died and in the next breath that He did not die?

C: I am not saying that God died.

I: Let me think this over again. The God-man died; and yet God did not die. So there must be some distinction that I do not yet detect between saying the God-man died and God died.

C: Yes. Can you figure out what the difference is?

I: I will try, though I know you will say this is wrong. You say that the God-man died, but God did not die. Then, at the time of His death, the divine nature and the human nature were separated and only the man Christ Jesus actually died.

C: No. Remember that when we discussed the person of Christ, we insisted that His union with the human nature was forever.

I: Yes. That is why I thought you must be saying that God died. You stressed that God entered into a permanent and inseparable union with the human nature. So I was sure that you meant the death of the God-man must have included His Godhood as well as His manhood.

C: Surely you recognize that there is something wrong in saying that God died. I am a bit disappointed in you.

I: I know what you mean. God is life—eternal, unchangeable life. He cannot die. I choked on those words myself. Nevertheless, Jesus Christ is in inseparable union with God, and Jesus Christ died in an inseparable union with God. It seems impossible to deny that God died. Are you not going to help me with this problem?

C: I could, but I think it is better for you to help yourself. You have all the basic data needed to resolve the difficulty and to articulate a great Christian doctrine.

I: Okay. I will struggle a little longer. First, Christ died. Second, that includes His human nature. Third, that human nature was indissolubly united with the divine nature. Fourth, nevertheless, the divine nature could not possibly die. Fifth, and yet, the God-man died. Sixth, therefore the God-man died, but God did not die. That's my problem.

Seventh . . . what is the solution? Obviously God was with the human nature—inseparably with the human nature—when the human nature died. Aha! I have it now. The divine nature was with the human nature—inseparably with it—when the *human* nature underwent death, which the divine nature could never undergo. So, though God did not die, the man who died was God. He did not cease to be God when He died, as the divine nature did not die, but only the human nature. Am I moving in the right direction?

C: Not only in the right direction, you have answered the question.

I: I have?

C: You correctly stated that the God-man, who is inseparably one person forever, has undergone death in the only nature in which such an experience was possible.

I: And it was the death of God in the sense that the man who died was God, though He did not die in the divine nature. His human death, though finite, was of infinite value because it was the death of a man who is God. In that sense of the word, God died. Or that experience which the divine human person, Jesus Christ, underwent was an experience that pertained to both natures, though it was undergone in only one.

C: You just stated what the early church needed several centuries to realize, after many controversies.

I: I was going to ask earlier how Christ's human death could have value to save a vast multitude of human beings, as the atonement is supposed to do. Now I know the answer to my own question. That death, though one of a finite individual, was nevertheless of infinite value because that human individual was indissolubly united with the divine nature, and therefore had infinite value.

C: Yes, you may recall that when we discussed Christology proper, we commented on this "community of attributes."

I: Now that you have reminded me, I do remember.

C: So you see now what I mean by saying that the Lamb of God, who shed His blood for the remission of sin, was and was not God. There is a sense in which His death was a divine death, and there is a sense in which it was not.

I: I see that very clearly now, though I was baffled before.

C: And you see, then, that the atonement is the divine sacrifice in the sense we have explained. This is the nature of the Lamb of God who takes away the sin of the world by offering up Himself as a bloody sacrifice. In an earlier connection we mentioned that teaching from the apostle Paul in Acts 20:28. There he refers to the blood of God—the blood of a *man* who is God, the blood of the *Lamb* who is God. The sacrifice of the Son of God in His human nature is the propitiation for our sins. Because it is such a costly vicarious sacrifice, it is accepted as a proper punishment for our sins. Thus, it produces in those for whom it was made, and who appropriate it for themselves, the "at-one-ment."

I: Did you say "those for whom it was made"?

C: Yes.

I: You said earlier that this atonement or sacrifice was made for the sins of the world.

C: I did say that.

I: Are you now drawing back from that universal statement

to a particular one?

C: No. I am explaining that the world for whom Christ died is not everyone in the world, but everyone whom He has chosen out of the world.

I: That is a funny use of the word "world," is it not?

C: I do not think so. You talk about the world of science, the world of fashion, the world of literature. You often refer to a whole community of individuals described in a particular way. Here, when we are talking about the world of the redeemed, we are talking about all who are redeemed, which is not identical with all who live in this world of ours, any more than those other qualifying expressions are.

I: I can see the legitimacy of such use, but I still have a problem. I seem to remember a passage somewhere in the New Testament that says that Christ was the propitiation not only for our sins but for the sins of the whole world. I do not remember the text exactly, but that was the impression I got when I read it. The writer seemed to say that Christ's death was not just for that particular Christian group, but for everybody.

C: Undoubtedly you are thinking of 1 John 2:2, which reads, "He Himself is the propitiation for our sins, and not for ours only, but also for those of the whole world."

I: That is the one. Does it not plainly say that Christ's propitiation was not for the sins of Christians only, but for everyone?

C: It does not say that in so many words, does it?

I: No, not exactly. But we both agree that the Bible can say things without saying them "in so many words."

C: Yes. I admit that is a theoretical possibility. John could be saying Christ died not only for the sins of Christians, but for every human being. But for now, all I am driving at is that he does not expressly say that.

I: Granted.

C: I will also grant that John may be implying what he does not expressly say. But is he? Is John implying that Christ's sacrifice was made not only for Christians, who accept Him, but for everybody? Do you not see a problem if John were actually construed as saying that Christ made a propitiatory sacrifice for every last person?

I: I do see a problem there. That would spell universal salvation.

C: Yes. And why is that a problem?

I: Even I know that the Bible does not teach universal salvation. Since you have convinced me also that the Bible does not contradict itself, I realize that such an unbiblical inference would be ruled out as a possibility.

C: That is good thinking on your part. I have granted it theoretical possibility, in that it is a thinkable idea in itself. But when compared with the teaching of the Bible as a whole, it is no longer thinkable.

I: So what are we to think in this case?

C: It forces us back to what we talked about earlier—not the world in general, but the world of believers. In the light of that, can you see what 1 John 2:2 would mean?

I: I suppose John's point is that the propitiation is not only for the local Christians to whom he was writing, but to

Christians everywhere.

C: Exactly. The atonement is not for any one group of believers, but for all believers everywhere in the world. But on the other hand, it is restricted to those for whom the sacrifice was made and who would believe in it.

I: That answers my question.

C: Bear in mind that we have looked at only a few biblical expressions of the atonement, such as the Day of Atonement and the Lamb of God who takes away the sin of the world, and the blood of God. The Bible is full of such passages. And Jesus Christ Himself says so.

I: He does?

C: Yes. Before His death, as recorded in John 16:12, He said He had many things to tell His disciples, but they could not bear them. After His death, however, on the way to Emmaus, as we read in Luke 24, He told two of the disciples how the whole Old Testament predicted that He would die as a sacrifice for the sins of His people.

I: I remember that. What did He mean, though? Why could the disciples not bear, before His death, what He later told them after His resurrection?

C: Remember that they just did not believe the Messiah was going to die, but they had the erroneous notion that His ultimate reign would be achieved at His first advent. He gently corrected them and quietly prepared them for His death, but they still were incredulous the very night before the crucifixion.

I: So He could not tell them what weighed most heavily on His heart, the inevitability and meaning of His death, because they were not prepared to accept that awful fact?

C: Yes. That is the most poignant part of the incarnation story. Christ was born to die, and those for whom He was going to die were utterly unprepared to accept that awesome display of divine love for them. So our Lord had to go to His cross alone, suffering for people who did not even realize He was suffering for them.

I: That certainly explains to me, as nothing else does, the need for the atonement. We sinners need atonement for our sins.

C: How true. Would you like me to cite a number of passages to which Christ no doubt alluded, along with other New Testament passages on the atonement, or shall we continue the discussion assuming the existence of such passages?

I: I believe you when you say there are many such passages. But I think it may be good to hear some of them. That may answer the questions I still have.

C: Very well. Let me read two dozen:

> Sacrifice and offering Thou didst not desire; mine ears hast Thou opened: burnt offering and sin offering hast Thou not required. Then said I, Lo, I come: in the volume of the book it is written of me, I delight to do Thy will, O my God: yea, Thy law is within my heart (Psalm 40:6–8; see Hebrews 10:5–9).

> Surely He hath borne our griefs and carried our sorrows: yet we did esteem Him stricken, smitten of God, and afflicted. But He was wounded for our transgressions, He was bruised for our iniquities; the chastisement of our peace was upon Him: and with His stripes we are healed. All we like sheep have gone astray: we have turned every one to His own way; and the Lord

hath laid on Him the iniquity of us all. He was oppressed and He was afflicted, yet He opened not His mouth: He is brought as a lamb to the slaughter, and as a sheep before her shearers is dumb, so He openeth not His mouth. He was taken from prison and from judgment: and who shall declare His generation? for He was cut off out of the land of the living: for the transgression of my people was He stricken . . . . Yet it pleased the Lord to bruise Him; He hath put Him to grief: when thou shalt make His soul an offering for sin, He shall see His seed, He shall prolong His days, and the pleasure of the Lord shall prosper in His hand. He shall see the travail of His soul, and shall be satisfied: by His knowledge shall my righteous servant justify many; for He shall bear their iniquities. Therefore will I divide him a portion with the great, and He shall divide the spoil with the strong: because He has poured out His soul unto death: and He was numbered with the transgressors; and He bare the sin of many, and made intercession for the transgressors (Isaiah 53:4–8, 10–12).

In that day there shall be a fountain opened in the house of David and to the inhabitants of Jerusalem for sin and for uncleanness (Zechariah 13:1).

For this is my blood of the new testament, which is shed for many for the remission of sins (Matthew 26:28; Luke 22:30).

And [Jesus] said unto them, Thus it is written, and thus it behooved Christ to suffer, and to rise from the dead the third day: And that repentance and remission of sins should be preached in his name among all nations, beginning at Jerusalem (Luke 24:46–47).

[We are] Being justified freely by his grace through the redemption that is in Christ Jesus: Whom God hath set forth to be a propitiation through faith in his blood, to declare his righteousness for the remission of sins that are past, through the forbearance of God: To declare, I say, at this time his righteousness: that he might be just, and the justifier of him which believeth in Jesus (Romans 3:24–26).

[He] was delivered for our offenses, and was raised again for our justification (Romans 4:25).

For I delivered unto you first of all that which I also received, how that Christ died for our sins according to the scriptures (1 Corinthians 15:3).

Grace be to you, and peace, from God the Father, and from our Lord Jesus Christ, who gave himself for our sins, that he might deliver us from this present evil world, according to the will of God and our Father (Galatians 1:3–4).

In [Him] we have redemption through his blood, the forgiveness of sins, according to the riches of his grace (Ephesians 1:7).

But now in Christ Jesus ye who sometimes were far off are made nigh by the blood of Christ. For he is our peace, who hath made both one, and hath broken down the middle wall of partition between us; having abolished in his flesh the enmity, even the law of commandments contained in ordinances; for to make in himself of twain one new man, so making peace; and that he might reconcile both unto God in one body by the cross, having slain the enmity thereby: And came and preached peace to you which were afar off, and to them that were nigh. For through him we both have access by one Spirit unto the Father (Ephesians 2:13–18).

In [Him] we have redemption through his blood, even the forgiveness of sins . . . . For it pleased the Father that in him should all fullness dwell; And, having made peace through the blood of his cross, by him to reconcile all things unto himself; by Him, I say, whether they be things in earth, or things in heaven. And you, that were sometime alienated and enemies in your mind by wicked works, yet now hath He reconciled in the body of His flesh through death, to present you holy and unblamable and unreprovable in His sight (Colossians 1:14, 19–22).

For there is one God, and one mediator between God and men, the man Christ Jesus: Who gave himself a ransom for all, to be testified in due time (I Timothy 2:5–6).

[He] gave himself for us, that he might redeem us from all iniquity, and purify unto himself a peculiar people, zealous of good works (Titus 2:14).

. . . by the grace of God [Jesus] should taste death for every man . . . . Wherefore in all things it behooved him to be made like unto his brethren, that he might be a merciful and faithful high priest in things pertaining to God, to make reconciliation for the sins of the people (Hebrews 2:9, 17).

Neither by the blood of goats and calves, but by his own blood he entered in once into the holy place, having obtained eternal redemption for us. For if the blood of bulls and of goats, and the ashes of an heifer sprinkling the unclean, sanctifieth to the purifying of the flesh: How much more shall the blood of Christ, who through the eternal Spirit offered himself without spot to God, purge your conscience from dead works to serve the living God? And for this cause he is the mediator of the new testament, that by means of death, for the redemption of the transgressions that were under the first testament, they which are called might receive the promise of eternal inheritance . . . . Nor yet that he should offer himself often, as the high priest entereth into the holy place every year with blood of others; For then he must often have suffered since the foundation of the world: but now once in the end of the world hath he appeared to put away sin by the sacrifice of himself (Hebrews 9:12–15, 25–26).

[We have come] to Jesus the mediator of the new covenant, and to the blood of sprinkling, that speaketh better things than that of Abel (Hebrews 12:24).

Wherefore Jesus also, that he might sanctify the people with his own blood, suffered without the gate . . . . Now the God of peace, that brought again from the dead our Lord Jesus, that great shepherd of the sheep, through the blood of the everlasting covenant, make you perfect in every good work to do his will (Hebrews 13:12, 20–21).

Forasmuch that ye know that ye were not redeemed with corruptible things, as silver and gold, from your vain conversation received by tradition from your fathers; But with the precious blood of Christ, as of a lamb without blemish and without spot: Who verily was foreordained before the foundation of the world, but was manifest in these last times for you (1 Peter 1:18–20).

[Jesus Himself] bare our sins in his own body on the tree, that we, being dead to sins, should live unto righteousness: by whose stripes ye were healed (1 Peter 2:24).

For Christ also hath once suffered for sins, the just for the unjust, that he might bring us to God, being put to death in the flesh, but quickened by the Spirit (I Peter 3:18).

The blood of Jesus Christ His Son cleanseth us from all sin (1 John 1:7).

Unto him that loved us, and washed us from our sins in his own blood. . . . (Revelation 1:5).

And they sang a new song, saying, Thou art worthy to take the book, and to open the seals thereof: for thou wast slain, and hast redeemed us to God by thy blood out of every kindred, and tongue, and people, and nation (Revelation 5:9).

I: That is really impressive. And I understand that there are many other passages you have not read here. The atonement is much more central to the Bible than I realized. But I still have some questions.

C: Please raise them.

I: I almost hate to ask this in the light of things we have just been saying and learning about the actual sacrifice He made.

C: I am sure that Christ will not be offended by honest questions about anything in His Word.

I: Suppose I am the sinner the Bible claims, and suppose Jesus Christ offers His blood for the remission of my sins, as it also claims. Really, is that fair either to Him or to me? On the surface of it, I cannot see how it is fair for Him to be judged or for me not to be judged.

C: That is a fair question. Let us first address whether it is fair to Christ to be judged for the sins of His people. I think we would both insist immediately that, if it were imposed upon Him to suffer for something He had not done, that would surely not be fair.

I: Agreed. The God of all the earth could not be just and arbitrarily condemn someone for somebody else's sin. If He arbitrarily inflicts the punishment for your sin and mine on Jesus, who is in no way guilty of those sins, that would surely be unfair.

C: On the other hand, if God does not impose that on Jesus, but Jesus asks it for Himself, would that not change the matter?

I: I guess it would, though I cannot imagine why someone would want to suffer for somebody else's sin.

C: The point is, if someone did choose to suffer for somebody else's sins, for whatever reason, assuming the person is in his right mind, it would not be unfair if he were then punished for the guilt of their sins, would it?

I: I guess not. No.

C: Then our first problem is solved.

I: Why?

C: The Bible makes it very plain that Christ voluntarily took others' sins upon Himself. They were not laid upon Him without His consent.

I: Where does the Bible say that?

C: While it does not say that in so many words, the Bible does nevertheless teach, first of all, that Jesus Christ is the *Logos*, the Word, the second person of the Trinity. That is to say, He is a full member of the Godhead. As such, He is absolutely sovereign. No one can impose his will on the deity.

I: I see. But as we have already noticed, He did not suffer as deity; He suffered in His humanity. That punishment for other people's sin was laid upon Him as a human being, was it not?

C: Yes, it was as a man that He suffered the punishment for our sins, but as God that He submitted Himself to do so.

I: Run that by me again.

C: As God, the second person in the Godhead, He must have agreed to undertake this redemptive role. To suffer the punishment of His people's sin involved His taking upon Himself, voluntarily, a human nature in which He could thus suffer. So, though He suffered as a man, and the punishment of our sins was laid upon Him by the deity, as deity He Himself concurred in His own incarnation and atonement.

I: I see. We can truly say that Jesus Christ, as deity, voluntarily undertook to suffer for the sins of His people. He subjected Himself to that vicarious atonement.

C: Yes. And in a sense, even as to His human nature, He voluntarily submitted to the cross. He came to do the Father's will. Jesus had said, "The Father is greater than I," referring apparently to His human nature. As a human being, He submitted Himself to the Father's will.

I: That is the significance of Gethsemane, is it not?

C: Yes. Christ said, "Not my will, but Thy will be done." His will, at that time, was to avoid the awful suffering of the cross on the next day. "If it be possible," He had prayed, "let this cup pass from me." His will as a human being was to avoid the incredible anguish of Calvary, if it were "possible."

I: But when He realized it was not possible, then He voluntarily, as a human facing the wrath of God on the cross, said, "Thy will be done."

C: Right. The very statement, "Not my will, but Thy will be done," really means that Christ's will as a human being was submissive to the will of the divine being. He was saying in effect that His will as a human being, shrinking naturally from the ordeal of the cross, was to avoid such if at all possible, but only if possible. When it became obvious that it was not possible to avoid the cross and still accomplish His redemptive work, then of course His will was to do God's will, which was to suffer in place of His people. Thus, as a human, Jesus chose to submit to the will of God. His will, as a human, was to do God's will.

I: I am satisfied on this first point. It was not unfair for Jesus Christ to suffer for His people's sins because He

Himself (both as divine and human) voluntarily undertook to do that. He was not forced to suffer against His will. But we still have another part to the problem. I was asking if it is fair for the guilty person to have someone else suffer for his guilt, while he goes free.

C: I recall. The unfairness, or alleged unfairness, would be the guilty person's not having to suffer the proper punishment for his crime. Is that it?

I: That is precisely my question.

C: You will notice that the guilty person does not go unpunished.

I: I had not noticed that at all. It seems to me that the guilty person does go unpunished. After all, we sinners are forgiven without ever having suffered the damnation of hell for our sins. Am I not correct?

C: I am afraid not.

I: What am I missing? Surely Jesus paid it all. I did not pay anything. What is that but going scot-free from the punishment for my crime? I must be obtuse. I cannot see any way to alleviate that part of the problem.

C: Think about it. When we talked about Christ's suffering, we said it was "vicarious."

I: Yes, meaning He was our substitute. Ah, the light is beginning to dawn.

C: What do you see?

I: If Christ voluntarily suffered for my sins, then He did suffer for *my* sins. He was punished in *my* place.

Vicariously He endured for *me*. In that profound sense, *I* was punished in Him. Is that what we are saying?

C: Excellent.

I: Christ was my vicar, my substitute. In my place, He suffered my punishment. So in a very real way, *I was punished for my sin*. I did not go free. My debt was paid in full by me.

C: Exactly. It was paid in full by *you*.

I: Not by me in person, but by me in my representative, my vicar, my substitute, my vicarious sacrifice.

C: Amen.

I: That is truly amazing. I pay for my guilt in a way that, left to myself, I could never have done, even in eternal torment in hell.

C: Precisely. Inasmuch as Christ's sacrifice of infinite value was in your place, you paid the infinite price for your guilt.

I: I notice you say that believers are identified with Christ's suffering on their behalf. Unbelievers, I take it, are not?

C: How can they be when they refuse to be?

I: Yet Christ died for the elect before they believe, did He not?

C: Yes. I can see where you are heading.

I: It is Christ's dying for people that brings them faith, and not their own faith that applies His death to them. Is that not so?

C: It is.

I: Then if all for whom Christ died are unbelievers, why would it not be true that He died for all of us?

C: It would not logically follow that because Jesus died for unbelievers, to make them believers, He therefore died also for *all* unbelievers.

I: I admit that would be a logical non sequitur. And, of course, it would follow that if the atonement benefited only certain unbelievers, it was meant for no others. The whole doctrine of election, which we have seen to be a biblical teaching, means that Christ died only for particular unbelievers. He died for Peter and not for Judas.

C: Yes, but He died for Peter not because Peter was a believer, but in order to make him a believer.

I: I will not ask the question that comes surging to the surface every time we get on this subject, namely, why did He not die to make Judas a believer? I know the answer to my own question. He is sovereign in His grace. "I will have mercy on whom I will have mercy," He said.

C: And the mercy to which He refers there is the gift of Jesus Christ specifically for His chosen people.

I: Is there a name for that doctrine?

C: Yes. There is a popular and misleading name, and there is a proper name.

I: What is the misleading name?

C: It is often called "limited atonement."

I: Obviously it is limited to the elect, so how is that misleading?

C: As you say, it is limited in its design to save the elect. But many people read into that word "limited" associations which do not belong to it.

I: Such as?

C: Some make it mean that it is limited in its sufficiency, which it is not.

I: And others?

C: Others think it is limited in its offer, which it is not.

I: That is puzzling. I thought we decided that the offer of the gospel of Christ's death and redemption was to the elect only.

C: Yes, in a sense we have shown that to be the case. But you realize it is unlimited in another sense. The offer of the gospel goes forth to everyone's ears and hearing. As a Christian minister, for example, I do not hesitate to offer it in the hearing of every soul. As a person hears it, however, he recognizes that it is for *sinners* only. If the hearer considers himself righteous, then that invitation is not to him. He feels no need for it.

I: So there is a sense in which the offer of the gospel is unlimited?

C: Yes.

I: And yet limited. What you have just said raises another question.

C: What is that?

I: You just explained that when Christ made atonement by His life and death, He did it for the elect. I understand you on that, and you are quite persuasive that the Bible teaches divine election. But my question is this: Are Christians not supposed to extend the invitation of Christ's sacrifice to everyone, and not only to those who are elect? And, if to everyone, how does a Christian know whether a person is elect and supposed to receive the message?

C: The Christian is supposed to declare to everyone with whom he has an opportunity that Christ calls everyone to repentance and faith and salvation.

I: Then the call is universal?

C: Quite right.

I: But the intention of the call is particular and only for the elect?

C: Correct again.

I: I am confused. How can I make a universal call to only specific individuals? How can the call be *universal* to everyone, and *actually* only for that segment of mankind called the elect?

C: It is possible.

I: A universal call that is exclusively for particular individuals? If that is possible, the possibility certainly escapes me.

C: Listen very carefully to the call and see if you do not see my point. I will give you a sample call that is simultaneously universal and individualistic.

I: I cannot for the life of me see how you can do it. But I am listening.

C: Here it is: "Jesus Christ calls everyone, everywhere to confess his sin and trust in Jesus for his salvation and deliverance."

I: That is definitely a universal call. But I do not see how it is a particular and exclusive call. You do sincerely invite everyone, everywhere to come to Jesus Christ to be saved.

C: Yes, I do.

I: Do you not see that such a universal call is not restricted at all?

C: Are you sure?

I: You are asking me the questions now, are you?

C: Yes, I am asking. Is that call you have just heard not restricted?

I: I do not see what you are driving at. The call is to everyone, everywhere, and presumably at all times.

C: It is indeed.

I: I know I am supposed to see something that I am not. But frankly I do not see any exclusiveness in it whatsoever. You are saying that anyone, anywhere at any time who will confess his sins and come to Jesus Christ will most certainly be saved.

C: That is exactly what I am saying. But do you not see that it is very particular?

I: Very particular? I have talked to you often enough to know that what sometimes baffles me at the beginning of a dialogue becomes embarrassingly obvious before we are finished. And I suspect that it will be that way again. But for the moment, I cannot see it. What am I missing?

C: Listen again very closely. I call everyone, everywhere to come who will acknowledge his sin and bring his guilt and need to Jesus Christ, and I assure him, without any qualification, that in doing that he will most certainly be saved eternally by the blood of Jesus Christ. Now do you see what is very particular here?

I: You are saying that anyone who will acknowledge his sin and bring his guilt to Jesus will be saved. Now that is a precise description, I see. You are universally inviting anybody who fits the description?

C: You are certainly closing in on it. Can you finish?

I: Let me see. The call is universally extended to that group of people who acknowledge their sin, bring it to Jesus, and are thus assured of everlasting salvation. The particularity there is that these people acknowledge their sin and bring it to Jesus. I see that. But are not all men everywhere sinful and guilty, and therefore invited to come to Jesus Christ, so that the call, even with that precision, is at the same time absolutely universal?

C: You are right that everyone, everywhere is guilty and in need of salvation through Jesus Christ. But I want to ask you a question: Is everybody, everywhere aware of his guiltiness and need?

I: Now I see what you mean. The answer is very easy. No. Men do not universally acknowledge the guilt they universally have.

C: That is my point, and yours as well, is it not?

I: Yes. I grant that though people universally have guilt and need Jesus Christ for their salvation, they do not universally feel or acknowledge that guilt. In fact, I have friends who would be insulted if you told them that they were guilty sinners in need of salvation by the blood of Jesus Christ. And I know that there are vast multitudes in the world who meet that description.

C: The vast majority of mankind does not acknowledge their guilt, but categorically denies it. They even resent anybody who suggests they have it and ultimately resent Jesus Christ for inviting them, which implies that they need the salvation.

I: I guess that is true. And I certainly see the point now. The call to come to Jesus Christ is universal to everyone within its hearing who is guilty and will come to Christ for forgiveness. And the people who meet that description are a minority, so that this universal call, when looked at closely, is a call only to those who acknowledge their need of the Christ to whom they are invited.

C: Very well said. You have made it clearer than I have ever made it myself—that the universal call is at the same time personal, being addressed to a minority of mankind.

I: What I thought to be a contradiction in terms just five minutes ago is now obvious to me. Unfortunately that is not my last question.

C: Do not say "unfortunately." I think it is fortunate that you do think so deeply and honestly about these questions. Christ has not called for any crucifixion of the intellect. He does not rule out legitimate questions. On the contrary, He is the truth, and He wants people to understand what He is saying, so that when they decide for or against Him, they know who He is and what He is offering. The all-wise God does not rejoice in the worship of fools. So go ahead with whatever questions you feel are germane to this basic matter of the atonement of Jesus Christ.

I: Something has always profoundly disturbed me about the very idea of an atonement like the one taught by Christianity. I understand the biblical doctrine is that Jesus Christ was offered up as a sacrifice to divine justice. And He paid for our sins by enduring our punishment, or receiving our wages of sin in His death. What bothers me about the idea is that it seems to wipe out what I have always thought of as the very heart of the Christian religion.

C: What do you mean?

I: I have understood from my childhood, when I was taught about the Christian religion, that God was a God of mercy and pardon and forgiveness.

C: You were well instructed. He is a God of infinite mercy. Do you think the satisfaction of Jesus Christ is inconsistent with the mercy of God?

I: That does trouble me. I am puzzled that you do not see the problem here. Do you not see a contradiction in saying that God was satisfied totally because payment was made in full for the guilt of our sins, and yet saying that God is a God of mercy? If you were preaching a God of justice, I could see how the atonement, with its full payment for sins, would be consistent with that. But how in the world can the atonement exist alongside of mercy?

C: Before I address that question, may I remind you that earlier in our conversation it was the justice of the atonement that bothered you?

I: Yes, I remember. You have answered persuasively that God's justice is not obliterated by the atonement, but is actually fulfilled in infinite fullness. But now my question is whether the price of vindicating divine justice has not been the obliteration of divine mercy.

C: I am a little confused on this point. Would you explain a little more why you feel that the satisfaction of justice in Christ's death is somehow incompatible with His mercy? I understand how justice could look like the opposite of mercy, but I do not quite see why you feel that something in this gift of divine justice contradicts the mercy of God. Would you go over it again?

I: If God's justice is utterly satisfied for the sinner who comes to Jesus Christ, then whatever benefits result from that absolutely adequate sacrifice are the sinner's due. Therefore God *owes* something to the sinner who comes in the name of Jesus Christ?

C: Yes, He does, on the basis of Jesus' full payment. I am beginning to see what you mean. I apologize for lagging behind. What you are asking is that since God has been paid in full and *owes* the sinner the pardon purchased by Christ for him, how can that be called a demonstration of divine mercy? Am I understanding you now?

I: That is the problem as I see it. Do you not see that as a problem?

C: Yes, when stated that way. And I realize now why I was slow to catch on. My thinking was absorbed with the implied mercy of God, which is in the background and not in the foreground of our discussion.

I: Now you are losing me.

C: Sorry. It is just that my mind was in another area of the discussion, which we have not yet brought to the foreground—that the mercy of God was what sent Jesus Christ to pay the full price for the remission of the penitent's sins. Do you follow?

I: Now I do. There is mercy here, though it is at a different point from where I was looking. In a certain sense there is no mercy in pardoning the sinner whose guilt has been paid in full by Jesus Christ. At that point, it is a matter of absolute justice. And if God is a God of justice, then He must acknowledge that the sinner who claims the atonement of Jesus Christ is totally expiated of his guilt and reconciled to God. But what I failed to ask was, where did that payment come from? When I answer that question, I have to say it came from the mercy of God. Is that what you are suggesting?

C: That is the idea. It is by the mercy of God that Christ's full payment of God's justice makes it absolutely obligatory for that just God to receive a repentant sinner, who trusts in Jesus Christ. God's mercy, in other words, satisfied His justice. Or to put it another way, God's willingness to be merciful is what led Him to "so love the world that He gave His only begotten Son, that whosoever believes in Him should not perish, but have everlasting life." His love, in the form of mercy, led to His satisfying His justice by the gift of Jesus Christ. Or to put it still another way, that gift of mercy was the satisfaction of divine justice.

I: That is truly sublime. The justice of God in the atonement of Jesus Christ, which on the surface seems to be the enemy of mercy, is actually the supreme demonstration of it.

C: You see why I so often say that the Christian religion has a built-in apologetic. When one understands it, he is compelled by the obvious, irresistible truth of it. A truth so sublime can only come from God.

I: Yes, I have seen that time and time again, though this is the first time I have seen it with respect to the atonement. It amazes me to think of the number of people who reject the atonement because they say they believe in the forgiveness of God.

C: Yes. What they should say is they *believe* in the atonement because they believe in the forgiveness of a holy God who would by no means clear the guilty except in the only way they could truly be cleared.

I: That must be the meaning of the biblical expression, "that God might be just and the justifier of the ungodly."

C: Yes, it comes from Romans 3:26: "That He might be just and the justifier of the one who has faith in Jesus." God is both just and the justifier of the ungodly. Normally when a person is the justifier of the ungodly, it is because he is not a just person. Any human being who declares a guilty person innocent is himself guilty, and not an honorable judge. And on the surface of it God could be mistaken for the ultimate unjust judge. But inasmuch as His justification of the ungodly is based on the punishment of their sin in Jesus Christ, God is clearly just when He justifies the ungodly, and they are made godly in the righteousness of Jesus Christ reckoned to them. Have you run the gamut of your questions on the atonement?

I: For the most part. But there is another formidable question I would like to raise. I think I know the answer, but I am not sure. Even if I do know the answer, I cannot state it very well.

C: What is the question?

I: Let me work up to it. First of all, it is true that Christ was offered as a propitiation to satisfy divine justice.

C: Yes.

I: That offering or sacrifice was made to God, correct?

C: Yes.

I: And obviously that sacrifice was made by the Son of God.

C: Correct.

I: All right. I have my facts straight now, and that leads me to ask, does this doctrine of the atonement mean that God the Son *placates* God the Father?

C: Yes, in a sense.

I: What sense? If God the Son, by His sacrifice, placates God the Father, does that not imply a split in the Godhead?

C: I think I know what you mean, but I would like to have you spell it out more fully.

I: If the Son placates the Father, that would seem to suggest that the Son is friendly to lost sinners (at least some of them), but the Father is hostile to them; and thus there is a profound split in the Godhead—a real antagonism between the Father, who is angry with the sinners and is ready to plunge them into hell at any moment, and the Son who loves them so much that He is willing to die for them. Is that not a profound split right in the heart of the divine Trinity, militating against any notion of eternal love and unified purpose shared by the members of the Trinity? Could you live with the idea that the Father and the Son are at loggerheads, in such a way as this?

C: Thank you for that elucidation of the question. I see your point. No, I could not live with the idea that the Father and the Son are at any kind of antagonism in their relationship with one another.

I: So you grant my point?

C: I grant that the idea of the Father and Son in conflict is not compatible with the very notion of the ever-blessed divine Trinity.

I: Are you being especially cagey here? On the one hand you seem to admit my point, and yet you seem not to admit it. I notice you speak of the "idea" that the Father and the Son are hostile to each other. Is it not clear that they are? Have you not said that the Father is propitiated by the Son, and that if that had not been done, the Father, in spite of the Son's affection for sinners, would have plunged them into eternal condemnation?

C: Be patient with me; I did not really say that. Let us go over it a little more carefully. It is true that God is propitiated by the sacrifice of His Son.

I: That is exactly my point. You agree, then, that the Godhead (especially the Father) is estranged from men, and He is reconciled to them by the friendly Son offering Himself as a sacrifice for them.

C: Not exactly, though I can certainly understand why you see it that way. And I may have even been negligent in not making certain aspects of the atonement clearer before now. But that is not what we are saying.

I: Okay. Say it again, and I will listen very carefully.

C: We are saying that God is estranged from man the sinner and infinitely angry with him, and, if there is no way to clear the sinner from his guilt, God will pour out eternal wrath upon him.

I: I see the subtle difference you are introducing, which I had not heard before. You are saying that the Godhead, not just the Father, is estranged from man?

C: I am.

I: The Godhead includes the Father, Son, and Holy Spirit.

C: It does.

I: Then you are saying that the Son, as well as the Father, is hostile toward the sinner. Are you also saying that the Son of God is infinitely angry with sinners, even elect sinners?

C: That is what I am saying.

I: That raises an even deeper problem for me.

C: What is that?

I: Now you are asking me to believe that the Son is both infinitely angry with the sinner and yet dies for his salvation! Can you possibly mean that?

C: Yes.

I: You mean to say that the same person, the Son of God, infinitely hates and infinitely loves the elect sinner at the same time? Is that not a contradiction in terms—a split not in the Godhead, but in the second person of the Godhead?

C: Is it not possible for a person to hate with a holy hatred absolutely wicked persons (such as fallen men are) yet at the same time desire their salvation? Is that a contradiction?

I: Let me think that over. It certainly looks like a contradiction. How could Christ have a perfect hatred and a perfect love at the same time for the same guilty sinners?

C: Before I try to answer that deep question, let me observe one thing in passing.

I: Please do.

C: You realize that this is the very heart of the gospel: God the Son died for those whom He infinitely detested. I am not dealing with the problem of how that could be; I am just pausing for a station break here. I am reminding you that here is the whole wonder of the gospel, the incredibility of divine grace. As Paul puts it in Romans 5:6–7, no one would die for a righteous man, "though perhaps someone would, for a good man, even dare to die; but God [especially the Son] demonstrates His love for us in that while we were yet sinners, Christ died for us." What you are having difficulty with is nothing less than the gospel in its quintessence. The all-gracious Son of God loved sinners so much that those whom He hated as sinners He died to deliver from sin.

I: Thank you for impressing that upon me. While, as you admit, that does not answer my question, it does, in a way, disarm me. It almost convinces me emotionally, even while I am intellectually still on the rack. I know that is what makes Christianity tick. That is the Christian religion, the gospel itself. And yet I find myself asking, does the gospel make sense, intelligible sense? I feel almost wicked raising the question when I realize that my only hope for salvation is that this not only could have happened, but did happen.

C: Most feel there must be an answer. Is it possible for

someone simultaneously to have an infinite hatred and an infinite love for the same guilty persons? The answer is in terms of an ethical concept: the difference between a love of complacency and a love of benevolence.

I: Refresh my mind on these terms, please.

C: A love of complacency is based on an admiration and affection for a morally worthy individual—a person so excellent that one has complacency or pleasure in that person's character.

I: And a love of benevolence?

C: A love of benevolence is good will toward a person. That person need not be worthy of admiration and affection because of any excellence in his character. The love is simply a desire to do good to a person irrespective of his character.

I: All right, I understand those terms. How do they solve our problem?

C: When we say the Son of God both loves and hates the same sinners at the same time, we are talking in terms of those two kinds of love. The Son of God does not have any love of complacency for sinners. They are absolutely obnoxious to Him. Without holiness, no man will see the Lord. Only the pure in heart will see God. God will by no means clear the guilty. So, as God, Jesus Christ has only absolute "displacency" or displeasure with sinners. They warrant holy hatred because they are utterly detestable and worthy only of condemnation.

I: So the Son's love for sinners has no complacency in it, since they deserve infinite hatred; it is, instead, a love of benevolence or good will.

C: That is precisely the point. Jesus, who has an infinite hatred of the wicked person, may at the same time have a love of benevolence for him. In His good will toward sinners, He desires to bring blessing to them.

I: I think I can carry the ball from here. If the Son of God has such a will as that, I will have to admit that there is no contradiction. It would be up to Him to remove a person's sin and bring him to a state of moral excellence, in which state He could have a love of complacency for him. Am I right?

C: Yes. That is exactly it. And you have answered how the same person, the Son of God, could have infinite hatred for the elect sinner and, at the same time, an infinite love of benevolence for the sinner. You even explained how the good that Jesus provides the sinner in His love of benevolence is the deliverance from sin and reconciliation toward God. That love of benevolence for this utterly unworthy person is what compels Jesus to redeem that person by shedding His blood for the remission of the person's guilt.

I: You not only answered my question, but addressed my next concern as well.

C: You are ahead of me. Explain, please.

I: You have solved two problems with one observation. In pointing out that the Son of God could have both a love of benevolence and an infinite hatred for the same person, you have also shown me how God the Father and the Spirit could likewise simultaneously love and hate sinners. So instead of the doctrine of the atonement pitting the Father against the Son, the Father could very well have exactly the same disposition toward sinners as Jesus the Son does.

C: I see what you mean. I think that is implied, though you noted it before I did. Yes, the Father and the Son had this infinite hatred, and God had to be propitiated if the sinner was to be acceptable to Him. The Father and the Son, and the Holy Spirit as well, have exactly the same dealings. And you would see what the Son's role in His atonement and expiation actually was, would you not?

I: Yes. That is very easy now. The three persons of the Godhead all agreed to show love of benevolence for certain sinners. They agreed further that, to make those persons acceptable to them and an object of complacency, their guilt would have to be taken and expiated. And they agreed that the second person of the Godhead would take upon Himself human nature and suffer the sacrifice necessary to propitiate divine justice. In other words, it was the justice of the triune God and not merely the justice of the Father.

C: Precisely. I could wish that more professional theologians could understand this as well as you do. You are not a professional nor even sure of your own Christian faith, but merely a seeker of salvation! You put it very well indeed. So you see there is absolute harmony in the Godhead, *especially* in the atonement; there is no trace of antagonism or opposition. The Son does not propitiate the Father in that sense of the word; He propitiates as far as the essential Trinity is concerned. All three persons are involved in infinite hatred, infinite propitiation, infinite acceptance, and infinite complacency in the elect for whom Jesus Christ died. The difference is simply in the roles played by the utterly unanimous essential Trinity. The Father exercises the executive and judgmental right. He is the one who passes the judgment of condemnation on the wicked. The Son, by common consent of the Godhead and on behalf of the entire Trinity, provides the satisfaction to the Father, who exercises the executive right of judgment, as well as acquittal.

I: Yes. One sees how these doctrines mesh together so beautifully. We had a fine discussion of the Trinity earlier.

And this is where the understanding of the Trinity is so important to understanding the atonement. If one does not remember the doctrine of the Trinity, including the essential Trinity and the economic Trinity, he will get into the very kind of confusion that I suffered from. He would be led to the same kind of objections, false objections based upon a misunderstanding that, until now, I labored under. I know hundreds of people who labor under such misunderstandings. But now I realize that, far from any antagonism in the Godhead, there is the most sublime and perfect unity, especially in the atonement.

C: *Soli Deo Gloria!*

# A

# Primer

# on

# Reconciliation

# Contents

# Part I

## Introduction

### 1. Our Domesticated God

According to the Bible, God's in His heaven, but all's not well with the world. "The wrath of God," says Paul, "is revealed from heaven against all ungodliness and wickedness of men who by their wickedness suppress the truth" (Romans 1:18). The hymn says:

*This is my Father's world: Oh, let me ne'er forget,*
*That though the wrong seems oft so strong,*
*God is the Ruler yet.*

According to the Bible, God is the ruler in and through these very things which seem so contrary to His purposes. He makes the wrath of men to praise Him (Psalm 76:10). He hardens the heart of Pharaoh (Exodus 4:21). The raging of Herod was of His ordination (Acts 4:27–28). Assyria is the rod of His anger (Isaiah 10:5). He forms light and creates darkness (Isaiah 45:7). So God is indeed in His heaven, but He is ruling over, in, and through evil as well as good. His being in heaven, therefore, is no guarantee that all is well on earth.

Men, the Bible says, are taking a false consolation from the fact that God is in heaven. "He's got the whole world in His hands" is the theme of a popular song, even the little baby. This is meant to be a reassuring hymn from which people in general derive great comfort. But the most famous and terrifying sermon preached in America is entitled "Sinners in the Hands of an Angry God." Jonathan Edwards did not consider it tranquilizing to be told that our lives are in the hands of God. On the contrary: "God is a great deal more angry with great numbers that are now on earth; yea,

371

doubtless with many that are now in this congregation, who it may be are at ease, than He is with many of those who are now in the flames of hell. So it is not because God is unmindful of their wickedness and does not resent it, that he does not let loose his hand and cut them off . . . . The wrath of God burns against them; their damnation does not slumber; the pit is prepared, the fire is made ready, the furnace is now hot and ready to receive them; the flames do now rage and glow. The glittering sword is whet, and held over them, and the pit has opened its mouth under them."

So it all depends on whether we are in the hands of an angry or a reconciled God. Power is comforting or discomforting depending on the one who wields it. If God be for us, asks the Scripture, who can stand against us? (Romans 8:31). But on the other hand, if God be against us who can stand for us?

The terrifying teaching of the Word of God is that the God in heaven is not for us, but against us. This admittedly is not "positive thinking." We "moderns" can no longer accept such ideas. We either domesticate God as a household pet or put Him out if He will not be housebroken. God must be friendly toward us or we will get ourselves one who is. If the Bible tells us that God is love, that is acceptable. If it speaks of the wrath and judgment of God, that is obsolete.

To show how common this opinion is, and also how tenaciously it is held, let me relate an incident. In a city in Pennsylvania I preached on Christ's commandment, "Love your enemies." In the application I said that, although Christians are not to take vengeance, they need not fear that justice may not be done. On the contrary, we are not to take vengeance because God intends to do precisely that, and He is far more capable of executing justice than are His servants. In that connection I cited the Biblical statement: "Vengeance is mine, saith the Lord; I will repay." After the service one elderly gentleman, with considerable feeling and tears of indignation in his eyes, said that he did not agree with my "notion." I asked him if he was taking exception to the command, "Love your enemies."

"Of course not," he said. He referred to the sentiment I had expressed in the one sentence of the sermon concerning the divine vengeance. He did not agree with "your idea" that God would take vengeance. I answered that I had quoted the Word of God itself, so that he was disagreeing with God's Word and not mine. Indignantly, he said, "No, I don't believe the Word of God teaches that. I disagree with *you*."

There you have it. This was an actual quotation from Scripture, as I told the man. It was God saying, "Vengeance is mine; I will repay." But the man was so opposed to the idea that he would not even concede that the Bible presented it, but, on the contrary, insisted, in spite of my disclaimer, that it was my peculiar notion.

Most Christians seem to believe that the statement "God is love" rules out "Vengeance is mine." Even when the wrath of God itself is acknowledged it is frequently construed in such a way as denies the vengeance of God. Wrath is presented as an ameliorative purging away of the defects of human character, and thus is designed for the person's ultimate good. So that while wrath may be painful in the administration, it is fundamentally a merciful and benevolent action on the part of God; anything but vengeance. Vengeance, however, is retributive justice. It means that God punishes persons because of their evil and for no other reason, as far as they are concerned. It expresses His infinite displeasure with their evil deeds. Many today simply will not grant that God hates sin so utterly that He will make men pay for it to the "uttermost farthing." They simply will not believe that He is of such a nature that He cannot abide the despising of His commandments, but will enforce vindictive justice to maintain the majesty of His own law and holiness. These persons seem to think that God is able to resent all types of indignity against His honor, but is not morally able to take vengeance on the evildoers.

*1. God is love.*

There are various ways by which men, even Christian men, have argued that God will not take vengeance. The main argument runs like this: since God is love, He cannot be vengeful. It is thought that love and vengeance are incompatible dispositions. A person cannot be both loving and vengeful. If he is loving, he cannot be vengeful; if he is vengeful, he is not loving. Love is of a benevolent disposition which leads to doing good toward other persons; vengeance is a disposition of hate which leads to doing evil to other persons. The two ideas are thought to be utterly opposite to each other. God could not possess both of these attributes. If He did He would be schizophrenic.

We cannot help but make an observation parenthetically at this point. The main reason the "modern" theologian would rule out the vengeance of God is the principle of consistency. Because vengeance is supposed to be inconsistent with love, it is repudiated. Usually, however, neo-orthodox theologians have no concern for consistency. It never bothers them in most of their thinking. As a matter of fact, they often maintain that revelation of the divine nature would necessarily appear to be inconsistent. Some of their theologians go so far as to say it would be a mark of divine revelation that it was paradoxical or inconsistent. It is rather odd, therefore, that modern theologians rule out the possibility of the divine vengeance because it is thought to be inconsistent with the divine love.

We will comment on the validity of this charge of inconsistency between divine love and divine vengeance later. Now we just put it on the record as one of the reasons that many Christian persons and Bible believers are unbable to entertain the notion that God will avenge Himself.

*2. God would not do what He forbids men to do.*

A second reason that many persons disbelieve the doctrine of the divine vengeance runs like this: It is a Christian's duty not to take vengeance. We are specifically taught by Christ to return good for evil, to love those who hate us, to pray for those who despitefully use us (Matthew 5:44ff.). We not only are not to return evil for evil by way of taking vengeance, but, on the contrary, we are to return good in the place of evil. So far as evil is concerned, we are to submit to yet more of it. In the words of Christ, "if a man smite thee on the one cheek, turn to him the other also." It is clearly the teaching of our Lord that we are to bear the injustices of men; to bear with men, not to bear a grudge against them; to be forgiving rather than avenging.

Furthermore, our Lord grounds this teaching on the very example of God: ". . . so that you may be sons of your Father who is in heaven; for He makes His sun to rise on the evil and the good, and sends rain on the just and on the unjust." So we are not to be vengeful because God is not vengeful. We are to live perfectly, that is, returning good for evil, because God lives perfectly. We are not to return evil for evil, but good for evil, just as God sends His good rain and His good sunshine upon the wicked and the unjust as well as on the just. This seems to be a very conclusive case for the virtuousness of non-vengeance, the viciousness of vengeance, and for the fact that it is a duty of men not to take vengeance precisely because God does not do so.

### 3. Men aren't so bad after all.

A third reason for insisting that God is not capable of vengeance is the feeling that there is no basis of distinction between good and evil persons. All good persons are somewhat evil and all evil persons are somewhat good. If God were to take vengeance on anyone, He would have to take vengeance on everyone. If He did not take vengeance on everyone, He could not take vengeance on anyone. But there is the biblical fact that some persons are accepted of God, reconciled to God, destined to be with God forever in heaven. That seems to rule out the possibility, in the thinking of these people, that God can take vengeance on any for, if He does, no man can be justified. If God should mark iniquity "Who, O Lord, shall stand?" (Psalm 130:3). But some people do stand. Some people are accepted. And if some people are reconciled, then God cannot be a strictly vengeful deity.

In other words, the advocates of our present theory seem to feel that we are caught in a dilemma when we consider the facts of the Bible. If God were a vengeful deity He would have to destroy all men because there is "none who does good, no, not one." But God does spare some, so He cannot be a vengeful deity because these are sinners who are dealt with in a way of mercy rather than in a way of vengeance. So our theorists maintain that God is not a God of vengeance. If He were, all men would have to be destroyed; but the evidence is that at least some men are not destroyed, and so, they say, God cannot be a vengeful deity. From that they infer that He cannot take revenge on anyone without violating the very justice for which He would be taking vengeance.

# Part II

## The Need of Reconciliation

### 2. Does God's Love Prevent His Vengeance?

We propose now to examine and refute the arguments which have been presented to prove that God does not avenge His holy law. Let us show that, in spite of the apparent feasibility of the attempts to domesticate God, they are futile. God's hands are not tied. His glory has not departed. His wrath is not dissipated and the fires of hell have not been put out.

There were three arguments set forth in the last section that shall be criticized in the following three: first, God's love prevents His wrath; second, His prohibition of our wrath prevents His own; third, His saving of some prevents His wrath on others. In this section we consider the appeal to God's love as being inimical to His wrath.

### 1. God's love is of two kinds.

Let us now examine this statement that vengeance and love are incompatible, and that since the deity is a God of love He cannot be a God of vengeance. There are two distinct sentiments which go by the name of "love." The ethicists call them the love of complacency and the love of benevolence. By the love of complacency is meant a love for another being because that other being is a worthy, moral person. His character and behavior is such that it commends itself to a holy being and pleases that holy being, who properly responds with affection for it. This is a love of complacency for a worthy person because of his excellency, because he deserves such praise and affection, because it is proper that he should be loved.

Now it is evident that vengeance is inconsistent with such a love of complacency. We presume that those who urge this present argument, while they do not commonly indicate that it is the love of complacency of which they speak, are nevertheless thinking of just such love. It is evident to them, and it is evident to us also, that it is a psychological impossibility for God to have a love of complacency and take vengeance on the person thus loved. That would be tantamount to God's loving and not loving the same person in the same respect at the same time. It would be maintaining God is angry with a person with whom He is pleased; God's hating a person whom He loves; God's punishing a person whom He praises. It is manifest nonsense to speak of God's taking vengeance on a person whom He admires and who pleases Him so much that He rewards that individual with His affection and pleasure. We admit, therefore, that if God is pleased with men, completely pleased with them, He will have no occasion for taking vengeance on them. With love, in that sense, vengeance is incompatible. It is, we grant, impossible for God to be a vengeful deity if He has a love of complacency for mankind.

However, love is used in another sense also, namely the love of benevolence. This means a love that consists in a good will toward another being. The person thus loving has a disposition to bless another person. Nothing is said about that other person's worthiness. Nothing is said about any complacency in that other person's worthiness. All that this love signifies is that a person wishes and does well toward his neighbor though that one may not at all deserve it. The neighbor may deserve the very opposite. Now, God may have this type of love existing in spite of the person loved rather than because of him.

Here again it is evident, and we concede this to our opponents, that if God has a love of good will toward another person, that will lead God not to take vengeance, but on the contrary to bestow favors. It would be impossible for God to have a good will toward a person while actually destroying that person. His destroying of that person would destroy His love of benevolence. Or His love of benevolence would prevent His destroying the person. It is admitted that at the moment of vengeance God could not have a love of benevolence that would prevent His destroying the person. It is admitted that at the moment of vengeance God could not have a love of benevolence, or that at the moment of a love of benevolence God could not take vengeance.

We may sum up the matter by saying that at the moment God has a love of complacency or a love of benevolence He cannot take vengeance. At the moment that He has a love of complacency He cannot take vengeance because there would be no object that would elicit a desire for vengeance. Vengeance is a reprisal for evil doing. By supposition, the person is not guilty of evil doing. He is an excellent being who illicits God's love of complacency. So there would be no ground at the moment God has a love of complacency for a person to visit him with vengeance, which assumes that God does not have a love of complacency. It is also true that at the moment of God's love of benevolence He cannot take vengeance because, although the person may deserve the divine vengeance, God would be psychologically incapable of administering it because, by hypothesis, He would have a love of benevolence or well-doing. This love of benevolence would lead Him to act mercifully toward the person and not in wrath. So that at the moment God has this love of benevolence He would be incapable of taking vengeance even though the person might deserve this vengeance. All this is admitted by way of concession and agreement with our opponents. Now we come to the specific criticism of the error in their overall position, which exists in spite of this area of sound ethical thought.

### 2. God's love of complacency cannot change.

In our entire discussion, when we were making concessions to the opposition, we always said that *at the time of this love* it was impossible for God to take vengeance. Whether it was a love of benevolence or complacency at the particular time, in that particular respect, vengeance would be ruled out as an incompatible disposition and behavior. But suppose the loved person's excellent and perfect moral character changed? That would immediately destroy a love of complacency. By definition, a love of complacency is a love based upon the excellency of the loved one's character. If that character changed, the basis for a love of complacency would be removed. It would then be impossible for God to have such a love. So far, then, as a love of complacency is concerned, it is at least possible for God to change to wrath, anger, and hatred which would lead Him to take vengeance upon the person in whom He previously had a love of complacency. The change in God in this instance would be traceable to the object of His former love, and not to a change in the divine will independently considered, which would remain constantly favorable to an excellent character.

Now consider God's love of benevolence toward a person in whom He does not have complacency. We do not

necessarily know why God would have a love of benevolence toward a person in whom He is not well pleased, but
it is thinkable that He has such a love. However, inasmuch
as that love is not required by justice, but exists for some
other reason, it could presumably change at any moment
without any change in the object of it. While, with respect
to a love of complacency, the loved object would have to
change (otherwise God's love of complacency would necessarily continue), a love of benevolence could change without
any change in the object. Our only point here is that, in any
case, God's love could change. If it is possible that God's
love of complacency or of benevolence could change, then
He could take an attitude of vengeance. In other words,
while it is true that at the moment of love, either of complacency or benevolence, it would be ethically or psychologically impossible for God to take vengeance if God's love did
change (and we have indicated that it could, and there is no
reason why it could not), then God could take vengeance
without this being inconsistent with His loving nature.

"True enough, but quite irrelevant," our opponents
may say. "We know that if God's love should change it
could be replaced by an attitude of hatred which could be,
we admit, a basis for vengeance. But our whole contention,"
they continue, "is that God's love does *not* change. Love is
no incidental aspect of the divine being, but a fundamental
attribute. He is defined in Scripture as being love, not
merely as having love or exercising love." Our opponents
may go on: "All of your arguments have had to do with,
and have relevance only to, the supposition that God's nature is not love, but that His behavior at certain times is
loving. Inasmuch as God's nature is love, and God's nature
cannot change, our argument stands that He will not be
able to take vengeance. "So," our opponents conclude, "we
agree with the consistency of your argument, namely that if
God's attitude could change, His behavior could change. But
we repudiate the soundness of the argument on the very
ground that since His nature cannot change, and His nature

is love, He cannot take vengeance."

We agree that the crucial part of this discussion is whether the love of God is an unchangeable attribute. We also insist that it is also a major question whether the love of God, if it is an unchangeable attribute, is the love of complacency or the love of benevolence. Let us, therefore, address ourselves to this question. It is evident, is it not, and goes almost without argument, that God's love of complacency is indeed an unchanging attribute. That is, all of Scripture represents God as unalterably pleased with holiness and unalterably displeased with unholiness. He is declared to be a Holy Being. It is therefore said that without holiness no man shall see the Lord (Hebrews 12:14). Only those with clean hands and a pure heart shall ascend into His holy hill (Psalm 15:2). And God will never be otherwise. It seems utterly obvious that God will never be otherwise. It seems utterly obvious that God, as He is represented in the Bible, will never come to be pleased with wickedness and displeased with goodness. Is it not enough merely for us to assert this? Will our reader not give us instantaneous assent?

Very well, then, it is admitted on all sides that "God is love" in the sense that He possesses this very nature, a love of complacency toward excellence, and He is unalterably so constituted as to love the excellent and hate the evil. As far as we have proceeded we have been (we think our opponents will see) working against their position. It is clear, is it not, that if God's love, which is unalterable, is a love of complacency, this spells vengeance for those in whom God has no complacency. Such a complacent love, as an unalterable attribute of the deity, so far from precluding His taking vengeance, virtually demands it. So far from vengeance being incompatible with such a love, it is inextricably associated with it. For if God's pleasure is in goodness, His displeasure will be in evil. If His pleasure leads to favorable action, His displeasure will lead to unfavorable acts, or the taking of vengeance.

*3. God's love of benevolence may change.*

The whole case, therefore, of the opposition must rest on the only remaining alternative—that God's love of benevolence is unalterable. That is, irrespective of the character of the person, God has, by nature and unalterably, a love of benevolence. If this is what is meant by saying that "God is love," this does rule out the possibility of God's ever being displeased and taking vengeance. This we admit; namely that if this is what is meant by the love of God vengeance is forever gone. On the other hand, our opponents will have to concede that if this is not what is meant, then all that remains is the love of complacency as an unalterable character of God, and this, as we have already shown, so far from precluding vengeance, requires it.

So let us address ourselves to the question whether God's love of benevolence is an unalterable attribute. We wish now to show that the unalterable attribute of God is not His love of benevolence.

*4. If God's love of benevolence were unchangeable, the*
*   Bible would not speak of His eternal wrath.*

Our reason for thus contending is that the Bible, anyone will admit, makes it very plain that God is capable of wrath. He does become angry. He does punish. Someone will immediately say, "Well, this is the whole point under debate. You are now begging the question, which is whether God actually does punish people. You, presumably, are arguing for the fact that He does. But now you are simply bluntly saying in so many words that He does. But that is precisely the point at issue."

It is not the point at issue just now. What we are here examining is whether God's love prevents His vengeance. We are denying it and submitting in proof that God Himself in His Word says that He takes vengeance. The reasoning is simply that the God who says He is love says He in wrath punishes evildoers. Love itself, therefore, sees no inconsistency in taking vengeance. If there is an inconsistency, as some allege, God is inconsistent! But this is as absurd as it is blasphemous, for if love itself does not know what is consistent with itself, how could anyone else know? Furthermore, if God were capable of inconsistency, how could creatures in His image ever detect it? Still further, if God contradicted Himself, how could He understand Himself, reveal Himself, or be understood by any other intelligence?

It is even more preposterous to deny that the Word of God does teach the wrath of God. We have already cited illustrations enough. One scholar has shown that for every single statement in Scripture concerning the mercy and grace of God there are three referring to His wrath and judgment. Apparently many more experience God's wrath than His saving grace for "the gate is wide and the way is easy that leads to destruction, and those who enter by it are many. For the gate is narrow and the way is hard that leads to life, and those who find it are few" (Matthew 7:13–14).

If God's benevolence to the wicked can change to wrath, His present love does not preclude His future vengeance.

*5. If God's love of benevolence were unchangeable, His love of complacency could not be.*

A second argument against the notion that God's love of benevolence is an unchangeable attribute is that, if this were, so it would rule out His love of complacency. But this, we have already shown, is an immutable attribute.

Let us explain. If God had, as an immutable attribute, a love of benevolence, He would always feel toward wicked persons the same way He feels toward virtuous persons. He would show toward people who despise Him and His laws the same face that He shows toward those who love Him and obey His commandments. As far as God's actual feelings or behavior are concerned, there would be no difference between the evil and the good. God would feel and act no differently toward filthy creatures than toward holy ones. There would be no meaning to the statement, "The wages of sin is death" (Romans 6:23). On the contrary, the wages of sin would be life. God would reward wickedness with blessings. To be sure, He would reward virtue with blessing, but He would also reward the lack of virtue with blessing. There would be no distinction between the two as far as God's attitude and action are concerned. The wicked could say with justice, "Let us eat, drink and be merry, for tomorrow we live." There would be no fear of God before anyone's eyes because there would be nothing in God to fear. If a person were disposed to be honest, he could no more count on the love of God than if he were disposed to be dishonest. If he chose to do good to his neighbor, he would please God no more than if he chose to torture and kill his neighbor. God's love would be the same in either case.

No one can say at this point, "Ah, but the wicked would have an inner torment, an uneasy conscience," for we must remember that inner torment, or an uneasy conscience, is itself a divine punishment. If God had nothing but a love of benevolence, He would not punish the soul anymore than He would punish the body. He would not punish inwardly any more than He would inflict the wicked with the adversities of circumstance. Moreover, how could a person be tormented in conscience if he believed that God unchangeably loved him?

If someone says further, "Ah, but God does exactly what you are saying He does not do. You admit that He makes His sun to shine and His rain to fall on the evil as well as the good." We admit that God makes His sun to shine and His rain to fall on the wicked, but we do not admit that He does what this supposition would have Him doing. For one thing, we can and do say that God's displeasure is expressed in the torments of conscience, which conscience suffers even while the sun shines and the rains are coming upon wicked persons. Furthermore, we say that God's love of benevolence is expressed temporarily and not unchangeably merely as an opportunity for repentance (Romans

2:4). Whereas, in the hypothesis before us, God has an immutable love of benevolence, and will therefore eternally show favor toward the wicked. There is a vast difference between this unchangeable love of benevolence and our (which we believe to be the Biblical) position. The two cannot be confused.

All arguments for the immutability of God's love of benevolence for the wicked perish with them in hell. If hell is eternal, as the Bible teaches, God's love for the wicked is not. This is so self-evident to everyone that the doctrine of hell has become as intolerable as hell itself. But the eternal fires will never be put out by wishful or frantic thinking. Here we rather assume than prove hell. Those who would survey the evidence may consult any standard theology such as Calvin, Hodge, Strong, or Shedd. The latter wrote a definitive monograph entitled *The Doctrine of Endless Punishment.* Harry Buis' work, *The Doctrine of Eternal Punishment,* is also useful.

> 6. *If God's love of benevolence were unchangeable it would obscure God's loving nature.*

A third argument against the doctrine under review is that not only would the outworking of this theory be preposterous, as we have just shown, but the in-workings would be preposterous also. The permanent expression of God's benevolent love must be a true indication of His intention and disposition. An expression can be temporary, and thus not an expression of the inner disposition. But permanent expression would surely have to be the expression of the inner disposition. If this were not so, the creature would never be able to understand anything of the nature of God. It is evident that creatures cannot have a perfect understanding of the mind of God. They cannot know it intuitively as God knows it. They are finite and He is infinite. Their only clues to His nature are what God is pleased to express or manifest. If therefore He shows Himself to be indifferent to morality; if by His expression He indicated that He was as pleased with wickedness as with virtue (which even our opponents admit is not the case), then the creature would be utterly misled. He could not help but think something of God which was not true of God. God would therefore be involved in hypocrisy. He would be deliberately manifesting Himself to be what He is not. If that were thinkable, which it is not, it would be a dreadfully immoral thing to attribute to God.

Our opponents may say, "But aren't you faced with the same problem? Don't you, in your admission that there is such a thing as a love of benevolence toward wicked men, face the fact that God does show Himself to be pleased with that which does not please Him?" By no means. First of all, God manifests this love of benevolence only temporarily. The Bible indicates, in our view of things, that it is temporary. The forbearance of God is meant to lead to repentance. If this repentance is not forthcoming, the forbearance of God will be withdrawn. That is the teaching of the Bible. The wicked are not permitted to conclude that, because God permits His sun to shine and His rain to fall upon them as well as upon the righteous, it shall always be so. On the contrary, the Bible teaches plainly, in our view, that it shall not be so in the world to come. This benevolence is strictly temporary, and for a purpose.

Second, we showed on our view that God torments the conscience of persons even while He outwardly blesses them, so that they cannot be led to conclude from this temporal prosperity that they have secured the favor of God. His tormenting of their conscience would disabuse their mind of that immediately, and would direct their queries to the questions: "What must I do to be saved while I have the opportunity in the divine forbearance? What must I do to improve my relationship with God before he expresses his anger outwardly and forever?"

*7. If God's love of benevolence were unchangeable He would be foolish.*

A fourth argument against unchangeable benevolence is as follows: Immutable, benevolent love would destroy the wisdom of God. We know that God is one, harmonious, blessed Being. If His attributes were in conflict He could not possibly be one, harmonious, or blessed. But, if God's love of benevolence were an immutable attribute, it would be in hopeless conflict with His wisdom. The wisdom of God is an attribute which no one denies. It leads to the accomplishment of all His infinite purposes in the most expeditious manner. Now if God felt an unchangeable love of benevolence for all men, irrespective of their characters, that would promote evil and tend to destroy good in the creatures. They would succumb to temptation without any deterrent. Any difficulties in the path of duty would be easily avoided by simply turning away into the path of evildoing. God's whole purpose to promote good works, to restore the divine image, to lead men in paths of righteousness for His name's sake, would be frustrated. God would appear as infinitely stupid. He would avowedly desire to promote righteousness, and then, according to this theory, would choose the method most perfectly fitted to destroy it. His aim would be to eradicate evil, but the method He employed would be perfectly suited to establishing it. God's house would indeed be divided against itself. His purposes and His methods would be in open conflict. This would be an insufferable insult to the divine intelligence. Instead of being infinitely wise, God would appear infinitely foolish.

Our opponents may say, "Aren't you overestimating your own intelligence here? Aren't you assuming that we creatures know more than we do? Aren't you ruling out the possibility that the event will be different than it appears, and that God may have a secret way of working here that you can't anticipate?"

We reply that such an insinuation as this certainly denies all human intelligence including the intelligence of the person who makes the assertion. We do not have an infinite mind, to be sure, but we have been given a mind able to make judgments for which we are held responsible. How could anyone help but conclude that if God expresses pleasure in evildoing this will promote evildoing? And that if God expresses no displeasure in wickedness, the ultimate deterrent to such behavior would be removed? If this is not self-evident, then there is no such thing as the obvious. If human intelligence is not to be relied upon not only are we out of line, but our opponents also when they make their criticisms. Let us forget such foolishness. Let us rely on our own ability to make responsible judgments. Let us both admit that there is nothing obscure here, that God's possessing such an unchangeable attribute as this can only have the effect in this world and the world to come, in time and in eternity, of favoring evil and discouraging good and, inevitably. reflecting on God's wisdom.

In conclusion (we conclude not because all has been said which can be said, but because all has been said which seems to be necessary) let us say this: God is a vengeful being. This is clear because, as a holy person, He must be opposed to the unholy, and this opposition must be expressed to His creatures. This fact, furthermore, has been revealed in the Sacred Word.

The objections which have been raised against this position we have answered as clearly and fairly as we can. We have dealt with them as honestly and as thoroughly as we could in the space at our command. It seems to us very clear that God, though He is a God of complacent love and a wise, benevolent love, is also a God who does and must say, "Vengeance is mine; I will repay." There is no inconsistency between such a disposition to vengeance and His love, either of complacency or benevolence. We have not explored in this chapter (because it has not seemed pertinent) why God does show this love of benevolence for a limited time. Suffice it to remark that it must be a part of His infinite wisdom. It would not be at all difficult to show the wisdom of it. That, however, is not the question under discussion. Rather, the question we have been discussing is whether it is consistent with the loving character of God for Him to take vengeance. That it is, we believe we have demonstrated.

### 3. Does God's Prohibition of Our Vengeance Prevent His?

We come now to the second argument, namely that since Scripture represents it as a Christian duty for men to love those who do evil and not to take vengeance, God Himself would not do otherwise. We admit, of course, that the Bible teaches Christians are not to take vengeance. It forbids their returning evil for evil. There is agreement between us and those who oppose us with respect to this fact of Christian duty. However, we immediately insist that the fact that we creatures have the God-given duty not to take vengeance does not necessarily imply that God Himself should not or would not take vengeance. Theoretically it is altogether possible that God is going to take vengeance, and precisely because He is going to take vengeance He may forbid any creature taking vengeance. There is nothing in the nature of the case that argues that because God has forbidden us to take vengeance that He, therefore, will not take vengeance Himself. Yet this implication would have to be true if our opponents are to have any cogency in their argument. They must be thinking that, because God forbids us to take vengeance, He, therefore, Himself may not take vengeance. We do not find the proponents of this theory actually arguing this case. They state the Christian duty not to take vengeance, and seem to feel that that fact carries with it the implication that God will also be duty-bound not to take vengeance. We must insist that, if our opponents are reasoning in this manner, they are making an utterly gratuitous assumption. As we say, repeating, there is nothing in the nature of the case which argues that because God forbids us to take vengeance He Himself will not take vengeance. Anyone who is going to appeal to our duty as an argument against God's vengefulness is going to have to show a connection which our opponents do not even attempt to show.

It does not behoove us to prove why God would forbid our taking vengeance if He Himself were intending to take vengeance. The burden of the proof is upon those who say that because He forbids our taking vengeance He cannot Himself take vengeance. Nevertheless, though the burden of the proof is not on us, it may not be out of the way for us to indicate why we believe God forbids us to take vengeance even though He Himself intends so to do.

*1. We are too unjust to take vengeance.*

One reason, no doubt, is the fact that we, being sinful creatures, cannot take a proper vengeance. We, frequently, when we are greatly angered, act in an extreme manner toward the person who angers us. For example, Lamech boasted: "I have slain a man for wounding me, a young man for striking me" (Genesis 4:23). In that text it suggests that Lamech, a wicked man, when he was even wounded, took vengeance by killing the person who had merely injured him.

We read once of a grotesque crime committed in the city of New York. A man brushed into a young boy. This boy was so infuriated by the little bump he received from this passerby that he turned on the man, pursued him for four blocks, and, when he overtook him, killed him. This is an extreme, a dreadful extreme, of course; but it is, at the same time, an illustration of how sinful men sometimes take vengeance. God is sufficiently concerned with justice that He will not turn over its administration to those upon whose integrity He cannot rely. So, from this standpoint, God's forbidding us to take vengeance, so far from carrying the implication that He Himself will not take vengeance, implies precisely the opposite. That is to say, God forbids our taking vengeance because of our inability to take it properly, and for that reason He, the Judge of all the earth who cannot do wrong, must take this important matter into His own hands.

### 2. We are too unloving to take vengeance.

A second reason God refuses to permit His creatures to take vengeance seems to be this: If we were to punish all offenses against us we would, in our present state of sin, undoubtedly have many unholy passions mingled with a fundamentally proper ethical sentiment of vengeance. It is not only that we would be prone to take an extreme vengeance, that is, more than an eye for an eye and more than a tooth for a tooth, but, also, we would have unholy hatred and animosity involved in the act as well. The first reason which we gave referred strictly to the punishment itself, to the outward administration of vengeance. This second reason refers to the attitude of heart which we would have in the act of taking vengeance. We would not take it as we should, as persons who are utterly committed to rectitude, who are lovers of justice and who punish because they love holiness and hate evil. On the contrary, we would have an unholy malice mixed up with this holy sentiment in every instance of our administration. God seems to consider this matter of vengeance of such great importance that He will not turn it over to persons who cannot administer it without doing so in an unholy manner. Therefore He will reserve this prerogative to Himself alone.

### 3. We are too busy to take vengeance.

A third reason God Himself will take vengeance, and will not permit creatures to do so, is this: Their taking vengeance would take all their time. That is, there is so much inequity in the world, so many offenses committed that require punishment, that if perfect justice were to be done every individual would be totally engaged, all the time, in meting out punishment and having punishment meted out to him. God Himself says that every idle word shall be brought into judgment. This means that there is nothing which a creature does, however trifling, as trifling as an idle word, which does not deserve and will not receive punishment. God is able to weigh every offense, to administer the perfect punishment for each transgression. We creatures, however, are able neither to weigh the offense nor to administer the justice required in every instance. Even to endeavor to do so, as we say, would take all of our time. We would be able to perform no other duty save the duty of judging our fellow creatures and being judged by them.

*4. We are too sinfully vengeful to have vengeance taken on us.*

A fourth reason that God refuses the taking of vengeance to His creatures while reserving that prerogative to Himself is this: the taking of vengeance by one creature against another creature in this present sinful state of affairs would only antagonize the creature against whom the vengeance is taken. He in turn would retaliate against his punisher. The punisher in turn would retaliate against the punisher. Every man would be embroiled in an endless war with every other man all the time; especially if we remember, as we have said earlier, that when a fallen creature takes vengeance on another fallen creature, even though the vengeance should be a just one, he would have animosity, ill-temper, and other unholy sentiments in his own soul as he administered this punishment. Such animosity and hatred is designed to stir up the same in these other persons to whom the discipline would be administered.

*5. Men will be associated with God in vengeance when they are worthy.*

We hardly need continue enumerating reasons which God evidently displays in His chosen economy of justice. Surely even these are sufficient to indicate this much: that it would be perfectly consistent for an avenging deity's refusing to permit His creatures to be delegated with that particular authority, at least in this world. We add that expression "at least in this world" in order to remind the reader that, according to the Scriptures, just men made perfect in the other world will be joined with Jesus Christ in the judgment of mankind. "Do you not know that the saints will judge the world? Do you not know that we are to judge angels?" (1 Corinthians 6:2–3).

We can see how proper it is for God to permit men in the next world to be associated with the Son of God in the Judgment. At that time they will be perfectly just men. Corruption, pollution, animosity, hatred, violence will be gone from their souls. They will see truth and love it and desire its execution. They will be joined perfectly in sentiment with the righteous Judge of heaven and earth, Jesus Christ. It will be altogether appropriate at that time for them to judge the world, and they shall do so. However, as long as sin remains, as long as we are in this present world, devoid of that perfection which shall come only at death, it is just as evidently improper and unsuitable for us to be entrusted with this holy task of judging our fellow creatures.

Matthew Henry once quaintly observed that many Christians transgress the will of Christ by their impatience in assuming the judgment seat. He meant that it is the prerogative of Christians to judge the world—but not now, later. When Christians in this world presume to take vengeance upon their adversaries, they show themselves to be impatient with God's way of doing things, unwilling to await the proper time. But they must. Insofar as they understand the will of God, they will wait until God perfects them for the delicate task of judging their fellow creatures. Meanwhile, "vengeance is mine. I will repay, says the Lord."

*6. God's present example is not His eternal one.*

The opponents of the doctrine that God takes vengeance may object at this point: "You overlook the fact that God not only forbids Christians taking vengeance, but He forbids them precisely because He Himself does not take vengeance." They may continue, "You argue that it is proper for Christians to be forbidden to take vengeance while God Himself reserves that perogative to Himself. True, but have you not overlooked the fact that God does not reserve this prerogative to Himself? On the contrary, He refrains from it and grounds His commands to his servants on the fact that He Himself does not take vengeance. 'Be ye perfect as your Father in heaven is perfect,' is the context in which Jesus has observed that God sends His sun and His rain upon the evil and the unjust as well as upon virtuous persons."

We reply that this passage proves only that God does not now, all the time, take vengeance against sinful creatures. He not only does not take vengeance now all the time against all sinful creatures, but He bestows favors upon these sinful persons at this time in this world. But the passage does not say that God never will take vengeance at any time against any of His creatures. It does not say He will always do good to them. It says simply, we repeat, that God shows certain favors to certain wicked persons in this present world. More than that it does not say. More than that He does not imply. There is nothing in what it does say which is inconsistent with the doctrine that God does take full vengeance upon the wicked, at some time, in some world.

If we have established our case that the Bible teaches plainly that God does take vengeance at some time against wicked persons in some world, then surely, this particular passage cannot be adduced as in any way opposed to that doctrine. It merely reminds us that the full vengeance which God is going to take He is not taking at the present time, but, on the contrary, is showing certain favors. That fact is used as a pattern for the behavior of God's servants. That is, He commands them to love their enemies and turn the other cheek, giving them as an object lesson His own behavior towards the wicked in this present world. Just as there is no inconsistency between the disciples being forbidden at the present time to take vengeance, and yet being told that at some future time they will be associated with Jesus Christ Himself in taking vengeance, so there is no inconsistency in being told that God at the present time in this world does not take full vengeance against the wicked, but at the same time will take full vengeance against them in another world at another time.

Notice how the passage in Romans 12:19–21 states the same duties as binding on Christians, but also explicitly mentions what is omitted in Matthew 5, that God will take vengeance on those whom He and His servants now benevolently love: "Beloved, never avenge yourselves, but leave it to the wrath of God; for it is written, 'Vengeance is mine, I will repay, says the Lord.' No, 'if your enemy is hungry, feed him; if he is thirsty, give him drink; for by so doing you will heap burning coals upon his head.' Do not be overcome by evil, but overcome evil with good."

## 4. Does God's Saving of Some Prevent
## His Taking Vengeance on Others?

The third and last objection was that God cannot take vengeance on some since He is gracious to others. Again, we agree with our opponents in the facts to which they allude. We and they alike admit that God shows mercy, saving mercy, to some persons in this world. However, our critics deduce from that acknowledged fact this *non sequitur*: because God shows mercy to some persons in this world He cannot be a God of vengeance to them. If He is not a God of vengeance to these persons, He cannot be a God of vengeance toward other persons, since all persons are contaminated with sin. The argument, therefore, is this: because God does not take vengeance on some sinners, He cannot consistently take vengeance on any sinners, and therefore He is not a God of vengeance.

While this is sound enough in its own pattern of

thought, it overlooks an essential truth. The neglected essential truth is the Biblical doctrine that Jesus Christ made satisfaction for the sins of believers. The doctrine of satisfaction means that Jesus Christ endured the vengeance of God on behalf of those who put their trust in Him. As the Scripture says, "For our sake He made Him to be sin who knew no sin, so that in Him we might become the righteousness of God" (2 Corinthians 5:21). We will have much more to say of this later.

If it is true that Christ endures the wrath of God for believers, God's grace to some does not imply that He is not a God of vengeance to others. When we understand the reason or basis for His showing mercy to these persons, we see a most compelling demonstration that God does take vengeance. The basis for the divine forgiveness is nothing less than the expiatory death of Jesus Christ. The fact that such a vicarious and expiatory death is necessary in order to reconcile sinners to God shows demonstrably how unalterably God is opposed to sinners. It clearly declares that He will not be reconciled without being satisfied. His holiness demands vindication. His justice must be maintained. Even His mercy is unable to override His justice. His mercy cannot override, but it can satisfy. On the basis of that satisfaction, that is to say, on the basis of the satisfaction of God's vengeance upon a substitute, and only upon that basis, will God extend forgiveness to sinful men who believe. How can there be more convincing evidence that God is a God of vengeance than is provided in the fact of the atonement, which declares that God will pardon no one except as His vengeance has been endured. If God were not a God of vengeance it would be possible for Him to forgive sinners without atonement. The fact that it is not possible for Him to forgive without atonement shows that He is a God of vengeance, and that He must be satisfied. His wrath is to be poured out either on the guilty person, or on the person who has assumed His guilt. So we see that the mercy of God, which does indeed secure the salvation of some men, nevertheless does not represent an abandonment of the divine vengeance, but a satisfaction of it. Therefore the fact that some persons are saved is another argument in proof of the fact that God does take vengeance rather than an argument against that doctrine. It certainly does not mean that they are saved because God is indifferent to their sins, and thus to the sins of all men.

Summarizing this part we may say that it is not we, but God, who must be reconciled. We have come to imagine that God needs to be reconciled to us rather than we to Him. In fact, we have reconciled Him to us, or domesticated Him. But the God we have domesticated is no longer God. The God whom we have reconciled to us is no longer worth reconciling. The very fact that we in our arrogance could suppose for a moment that God needs to be reconciled to us shows how much we need to be reconciled to Him. Our sin against Him is so great that we fancy He has sinned against us. We will never be reconciled until we admit that we need to be. He may be ready to forgive us, waiting to receive us as prodigals while we are afar off, but not before we admit our bankruptcy and need of Him.

# Part III

## The Nature of Reconciliation

### 5. God Chose Us in Christ Eternally.

Here is our situation to the present. God is of purer eyes than to behold iniquity. He will by no means clear the guilty. He could not care more about sin. His inexorable law is: "The wages of sin is death." Nor can God be bought, fooled, ignored, cajoled or frustrated. Man, on the other hand, has guilt, all guilt, and nothing but guilt. The thoughts and intents of his heart are only evil continually (Genesis 6:5). He has no excuse, and his alibis are illustrations of his guilt. If he really were innocent (as the insane are), he would not understand the charge of guilt, much less be ready with a defense. There is no possibility that man is not guilty as charged. His efforts to prove that he is not proves, therefore, that he is. That he says he is innocent makes him more guilty. So, God will not clear the guilty; man is guilty; therefore, God will not clear man.

There is only one possible outcome: death. There can be no other possibility—none at all. No last minute rescue. No conceivable change of God's mind or man's condition. Man must die or justice must. Man must die or God must. God cannot die. Therefore, man must die.

So reconciliation would not seem possible. Alienation would seem inalienable. Atonement appears unthinkable. Eternal separation is inevitable.

Only one way would be viable if it were do-able: if somehow someone could identify himself with man, undergo his due and yet not be destroyed. Each one of those things seems unthinkable and undoable. It seems unthinkable that anyone could do it if he would, and even more unthinkable than he would do it if he could.

According to the Bible there is one whose ability is as great as His willingness and His willingness as great as his ability—omnipotent and omnivolent. There is one who has perfect power and infinite love. There is one who identifies Himself utterly with His people and suffers utterly in their stead. It was in Christ that God was reconciling the world (2 Corinthians 5:19), for the most exacting job description of a reconciler was met fully in Him.

Christ perfectly identified Himself with His people, His elect. Union with Christ is a doctrine not adequately expounded by the theologians, but is the foundation nonetheless of reconciliation.

Christ's identification with His people is eternal. "He hath chosen us in Him before the foundation of the world" (Ephesians 1:4). We tend to construe these words in this manner: From all eternity God chose us to be in Christ.

God is eternal, Christ is eternal, and their choices are eternal. But, we say, we are not eternal. Therefore, although God chose us in Christ eternally, He could not have chosen us eternally because we do not exist as God does, eternally. So the verse must mean, we conclude, that God eternally chose us to be in Christ in time. Our identification with Christ is not eternal, but God's choice that we should be identified is eternal. What follows in the text seems to confirm this common sense interpretation "that we should walk before Him in love." Surely we do not do that eternally. We cannot walk before we are. We are not eternally, and therefore we do not walk eternally before God in love. Nor are we eternally in Christ, but are chosen from eternity to be in Christ.

In spite of the apparent good sense of this interpretation, it raises one problem—it is not what the text says. The text says that we were chosen in Christ (not, to be in Christ) before the foundation of the world. How, it is properly asked, can we, who are not, be? How can we be in Christ when we have no being? We cannot answer that. Our inability to explain, however, is no argument against the existence of anything. We cannot explain how we exist in time much less in eternity, but no one regards that admission as an argument against our present being.

Although we cannot explain how we can be in Christ when we have no being, God says that this is the case. So we have a conclusive argument in favor of our eternal existence in some sense, namely God affirms it. We have no argument against it. Even if we thought that we did have arguments against it, could they prevail in the presence of one word from God? But, in fact, we have no argument; merely a difficulty! an incomprehensibility! in other words, nothing! In summary, we have perfect evidence for our being in Christ eternally, and precisely nothing against it. We conclude, then, that we have been united with Christ eternally. We have been chosen by God as long as God has existed. We have been in Christ as long as He existed. To put this another way: God has not existed longer than we have. His existence is of a different kind, but not of a different duration.

This is breathtaking. We dare not say it. But we dare not *not* say it. In fact, we do not say it. God says it. When He speaks we may not be silent.

We hear cries of "pantheism" and "blasphemy!" But we have not said that we are God or Christ. On the contrary, we have said that the inspired Apostle says that we are chosen by God in Christ eternally. To be in God eternally is to be other than God eternally. Also, we are limited or finite, and not infinite as God is. We are in God, He is not in us. Likewise, we are dependent on Him, not He on us. We have said, and this is all that we have said, but we have said all of this: we are in Christ eternally.

Will someone quibble, "The text does not say 'eternally'? It says 'before the foundation of the world.' "

True, "before the foundation of the world" is not necessarily eternally. But God's choosing is necesarily eternal. His choice is either eternal or not eternal. If it is not eternal then it is in time, But why? Did He have to wait, as we do, to discover how things would turn out? If so, He is neither omnipotent nor omniscient. In a word, He would not be God. So, His choice must be eternal, and He chose us eternally. And, if He chose us eternally, we are eternal.

Which is blasphemy, to believe or to disbelieve God's Word? But if we did disbelieve it, on what basis would we do so? Because we cannot "understand" it! Is what God does not say easier to "understand" than what He does say? Do we disbelieve what He does say and believe what He does not say? Why? Because our minds are more comfortable that way! Our finitude becomes the measure of His infinitude. This is piety? This is humility? Which is the Christian thing to do? To believe God when He says that we are eternal, or to insist "Not so, Lord"?

Nevertheless, the persistent question keeps rising. How can we be eternal? Is this the heretical doctrine of the pre-existence of souls? But nothing has been said about "souls."

The text says that "we" were chosen in Christ before the foundation of the world. But are "we" not souls? Yes, we are now. Does it necessarily follow that we always have been? I do not know how this could be proved or disproved. Unless God informs us directly in His Word, we know of nothing elsewhere which could afford an answer. But why do we need an answer? Is it not enough that God has said we have existed eternally? Must we know in what form? Perhaps it was in the form of idea in God's mind. Who but God knows?

"Ah," you say "a mere idea!" But why do you say "mere" idea? Mind you, we are not saying, we cannot say, that that is what the text is implying. But if it were, why do you say "mere" idea? If the text does imply that you were in Christ as an idea, then *you* were in Christ as an idea. You were that idea in the mind of God. That idea in the mind of God was you. How wonderful that would be! If God identifies me with the eternal idea of me which is in His mind, I am delighted and honored to know my pedigree. That pre-existence would be different from my present existence, for I am now more than, or other than, an idea. But it would also be identical with my present existence because that idea was I, you. My body undergoes constant change, but remains my body. It is God and not I who constitutes the identity. What if He constitutes an identity between the I who now am and the idea which eternally was? We repeat, we do not have to answer these questions if we could, and could not if we would. We submit these "may-be"'s only in reply to the "can't-be"'s.

We had to spend all this time with the "metaphysical" identity because so many questions arise at this point. However, the truly wonderful part of the text is not the implied metaphysical, wonderful as that may be, but the asserted spiritual identity. We are chosen in Christ. It is interesting that we existed eternally; it is sublime that we are in Christ eternally. Existence eternally is mere duration without end. Existence in Christ is life eternal. The one fascinates the mind; the other grips the entire person.

Being in Christ from all eternity means that we were in Christ before we were ever out of Him, and out of Him only to be brought back into Him. The statement that "He chose us in Him before the foundation of the world, that we should be holy and blameless before Him" seems to mean: (1) we were in Him eternally; (2) we were chosen in Him eternally; (3) we were ordained to fall (this is implied rather than stated here; the reference to redemption and conversion that occurs in the context imply that there was some sort of alienation from this original union with Christ); (4) we were chosen to be restored in time through the blood of Christ and the work of His Spirit—this is the reconciliation to which the Bible refers, and with which our little book is primarily concerned.

The first two items above have already been sufficiently discussed. The third is only incidental to our primary purpose, but needs more elaboration even here. The theme is more fully discussed by Paul in the first chapters of the Romans and the first verses of the second chapter of the Ephesian epistle. From the third chapter of Genesis it occupies a central position in the unfolding human story. Grace only superabounded where sin first abounded. Where there is no law there is no sin, and where there is no sin there is no grace. In Ephesians 1:4 it is very much in the background. In fact, one would hardly suspect its presence in this chapter if Paul did not refer to redemption by the blood of Christ. This reference, however, immediately alerts us to the fact that the Apostle has left this perfect union with Christ to consider a present fallen condition which requires bloody redemption in order to restore this broken unity. The inference is spelled out in full detail in the next chapter where we read:

> And you He made alive, when you were dead through the trespasses and sins in which you once walked, following the course of this world, following the prince of the power of the air, the spirit that is now at work

in the sons of disobedience. Among these we all once
lived in the passions of our flesh, following the desires
of body and mind, and so we were by nature children
of wrath, like the rest of mankind.

Thus being born in trespasses and sins we were no
longer in union with God in Christ, but became the children of wrath and of the devil. So union is followed by alienation. We are out of Christ and in union with the spirit that
"now worketh in the children of disobedience."

Now let us notice (4) how reconciliation comes about.
In 1:4 we are simply told that God had chosen us that we
should be holy and without blame before Him in love. We
are not told how this decree was to be effected. This is explained now in 2:4f.: "But God, who is rich in mercy, out of
the great love with which He loved us (a reminder of the
eternal love already expressed) hath even when we were
dead through our trespasses, made us alive together with
Christ." Thus this great love leads Christ, from whom we
had become separated by sin, to make us alive again and
then unite Himself with us ("and raised us up with Him,
and made us sit with him in the heavenly places").

This divine procedure seems parallel to the eternal one.
In eternity, He brings us into being and then unites us
with Himself. In time, He brings us into new being and
unites us with the Author of our new being. Lazarus' raising was a miracle which illustrates the spiritual reality before us. Corrupt and stinking Lazarus was not even fit for
the presence of men, much less of God. Christ said,
"Lazarus, come forth." When he came forth a new and
whole man, Christ no doubt embraced him in tender fellowship, broken for the moment but now restored forever.

Thus the order of salvation events would seem to be as
follows: 1. eternally chosen in Christ; 2. fallen from Christ
in sin; 3. quickened from the death and defilement of sin by
Christ's power; 4. re-united with Christ in grace. There is a
sense in which union with Christ precedes, and a sense in

which union with Christ follows, reconciliation. The eternal (past) union with Christ precedes and forms the basis of reconciliation; but reconciliation precedes and forms the basis of the eternal (future) union with Christ. The first union with Christ had no beginning; the second has no end.

## 6. Christ Reconciles Eternally by Reconciling God

Now that we have seen something of the eternal span of God's plan, it is time to look more closely at this matter of how a God so holy can admit a man so unholy into His presence, reconciled. Granted that Christ raised and sanctified men by His power. This does not solve the problem; it creates it. The wages of sin were said to be death, but here they seem to be life. According to all that has already been shown from Scripture, God would have to use His power to destroy, not to save. If He saved man He would destroy Himself; if He destroyed man He would save Himself. The fact that man, subsequent to such an exertion of divine power, would be fit for the divine presence does not explain how that divine power was exerted when man was fit only for judgment.

We must look elsewhere in our passage for the answer to this question. This search brings us to His "blood" (1:7). "In Him we have redemption through His blood."

Now, why would the Holy One shed His blood? This is a problem in the opposite direction. How could God raise sinners? we asked. Now, how could He destroy saints? we must wonder. Disconnected these two facts defy explanation. Connected they may explain one another. The Holy One's shedding His blood may explain why the unholy ones do not shed theirs.

But how? There must have been a juxtaposition. The Holy One must have become identified with the unholy ones, and the unholy ones with the Holy One. That could explain everything, and that alone could explain anything. If He, by identification with them, became unholy He must die. If they, by identification with Him, become holy they must live. Thus He is killed and they are quickened.

Christ's identification with His people is implied, but not stated in Ephesians. It is stated in express terms: "He made Him to be sin who knew no sin, so that in Him we might become the righteousness of God" (2 Corinthians 5:21). Does this mean that Christ became a sinner? Of course not, for if He had then the text would read: "He was made sin by sinning that in Him we might become the unrighteousness of God." God forbid! The only way by which Christ's becoming sin could enable us to become righteous was by His not becoming a sinner. If He became a sinner He would die *with* us, not *for* us. He would die for Himself, not for us.

But if becoming sin does not mean becoming a sinner, what does it mean? It must mean that He became sin in the sense of being identified with sin, associated with sin, guilty of sin. On the surface of it this is preposterous. How could He who knew no sin become identified with it? guilty of it? We would be back again with the unrighteousness of God. God would not be saving people who deserved to die, but condemning a person who deserved to live. In the former case the Holy One would be beholding iniquity, which He cannot do; in this case, the Holy One would be not beholding righteousness, which He must do. So Christ cannot become sin in the sense of being identified with, guilty of, or charged with a sin of which He was not guilty. But He did become sin; therefore He must have been guilty. Yet He committed no sin. Then, He was guilty of someone else's sins. But that would be unfair, unjust. Not if He voluntarily took it. There it is. He must have voluntarily identified Himself with the guilt of these others. That would explain everything. That would explain how He became sin who knew no sin, and how they became the righteousness of God who knew no righteousness.

The picture is becoming clearer. Jesus Christ is the person who could as He would and would as He could. He could identify Himself with sinners and endure the pun-

ishment which was their due. As God He was able to assume a human nature. This wonderful thing He did.
"Christ Jesus, who, though He was in the form of God, did
not count equality with God a thing to be grasped, but
emptied Himself, taking the form of a servant, being found
in the likeness of men" (Philippians 2:5–7). Being man He
could obey and fulfill the law's righteous demands. This
wonderful thing He did: "And being found in human form
He humbled Himself and became obedient unto death, even
death on a cross" (Philippians 2:7–8). Being obedient man
He was able to suffer for the infractions of the righteous
law, which sinful man was all too able to commit.

The reader will have noticed that much of our discussion here was in general terms of God and man. This is because our discussion concerned these two principals and in
contrast with one another. We never meant by "man" each
and every human individual The casual reader may sometimes have read that understanding into our text. But we
never said it, we never intended it, and we never implied it.
We are laboring this rather obvious point because we think
that Scripture often proceeds in a similar way discussing
the theme in terms of the two principals, without any special reference to the particular individuals meant by the general term "man."

Many casual readers have a tendency to read universalism into these passages although the Scripture neither
teaches nor implies such. When it does become specific on
the matter it is very clearly particularistic and not universalistic. For example, Christ Himself was constantly
speaking about those whom the Father had given Him,
"My sheep," "blessed are your ears," "your eyes," "he that
hath ears to hear let him hear," "no man cometh unto Me
except the Father draw him," "I am praying for them; I am
not praying for the world, but for those Thou hast given
Me." (John 17:9), and "Come, ye blessed of My Father,
inherit the kingdom prepared for you from the foundation of
the world" (Matthew 25:34)—all which expressions are not

universalistic but particularistic.

Paul, and the Bible in general, teach to the same effect, but let us look more closely at the golden text of modern universalism, 2 Corinthians 5:19: "God was in Christ reconciling the world to Himself." First of all, the word "world" in Scripture does not necessarily refer to each and every human inhabitant of it. Let us take two examples which superficially seem to be using world that way. If these can be shown not necessarily so to signify, we may assume that no other passages do. Matthew 13:24–30 and 36–43 tells the familiar parable of the Wheat and the Tares. There is a field in which the owner sowed wheat, and his enemy, at night, planted tares in their midst. When Christ Himself interprets this parable He says: "The field is the world." Yet He clearly means the church in the world and not the entire population. It is only in the church that men pretend to be believers of the Word. Those outside, by definition, make no profession of faith. So we have here a deliberate and precise use of the word "world" in which an actual minority of the human population is in view. Consider John 3:16. This famous passage does not teach that God so loved each and every individual that He gave His only Son that they might have everlasting life. What it says is that He so loved mankind that He gave His Son so that every believer in the world should have eternal life. In other words, John 3:16 does not tell of God's love for each human being, but only for each and every believing human being. There is Scriptural warrant, to be sure, for the doctrine that God does have a love for each and every human individual, but this text does not teach it, though it uses the word "world."

We do not propose in this brief work to go into any exhaustive investigation of the word "world." Sufficient to say that in the Bible it does not always mean "each and every human individual." There is a question whether it ever does. Clearly the fact that God was in Christ reconciling the world does not necessarily mean that He was reconciling each and every individual in it.

Second, the immediate context shows that not all men were being reconciled by Christ or the Apostle to whom the ministry of reconciliation was given. The very appeal to be reconciled implies that. Furthermore, in 6:14 Paul commands the professed believers: "Do not be mismated with unbelievers." Obviously Christ and the Apostles were not reconciling all men—some were "unbelievers."

Third, the ministry of reconciliation given to the Apostle was the proclamation of Christ's work of reconciliation. This has not even today reached the entire world. So only a minority of mankind has heard the ministry of reconciliation, and only a minority of them has believed it.

Fourth, and finally, the ministry of reconciliation is not a declaration of an accomplished fact, but a call to experience a potential reality. The basis of reconciliation is indeed an accomplished fact, but reconciliation does not become an accomplished fact until the basis becomes the individual's. The basis of reconciliation is objective, that is, it means that an actual propitiation of an angry God, by a vicarious sacrifice which satisfied His justice fully, has been effected. All this I have explained above. Apart from this actual propitiation of a holy God, there would never have been any ministry of reconciliation or call of men to be reconciled to God. For how could they ever be reconciled to a holy God, of purer eyes than to behold their iniquity, and burning with wrath against their outrages against His law? It is because Christ has satisfied that holy wrath and reconciled the Holy One that sinful, frightened men, hiding in the bushes, covering their nakedness with the filthy rags of their righteousness, at enmity and at war with a God whom they never could have placated, may hear the welcome sound: "Be ye reconciled to God."

*This is the message that I bring,*
*A message angels fain would sing:*
*"Oh, be ye reconciled," thus saith my Lord and King,*
*"Oh, be ye reconciled to God."*

# Appendix

## "The Confession of 1967"
## (of the United Presbyterian Church in the
## USA) and Reconciliation-Universalistic?

In describing rules for debate on the "Confession of 1967", it has been suggested that the presentation of opposing views should be so accurate and fair that they will be recognized and acknowledged by the advocates of these views. To this we shall earnestly try to conform. However, when we set forth the new creed's doctrine of reconciliation some even of those indisposed to this creed, not to mention its advocates, will sincerely believe that we have misconceived its teaching so grossly as to be guilty of unintentional slander. Some of these may wonder if the slander is unintentional. All we can say, as we beg everyone for an open-minded hearing, is that we are not slandering anyone even unintentionally; that, in fact, we shall so fairly state and prove our position that even the gifted chairman of the committee will not deny it if he will be as candid as he is capable.

The new creed's doctrine of reconciliation is simply this: universalism. It teaches this heresy as plainly as if it said, what it studiously avoids saying: We believe in universal salvation.

For brevity's sake we shall present only three lines of proof for this most grave charge. First, the new creed maintains that God accepts men as they are and in spite of what they are: this is universalism. We quote: "The new life takes shape in a community in which men know that God loves and accepts them in spite of what they are. They therefore accept themselves and love others, knowing that

409

no man has any ground on which to stand except God's grace" (150-153).

No doubt there are those who have read this—perhaps even those who have written it—who immediately placed an evangelical interpretation on these words. Some may have thought this was another way of saying: "Just as I am, without one plea, but that thy blood was shed for me. I come to thee." But the creed is maintaining that men are or will be saved—reconciled—whether they come to Christ or not; whether they have heard of Christ or not; whether they reject Christ or not.

The new life, to be sure, takes place where men "know" that God accepts them as they are. Presumably, it is true of all men that God accepts them as they are. But all do not know it and therefore are not in the Christian community or church. All men, therefore, are accepted or reconciled but are not aware of it. The good news the church is to proclaim is not that men may be accepted but that they already are. The new confession conceives of 1 Corinthians 5:19 as meaning: not—"Be reconciled to God"; but, "be aware of your reconciliation." Or else it restricts the word "reconcile" to man (rather than God) and construes the exhortation "be reconciled to God" to mean accept, experience and have joy in God because he has already accepted you. The all-important point in the Confession is: God has accepted all men—it remains for men to accept his acceptance ("be reconciled").

If someone should say, "Granted that this teaching is implicitly universalistic; that it does not, in fact, allow us to believe that any could be lost if all are accepted just as they are (whether believing or unbelieving, whether penitent or impenitent, whether obedient or disobedient), still it is merely implicit; it does not say in so many words 'he that believeth not shall not see life but the wrath of God abideth upon him'."

For these persons we shall show, second, that the creed becomes still clearer on this matter when it says: "God expresses his love as wrath" (33:96). Even God's wrath is love. This would seem to say that even damnation is salvation. Hell must be a heavenly place. Some may legitimately ask if we are not guilty of a logical blunder here.

Just because the creed says that "God expresses his love as wrath" it does not necessarily follow that *all* of divine wrath is an expression of His love. We admit that our deduction does not necessarily follow *from these words as such*, but in the context, of which they are a part, it does necessarily follow. Let any logically-minded person consider the fuller statement: "God's love never changes. Against all that opposes him, God expresses his love as wrath." We can see from this that all of God's wrath is (according to this creed) an expression of God's unchanging love.

Let us apply this to the doctrine of the eternal wrath of God which is taught in our present (and continuing) standards. If God's love expresses itself as wrath, eternal wrath, then God's love is inconceivably frightful. John the Baptist would have had to warn sinners to flee from the love of God which is to come. Instead of gladly singing "O love that will not let me go", in agony sinners would pray, "O love, please let me go."

We hear our friends of the opposition saying, "That is the whole point: the love of God is expressed as wrath so that men will flee their sins and come to repentance." But we say to them, "Please remember, we are now considering your doctrine in relation to the eternal wrath of God, in relation to hell which our Reformed standards teach. If wrath is always an expression of God's unchanging love then the love of God to those in hell is the most frightening thing conceivable."

We know that our opponents do not want to say that there is such an eternal wrath of God. We suspect that some of them reject the notion that hell's eternal torments could be conceived as the love of God in action. We know that they believe that God's love expressed as wrath tends

to lead to repentance and deliverance from this painful manifestation of divine mercy. But we want them to see that if it
does not always bring to repentance—as the doctrine of hell
plainly teaches—then they must reject their own teaching
that God's wrath always expresses itself as love. But, on
the other hand, if they insist, as their confession implies,
that God's love as wrath always does lead to repentance and
salvation, then let them admit their doctrine is universal
salvation.

If even this is not clear enough for some, let us submit,
third, an explicit statement of universalism. "In the power
of the risen Christ and the hope of his coming the church
sees the promise of God's forgiveness for all wrong and the
renewal of society in all aspects of its life" (221). There
could scarcely be a more succinct definition of universal
salvation than the "forgiveness for all wrong and the renewal of society in all aspects of its life."

We believe that the implicit universalism of this document is beyond serious question. If any shadow of a defense is to appear it will probably take two prongs: one, a
doctrine (divine sovereignty); the other, an express statement (77, 78).

First, the general principle which has been frequently
cited today to stave off the charge (that neo-orthodox doctrine is universalistic) is the sovereignity of God. Since God
is absolutely sovereign, this school argues, we cannot say
whether He will or will not save all men.

This contention is refuted by several considerations.
First, the "Confession of 1967" has said that God will save
all men. Our whole argument above, unless it is totally erroneous, has shown that these creedalists teach that God
accepts men in spite of what they are, His very wrath is
only love in disguise, and that He will utterly remove all
evil from His creation. Such positions say only one thing:
God accepts all men, in principle, now; in actuality, sooner
or later. This says "universal salvation." Avoidance of that
language in no way avoids that idea. An indubitable infer-

ence is equal to an express statement so far as meaning is concerned. If these credalists do not want to teach universalism, they do not avoid it simply by avoiding shibboleth expressions. If affirming that God accepts all men violates divine sovereignty, then this "Confession" is violating divine sovereignty.

A second argument, by way of refuting the use of the sovereignty doctrine as a defense of this Confession's universalism, is that this and all creeds would be violating God's sovereignty in saying anything about God. There are 4200 words in this "Confession," all of them saying something directly or indirectly about God. If we cannot say anything about what God will ultimately do about the salvation of mankind because of His sovereignty, how can we say anything about what He will do today? To say such "binds" God just as much. To say that "those joined to him (Christ) by faith are set right with God and commissioned" is surely predicting what God will do today, and thus, according to the reasoning under examination, infringing His sovereignty.

Again, third, the very doctrine of sovereignty itself is against this defense by means of sovereignty. It overlooks the fact that God can sovereignly bind Himself by His own promises or threats. If He cannot do this, how sovereign is He?

Furthermore, fourth, God has sovereignly committed Himself. The Scripture is full of His promises and His threats. One of these Bible promises, which these Confessionalists are glad to acknowledge, is that those who believe in Christ are set right with God. One of these Bible threats, which these Confessionalists are knowledgeable enough to understand, but indisposed to admit, is that those not joined to Christ will not be set right with God, but will have to pay the eternal wages of sin.

But this brings us to the second argument which may be used in defending this new creed against the charge of universalism—an express statement. "To receive life from

the Risen Lord is to have life eternal; to refuse life from him
is to be separate from God in death" (76–78). It is no accident that in the parallelism of these statements "life eternal"
is balanced by "death." "Death eternal" was called for by the
correlation. "Death eternal" was called for by the Bible.
"Death eternal" was called for by the Westminster standards. "Death eternal" was called for by the "Book of Confes-
sions." "Death eternal" would, by the mere addition of that
one word, have repudiated universalism and affirmed par-
ticularism. But it is not there, and cannot be there, because
that orthodox doctrine is not in this "Confession," or apparently in the minds of its composers.

Since "death eternal" is not there the "death" that is there
can easily be swallowed up in the victory of Christ's final
triumph when "the promise of God's forgiveness for all
wrong and the renewal of society in all aspects of its life"
comes. This "death" therefore, in the context of the "Confession of 1967" is temporary and must yield to the ultimate victory of Christ.

In closing we must observe that even this "death" must
be acceptable to God. It does not mean non-being because it
describes men who presently "refuse life." And God, we
have been told, accepts men "in spite of what they are." So
He must accept men in spite of unbelief as well as in belief;
in spite of death, no less than in life.

# The

# Problem

# of

# Pleasure

# Contents

Just about everybody thinks there is a problem of pain. Even philosophers assume that the most formidable theoretical problem is that of suffering. The most grievous question, however, is why pain constitutes a problem, for the real problem lies elsewhere. It may trouble you as a reader to learn of someone who thinks pain is not a problem. You have thought it obvious not only that there is pain, but also that pain in a world created by a good God is indeed a problem. Since no one in this world escapes adversity altogether, no one doubts that there is pain in the world. Some of this pain is excruciating. In fact, some people face more distress than comfort. Apart from Christian Scientists, no one we know denies that pain hurts.

## The Non-Problem of Pain

Pain and suffering raise a dilemma. Philosophers commonly argue: "If God is good, then He is not all-powerful; and if He is all-powerful, then He is not good." Suffering, they insist, is not compatible with an omnipotent, benevolent deity. If God were both good and omnipotent, He would never allow suffering. Since misery and suffering do occur, He is either not good or He is not all-powerful.

A few theologians say that God is omnipotent though not good. They think of Him as being beyond good and evil and indifferent to finite happenings, or as having created the world in such a way that pain simply comes about when people violate the laws of the created universe. God, somewhat abstracted from it all, could not care less about the relentlessness of created nature. It is a kind of self-correcting universe; people have to pay the price of pain when they tinker with it. God Himself does not tinker with it, and thus there are no miracles.

The Indian god, Bhagwan, exemplifies this thought. A picture on the temple wall showed this deity bending over the prone figure of a human being and pulling out the victim's entrails. One tourist asked the meaning of the painting and was told that it "shows Bhagwan's power." Apparently Bhagwan, though not good, was irresistible and did not hesitate to show his strength by torturing those less powerful than he.

The more common philosophical solution, however, is to give up not the goodness of God, but rather His omnipotence. God is indeed good, but suffering proves that He simply is not able to achieve universal happiness. He would like to, and if He were able He would. Since He does not, He is not able. When God is put in the dock, He is cleared of any guilt of ill will. He is simply less powerful than He is benevolent.

The idea of a finite God has had a long history from Plato to Edgar Sheffield Brightman. God may be infinite in His goodness, but He is finite in other qualities, especially power. He is a limited deity as far as His ability to execute His desires is concerned. The result is the tragic story of human misery. William James, one of the most noted preachers of the finite God, goes even further than that. In one of his most noted comments, he remarked that there is a problem of suffering as long as one cockroach pines in unrequited love. I myself will have to admit that my faith was challenged when in a museum many years ago I saw an artificial representation of a hawk pulling apart a tiny bird. "Nature red in tooth and claw" nearly overpowered my belief in an omnipotently good deity. We sympathize with William James's suffering cockroach, and agree with him that, if there is a problem of pain at all, it is not restricted to human beings. Wherever there is any anguish, there is the problem of pain.

We need not further illustrate what is meant by the problem of pain. What probably troubles the reader is having been told that there is *no* problem of pain—especially since the writer is not a Christian Scientist, but actually admits that pain hurts. How could anyone imagine that pain raises no problem in a universe in which an omnipotently benevolent deity reigns supreme?

The answer to that so-called problem of pain is sin. As long as there is sin, there can be no problem of pain. A good God, if He is omnipotent, would have to make the sinner suffer.

A dilemma would exist only if there were no suffering in a sinful world. Then we would have to say there cannot be a true God. Were there no adversity in a sinful world, God either would not be good or would not be omnipotent. Either He would be unconcerned about sin's being unpunished, and therefore not good, or He would be unable to punish sin, and therefore not omnipotent. That would be a real problem in our world, where sin obviously abounds.

What could you possibly expect in a sinful world but suffering? If there were no suffering, then you would have an absolutely unanswerable problem: How could God be all-powerful and all-good and allow sin to go unpunished?

## The Real Problem Is Pleasure

Troubled by the non-problem of pain, most people do not feel the real problem. The real difficulty is the problem of pleasure. While in a sinful world, pain is to be expected, and pleasure is not to be expected. We should be constantly amazed at the presence of pleasure in a world such as ours.

It is easy to understand why this confusion has come about. Pain is a painful subject. Pleasure is a pleasurable subject. People do not like pain. They do like pleasure. And people associate problems with what they do not like. Because they do not like pain, they call it a problem.

The fact is that pain is no problem, whereas pleasure is an excruciating problem; and if one ever begins to think about that it can become intolerable. How could there be pleasure in a sinful world? People do not like thinking about pleasure in such a light because then they must admit their own sinfulness.

On the other hand, there is a kind of relief from pain in viewing it as an undeserved problem. We imply that the blame for our affliction lies elsewhere. That soothes our pain a little by assuring us that we do not deserve such misery. But if pain is a non-problem, it is so because we deserve punishment. Calling it a "non-problem" is a frank admission that we are sinners and, therefore, may not complain about it.

So when we call pain a problem, we claim we do not deserve it. We are even prepared to scuttle God to maintain our own innocence. We will say that God is not able to do what He would like, or He would never permit persons such as ourselves to suffer. That puffs up our egos and soothes our griefs at the same time. "How could God do this to *me*?" is at once an admission of pain and a soporific for it. It reduces our personal grief by eradicating the deity. Drastic medicine, indeed, that only a human ego, run wild, could possibly imagine.

## Why Pain Is Not the Problem

So that there are no doubts that pain is a non-problem, three points may be made: first, there is sin; second, sin requires suffering; and, third, therefore, suffering is not a problem, not even eternal suffering, which is the ultimate form of it.

### The Fact of Sin

First, then, the easy part, that there is sin in the world. Karl Menninger recently wrote a book entitled, *Whatever Happened to Sin?* Well, as the doctor admits, sin is still here. It is just that people do not so willingly acknowledge that fact. A spade is no longer called a spade, but some euphemism. The little boy says to his mother, "Why is it that whenever I do anything bad, it's because I'm a bad boy; but whenever you do anything bad, it's because you're nervous?" It is nerves rather than sin. It is our glands rather than sin. It is what we eat, the environment, our biorhythm, rather than sin. In fact, it is anything but sin.

Sin denies that it is sin. The ultimate form of any vice is to deny that it is a vice, and rather to rejoice in it. That is denial with a vengeance, actually making a virtue of it. John Barrymore used to say that he did not like to be obscene and not heard. His obscenity, for him, was a virtue that deserved to be displayed and admired; he wanted praise for it. Whether or not we have become hardened so as to make sin a virtue, we certainly have made sin sinless.

No one would ever read the Bible and get the impression that God is in His Heaven and all's well with the world. Sin started with the first man, according to the Bible. In Adam all sinned. Sin came into the world through the transgression of one man. But many view the Bible as antiquated and obsolete. People who deny sin deny what I am saying right now as I affirm sin. They will say, "Nonsense." When they realize that I have a Ph.D. from Harvard, they will say, "That is utterly inexcusable for a person such as he not to know that sin is a mere name, and not a real entity at all." As a matter of fact, they could get up quite a head of steam and even tell me: "You *ought* to know better." When a person says to me, "You ought to know better," he means that I am sinning by saying what I do. I am doing what is wrong, and I am inexcusable because I should know better. That is essentially what we mean by sin, violating the moral law. One ought to act according to his understanding of truth. These persons feel that I should understand the truth that there is no such thing as sin. Consequently, by affirming sin, I am telling a falsehood, which I should not do. They blame me for this and reprimand me for this wrongdoing. They say to me that I am not the type of person I ought to be. That is a rebuke as well as a definition. It is showing what sin means, and that I am a sinner, and that I deserve the verbal punishment (at least) that they give me by so labeling me.

So while they deny sin, they affirm sin. If they really did not believe that there is such a thing as sin, they would not, in effect, call me a sinner. But if they do call me a sinner, by that word or by a euphemism, then they show that they do not believe that sin is obsolete. So they find themselves in a predicament of wanting to deny sin, but unable to do so without affirming it. Sin is not only not obsolete, it is not obsolescent; and, indeed, it never can become obsolete while this world remains as it is. God's Word has not fallen too far behind the avalanche of contemporary literature. We may tell Dr. Menninger that the only thing that has happened to sin is that people now, rather than affirming it by affirming it, prefer to affirm it by denying it.

Those who affirm sin by denying it are doubly sinners. When they call me a sinner because I ought to know better than to affirm sin, they are themselves affirming sin. Though sinning itself is bad enough, denying sin is an additional sin, so that those who deny sin are actually double sinners. In a certain sense, they argue more strenuously for sin than we traditionalists do. And they have more opportunity for sinning than we do because denying that sin exists is not a possibility for those who believe the Bible.

So, then, there is sin. Not only does the Word of God say so, but, what is far more impressive to our culture, twentieth-century intellectuals say so with a vengeance.

### Sin Requires Punishment
Second, sin deserves punishment. Dr. Karl Menninger asks, *Whatever Happened to Sin?* He should write another book entitled, *Whatever Happened to Punishment?* In the opinion of many, not only does crime not deserve punishment, but punishment is the crime. Menninger himself wrote *The Crime of Punishment.* But when a person says that crime does not deserve punishment, he is taking the heinousness out of the criminal act. He thinks that crime does not spring from the actor, but from some external circumstance—his ghetto background or his privileged status with its irresponsibilities. "It's not your son's fault," said the maid to Reinhold Niebuhr. The son of the famous theologian had been in a neighborhood brawl and was some-

what worse for wear when the maid interceded with the father, who was about to finish what the neighborhood kids had started. "It is not your son's fault—it is the company he keeps." Neibuhr's response to the maid's entreaty was, "It is not the company he keeps; it is his own little black heart." The maid championed the thesis that there is no crime except punishment, whereas Niebuhr, in this case, expressed the sentiment that there is crime, and it does deserve punishment.

I think we would all agree that crime deserves punishment. Those who say that it does not say so quite consistently, because they argue that it is *not* crime. We agree that where there is no crime, there needs be no punishment. The question is a matter of fact rather than value judgment.

Is there such a thing as crime? We have already answered that question. If there is such a thing as sin, there is such a thing as crime, a specific form of sin. And if we all agree that there is such a thing as crime, or sin, then it deserves punishment. When I am told, "You *ought* to know better," I am not only being informed, I am being rebuked. That indictment amounts to a punishment for my sin of saying there is such a thing as sin. So those who say such things prove both points—that there is sin, and that sin ought to be punished. If they rebuke me verbally, and I do not mend my ways, the question could well come up whether I ought to receive some other form of punishment. They are convinced of one thing: I ought to be punished in the most effective way.

Most intellectuals are opposed to corporal punishment because they do not think it is effective, and they argue against capital punishment, that it does not deter crime. Futile punishment ought not to be administered. Capital punishment, since these people think it is futile, is resisted not because it is punishment, but because it is not punishment, that is, it is ineffective. They want crime deterred, but by an effective form of punishment. It seems, no matter how people express it, they must acknowledge that there is sin, and that sin deserves to be punished. The only differences among us have to do with the names we give to sin and the shape punishment should take.

Consider our opinion about capital punishment with respect to the killing of police officers. Why would that question ever come up? If punishment is a crime, then of course the killing of a policeman should not be punished either. When we make distinctions between killing civilians and killing policemen, we show that certain kinds of crime, at least, deserve punishment. But no one is saying that crimes do not deserve punishment. The question is *what* crimes do, and what punishment is effective. Apparently, some believe that though capital punishment is not effective with civilians when civilians are the victims, it may be effective and necessary when policemen are the victims. There seems to be a general impression that capital punishment in the case of murderers of police is a deterrent and therefore ought to be administered.

One form of capital punishment everybody seems to approve: killing an attacker in self-defense. That is, most people will defend saving one's own life, even if it requires taking the life of the would-be killer. There is a great division of opinion among us at the present time whether killers, *after* they have killed, should be killed. But there is virtually no difference of opinion that killers, *before* they are successful in killing, should be killed, if that is the only way that they can be stopped.

*Punishment Requires Pain*

Third, suffering is necessary. If there is such a thing as sin, and sin deserves to be punished, then the punishment must be administered, and punishment that does not hurt is not punishment. We may insist that the punishment is ameliorative or helpful, ultimately, but nobody is drawing up a proposition that punishment is not painful. It is self-evident that if punishment is not painful, it is not punishment. The only point of punishment is the administration of pain. The person who does sin, who commits a crime, deserves to be punished; he deserves to suffer. One hopes that suffering will cure him of his sinfulness. At least, it will correct his behavior. He will be "scared straight" in behavior, if not softened in spirit.

In human affairs, pain is no problem. Even in *our* conduct, if we did not administer pain under certain circumstances, that would be a problem. It would, we think, be wrong.

Our main problem is that so much crime goes unpunished. Murderers—proven, demonstrated murderers—serve an average of about eight years in prison for killing another human being in cold blood. But most murderers are not caught at all and not punished at all. Our thinking is loose and our laws are not what they ought to be. Even judging our performance according to our own inadequate standards, we are far short of the mark. We recognize that our crime lies in nonpunishment rather than in punishment, though occasionally the punishment itself is the crime when it is excessive or when it is punishment of the wrong person. Fundamentally, our own culture in our own estimate falls under our own condemnation of not fitting the punishment to the crime, even approximately.

But when we consider God, we realize that He would see sin perfectly because sin, in the last analysis, is against Him. He is the author of the moral law by which we are constrained. "Where there is no law there is no sin." Furthermore, if even we can see that sin should be punished, He would see with perfect and infinite vision that sin should be punished. Most important of all, if we punish crime (very, very imperfectly), He will punish it perfectly, precisely because He is both good and omnipotent. Therefore, we have no problem with pain inflicted by God, if it can be shown that the person suffering it deserves it, and that it is in the measure which he deserves. These two characteristics we assume, of course, would describe a divine act of punishment or infliction of pain.

Because every man is a sinner, every man deserves the wrath of God. Manifestly, he is not getting anything that approximates, much less exceeds, the wrath of God in this world. Manifestly, "he" is all of us, since we all are sinners. We deserve to suffer because, without exception, we are sinners; and in fact, we all deserve far more than we receive.

If someone says, "Look, I read in the paper just today about some gangsters exchanging bullets and an *innocent* bystander being killed. The innocent bystander was killed. You don't call that divine justice, do you? Maybe the gangsters deserved to kill each other and be killed, but the innocent bystander, by definition, didn't deserve to be killed, did he?"

"You're right," we reply. "Innocent people don't deserve to be killed. And the man was innocent of any particular crime that concerned these two who were exchanging bullets." Those two men would agree that he didn't deserve to die. It was the other criminal, the first criminal will insist, who deserved to die. He will even say, "I didn't mean to kill that bystander. He should have watched himself and stayed out of the fire. Too bad. But the other guy I was trying to shoot deserved to be killed. I'm glad I got him. I'm sorry about this innocent bystander."

Yes, the man was innocent as far *as their quarrel was concerned*, but was he an innocent bystander in the sight of God? Obviously not, if what we have already said is true. He was a sinner under the wrath of God who had not begun to receive the full punishment he deserved. So, as far as God was concerned, he deserved that bullet. As far as God was concerned, he was not an innocent bystander. As far as God was concerned, he was a criminal too, who was receiving a deserved bullet which the *gangster* had no right to shoot, but which *God* had every right to allow to be shot. This bystander was innocent before the man who shot him, but guilty before the God who ordained permissively that he be shot.

Do people really deserve to suffer at God's hand, and are

they fairly punished? It is clear that they deserve to be punished because they are sinners, and that they have been fairly, not excessively, punished because they are sinners against God, against an infinite God.

## Why Do the "Righteous" Suffer?

Again, a protest arises: "What about the suffering of the righteous? Is the Bible not full of the complaints of godly people who are afflicted while the wicked flourish as a green bay tree? Is the Bible not against you in saying that some righteous do suffer and some sinners do not suffer?"

Take, first, the charge that the wicked prosper rather than suffer. That is the lament of the godly at times. The Bible grants that many wicked persons continue to live and flourish in this world, much to the dismay of the righteous. But the Bible does not teach that the wicked do not suffer. It does teach that they suffer, but not as much as they deserve to suffer. In many instances, they do not endure as much physical suffering as the saints, who are often martyred. But the Bible does not present the wicked as not being punished. It simply says they do not receive their full punishment in this world. God has a better way of administering justice than that.

Likewise, the godly do suffer and complain about it at times. But the Bible teaches plainly that their suffering, even after their conversion and reconciliation to God, is not punishment any longer, but chastening. It is not the punishment of a God who is angry with them, but the chastening of a God who is reconciled to them. Whom God loves, the Scripture says, He chastens. He makes all things, including pain, "work together for good for them that love God, and are called according to His purpose." This should be the consolation and strength of saints. They are far from perfect, so they lapse into complaining at times. They forget the divine purpose, momentarily, under the smarting of their grief. But the Bible does not say that the righteous suffer, any more than it says that the unrighteous do not suffer. The unrighteous suffer, but not as much as they deserve to or ultimately will suffer; and the righteous painfully suffer, but they do not suffer pain. That affliction is actually a blessing in disguise. At times, they can see through the disguise. At other times, the pain hurts so much that they cannot, through their tears, see the disguise. Momentarily they lament the heavy hand of God upon them, but when they are thinking in their most saintly character, they praise God. His rod and staff comfort them.

Job, for example, was permitted some awesome catastrophes for the good of his soul. It did indeed do his soul, and ultimately his body, great good, as we know from that famous book of the Old Testament. Job was like a modern saint who suffered so dreadfully, but said that he did not "have a pain to spare." When pain is present it is difficult to bear; but when a Christian, even in anguish, realizes that this is the heavy hand of a loving God upon him, he blesses God in his suffering and for his suffering, which he knows is for his own good and for his everlasting blessedness.

So, in spite of all the intellectual agonizing about the problem of pain, the only problem is explaining why pain is a *problem*. In a sinful world pain is axiomatic. No one should ever have been surprised about its presence. It would have been a problem only if it did not exist. If this is the imperial problem of philosophers and theologians, this emperor has no clothes.

Only as an emotional and physical "problem" is pain real, and, as such, the only real problem is that pain hurts. That is easy to understand, but insuperably difficult to endure. So mankind should expend its intellectual energies not on a non-problem of pain, but on how to escape it. "What must I do to be saved?"

*Absence of Pain Would Be a Real Problem*
If there were no pain in this world, there would be a real

problem. But, since there is pain, there is no dilemma because we know that this sinful world deserves precisely that. The present pain is not sufficient to our crimes, so that we can ask, Why so little pain? Why so much pleasure? Why *any* pleasure?

This is the real difficulty. Why is there any pleasure in this world? There is no problem of pain, but there is an omnipresent problem of pleasure. If God was in His heaven, and all were well with the world, then we would know that this world is indeed a paradise. Since, though God is in heaven, all is not well in the world, the question is, Why so little punishment? God is a being of infinite glory. Sin against Him is sin of infinite enormity. We say that sin is sin. But there is another sense in which sin is not sin. One sin is vastly different from another sin. It has the same nature, to be sure, but the different degree of it eclipses what it has in common.

For example, two boys get into a scrap, and one of them gets beaten up more than the other. Suppose he deserved it, had done something which required a bit of thrashing. Nobody's eyebrows are raised much as long as there has been no permanent damage. Just two kids fighting it out over some grievance.

Suppose the same kid, however, beat up his mother as much as he beat up his friend. Would anyone ever say that is the same sin? The beating is the same, but the offense is vastly greater. Why? Because the boys are peers; they are more or less equal to one another. But in their filial relationships, the mother is nearer than the boy's peers. She is also much more significant than her son as the source and preservation of his being. He has a divine command to honor and obey her. He owes everything to her, including life itself. For him to be disobedient to her would be a very great offense, but actually to beat her would be an unspeakable one because she is his mother. We would say that if he only spoke back disrespectfully to his mother, without even touching her, that offense would be greater than giving his neighbor a severe thrashing.

We see this principle generally in human affairs. Even our soft culture (where capital punishment is considered the crime) recognizes a difference between killing a policeman and killing a civilian. It is the same murder, to be sure, but to murder a person risking his life to prevent murder is considered more iniquitous than to murder the person, for example, who may have provoked it. Both are just as dead, but we recognize the difference between the two murders.

Again, a man kills a peer; that is terrible. But if he attacks and kills a defenseless old lady who has befriended him all his life, does anyone say that is the same crime? It is the same murder. Both persons are equally dead. But more is owed to one than to the other. Consequently, a violation of that obligation makes one crime more heinous than the other.

There is no comparison at all between God and any of His creatures. In fact, all our sins against our fellowman are ultimately sins only because God has forbidden these deeds. "Against Thee and Thee only have I sinned," cried David, after committing adultery and murder. In sexually contaminating Bathsheba, and politically executing her innocent husband, David was guilty of two capital crimes. Each one of these, however, was a crime in any degree only because it was a violation of the divine commandment. "Against Thee and Thee only have I sinned." In adultery and murder, lying and theft, and any other particular sin, we have sinned "against Thee and Thee only." Instead of reducing the severity of these crimes because they are directed against one person only, it aggravates them, because that one person is infinitely more valuable than all the creatures combined. And if we recognize degrees of heinousness between a crime against one human being and another, we can see that the difference between a crime against a human and against the divine Being is infinite, and requires an infinitely more severe punishment.

*The Problem: Why So Little Pain?*

This is a sinful world, and sin is ultimately against its Creator, God. That sin is infinitely heinous and deserving of infinite punishment. All that mankind has suffered, in all of the ages at the hands of an angry God whose holiness has been obscured and whose justice has been violated, does not add up to one offense against the deity.

In this light, we see the problem of pleasure. Manifestly, as sinners against an infinitely glorious God, we deserve an immediate and infinite, condign, irremediable punishment from His holy, powerful hands. Nothing that we have ever received, that anyone has ever received, in all this world, has even approximated an adequate punishment for the crimes we commit in any one moment. How, therefore, do we continue to live? Why are we not plunged into eternal torment now, immediately?

What irony that sinners consider the greatest problem they face in this world to be the problem of pain. The ultimate insult against God is that man thinks he has a problem of pain. Man, who deserves to be plunged into hell at this moment, and is indescribably fortunate that he is breathing normally, complains about unhappiness. Instead of falling on his knees in the profoundest possible gratitude that God holds back His wrath and infinite fury, the sinner shakes his fist in heaven's face and complains against what he calls "pain." When he receives his due, he will look back on his present condition as paradisaical. What he now calls misery, he will then consider exquisite pleasure. The most severe torment anyone has ever known in this life will seem like heaven in comparison with one moment of the full fury of the divine Being.

The most foolish thing a human being ever says is that "the only hell there is is in this world." The truth of the matter is that, for that person, the only *heaven* there is is in this world. When he goes to hell for his unbelief, he will realize that the only heaven he ever knew was in this world, which he called "hell." How he will then cry out for a moment of what he now calls "hell!"

Anyone who is aware of the existence of God and of sin cannot help but wonder about the problem of pleasure. "How long, O Lord, how long?" the saints cry out. They are especially aware of the predicament when they see the wicked flourish as the green bay tree. But the thoughtful saint, when he sees the wicked existing in the most miserable circumstances (as far as possible from flourishing as the green bay tree), wonders how long the Lord will put up with such iniquity and so little punishment. Time and again the psalmist cries to God as if he thinks God were sleeping. God punishes so little the evil which deserves so much that the psalmist, in his moments of despair, concludes that God must be sleeping. He would shake Him and wake Him up so that God would show how angry He is against the wicked. The Scripture says that God is "angry with the wicked every day." The saint knows that, but wonders why, if God is angry, infinitely angry with the wicked every day, He shows so little of His wrath.

The wicked, in turn, draw a false consolation from their relative comfort. When they flourish, they suppose that "the Man upstairs" is pleased with them, that He is blind to their faults, that they are able to pull the wool over His eyes as they do over their business associates and others who are their victims. Some of them get away, literally with murder. Nothing happens to them. The "Lucky Lucianos," as they are called, come and go. They kill, they rape, they steal, they lie, they threaten. So far from being punished for it, they seem to be blessed by it. Honesty pays, but it is not obvious in their cases. Crime is not supposed to pay, but it certainly seems as if it is very lucrative, especially in an age such as ours when more of the sympathy is for the victimizer than for his victims.

The Bible indicates that God hates the wicked. He is not only angry with them, He actually hates them. "Thou dost hate all who do iniquity" (Psalm 5:5). "The one who loves violence His soul hates" (Psalm 11:5). He hates liars and covenant breakers. He hates persons such as Esau, who prefer their mess of pottage to their spiritual birthright.

Yet, as the Lord says, He makes the sun to shine and the rain to fall on the unjust and the wicked as well as on the godly. And His followers are required to act accordingly. Christ commands us to love our enemies, and uses as His model the fact that God from heaven showers His blessings on the wicked. We see that God actually hates and is infinitely angry with persons upon whom He pours great blessings. We are not allowed to hate persons, but are commanded to love them. We cannot, of course, be pleased with persons who hate God and hate us, but we can behave lovingly toward them and pray for them. In so doing, we follow the model of God.

All of this only accentuates our problem—the problem of pleasure. We observe in life that mankind generally prospers. There is much sickness, suffering, loneliness, emptiness, and sorrow, to be sure; but it is not in any proportion to the blessing most people receive. One would hardly believe that God really hates the wicked and is infinitely angry with them, judging from the way He behaves toward them. It perplexes the godly and is misinterpreted by the wicked themselves, as if it were a token of divine permission at least, and favor at most. So the Bible, instead of relieving the problem at this point, seems to aggravate it. It reveals God as knowingly participating in this crime; that is, He is visiting untold blessings upon people whom He actually hates. Coupled with His anger, which is unceasing toward the wicked, He gives them many tokens of forbearance and love.

## Why Does God Permit Pleasure?

What is the solution to the problem of pleasure? Suppose there was no revelation from God, and we only knew that there is a holy God, and we had some familiarity with the history of our race. What conclusion would we

reach when we contemplate the problem of pleasure? One
does not need the Bible to know that we are a morally culpable race, and that there is a holy God. When we ponder
the problem of pleasure, what would we think is the solution?

*Is God Fattening Us For Slaughter?*
It seems to me there are only two possibilities that
could very well occur to us. One is that God is fattening the
sheep for slaughter. That is, men are obviously wicked and
God is even more obviously holy. God must be angry with
us, and our troubled consciences confirm it. A moment's
reflection would tell us that we do not receive adequate
punishment in this world for our sins. Even though we are
hardened and calloused, and some of us have seared consciences, the generality of people know full well that we
have not been dealt with adequately by an infinitely holy
God, who we know must exist. We know that we are not
getting away with anything that He is not permitting us to
get away with. We know He is an infinitely powerful God,
who could take us in hand at any moment. We are equally
aware of the fact that He is not doing so. So we wonder, as
we tremble, whether He is simply allowing us to go on
until we are fat enough for His divine slaughter. It is an
awesome thought, to be sure, but an inevitable one when
we put one and one together: that is, the holiness of God
and the sinfulness of man.
We know there has to be a judgment coming. We also
know that our judgment will be according to our sins. We
recognize the gradations of sins among ourselves and in our
own law courts. We are aware that sin against God must be
infinitely more dreadful than any crime we commit against
one another. We try to fit our punishment to the crime, for
justice demands it, and we know that infinite justice must
do the same thing. We know that we are adding up sins
every day we live, which becomes less and less excusable
as we have more and more experience and knowledge about

God and the moral law. (If we are learning less and less, we are aware of the fact that that itself is a blameworthy thing.) We should be learning more and more, and that would make us more and more aware that we are becoming guiltier and guiltier. We obviously are built to learn from experience. If the more experience we have the less we learn, the more blameworthy we realize that we are.

We are infuriating the deity more and more. If He is a just and holy being, as we are led to believe, we are simply asking for it. Some criminals are so powerful that they can say to people whom they have marked out for death, "You're dead." They are not boasting; they have so much underworld power that they can liquidate most people they set their minds to remove. It is a dreadfully wicked power; but what power do they have except that which comes ultimately from the One who made them and sustains them, and without whose power they would not have any life, not to mention power, of their own?

There is no possibility of escaping God. Sometimes people get new identities and manage to escape the hitmen of the underworld. But who is ever going to escape God? Certainly not these criminals who have the audacity to say to innocent human beings, "You're dead." But not only they; they are just gross offenders. We are more sophisticated and refined ones. The more refined we are, the more aware we are that our sin can very well be more heinous than that of these crass professional criminals. No crime escapes the all-searching mind of the omniscient God.

The only reason we are getting away with it at the moment is that the Judge of heaven and earth has not seen fit to call us to account at this particular moment. We know we cannot escape. We know that we are only angering Him more and more with each passing day. We know that He, therefore, is permitting us to add sin to sin and become worthier and worthier of judgment, and so be certain recipients of an ever more terrible wrath.

We ask ourselves, "Is God letting us get away with it so

that, when our time is up, we will have accumulated enough sin to merit the wrath He has in store for us?" That is frightening, but no thoughtful person can deny its possibility. We see cattle grazing in the meadows and know that the farmer is feeding them for one ultimate purpose, namely to take them to market. Why are we sinners prospering?

### Is God Waiting To Be Merciful?

The second thing that could occur to us as we ponder a God who is infinitely angry with us, yet not only withholding His infinite wrath, but actually showing us tokens of divine favor is this: He really loves us and wants us to turn away from our sins. If He passed final judgment now, we would have no such opportunity; that would be the end of time for us. He has sufficient provocation to do so; that we recognize. We have sinned enough to deserve His infinite wrath at any moment, but we do not receive it. We have an opportunity, therefore, to turn away from our sin and to turn to God. Instead of continuing to offend Him, we can plead for forgiveness and seek to please Him. While there is yet life, that is possible.

We are talking now as if there were no Bible, as if God had never revealed His purposes to us. As a mere guess, we could entertain the hope that God is sparing us now not to fatten us for the slaughter, but to save us from the slaughter.

Of course, He would have to be *merciful*. All He has to be to account for our judgment is holy and powerful. We know He is holy. We know He is powerful. To account for our being spared with the possibility of being saved from His wrath, He would have to be merciful.

Do we have any ground for hoping (other than the sheerest possibility) that He is a merciful God? There is nothing to stop us from hoping that He is. Since we know that we live on borrowed time and do not deserve a second more, we cannot help hoping that He may be sparing us in order to save us. We do not *know* that. We can prove from the existence of the world that He is all-powerful. We can prove from the way in which it is put together that He is all-wise. We can prove from our conscience that He is all-holy. What do we have to support the idea that He may also be merciful?

Mercy even with us is an optional virtue; we do not have to be merciful. We usually admire people who are, but we do not say that people must be so. We say everybody must be just. We say, for example, an employer, if he agrees to pay a certain wage, must pay that particular wage. If he does not pay it, then he is unjust and is liable to a lawsuit. All our contracts are based on the integrity and honesty and justice of people with whom we do business. They are actually subject to trials and imprisonment and even execution if they violate their duty of man to man. What about mercy among men? We love it. We admire it. We encourage it. We sometimes practice it. But we do not say mercy is obligatory.

Let us go back to that employer who must pay the worker what he has promised he would for an honest day's work. Does he have an obligation to give him a Christmas present? No. Does he have an obligation to pay his hospital bill? Not unless he has made it a part of his contract. Does he have an obligation to visit his employee when he is sick? No. That is not a part of any contract. Does he have to entertain his workers at his own home with his own family, or be friendly to them beyond his actual obligations? The answer is always "No." A worker may very well appreciate such actions when done by an employer, but he cannot demand them. He cannot fault the employer if he does not give them.

As a professor for thirty years, I had an obligation to teach my courses adequately, to grade students fairly, and to give them a proper basis for passing their examinations in accordance with their abilities. I could be faulted if I did not do those things, or even be reported to the president and the board, and ultimately fired if I failed to deliver on these obligations. Did I have an obligation to help a student outside of class? to give him extra hours? to spend time with him before examinations? and after the examinations to point out his mistakes and see if he could correct them so that the next time he would do better? No, none of those things was necessary. Some of us professors would do those things. No student could ever demand them. He had an obligation to be grateful for them if we gave them to him. On the other hand, our basic responsibilities were required, and a student could expect them, and we were reprehensible if we did not deliver. He did not have to thank us for them.

So we see, even in human affairs, that mercy is desirable. It is never, however, obligatory. We admire it when present. We do not censure for its absence.

If this is true even of human affairs, we can see immediately that God does not have to be merciful. He gave us life and conscience. He gave us intelligence to meet our obligations, and He has a right to hold us responsible for using them. He has no further obligation to forgive us if we do not. We say that the Judge of all the earth cannot do wrong, but we cannot say that the Judge of all the earth must be merciful.

As a matter of fact, and this is a frightening thought, there are grounds for thinking that God could not be merciful. If God were merciful, that would upset the balances of justice. If, as a professor, I had become compassionate with poor students and given them C's instead of F's, what an injustice that would be to the students who *earned* their C's. And students who earned F's would consider them of no significance. I would be an arbitrary professor who gave grades as I pleased. While I could not be just and give an A student a C, nevertheless I could be merciful and give a C student an A or an F student a C. The whole grading system would collapse. Good work and bad work would be indistinguishable.

Or, compare a judge who hears a case, but is allowed to exhibit mercy. He sees an individual who has committed a simple murder, but he feels compassionate toward him and sees fit to pardon him. He is a merciful judge and so that murderer goes free, but justice goes a-begging. We could never tolerate such behavior in a teacher, and certainly not in a judge. Our whole social fabric would be torn apart if mercy were allowed to make justice of no effect. Justice is obligatory; mercy is not. If mercy, which is optional, actually ruined justice, which is mandatory, mercy could not be permitted.

But thank God there is a place in human affairs where mercy may legitimately exist and not violate justice. If a judge, for example, after passing a proper and fair judgment on a criminal, does everything in his power to alleviate the suffering of the criminal's family and correct the behavior of that criminal, going far beyond the call of duty and doing something that is not necessary, that certainly would not harm justice. On the contrary, it would accentuate justice. This man would be an inflexibly righteous judge who never allowed mercy to cloud his judgment at the bench; but he would at the same time be a merciful person who, outside the courtroom and at a point where it never infringed on the justice of any of his sentences, went out of his way to be helpful to those whom justice condemned.

So we could begin to hope again. God could be merciful if He could be merciful in a way that did not violate His justice. His justice must be inflexible. Though God is merciful, He cannot throw the scales of justice out of balance.

How could God ever find a way that He could be merciful to us sinners and at the same time be just? Sins must be punished. How can we be punished and, at the same time, be the beneficiaries of divine mercy?

Take the analogy of the teacher and his student. The professor has first of all to be just, and the student flunks the course. He has to flunk the course; then the teacher can be merciful afterwards, going out of his way to help the student understand the course and prepare him so that, when he repeats the course, he will be able to meet the demands and pass it successfully, perhaps even well.

Apply that analogy to God. God has to punish us for our sins. That must be done, just as the F must be given by the professor. But an F by a professor is something which can be overcome. It is, after all, a temporal punishment, and it can be temporally corrected. Sins against God are of infinite enormity. When God punishes us for our sins, that means infinite wrath. If one goes under the unending wrath of God, how can mercy possibly help? The student with an F has a hope in this world. The person who goes into the next world under God's wrath has no hope.

This venture into speculative theology leaves us despairing, with a just God whose justice cannot be compromised. Therefore, He must punish us for our sins ultimately. That answers the problem of pleasure.

We have solved the problem of pleasure, a grim solution but a sound one. We are allowed to "enjoy" ourselves while the wrath of God remains over us only until He is ready to pour it out upon us. God is not mocked. Sinners are not really prospering. What is pleasure now turns out to be only a time of gathering an ever greater bundle of sticks for the sinner's own burning. "Whatever a man sows that shall he reap." The law of karma means an endless cycle of torments without any hope of nirvana. The Hindu religion senses this, but is afraid to say it. Most other religions sense it too, but try to whistle in the dark.

## Where Mercy and Justice Meet

Only the Christian gospel resolves the problem of pleasure, and then offers a way that genuinely delivers us from it in a way in which justice and mercy kiss each other. Only Christ provides a true way of salvation from the dreadful predicament in which the problem of pleasure places man.

First, Christianity confirms the fact that justice must be satisfied. Sin must be condemned according to its demerit. This means eternal doom. The sinner must be damned because God must be inexorably holy and just. His all-powerful Being must vindicate His all-holy Being. Christianity never compromises the ever-blessed purity and excellency of the divine nature.

Second, Christianity alone finds a way to satisfy infinite justice and provide infinite mercy at the same time. What no other religion has dreamed of, Jesus Christ has accomplished. He underwent the infinite wrath of God against sin and lived to bestow His mercy on the damned sinners for whom He died. The infinite Son of God took upon Himself a human nature in which He underwent the full fury of the divine wrath. The omnipotent God satisfied His violated holiness by punishing sin completely in His blessed Son, who "became sin" for His people. The justice of God was vindicated in full in the substitute, His own Son, our Savior dear. He survived that awful vengeance and rose victor over the grave by the power of His own divinity. Now He offers to every sin-sick and "pleasure"-burdened soul an everlasting mercy. Perfect mercy and perfect justice in the gospel of the crucified One are here and now offered to you, dear reader.

Now the problem of pleasure has its answer in full. God has spared you, not that you be damned, but that you be saved from the damnation that otherwise would inevitably have been your destiny. Now Jesus Christ stands at the door of your heart and offers to come in and dwell with you forevermore: "Come unto Me, all ye who are weary and heavy-laden, and I will give you rest."

## Real Pleasure Forever

You who are burdened with your "pleasures" now have the opportunity to escape. Continue as you are and every moment you go on will be "pleasure" more or less ("hell" on earth is "heaven" for the lost); but that "pleasure" you do not deserve will only add to the everlasting condemnation you do deserve if you do not turn to Jesus Christ. Your present "pleasure" is your opportunity for real pleasure in the presence of a reconciled God, your Father. Spurn the offer of real pleasure and you will be damned by your spurious pleasure. Receive the offer of joy forevermore and you will realize the purpose for which you have your "pleasures" to this very moment: that you should be given this opportunity now to have *true pleasure forevermore*—

"At Thy right hand there are pleasures for evermore" (Psalm 16:11).

# A

# Primer

# on

# Dispensation-
alism

# Preface

This elementary presentation focuses on several crucial features of dispensationalism in its classic form, "Scofieldism."

Changes are taking place in that theology, and most of them are changes for the better. For example, regarding the Scofield Bible's view that the Holy Spirit did not regenerate the Old Testament people of God (compare the note on Zechariah 12:10), a number of dispensationalists are coming to a better view (even among the editors of the Scofield Bible itself).

Yet these changes (which I most cordially welcome) are not fundamental and systematic. They represent a tendency, but not a clear and clean break with the abominable heresy of antinomianism, which is endemic to dispensationalism.

I am certain that, if and when such a break occurs, those who are part of it will eagerly and candidly distance themselves from their former dispensational views, whatever the cost. It is my hope that this primer will spur them lovingly in that direction.

I owe my salvation, under God, to a dispensationalist. When I came to the Philadelphia School of the Bible in 1932 I was a professing Christian, but I did not really understand the way of salvation. The most crucial half-hour in my entire life began when I asked the Dean of that school the rather silly question, "What do you teach here?" He felt a question like that deserved the full treatment. For half an hour he told me what the Philadelphia School of the Bible taught, while I stood there transfixed. Although I had known something about Christ and His death, not until that moment did I understand that He died for the remission of our sins, and that the whole Bible, from beginning to end, was the telling of that wonderful story. My gratitude to that teacher, and to the whole dispensational school of theology which he represented, will linger with me through eternity.

Nevertheless, I believe the theology of dispensationalism, though intending evangelicalism, is a serious deviation from biblical doctrine, and even threatens its own evangelicalism. This primer will try to show the truth of that heavy charge. I show my gratitude to all dispensationalists by attempting to correct the errors I see in their system. My heart is sad to say these things, but, as God is my witness, it is a deep labor of love on my part. Never did anybody feel more affection for a group of people whom he had to criticize than I feel for dispensationalists past and present.

# The Fundamental Idea:
## Dividing Rather than Unifying the Bible

A central text of the dispensational theology is found in 2 Timothy 2:15: "Study to show thyself approved unto God, a workman that needeth not to be ashamed, rightly dividing the word of truth." (See C. I. Scofield's comment on this verse in his work *Rightly Dividing the Word of Truth*.)

From the beginning, dispensationalists have interpreted this statement to mean that the Bible is presented in sharply divided parts called "dispensations." Correctly interpreting the Bible is correctly dividing these dispensations from one another.

In itself, that is not an erroneous opinion. Paul's word *oikonomia* means "administration," and implies discerning or distinguishing the differences in the various periods of biblical revelation. As the Criswell Study Bible states, it is "the plain, straightforward understanding of the Scripture." The church has so understood it through the ages. What is peculiar about the dispensational way of understanding is not its seeing different, unfolding stages of revelation, but the way it sees those stages. Unlike traditional interpreters, dispensationalists "divide" these sections sharply into areas that *conflict with* one another rather than *unfold from* one another. Genuine biblical revelation is developmental; one stage unfolds naturally from another as the unfolding of the blossom of a flower. But, for dispensationalists, these periods are sharply divided rather than integrated, and they conflict rather than harmonize. Even "divide" is a sharper term than Paul's original requires, and dispensationalists have made it sharper still, a veritable scissor separation of one part from another.

Oswald Allis has noted that feature. As an Old Testament scholar, he was impressed with dispensationalism's similarity to radical biblical criticism. Dispensationalists are generally very conservative and anti-critical. They all agree that the Bible is the Word of God, unlike the Bible critic who assumes it is a mere product of men. Consequently, Allis notes with surprise that these ultra conservatives and ultra radicals close ranks by the radical way they cut up the Bible. Radical scholars divide the Old Testament into different and conflicting documents with varying theologies. Dispensationalists do not go about their job in quite the same way, but they end up with very similar results. Just as there are radical radicals who split the biblical documents to smithereens, so there are ultra dispensationalists (Bullingerites) who do the same.

As we shall see throughout this booklet, the dispensational interpretations resulting from such radical divisions of the biblical revelation are unjustified.

Generally speaking, dispensationalists consider themselves much more loyal than anti-dispensationalists to the teaching of Scripture. While they admit that many of us who oppose them believe just as fervently as they in the inerrancy of Scripture, they think they are humbler in accepting its straightforward teaching. We tend to be more sophisticated and less submissive. They are childlike in their faith; we are less so. They, to use the words of Isaiah, "tremble" more at God's Word than we do.

This difference in approach and attitude comes to the surface in dispensationalism's "literalism" versus our supposed "spiritualizing." Dispensationalists think they take the Bible at its word, whereas we make it conform to our anticipations They are more literal, willing to follow the words of Scripture wherever they lead. We, they think, make the Scripture fit into our own preconceived theology. When its literal meaning does not fit, we must spiritualize it, whereas they remain faithful to its literal teaching.

While dispensationalists see themselves as literalists and their opponents as spiritualizers, their conservative opponents maintain that they are wrong on both counts. First, dispensationalists themselves are not consistent literalists, and, second, their opponents do not spiritualize unless they feel Scripture itself, taken literally, has a spiritual or metaphorical meaning. Both groups try to follow, consciously or unconsciously, the dictum of Martin Luther: "Literal wherever possible." As Dr. Earl Radmacher has astutely observed, "Literalism is not letterism."

We all agree that most literature, including the Bible, is meant to be understood according to the literal construction of the words that are used. Even in common speech, we assume a person should be taken literally unless he is obviously using a metaphor, or is allegorizing, or is in some way alerting us that the usual meaning of his words is not in play at the moment. Then, and then only, will we interpret other than literally. The same is true with respect to the Bible.

But all literalists, at one point or another, interpret the Bible figuratively. There is not a dispensationalist living who believes that, when Christ said He was the vine, grapes were to be picked from His body. On the other hand, when our Lord said, "I am the way, the truth, and the life," no one doubts that He meant He was the only way anyone could come to the Father. That was no figure of speech, but an absolute, literal, dogmatic statement that He was the only way to eternal life.

The vast proportion of Scripture is either obviously literal or obviously figurative, both sides admit. Only in a relatively few disputed areas does the question arise whether the Scripture is to be taken literally or figuratively. We do not accuse dispensationalists of being absolute literalists, nor should they accuse us of being absolute spiritualizers.

We both are literalists up to a certain point. At the points where we differ, dispensationalists generally interpret the passage literally and nondispensationalists figuratively. But to say on the basis of that limited divergence of interpretation that the two schools represent fundamentally different hermeneutical approaches is unwarranted. Many on both sides think that this hermeneutical difference is more foundational than the theological. I profoundly disagree.

If the usual distinction between dispensationalists and nondispensationalists as literalists and spiritualizers is not a valid one, what is the issue here? As I said above, it comes back to this matter of *dividing* the Word of God as over against *unifying* the Word of God. The dispensationalist sees in various periods diverse dispensations rather than a harmonious unfolding of different dispensations. In other words, the difference here is not so much in the fundamental hermeneutical approach as in the interpretations.

As the dispensationalist approaches prophecy, he does not differ from the nondispensational conservative. They both believe they are addressing the Word of God; both have confidence in predictive prophecy; and both are endeavoring to understand what the Word of God means. But àt this point the two interpretations diverge into a separation versus an integration of the parts of Scripture.

It is very difficult to say which is the cart and which is the horse in this case. Is it the literalistic tendency that produces this divided Scripture, or is it the belief in a divided Scripture that drives the dispensationalist to ultra-literalism at some point? I think it is the latter, though that is not easy to prove.

I let this matter rest for now. The remainder of this pamphlet will look at the divergent interpretations and, incidentally, at the way the two groups do interpretation and why. Here it is sufficient to observe that the dispensationalist divides Scripture according to a common misconstruction of 2 Timothy 2:15, whereas the anti-dispensationalist, believing that is a misinterpretation of the text, sees an overriding unity in the Word of God.

## Applications of this Fundamental Idea

This radical disparateness of the Bible is the fundamental motif of dispensationalists, and it manifests itself in crucial areas. First, I will consider the dispensational conception of the people of God. Second, I will note the dispensationalist's idea of the predestination of the people of God. Third, I will examine the dispensational view of the salvation of the people of God. Fourth, I will conclude with the dispensationalist's view of the future of the people of God.

*Dispensationalism and the People of God*

John Calvin referred to some proto-dispensationalists of the Reformation period as reducing Israel to "a herd of swine." The "dispensationalists" of the time regarded the ancient people of God as merely temporal. Their life was in this world and their hope was in this world. They were satisfied if they could sit in peace under their own fig tree with no invading foe troubling them. Temporal prosperity was their heaven, and they did not look far beyond.

Calvin thought otherwise. In his *Institutes of the Christian Religion*, he devotes an entire chapter, "The Similarity of the Old and New Testaments," to the *spiritual* interests of the Old Testament people of God. In essence, they were the same as the New Testament saints. Some individuals of the old dispensation exceeded spiritually many in the new dispensation. Calvin begins with these words and continues in the same vein throughout the chapter: "It may now be evident that all those persons, from the beginning of the world, whom God has adopted into the society of His people, have been federally (convenantally) connected with Him by the same law and the same doctrine which are in force among us."

Of course, dispensationalists do not refer to Israel as a "herd of swine. " In fact, they resent such a description of their viewpoint. Nevertheless, they think of Israel as the "wife of Jehovah," in distinction from the New Testament people of God, who are described as the "bride of Christ." The wife of Jehovah would seem equivalent to the bride of Christ. Jehovah in the Old Testament is, of course, the Lord Jesus Christ. Nevertheless, dispensationalists confine the

Old Testament "wife of Jehovah" to earthly blessings, in distinction from the heavenly blessings of the "bride of Christ."

This division between the Old Testament people of God and the New Testament people of God is far reaching. For example, it divides at the point of regeneration and the new birth. To be a member of the New Testament people of God, one must be born of the Spirit. No matter how outwardly moral a person is, he is not saved and a member of the true church of Jesus Christ unless he is a new creature. By contrast, the Old Testament saint was not a born-again Christian. For example, Lewis Sperry Chafer says of Nicodemus that he was a perfected Jew under the Old Testament law. He was not born again, but a true Israelite. He was a genuine member of the Old Testament people of God though he, at that time, had not entered the company of the New Testament people of God. Dispensationalists see Paul, prior to his conversion, after the same model. Before his conversion, this Jew was "as touching the law, blameless." The dispensationalist takes this to mean that he met the Old Testament requirements. In that dispensation, he too was a "perfected Jew." Only when he was born again did he become a member of the church of Jesus Christ.

By contrast, the covenantal view of the people of God sees in both dispensations the same people of God. All are members of the church, all are born again, and all are saved by the one Mediator between God and man, the man Christ Jesus. The same church of Jesus Christ comprises both. One is not a swinish, earthly people and the other a regenerate, heavenly people. They are both the people of God, born of His Spirit, created anew by the Jesus Christ.

The church, says Chafer-Walvoord, is "the body of Christ . . . called out of the world and joined together with a living union in Christ. This concept is not found in the Old Testament . . . ." (*Major Bible Themes*, p. 234). That is to say, the body of Christ did not exist in the Old Testament. The Old Testament people of God were not called out of the world and joined together "with a living union in Christ." A dispensationalist will deny that this opens up the possibility of different ways of salvation; however one group has a living union with Christ and the other has none. A dispensationalist will say that all are saved by Jesus Christ, but they are not in living communion with Jesus Christ.

According to dispensationalists, there are three categories of people: (1) the Jew, (2) the Gentile, and (3) the church of God. The Jews, or Israel, are the descendants of Abraham and Jacob ("Israel") who have the earthly promises. (Abraham is said to have "spiritual" as well as temporal blessings but not regeneration, adoption, and "living union in Christ." He was the "channel" of such blessings, but not the recipient himself.) These Jews are now scattered in the whole world and later will be gathered together. The church consists of those Jews and Gentiles who have been born again and are members of Jesus Christ. The Gentiles are the rest of mankind who never had any kind of acceptable relationship to God. In other words, dispensationalists see three categories where the Bible sees only two: the people of God and those who are not the people of God. There are those who are saved and those who are not saved. There are those who are in Christ and those who are not in Christ. But what God has joined together (Old and New Testament church), I fear dispensationalists have rent asunder. The one undivided church of all time the dispensationalist divides in two irreconcilable parts: the Jewish, Israelitish people of God and the Christian people of God. And the church is not only separated in this world, but even in the world to come.

Abraham himself shows that the dispensational division between Israel and the church is erroneous. The Israelites descended from Abraham, but dispensationalists sever them, as well as Abraham himself, from the people in living union with Jesus Christ. Yet, in the New Testament, those who are in living union with Jesus Christ are the seed of Abraham. Christ Himself says to the Jews, "If you

are Abraham's children, do the deeds of Abraham . . . Your
father Abraham rejoiced to see my day; and he saw it and
was glad" (John 8:39, 56). According to our Lord, these lineal descendants of Abraham were not really the seed or
children of Abraham at all since they did not come to living
union with Jesus Christ. Those who have a living union
with Jesus Christ are the true Israelites. So we see that not
all lineal descendants of Abraham were necessarily the children of Abraham, but only those lineal descendants of
Abraham (as well as Gentiles) who came to Jesus Christ.
The true children or descendants of Abraham and the
Christian church are one and the same.

In Romans 4 Paul says the same thing: the children of
faith are the children of Abraham. He himself was an
Israelite, but he did not become a true child of Abraham
until he became a believer in union with Jesus Christ. In
other words, the New Testament teaches that New Testament saints belong to the church by a living union with
Jesus Christ, and as such they are in union with the people
of God in all dispensations who are the true children of
Abraham.

Christ is much more visible in the New Testament, of
course. Living union is much more apparent, but there is
no denying, even by the dispensationalists, that Christ is
the eternal Son of God and was very active in the Old
Testament, and that even the salvation of the Israelites
rested on faith in Jesus Christ.

Dispensationalists cannot have it both ways. If the Old
Testament people of God had no union with Christ, they
were not saved by Him. If they were saved by Christ, dispensationalists have to admit that the Israel of the Old
Testament and the church of the New are one and the same
body of people, all of them in union with Jesus Christ, and,
as such, the true sons of Abraham. God has joined the
people of God in all dispensations in Jesus Christ.
Dispensationalists have divided them.

*Predestination and the People of God*

Dispensationalists are popularly known as "four point" Calvinists. Many people know the five points of Calvinism by the famous acrostic TULIP:

T=total depravity
U=unconditional election
L=limited atonement
I=irresistible grace
P=perseverance of the saints.

Most dispensationalists claim to believe all of these biblical doctrines except limited atonement. In other words, they believe in total depravity, election, irresistible grace, and the perseverance of the saints. I am not accusing my dispensational friends of dishonesty, but of not understanding the doctrines they profess. If they did understand them, they would realize that they disagree with all five and not merely with one.

For example, dispensationalists profess to believe in unconditional election. They say a great deal about the subject and intend to affirm this great truth of Holy Scripture. But what do dispensationalists mean by their affirmation of unconditional election?

The Scofield Bible note on 1 Peter 5:13 ("The Church that is at Babylon, elected together with you") says that election is according to foreknowledge. It is unconditional *salvation* that dispensationalists are talking about. God foresees that the sinner will repent. Because God foresees this repentance and belief of the sinner, He chooses him to everlasting life without the sinner's having any virtue which recommends him for election.

All of this is quite true. But it is not what "unconditional election" means. That doctrine teaches that God elects the sinner while he is in his sin before he even turns away from sin or turns to faith. It is the *election* that is unconditional, not merely the resulting salvation. If God chooses or elects a person, foreseeing his repentance and faith, that may well be an unconditional *salvation*, but it is not an unconditional *election*. (In fact it would not even be an unconditional *salvation*, but salvation conditioned by a non-meritorious, necessary faith.)

Furthermore, dispensationalism repudiates Calvinism by its explicit rejection of the third point, limited atonement, and by its misinterpretation of the first, total depravity.

The dispensationalist explicitly rejects limited atonement. The very fact that he rejects the doctrine that Jesus Christ died to secure the salvation of only the unconditionally elected shows that the dispensationalist does not believe in unconditional election. If election is unconditional (that is, of sinners indisposed ever to repent or believe so long as they remained in their sins), then the only ones to benefit from Christ's atoning sacrifice are people specifically called by the Holy Spirit and enabled to repent and believe. The atonement is limited by God's choice to save some sinners and not others. All of this is alien to the dispensational mind because the doctrine of unconditional election is not really there either. So we say to the dispensationalist that he ought to stop affirming the unconditional election of totally depraved persons or else stop denying the limited design of the atonement. Since his denial of limited atonement is consistent with all of his teaching, he ought to see immediately that he cannot possibly affirm (consistently) the Calvinistic doctrine of unconditional election.

The dispensationalist also affirms total depravity. Again, I do not question his honesty, but I must deny his perceptiveness. How could a person believe that men are dead in trespasses and sins, that they hate God, are utterly indisposed to Christ, are totally depraved, and are morally unable to incline toward any virtue, least of all the virtue of coming to the spotless Lamb of God, and say in the next breath that God merely foresees these persons as repenting and believing? Corpses do not give birth to spiritual life. Men have to be unconditionally elected to repentance, faith, and the salvation Christ specifically purchased for them.

The dispensationalist has a genuine desire to honor the

predestinating, electing grace of God. There are so many passages in the Bible that affirm it, and dispensationalists are so biblical that inevitably they affirm it too. On the other hand, what the Bible means by the doctrine makes the dispensationalist uncomfortable. He cannot deny it because the words are in Scripture, but he cannot affirm it because the concept is not really acceptable to him.

The dispensationalist handles the problem by avoiding it. He gives lip service to divine sovereignty and human freedom. He constantly reminds us that both are taught in the Bible and both must be honored, but how they can be in harmony with one another is an inscrutable mystery. All that is true, but it does not explain what the doctrine is. A predestination of some corpses to live and some corpses to remain dead is what is manifestly meant by the Bible doctrine. Mankind is a valley of dry bones. Some of those dry bones are destined to live again and others are not. We have a sea of drowning sinners. Some are chosen to be rescued; some are left to drown. It is all very plain, but is not very palatable. The dispensationalist, as well as everybody else, shrinks from having to say that God lets many persons perish and chooses to save only some of the multitude. While they will not deny the doctrine outright, neither will they unambiguously affirm it.

Dispensationalists say that God has a plan. He knows even apart from that plan (*Major Christian Doctrines*, p. 233) what will inevitably happen. He lets it happen. That is about as far as the dispensationalist will go. But, to be true to the Bible, he must assert that God chooses to regenerate some and not to regenerate others. The dispensationalist will not deny it, but neither will he assert it. He makes predestination rest on foreknowledge, although he will not assert that unambiguously either. The dispensationalist finds himself between a rock and a hard place. He is biblical enough to know the Reformed truth and to want to believe it, but he cannot screw up enough courage to affirm it unconfusedly and unambiguously. He ends up with Arminianism, but he will not categorically affirm that either.

If anything is characteristically associated with Calvinism, it is predestinarianism. Calvinists believe all the classic, fundamental tenets of the Christian religion, of course. But what distinguishes them in the popular, and even in the academic, mind is their strong affirmation of the predestinating, unconditional election of almighty God. If a dispensationalist wants to be known as essentially Calvinistic, he cannot give any uncertain sound on this doctrine. Actually, he sounds the wrong note, but this is so subdued that dispensationalists themselves hardly detect it. They need to be aware, however, that they are not clearly, articulately, and emphatically stating what the Reformed faith has maintained down through the ages.

A clear comment on this subject comes in Scofield's note on 1 Peter 1:20. There he maintained that the relationship between election and foreknowledge is logically, first, omniscience, and second, divine decision, which includes foreordination, election, predestination, and foreknowledge. Yet, this is another instance of the hopeless obscurity of the doctrine in the dispensational mind. That statement would be truly Calvinistic if it unambiguously said that the divine decision (foreordination, election, and predestination) logically precedes foreknowledge, and this note does indicate that. Unfortunately, that is not all it says. It lists at the head of the logical verities *omniscience.* So, the order is omniscience, predestination, foreknowledge. That adds up to confusion—pure, simple, and eternal confusion. Omniscience means the knowledge of everything. But how could God have logically prior knowledge of everything before He has logically predestinated anything?

Furthermore, how can omniscience not include foreknowledge? How can God have all knowledge (omniscience) without foreknowledge (which dispensationalists represent as logically following on omniscience)? In other words, dispensationalists outdo typical Arminians here. Arminians erroneously teach that predestination logically follows foreknowledge, but even they do not make the further error of teaching that even foreknowledge logically follows omniscence. Foreknowledge, in the sense of prescience, is part of omniscience.

The first three doctrines of the five points go by the board in dispensational theology. It has no true doctrine of total depravity; it has no true doctrine of unconditional election; and it has no true doctrine of the specific design of the atonement. It is conscious only of the last deviation from the Reformed faith. I hope I have succeeded in making it conscious of the first two also. I pray that it will be consistent even if it has explicitly to repudiate all three great Reformed truths, but, rather than that, I hope that it will consistently affirm all three.

Dispensationalism rejects the other two of the five points as well. For example, Dallas Theological Seminary, which is the largest and most famous academic exponent of dispensationalism in the world, makes regeneration "come through" faith: "We believe that the new birth of the believer comes only through faith in Christ." (1981–82 Catalogue, Article VII), whereas, according to irresistible grace, faith "comes through" the new birth.

Not quite so explicitly, but clearly, Dallas repudiates the fifth point, the perseverance of the saints. The Catalogue, Article X, on "eternal security" shows that dispensationalism believes in the "security" of believers whether they "persevere" or not. When saints "persistently sin," God will "chasten them and correct them in infinite love; but having undertaken to save them and keep them forever, apart from all human merit, He, who cannot fail, will in the end present everyone of them faultless before the presence of His glory and conformed to the image of His Son." Sinners are secure even though they "persistently sin." This would be perseverance of the sinners, not perseverance of the saints.

*Salvation and the People of God*

Dispensationalism is not, as it usually claims to be, Calvinistic or Reformed. This is an extremely serious fault inasmuch as the teaching of the Bible, we believe, is Reformed throughout. Jesus Christ gave a mandate when He commissioned His church to teach people to observe whatsoever He had commanded them (Matthew 28:20). He has commanded in the Old and the New Testament the teaching of the "whole counsel" of God, which is indeed the Reformed system of theology. For dispensationalism to deviate from that is a serious fault. To claim *not* to do so, while doing so, is an even more serious fault. Nevertheless, it is not a *fatal* fault. It is possible, *very inconsistently*, to preserve the Christian religion while taking away its systematic character. It is sinfully possible to be faithful to the heart of the gospel even while departing from the context of it. I would by no means minimize the gravity of such defection, though I believe it is not fatal.

But what is indisputably, absolutely, uncompromisingly essential to the Christian religion is its doctrine of salvation. While a theologian may depart from the Reformed system and travel at his own peril, to depart from the essential salvation pattern is to depart from Christianity. Consequently, the doctrine which we now consider is of the essence. If dispensationalism has actually departed from the only way of salvation which the Christian religion teaches, then we must say it has departed from Christianity. No matter how many other important truths it proclaims, it cannot be called Christian if it empties Christianity of its essential message. We define a sect or cult as a group of people who claim to be Christian while voiding the essential message. If dispensationalism does this, then dispensationalism is a cult and not a branch of the Christian church. It is impossible to exaggerate the gravity of this situation.

What, then, does dispensationalism teach about the people of God and salvation? Happily, I find that all dispensationalists of whom I have ever heard or read maintain with vigor and emphasis that they believe that Jesus Christ is the only Savior in *all* dispensations. The cross of Christ is the way of justification for *everyone* from Adam to the last saint who will ever be saved. No matter how things appear on the surface, they insist that, at the bottom, the blood of Christ is the only ground of salvation for anybody at any time.

Our dispensational friends emphatically affirm their adherence to the essential Christian way of salvation. Whatever their intentions may be, they nonetheless fail to carry them out in their theology. However frequently they affirm their loyalty, their system of doctrine relentlessly militates against this.

They do not grasp that point, and I honor them for sincerely opposing my charge. But they cannot consistently maintain that opposition while teaching their system of doctrine. They must face this criticism fairly. Unless they can show some fallacy in it, *they must repudiate the dispensational system or else repudiate the gospel of Jesus Christ!* It cannot be placed in any less grim light than that. I admit my own fallibility. I am open to all counter criticism. I have been waiting for years to see a dispensationalist refute that proposition and demonstrate not only that he *intends* to glory in the cross, but that he actually *does* while maintaining the dispensational system of theology. No one has not done this so far. I am afraid that no one can do so. Many people will vigorously and indignantly reject this charge without even considering, much less weighing, it. That is not worthy of a Christian; what is appropriate at this point is either to refute or to recant. Rejection and repudiation of me is no substitute. Let the dispensationalist hear me fairly; then, let him submit to this criticism and abandon this false theology or attempt to refute it. Let him hear my response, and let us *all* follow where the truth leads. As God is my witness, if I see myself to be wrong, I will acknowledge it, beg forgiveness of all dispensationalists, correct my ways, and humbly teach the truth, the whole truth, and nothing but the truth.

Why do I say that the dispensational system is against the cross of Jesus Christ, which it professes to exalt? First, the dispensational distinction between Israel and the church implies a different way of salvation. Second, their very concept of predestination also implies a different way of salvation. Third, the very meaning of the term "dispensationalism" rules out the possibility of the Christian way of salvation. Fourth, their notion of the kingdom being offered by Jesus Christ, which, if accepted, would have made the cross unnecessary, is incompatible with the Christian way of salvation. Fifth, their view of the Old Testament people of God trusting in the coming of Christ rather than in the coming Christ is a fatal error. Sixth, and by far the most important incompatible element in the dispensational system, is its antinomianism, which precludes the possibility of the Christian way of salvation.

First, the dispensational distinction between Israel and the church implicitly repudiates the Christian way of salvation. Dispensationalists make a qualitative distinction between Israel and the church. They are two different peoples, not the same people of God. They have a different relationship to Him in this life and a different future.

If these are two different types of people, how can they have the same salvation? If, as dispensationalists maintain, Israel as well as the church is saved by the blood of Jesus Christ, how can there be this qualitative difference between them as peoples? Jesus Christ is the same yesterday, today, and forever. His salvation is the same yesterday, today, and forever. It may be administered in somewhat different ways, or in different contexts, but what is administered is the same: redemption by the blood of Jesus Christ. The whole church has taught down through the centuries, and even the dispensationalists profess to believe, that there cannot be two different categories of people. How can those who are saved in the same way, by the same Savior, through the same redemption, be a different people? How can Israel be reduced to a "herd of swine," and, at the same time, be the beneficiaries of the same blood of Christ from which we present-day Christians benefit?

It will not do to say that Israelites were the beneficiaries of the same redemption if they benefit in an entirely different manner. According to dispensationalists, the Old Testament people are not the heirs of the Holy Spirit and are not regenerated and grafted by Him into Christ in the same way that the New Testament people are. If Christ purchased the same thing for the Old Testament saints before He came that He did for the New Testament saints after He came, there cannot be a qualitative difference between them. There being clearly that difference, as the dispensationalists *vigorously maintain*, then there must be what the dispensationalists *vigorously deny*, a different basis of their acceptability with God.

The Bible teaches that the people of God are the same in all dispensations. They are, as Ephesians 2:20 says, built on the same foundation, "the prophets and apostles." The prophets of the Old Testament and the apostles of the New Testament are together a foundation for the church of God. The apostle Peter uses the same language for the New Testament church of God that was used for the ancient people of God in the Old Testament, calling them a royal priesthood and a holy nation: "But ye are a chosen generation, a royal priesthood, a holy nation, a people of his own, that ye should show forth the praises of him who hath called you . . ." (1 Peter 2:9).

In Paul's famous metaphor, the Jews were the original olive tree into which the Gentile believers were grafted (Romans 11:17f). They are the same plant; they have the same source of life; there is no difference between them except a temporal one. The early form of organization was displaced by the present form of organization, but the living stock of their lives, Jesus Christ, is the same in all periods. The Bible says this because it maintains what the dispensationalist only claims, namely that Christ is the one and only Savior of all time. It does not split the church, as dispensationalists do, but unifies the church in all ages because it sees that they are all saved by the same undivided Lord Jesus Christ.

Second, the dispensationalists' doctrine of predestination eliminates a sound doctrine of salvation. This is not so obvious as the first point, but it is equally true and can be demonstrated (with some difficulty) just as clearly.

If salvation comes to the individual by virtue of his foreseen faith, then, of course, his salvation is not the same as that which comes by God's predestinating grace. The salvation that comes to a mortally sick person, who can at least reach out and take and apply the medicine that cures him, is a very different thing from the salvation that comes to a corpse. Dispensational thought, growing out of the defection from the predestinarianism of the Bible, means that the sinner is still (though barely) alive. He can be restored to health by the exercise of his own weakened (but not destroyed) abilities. He is not saved by grace alone. He is saved by the offer of grace appropriated by his own remaining moral ability. Christ does not save him, but makes salvation possible for him. Surely there is a vast difference between Christ as an *aid* to a person's salvation and Christ *as* the person's salvation.

It is true that the dispensationalist will consistently say that a sinner cannot be saved without Christ, but that remnant of the gospel in their message is not the whole gospel. The gospel is not that Christ makes salvation possible, but that He makes it actual. He is not a potential Savior, but a real Savior of His people from their sins.

The dispensationalist really says that the sinner in his present condition is still acceptable to God. God will condemn sinners if they do not take steps toward God, but they still have the power to do that; and if they do what is in their power they will, by coming to Christ, save themselves. Christ enables people to save themselves. They initiate that act of salvation by appropriating the divine remedy offered in Jesus Christ. The dispensationalist will be outraged by this; he does not realize what he says because he puts so much verbal stress on the divinity of the remedy and the indispensability of the offer of the gospel. He cannot remain blind, however, to the conclusion that the sinner himself has it in his power to take this medicine, and, if he takes it, he most certainly (by applying Christ to himself) saves himself. It is perfectly clear to the dispensationalist that without Christ he could not save himself. He would certainly die apart from the rescue offered by Jesus Christ. Nevertheless, Christ alone does not save the sinner; the sinner appropriates the offer of Christ, so the sinner is the decisive one.

As an illustration, suppose there are twins in a given Christian family. They are reared by the same godly father and mother and, in their very young years, introduced to the same gospel of Jesus Christ. They are convicted of their sinfulness and their need of a Savior, and also that salvation has been offered in Jesus' blood and righteousness. One of these twins embraces the gospel which his parents present, and the other refuses to do so. The one who believes will be saved; the one who disbelieves will be lost. According to the dispensationalist, both of the boys have it in their power to believe Jesus Christ or to disbelieve Jesus Christ. The one brother believes Him; the other brother disbelieves Him. The one brother thus brings everlasting salvation to himself; the other brother brings everlasting damnation to himself. When we ask Paul's question, "Who has made you to differ?", we do not get the answer that the apostle Paul calls for. "For who maketh thee to differ from another? And what hast thou that thou didst not receive? Now if thou didst receive it, why dost thou glory, as if thou hadst not received it?" (1 Corinthians 4:7).

Clearly it is God who makes these persons to differ. Dispensationalists disagree. It is clearly the twins, not God. God is the same to both of them. Christ has died alike for each of them. The gospel is offered in the same terms to both boys. The difference between them is not God or Christ; the difference is within themselves. One exercises faith; the other one does not. One saves himself by believing in Christ; the other one damns himself by disbelieving in Christ. But it is the person himself, not the Lord Jesus Christ or the sovereign God, who causes them to differ.

Think of Jacob and Esau. How does Paul talk about those biblical twins? "For the children being not yet born, neither having done any good or evil, that the purpose of God according to election might stand, not of works, but of him that calleth, It was said unto her, the elder shall serve the younger. As it is written, Jacob have I loved, but Esau have I hated" (Romans 9:11–13). Jacob and Esau differ because the sovereign God loved Jacob and hated Esau. He made Jacob a vessel of mercy and left Esau a vessel of wrath.

A dispensationalist cannot say that. He would sooner choke than glory in himself; however, insofar as he is a dispensationalist, he does not glory in the cross but in his own acceptance of the cross. If this offends him, then thank God it offends him, because it means that in his heart he believes what by his mind he disavows. Let him bring his mind in line with his heart. It will never do for him to say that in his heart he trusts in Christ alone as the author as well as the finisher of his salvation, when he himself is the author of his salvation (and ultimately even the finisher of it). If he really believes God is the author, then let him say so. That, I believe, will be the end of his dispensationalism.

Third, the very meaning of the term "dispensation" militates against the Christian gospel of salvation. The definition of "dispensation," according to the revised Scofield Bible, is a period when persons are tested with reference to their "obedience to some specific revelation of the will of God" (Genesis 1:28). A person is acceptable or unacceptable to God by the way he behaves with respect to certain commandments in certain ages. Construed literally, this is a form of justification or salvation by works.

The dispensationalist will recoil from this charge. He will answer that Christ is the underlying basis of salvation in all dispensations. But if that is so, why does the dispensationalist say that a person is tested with respect to his conscience or his observance of government or the law, or something else? If the dispensationalist replies, "This is just a test of his sincerity and the reality of his faith," well and good. He immediately ceases to be a dispensationalist and becomes a covenant theologian. He cannot throw this in as a sop to satisfy his critics; he must articulate it. "Dispensation" is his fundamental concept. But while I read many statements about dispensations, I never read that all these tests are simply to show that a person is really trusting in Jesus Christ. If he did say that, the dispensationalist would have to say that these tests apply in all dispensations. That is, a Christian individual must always honor his enlightened conscience; he must always respect those in authority; he must even observe the various ecclesiastical laws of God (as the dispensationalist does say). But, what difference would there be between one dispensation and another except the clarity of unfolding revelation? Why would there be different economies of redemption if the one covenant of grace underlay all of them? Why would these dispensational theologians not insist that they are indeed *covenant* theologians, and that these dispensational differences are only what the Reformed theologians of the ages have been calling "modal" (not essential) differences. The essence of all dispensations is salvation by grace in the shed blood of Jesus Christ. That is what covenant theologians say and build their theology on. That is what dispensational theologians say, but they erect their theology on an entirely different foundation.

Dispensationalism *per se* denies covenantism at the same time that dispensationalists defend themselves from that charge by surreptitiously suggesting that they are covenant theologians. They do not use this language, but when we criticize them for offering differing schemes of salvation they say, "No, it is the same way; it is the same covenant; it is the same shed blood of Jesus Christ." If they are going to say that conscientiously, then they must stop saying the other. If they are going to say the other, it will not do to make this evangelical gesture, which is incompatible with the fundamental concept of dispensationalism.

Still, the dispensationalist does *not* say, strictly speaking, that Christ is the Savior in all dispensations. This most definitive Scofield note on "dispensation" explicitly *rejects* Christ in what is meant to affirm Him. According to that note, there are *not* separate ways of salvation. But why? Because even before the cross man was "saved in prospect of Christ's atoning sacrifice." Accordingly, those before the cross were not saved by "believing on the Lord Jesus Christ" but "in prospect of Christ's sacrifice." There is an infinite difference between being saved by Christ's sacrifice and being saved in "prospect" of it! If a dispensationalist replies that I am quibbling with language, he cannot be in earnest. That difference in the ways of salvation is the most crucial difference between the two theologies. If a dispensationalist gives up that distinction, he gives up his dispensationalism!

I do sense a trend among dispensationalists back to the orthodoxy from which they have departed. Even the differences between the revised Scofield Bible of 1967 and the original Scofield of the turn of the century show the revisers moving away from the older dispensationalism toward the more orthodox, Reformed theology. Nevertheless, I have to say that, though they may be moving in the right direction, they have not *departed* from the older, seriously defective doctrine. I pray with all my heart that this movement in the right direction will carry them back to where they belong—with us in the Reformed faith. But until then I cannot withdraw my criticism that this is another gospel, which is *not* another gospel. I am not saying they *intend* everything that they say and write. Nevertheless, as teachers in the church, they must teach soundly. They cannot excuse error on the ground that they *mean* truth. If they mean the truth in their hearts, then they must express it by their lips. It is out of the heart that either sin or righteousness proceeds, as our Lord says. He sees the heart; we creatures can only hear the mouth. This is no doubt the reason Paul insists that "if you confess with your mouth Jesus as Lord, and believe in your heart that God raised Him from the dead, you shall be saved" (Romans 10:9).

If in his heart the dispensationalist loves the gospel and believes that it is the same in all ages, and that all people are always saved only by that one way, let him say so consistently and repudiate everything in his system that is inconsistent.

He should not need any vigorous exhortation at this point. If he truly loves the gospel of Jesus Christ and considers this criticism fair, but is incapable of refuting it, then surely he will thank us, repudiate his error, embrace the truth, and be one with us in the covenant theology of the ages.

Fourth, the dispensationalists' conception of an offer of the kingdom which could have made the cross unnecessary is an appalling, implicit rejection of the gospel. In dispensational thinking of the most moderate character, Jesus Christ came to offer an earthly kingdom to Israel. That kingdom would have fully established the Old Testament legal system and its expansion through the whole world under the leadership of a revived Israel and her Messiah. All the errors that belong to the dispensational conception of the age of the law would have been reenacted at that time had Israel accepted their king, Jesus. Fortunately, for the dispensationalist and all of us, the Jews rejected Christ's supposed offer and doomed Him to the cross. Christ's death on the cross, which came about only because Israel did not accept Him as the king of Israel, is the basis of our salvation in this dispensation of grace, or the age of the church. In other words, the gospel was a happy accident for Christians. It depended

entirely on the faithlessness of the Jews. Had they responded as they ought to have responded, there would
never have been a gospel of Jesus Christ. This is surely an
appalling notion. How a Christian could entertain it, even
momentarily, is very difficult to understand.

Dispensationalists account for such an appalling concept by their view of divine sovereignty. They say that God
knew from all eternity that when the Jews were presented
with the kingdom by the Lord Christ they would refuse it.
Consequently, Christ could not have set up His kingdom at
that time, thus making the cross unnecessary. Many of
them say they are as shocked by the implication that the
cross of Christ might never have occurred as we are. But
they are tranquil because God knew that this would never
happen.

Ironically, dispensationalists think they are very Calvinistic at this point. God knows all things and, in a certain
sense, foreordains all things. They rest in that Calvinistic
doctrine to free themselves from any guilt in teaching this
incredible notion that the cross was, strictly speaking,
unnecessary. "No, it was necessary," they insist. God
knew that it *had* to take place. And God knew that it *would*
take place because He knew that the Jews would not accept
this offer which would have made the cross unnecessary.

God was offering Israel a very, very, very wicked option. According to dispensationalism, the Lord Jesus Christ
offered something to the Jews in good faith which, had they
accepted, would have destroyed the only way of man's salvation. God is an honest God. He is a sincere God. He,
therefore, truly offered the Jews a kingdom which would
have made the cross impossible. Now, obviously, if God
offered a kingdom which He could not have permitted to be
established, He could be neither honest nor sincere. The
dispensationalist tries to think that God was both honest
and sincere because He *knew* the way in which people
would respond to the offer. He was doing it safely, as it
were, because He knew that this dishonest and insincere

offer would never be accepted. The fact of the matter is He could not possibly have redeemed His promise had it been accepted. If the Jews had embraced Christ's offer, God would have had to say, "I am sorry, Christ cannot be elevated to the throne at this time. He must die on a cross." If the Jews expostulated and said, "But you offered us this," He would have had to say that it was not a sincere offer. "I thought that you would never accept it."

Of course, the dispensationalist in the background is saying, "No, that would never happen because God knew it would never happen." I am granting that it never could have happened. Still, the supposed offer was insincere. God was making an offer that He could never have redeemed, though He dishonestly implied that He would if it were accepted.

Dispensationalists counterattack at this point with considerable cogency because this is so highly hypothetical. They insist that what they are saying is no different from the Calvinistic interpretation of the "offer of the gospel." God knows who will and who will not accept it. The dispensationalist says to the Calvinist, "Suppose a person whom God had left to perish had chosen actually to believe. Could God have accepted that person's faith? Would He not have said, 'No, you were not chosen; therefore, you cannot have this gospel which you profess'? He could not have redeemed His promise. He offers it to everybody and if everybody actually were to accept it, then God could not actually save everybody, because He had already declared that everyone would not be saved. If He were to save everybody, he would prove Himself to be ignorant of what was going to happen and frustrated in all of His counsels and purposes. So what difference is there," the dispensationalist asks, "between our saying that God knew that the Jews would reject the kingdom and make the cross necessary, and your saying that God knew that certain persons would reject Jesus Christ and thereby make His predestination and foreknowledge true so that He would not have to make good on His insincere offer of salvation?"

Clearly, the whole gospel goes if God can lie. If His promise is not "Yea" and "Amen," we can never be persuaded that His offer of the gospel is genuine. The dispensationalist asks, "If we fall, do you not fall with us?" We answer, "No!" The dispensational representation of Reformed theology is a caricature at this point. We admit that, *if* we were guilty of what dispensationalists charge, our error *would* be as fatal as theirs. But, dispensationalists do not understand what we teach. We do not teach that God invites reprobates to believe and be saved, knowing full well that He will not give them a heart of faith. In fact, God does not call reprobates! Whom does He call? Sinners! Only those who recognize themselves to be sinners are called. Any *one* of them who comes will be saved. God never invited anyone who, if he responded, would be refused! God would never be embarrassed, even hypothetically, by someone's coming and being rejected because he was not predestinated and foreknown. No one has been refused, would be refused, will be refused, ever!

Even Reformed theologians sometimes state this "universal call" incorrectly, as if Christ were inviting the "righteous" to repentance.

However, according to Reformed theology, the call of the gospel is universally to all who are conscious of being "sinners," "poor in spirit," and aware of needing a Savior. It never was or will be offered to the "righteous," proud in spirit, and self sufficient. So Christ makes no insincere invitation to persons He would not accept if they did come (which is precisely what dispensational teaching says He does in reference to offering His kingdom to the Jews).

It is true that our Lord said that many were called but few were chosen, as if only a few of those sincerely invited were accepted when they came, if they came. What Christ was saying was that the call went everywhere, but only those who paid attention to the nature of that call and came running were chosen and were choosing. The self righteous recognized that the call was not for them, but for despised "sinners"—they did not choose and they were not chosen.

Fifth, the way dispensationalists conceive of the Old Testament believers is drastically different from the biblical way. According to dispensationalists, the Old Testament people are saved by believing in the *coming* of Christ while, in the biblical view, the Old Testament people are saved by believing *in the Christ* who is coming. In dispensationalism, a person is saved by anticipation; in the biblical system, a person is saved by Christ. If Christ is the only way of salvation in all dispensations, then in all dispensations, persons must be saved by Jesus Christ, and not by an anticipation of His coming.

This is no artificial distinction. The Old Testament people are not saved by Jesus Christ, according to dispensationalism; they are saved by hope in the coming of Christ. As such, they do not benefit from what Christ actually achieves when He comes. They are not regenerated; their hopes are not heavenly; they are an earthly "herd of swine." Another way of salvation connected with Christ, but not resting on Christ, is indeed a different way. The dispensationalist at this point is, unconsciously, perhaps, consistent. He does not regard the Old Testament people of God as second, third, or fourth class citizens, but they do not belong to the kingdom of God. They are not in the heavenlies with Christ Jesus. That is consistent with their not being saved by Jesus Christ, but it is inconsistent with being saved by Jesus Christ as the dispensationalists are always *saying*, while constantly, by their doctrine, *denying*.

Sixth, the antinomianism of dispensationalism is utterly incompatible with the one gospel of our Lord Jesus Christ. Dispensational theology does not honor the one way of salvation in other dispensations than the present one. It does not even honor the gospel of Jesus Christ in this so-called dispensation of grace or of the church. This is the dispensation in which the gospel is supposed to come into its glory; but in this very dispensation it becomes most patently obvious that the dispensational gospel is another gospel altogether. Antinomianism is anti-gospelism. One cannot be antinomian and Christian at the same time. If dispensationalists do not want to be anti-Christian, they must repudiate the antinomianism which is a part of the warp and woof of their "gospel."

Is dispensationalism truly antinomian? Antinomianism is the doctrine that a Christian is saved without any obligation to keep the law. "Apart from the law," in the antinomian mind, means apart from any *necessary* relation to the law. Their doctrine teaches that we are saved by faith alone. The usual way of stating Reformation doctrine is that we are "justified by faith alone, but not by the faith that is alone." That is, we are justified by our union with Jesus Christ by true faith; but that faith is not alone because it bears the fruit of good works. Antinomians say that justification is by faith alone, and by a faith that may be alone. The faith ought to bring forth good works, but, if it does not, that is not fatal to faith. The antinomian will never put it this way, but it amounts to justification by a faith without works, justification by a "dead" faith. James says plainly that faith without works is "dead." If faith may exist without works in antinomianism, then that justification may be by a dead faith, that is, by no faith at all. Therefore, this denies the gospel of justification by faith and repudiates Christianity.

Dispensationalism is inseparably connected with antinomianism. Dispensationalism teaches that justification may occur by a dead faith. It is, therefore, an enemy of the central doctrine of the Christian religion—justification by faith alone. It is a champion of possible justification by no faith at all, since it maintains that *may* occur. It does not recommend that it *ought* to occur.

Dispensationalists, in their opposition to the law, are not, however, totally opposed to it. They recommend the keeping of the law—the moral law, the Christian law. They maintain that a person who believes himself to be saved by

Christ ought to live for Christ. There is even a promise that *if* he abounds in the work of the Lord he will have a great reward. If, on the other hand, his faith is sterile, he will not enjoy *fellowship* with God. He will not be rejected by God, but neither will he be in happy communion with God. He is on his way to heaven, but he will not be happy along the way.

Some years ago, I was teaching a survey of church history to the staff members at Campus Crusade's summer Institute of Biblical Studies in Fort Collins, Colorado. Several times in the survey course antinomianism was mentioned. One day, one of the members of that class came up to me and said, "Dr. Gerstner, will you read this chapter of Dr. Ryrie's, and tell the class whether you think that is a modern expression of antinomianism?" I read that book of Dr. Ryrie's on Christian discipleship and particularly examined the chapter in question. The next day I said to the class, "This is modern antinomianism." I was very sorry to see that my friend, Dr. Ryrie, was guilty of this awful doctrine, and, since there were several of his students in the class, I urged them to relay to Dr. Ryrie my deep distress and concern about this unsound teaching in this particular book. I knew of this trend in dispensationalism. I must admit, however, that I had never looked at it so carefully and been so thoroughly persuaded that this doctrine was taught even by one of dispensationalism's very best theologians, Charles Ryrie.

Those students did not relay my message to Dr. Ryrie, as I discovered when I met him in person a couple of years later in Chicago. We had only time there for a fifteen minute conversation. During that conversation, Dr. Ryrie convinced me of one thing: he did not mean to be antinomian. I told him how happy I was of that. It assured me of what I thought was the case. At the same time, I said to him that his assurances did not convince me that he was not teaching the doctrine, but only that he did not mean to teach the doctrine. So we agreed to carry on a further correspondence.

Shortly after I returned home, I received a copy of Dr. Ryrie's book on *Grace* with a number of passages underlined, all of which were meant to indicate to me how anti-antinomian Dr. Ryrie was. I wrote him a letter of appreciation for his intention to avoid this fatal error. I saw why he thought he had avoided it, and why he thought these statements to which he had directed my attention supported his opposition to that doctrine. I spelled out to him in that five page letter that they did *not* succeed in doing what he thought they did. They did not prove that he was not antinomian. I gently charged him once again with antinomianism and hoped that he would carry on the correspondence, proving to me that I was mistaken and that actually he was an opponent of this fatal error.

A couple of years have gone by now and Dr. Ryrie has not answered my letter. When someone proposed that we have a public discussion on this subject, he declined that also. I am left with the unhappy conclusion that Dr. Ryrie is an antinomian who does not think he is an antinomian, and does not feel it necessary to try to prove to me that he is innocent of the charge. I am very sorry about this, because I have to say about my friend that he is an unsound teacher of this dreadful error.

As an example of antinomian teachers I cite one of dispensationalism's most able expositors, Dr. Alvin McClain, a reviser of the Scofield Bible. I can do no better than examine his thoughtful little book entitled *Law and Grace* (1967). He acutely argues that the New Testament expression "under the law" could have only one of two meanings. It referred to being under the law either as the basis of salvation or as a way of life. Since no one was ever, in any age, saved by keeping the law, the former possibility is excluded, and the expression can only refer to being "under the law" as a way of life. So when the New Testament says, as in Romans 6:14, that the Christian is not "under the law," it means that he is free from it as a way of life or standard of duty. Dr. McClain's mistake is certainly not in the sharpness of his reasoning. What then? He assumes that, although the Bible never taught that the law was the basis of salvation, the Jews did not so misconstrue the Bible. That is precisely what they did. For example, the rich young ruler thought that he had "kept" the law from his youth up (Matthew 19:20). Paul himself had thought that, before his conversion, he had been "touching the righteousness which is in the law, blameless" (Philippians 3:6). The Pharisees and Jews generally trusted in their own righteousness as keepers of the law (Luke 18:9; Romans 10:3). That "righteousness" is what, as a Christian, Paul found to be "dung," though he had cherished it before. So, in Romans 6:14, he says we are not "under the law" precisely in that sense. He saw that, when the Galatians had sought to be "justified by the law," they had, as it were, "fallen from grace" (Galatians 5:4). Consequently, Paul said that his doctrine "established" the (moral) law as the way of life—not as the meritorious ground for salvation. What Paul's doctrine of grace established, McClain's doctrine of grace destroyed. "Do we then make void the law through faith?" asks Paul . McClain answers, "Precisely!" Paul answers, "God forbid!" (Romans 3:31).

### The Future of the People of God

The doctrine of the future is the best known element in dispensational theology, and, at the same time, the least important. Ten million people have bought copies of Hal Lindsey's *Late Great Planet Earth*. John Walvoord's *Armageddon* has sold more than 100,000 copies. These themes interest people concerned with world politics, the Near East, OPEC problems, etc. I think dispensationalism is consistently wrong in this area, but my real concern is not with their eschatological opinions, but the underlying concept. That underlying concept is the difference between Israel and the church.

Most dispensationalists project this division between the people of God into all eternity. Israel is going to be a "herd of swine" for evermore. Her destiny is to be restored to a perfect condition on earth, everlastingly.

This is a classical instance of gaining the whole world and losing one's soul. Israel will gain the whole world, but will lose its soul as the true Israel of God. This false distinction between the two peoples of God is projected endlessly.

This alone would be a total liability in dispensational theology. It is impossible everlastingly to divide the one people of God. The Church is one in all ages. Those redeemed by the blood of Jesus Christ are the one body of Jesus Christ. That olive tree is the same olive tree. All the redeemed will come to sit down with Abraham, Isaac, and Jacob, as Jesus says. There is but one royal priesthood, one holy nation in all ages. Whatever differences there may be in time and condition under which the people of God live, they are reunited in the world to come, everlastingly one in the divine presence of the glorious Redeemer of God's elect of all ages.

Only a difference in the way of salvation could justify this eternal division. It is incredible that the same body of people, redeemed by the same blood of Jesus Christ, should be perpetually separate from one another. If the Church's one foundation is Jesus Christ her Lord, as the hymn says, she is one in heaven and on earth.

This eschatological concept is fundamental to dispensationalism, and the "rapture" is the most significant event on the eschatological calendar. Dispensationalists are full of this doctrine. We hear about it constantly. It is expected momentarily.

What is the "rapture" but the catching up of the Church from the world into the heavenlies with Christ Jesus, there to dwell with Him forevermore? According to dispensationalism, it is the prelude to the conversion of Israel and its glorified condition on earth. It is the prelude to the kingdom of heaven established in this world where the Jews are the servants of the Messiah and the proclaimers of His gospel in an earthly, legal form to the whole world. This "seventieth week" of Daniel is the burden of the whole last book of the Bible, the Revelation. There is contact with the past in the opening chapters and reference to the eternal future of the church in heaven in the closing chapters, but chapters 4 to 20 of Revelation are concerned with the seventieth week of Daniel, the ultimate restoration of Israel, and the Davidic kingdom of heaven. Almost the last thing that God does in His Word is make the unfortunately-conceived distinction between Israel and the church permanent. Dividing the people of God is the last great "redemptive" act in which the Almighty engages, according this unfortunate view.

I am not concerned here with eschatological details. To be absorbed in the details of Daniel's seventieth week, while ignoring the fact that the interpretation splits the church of God through all eternity, is pathetic, to say the least. Without an verse by verse refutation, it is obvious that any such interpretation is false. God clearly teaches that there is one Savior of God's elect in all ages. Any interpretation that obscures this is false. Jesus Christ's second coming is not to separate the Church from the Church, followed by a third coming to bring an end of the world.

Without even looking at a single dispensational commentary in detail, it is perfectly obvious that a commentary which makes that out of the last book of the Bible is wrong—just as a liberal interpretation of the Bible which reduces Christ to the status of a man and His gospel to works salvation is false. We need not bother with the details of its errors.

Dispensationalists and non-dispensationalists alike know that anyone who reduces Christ to the status of a man, and salvation to the status of human endeavor, has not grasped the elemental details of the gospel. He may have all sorts of insights and wisdom about this, that, and the other detail, but he has missed the main message of the Bible. So, then, whatever devotion dispensationalists have to the Bible, and with whatever knowledge they adorn their comments, they fundamentally misunderstand the Bible. If they make it lead up to a climactic separation of the body of Jesus Christ, which He has purchased with His own blood and unified in Himself all eternity, they have not so learned Christ.

# Conclusion

Although dispensationalism has been the instrument of salvation, its message, though well-intended, destroys the salvation message. It tears my heart to say this because dispensationalism has meant so much to me and multitudes of others in another context. Nevertheless, I believe that this primer proves that charge.

Dispensationalism divides rather than preserves the unity of the Bible. It divides the people of God. It divides predestination from the people of God. It divides salvation from the people of God. It divides the people of God into the endless future. These things are incompatible with a sound interpretation of the Bible. If nothing more than this is said, I believe this proves that dispensationalism is not a biblical doctrine, but is, in fact, anti-biblical at its essential level. Those who would like to study the matter more thoroughly may wish to consult the brief bibliography I have appended. I can only say to my dispensational friends, from the depth of my heart, "Please, unless you think you can refute this, acknowledge its truth. Repudiate this system of doctrine and soundly articulate the gospel you love and to which your life is devoted."

The reader may very well wonder how a person can attack as un-Christian a system of doctrine that has been the means of his own salvation. The explanation is fairly simple. There is enough truth in the dispensational system that a person understanding that truth apart from the rest of the system could very well be saved by it. Dispensationalism clearly teaches that the blood of Christ is the theme of the Bible throughout. In that, dispensationalism is absolutely correct. God used a dispensationalist dean in my conversion; from this teacher I learned that Christ's redemption is the central theme of the Bible and that redemption is essentially in the shedding of His blood. That was dispensationalism's contribution to me, and for that, I will be everlastingly grateful.

The dispensational system of doctrine, however, militates against that very emphasis. It actually vitiates the biblical doctrine of redemption by Jesus Christ; one can no longer trust in Jesus Christ alone as his Savior. In spite of all their declarations to the contrary, I have shown that dispensationalism makes the cross of Christ of no effect. It is obvious that it is of no saving effect in the whole Old Testament economy and in the anticipated kingdom. I have also made it evident that, because antinomianism is the essence of dispensational understanding of the age of grace, dispensationalism even vitiates the cross in this period in which we now live. So the dispensational system of theology is against the work of Jesus Christ in the Old Testament, in the New Testament, and in the kingdom of the world to come.

Just as truly as I was converted by hearing about the blood of Jesus from dispensational lips, so many of you may likewise have been converted under similar circumstances. Just as I came to learn that the blood of Christ was not really glorified in the dispensational system, and thus came to oppose the dispensational system, so I trust the same thing will be true of the reader. You may very well, for the rest of your lives, be grateful that you first came to know about Jesus Christ through some dispensational teacher or writing. If you learn properly about Jesus Christ, you will realize that those individuals who first brought the knowledge of Him to you actually undermine that knowledge in their full system of doctrine. So, grateful for the elemental truths (which come in their system though vitiated by their system), you can best show your gratitude by opposing them when they, thereafter, attack what they themselves declare. Just as I feel I am returning a debt of gratitude to dispensationalists for the truths which they proclaim by opposing the erroneous system in which they proclaim their error, so I trust that you may do the same.

May it be with them as it was with Apollos, whom Paul taught "a more excellent way." Whatever his error was, he was a true believer who, when shown a more excellent way, did not combat it, but believed it and became a consistent Christian teacher and preacher of the gospel. May all dispensationalists readily embrace this more excellent way and propagate it with a purified zeal born from above.

# Bibliography

**Dispensational Works:**
Chafer, L. S. *Systematic Theology*, 8 vols. Dallas: Dallas Seminary Press, 1947-48.

_____. *Major Bible Themes*. Revised by John F. Walvoord. Grand Rapids: Zondervan Publishing House, 1981.

**Covenantal Works:**
Allis, O. T. *Prophecy and the Church*. Phillipsburg, New Jersey: Presbyterian and Reformed Publishing Company, 1945.

Bass, C. *Backgrounds to Dispensationalism*. Grand Rapids: Eerdmans, 1960.

Calvin, J. *The Institutes of the Christian Religion*, Book II, Chapters X, XI.

Kevan, E. F. *The Grace of Law*. Morgan, PA: Soli Deo Gloria, 1993.

Warfield, B. B. Review of L. S. Chafer, "He That Is Spiritual," in *Princeton Theological Review* 17, 2 (April, 1919): 322-27.